Learning English

Challenge 21

Band 2

Herausgegeben von

Stephanie Ashford
Maria Dashöfer
Hermann Fischer
Beate Hegemann
Alexander Hick
Harald Peter
Barbara Ware-Thürwächter
Ephrem Wellenbrock

Ernst Klett Verlag
Stuttgart Düsseldorf Leipzig

Learning English · Challenge 21 · Band 2

Herausgegeben von
Stephanie Ashford, B.A. Hons., Villingen-Schwenningen; OStR'n Maria Dashöfer, Mannheim;
OStR Hermann Fischer, Münster; StD'n Beate Hegemann, Gladbeck; StR Alexander Hick, Weinheim; StD Harald Peter, Kirchzarten; StD'n Barbara Ware-Thürwächter, M.A., Karlsruhe; OStR Ephrem Wellenbrock, Dorsten

Beratende Mitarbeit
OStR Josef Isser, Stuttgart

Tonträger zu diesem Band

 Selected texts   ISBN 3-12-510615-X   Doppel-CD mit ausgewählten Texten aus dem Schülerbuch
 Additional texts   ISBN 3-12-510618-4   CD mit zusätzlichen Hörverstehenstexten

---

Symbols

● Supplementary activity

Text available on CD:
 selected texts from the students' book
 additional texts for listening comprehension

! Special attention necessary!

📖 Skills files

Abbreviations

abbrev.	abbreviation
adj.	adjective
AE	American English
BE	British English
Col.	column
e.g.	for example
esp.	especially
fig.	figuratively
i.e.	that is
lit.	literary
opp. of	opposite of
s.o.	someone
s.th.	something
usu.	usually

Disclaimer

All the websites were appropriate and correct at the time of printing. No responsibility can be assumed for further links connected with any websites.

---

1. Auflage   1 5 4 3 | 2007 2006 2005 2004

Alle Drucke dieser Auflage können im Unterricht nebeneinander benutzt werden, sie sind untereinander unverändert.
Die letzte Zahl bezeichnet das Jahr dieses Druckes.
© Ernst Klett Verlag GmbH, Stuttgart 2003. Alle Rechte vorbehalten.
Internetadresse: http://www.klett-verlag.de

Redaktion: Gillian Bathmaker, B.A. Hons.; Virginia Maier, M.A.; Andrea Thieme (Assistenz).

Umschlaggestaltung: Hanjo Schmidt, Stuttgart.
Grafik: Christian Dekelver, Weinstadt; Hanjo Schmidt, Stuttgart.
Reproduktion: Meyle + Müller Medien-Management, Pforzheim.
Druck: H. Stürtz AG, Würzburg.
Printed in Germany.
ISBN 3-12-510610-9

Contents

Text Tasks

1. Modern t@lking

		Text	Tasks
	Cartoons	8	9
E‑mails and the Internet			9
	A survey		9
	In an online chatroom keep it short and sweet .... *The Guardian Weekly*	11	10
🎧	Getting Wired: E‑mail from Bill .... from *Eyewitness to America* by John Seabrook	12	14
	E‑tailing .... *International Herald Tribune*	14	14
	We're off to the online mall .... *The Economist*	15	15
	Internet shopping 'could divide British society' .... *Daily Telegraph*	17	16
Online issues			18
★🎧	Listening comprehension		18
	Divorced mother logs on to see children .... *The Weekly Telegraph*	19	18
	Internet addiction	20	20
🎧	Can we get caught in the web? .... *Newsweek*	21	22
	Project: User's guide		23

2. World of work

		Text	Tasks
Why work?			24
🎧	Filling days .... from *About a Boy* by Nick Hornby	25	26
Where next?			26
	The right choice .... *Self‑Directed Search Assessment Booklet* (adapted)	27	27
	Personality types .... *Self‑Directed Search Assessment Booklet* (adapted)	28	27
	The right job		29
	Fair pay		29
	Getting the job	31	30
🎧	The Interview .... from *The Interview* by Mary Gladstone	32	33
Working women: past and present			34
	More and more women are working	34	34
	Courtauld silk mill workforce .... from *Under Control: Life in a 19th‑Century Silk Factory*	35	35
	Workers' testimonies .... from *Factory Inquiry Commission / Children Working Underground*	36	36
★🎧	Listening comprehension		36
	My working life .... *The Sunday Times*	37	37
	Working mothers .... *The Independent*	39	38
	Project 1: Decision making .... Choosing the right applicant		40
	Project 2: Research & present .... The changing world of work		41
	Project 3: Discussion & survey .... Drug testing		41

3. Business matters

		Text	Tasks
Entrepreneurs			42
🎧	Richard Branson (1950) – capitalist adventurer	42	43
🎧	Anita Roddick (1942) – caring capitalist	43	43
Dot‑coms and E‑tailing			44
	What went wrong at Boo.com? .... *The Week* (adapted)	45	44
The Day the World Turned			46
🎧	The Day the World Turned .... from *In a Land of Plenty* by Tim Pears	46	47

3

	Text	Tasks

Doing good business		48	
Ben & Jerry sell out as hippie ideal is licked	*The Daily Telegraph*	48	49
Recipe for success – a role play			50
Investing ethically			51
🎧 *Listening comprehension*			51
Communicating in business			51
Business tasks and correspondence		52	51
🎧 *Listening comprehension*			53
They do things differently round here			54
Do cultural differences matter?	by Michael Rössler	54	55
Project: International e-tailing			55

4 Energy & the environment

Global warming	cartoon	56	56
Climate change: scientific certainties and uncertainties	from the Natural Environment Research Council	58	56
🎧 *Listening comprehension*			56
Forms of energy			60
Kicking the carbon habit	*The Guardian*	61	60
Nuclear energy			62
Putting waste in its place	from *Oldbury a power in your life*	63	62
Using energy: saving energy			62
Energy & conservation			64
🎧 "Let our kids find their own oil."	by Art Buchwald	64	65
Energy user no. 1: the car			65
Evolution of Energy	*Detroit Free Press*	66	67
Car-sharing clubs			68
How CityCarClub improves city life and our environment	*CityCarClub* brochure	69	68
Ecology & the economy			70
Should you recycle this paper? Maybe not!	*The Independent*	71	70
How to make lots of money, and save the planet too	*The Economist*	73	72
🎧 Earth Song	song by Michael Jackson	74	75
Project: Research and report – local action			75

5 Science & technology

Futurology			76
Oops! They got it horribly wrong		76	77
Fifteen predictions which will change our world	*The European*	76	77
Ten advances that have already arrived	*The European*	77	77
We can beam you up, as long as you're a photon	*The Independent*	78	78
Computers and Robotics			79
Where next for the transistor?	*Daily Telegraph*	79	79
House 'brain' develops helping habit	*Saturday Telegraph*	80	80
Robonurse takes care of elderly	*The Sunday Times*	82	81
🎧 *Listening comprehension*			81
Scientist's responsibility			84
🎧 Send in the clones	*The Independent*	85	84
🎧 The Weapon	from *And the Gods Laughed* by Frederic Brown	88	
Project: Instruction manual			89

4

Text Tasks

6 Space – the final frontier?

Space travel 90
   Space Oddity .... song by David Bowie 91 90
   Listening comprehension 90
   The International Space Station .... *Improving Life on Earth and in Space* 93 92
   The ultimate thrill ride .... *Newsweek* 94 94
   Role play: talk show 96
   "If I Forget Thee, Oh Earth …" .... from *Across the Sea of Stars* by Sir Arthur C. Clarke ... 96 99
Satellites 100
   NOAA Satellites help rescue 166 people in U.S. in 2001 .... *NOAA news* 101 100
UFOs 102
   Independence Day – extracts from the screenplay .... from the screenplay *Independence Day* 102 104
   Life UFO poll .... *LIFE* 105 105

7 ¡Hola, USA!

In search of the American Dream 106
   Coyote's Game .... *TIME Magazine* 107 107
   Sweat of their brows reshapes economy .... *The Washington Post* 109 108
Hispanic influences 110
   U.S. population figures 110 110
   Hispanics abound, hard to pin down .... *Houston Chronicle* 112 111
   Legal Alien .... poem by Pat Mora 113 113
   Listening comprehension 113
   Courting a Sleeping Giant .... *TIME Magazine* 115 114
   The Legacy of Generation Ñ .... *Newsweek* 116 116

Project: Immigrants in Germany 117

8 Changing lifestyles

Families 118
   Cartoons 118 118
   Strange but true 119 119
   The modern family 120
   We're mixed up and very happy .... *The Observer* 121 120
Relationships 122
   To marry or not to marry? .... *The Guardian* 123 122
Birthrate trends 124
   Zero population .... by Art Buchwald 125 124
Future lifestyles 126
   Future scenarios .... From *Britain towards 2010* by Richard Scase 127 126
   Listening comprehension 126
   Leaving home .... by Ginny Maier 128 128
Living well 130
   Advice, like youth, probably just wasted on the young .... *Chicago Tribune* 130 130
   Warning .... poem by Jenny Joseph 132 133

Project: Lifestyle magazine launch 133

Text Tasks

9 Mad for ads

Analysing adverts		134	135
Advertising is …		136	136
Celebrities in advertising		137	137
Reaching the audience			138
Nascar's new campaign	*AdAge.com*	139	138
Listening comprehension			138
Leading advertisers		140	141
The Top 100 US Advertisers	*AdAge.com*	141	141
Advertising standards			142
Pot Noodle has learnt that it is just trash cuisine	*Education Guardian*	143	142
Advertising is everywhere	*The Guardian*	145	144
Consumerism			146
One woman in five is a shopaholic	*The Observer*	146	146
E-tailing			148
Shopping on the net could jam the roads	*The Times Higher Educational Supplement*	148	148

Project 1: Reaching teenagers 149
Project 2: Internet Project 149
Project 3: Glossary 149
Project 4: A TV spot 149

10 USA: People, politics, perspectives

What is an American?	cartoon	150	150
Americans about America		151	151
Becoming American	*American Progress*, painting by John Gast	152	152
Out of many, one	*The Washington Post*	153	152
The Oath of Allegiance		154	154
Governor Locke's remarks	speech by Gov. Gary Locke	155	154
Born on the Fourth of July	from *Born on the Fourth of July* by Ron Kovic	157	156
Listening comprehension			156
Annual meeting of the Bretton Woods Committee	The U.S. Department of State	158	158
The Weak at War With the Strong	*The New York Times*	161	160
Fact file: U.S. history and foreign policy			162

Project: Researching historical information 163

11 The voice of British politics

Quiz			164
National identity – an Island race?			165
'I call myself …'	*The Guardian*	165	165
Ben Bradshaw on the British people	exclusive interview		165
The future of Britishness	speech by Robin Cook	166	168
The legacy of Empire	*Observer Worldview*	169	170
Ben Bradshaw on the Commonwealth	exclusive interview		170
Fact file: The Commonwealth			171

Text Tasks

The Monarchy 172
- Ben Bradshaw on the Monarchy .... *exclusive interview* 172
- Politics and the Prince .... *The Guardian* 172 174

Britain in Europe 174
- *Listening comprehension* 174
- About the euro: An open letter to the PM's Press Secretary .... by Fay Weldon 174 176

Politics & the media 176
- Ben Bradshaw on politics & the media .... *exclusive interview* 176
- Stage-managing the Surf-Summit .... from *Whispers of Betrayal* by Michael Dobbs 177 179

Project: Political profile 179

Skills files

- **Mind maps** 180
- **Analysing style** 181
- **Translating** 182
- **Essay writing** 184
- **Connectives** 185
- **Writing a summary** 185
- **Making phone calls** 186
  - Social calls 187
  - Formal calls 187
- **Small talk** 188
- **Giving a talk or presentation** 189
- **Illustrations & photographs** 190
- **Cartoons** 190
- **Tips for an interview** 191
- **Having a discussion** 191
- **Useful phrases for discussions** 192
- **Collecting words** 193
- **Surviving without a dictionary** 194
- **Using an English-English dictionary** 194
  - Dictionary page 195
- **Letter writing** 196
  - Personal letters 196
  - Salutations & complimentary closes 196
  - A letter of application 197
  - A business letter 198
- **Writing a CV** 200
- **Projects & group work** 201
- **Questionnaires & surveys** 202
- **Memos** 204
- **Agendas** 204
- **A press release** 205
- **Writing a report** 206
- **Talking about statistics** 207

Glossary 208
A–Z 211

1 Modern t@lking

● Think of captions to go with each cartoon. Compare your version with what others in your class suggest and choose the most appropriate one.

Modern t@lking 1

E-mails and the internet

Looking at the cartoons
1. In one or two sentences say which aspect of modern communication is depicted in each of the cartoons (advantages, disadvantages, developments, effects, etc.).
2. Draw up a mind map on modern communications technology. Start with the aspects depicted in the cartoons and then add other aspects which you can think of.

> **Mind maps**
> See *Skills file* on p. 180.

A survey

Work in pairs or a small group.
Prepare and carry out a survey in your class (or year group) to find out about the types of communication used by your peers. Use the key words and ideas in the box below to devise questions (Q.) and answers (A.).
Analyse your answers and draw conclusions. Present these in the form of a text supported by statistics, graphs and diagrams, which you can create on the basis of your findings.

> **Questionnaires & surveys**
> See *Skills file* on pp. 202 & 203.

Using the internet

1. **Q.:** Own PC?
   A.: *Yes/No*
2. a) **Q.:** Internet access?
   A.: *Yes/No*
   b) **Q.:** Where: at home? school? …?
   A.: *multiple choice*
3. a) **Q.:** Use internet for?
   A.: *multiple choice:* information/games/e-mail/chatting/shopping/learning/music/homework/…
   b) **Q.:** Two most frequently used options?
   A.: *open-end*
4. **Q.:** Time spent online per day/week/month?
   A.: *multiple choice*
5. **Q.:** How much?
   A.: *multiple choice*
6. **Q.:** Who pays?
   A.: *multiple choice*

Using mobile phones

7. **Q.:** Own mobile?
   A.: *Yes/No*
8. **Q.:** Use?
   A.: *multiple choice:* talking/text messaging/playing/…
9. **Q.:** How much?
   A.: *multiple choice*
10. **Q.:** Who pays?
    A.: *multiple choice*

Writing and text messaging

11. **Q.:** How often used?
    A.: *Table, multiple choice:* fax/e-mail/post/text message – hour/day/week/…

Here are the original captions. Try and match them with the correct cartoon:

Stop talking now class. • I know you're on the bus, I'm just behind you. • What's that? • Typical men, always bragging about whose is smallest. • It's great, people can get you anywhere, so you get masses of calls, so I keep it turned off. • Hi. My name is Barry, and I check my e-mail two to three hundred times a day. • Mom, do I get my bedtime story? Yes dear, how do you want it, e-mail or mobile?

1 Modern t@lking

Before you read: In an online chatroom ...
- What common abbreviations do you use when sending e-mails or text-messages? Brainstorm as many as possible with a partner and make an alphabetical listing. What language are the abbreviations in? Are they internationally recognized/recognizable?

After reading

Working with the text
1. Add all the abbreviations used in the text to the list you made in the pre-reading task. Give their meanings in full.
2. Find information in the text and make notes under the following headings:
   - *Reasons for using "netcronyms"* (Col. 2, l. 43)
   - *Netcronym users*
   - *Chatroom-Style*
   - *Background/predecessors to e-mail/Chatroom language*
   - *Finding out more about netcronyms and instant messaging*

Language & style
1. Write a definition for "netcronym".
2. Find the colloquialisms in the text which mean:
   a) to know nothing at all about s.th.
   b) to interrupt
   c) to find s.th. very funny
   d) to be forgotten
3. Find other examples of colloquial language used in the text and rewrite the sentences using more formal language.
4. Descibe the article in terms of other elements of style (e.g. the rhetorical devices) used.
5. Why do you think Michael Ruane chose this type of language and style to write the article? Say whether you think it is appropriate or not and why.

A step further
Write an essay/comment with the title: "Netcronyms: Use and consequences".
Use the notes you made in "Working with the text" task 2. to describe the current situation then draw your own conclusions on what the consequences of using this type of language might be. (Consider consequences for face-to-face communication, the generation gap, language development, globalization, etc.)

> **Analysing style**
> See *Skills file* on p. 181.

> Solutions: see p. 223.

Just for fun! :-)

What do these acronyms mean?

B4N	MYOB
CSL	OTOH
F2F	rehi
FYA	STYS
FYI	TYVM
ILY	WB
LMK	XOXOXO

... and these emoticons ?

>:-(	[:-)
:( )	X
(:-D)	0
:-@	
@>--->---	

Use a search engine (e.g. Google) and enter "chat dictionary" or "emoticons" to find out more or add some of your own!

And how can you recognise an emoticon beginner?

If you type in capitals WHAT ARE YOU TRYING TO SAY?

In an online chatroom keep it short and sweet

by Michael E. Ruane

U may have noticed some odd phrases slipping into ur kids' e-mails. Like when they mention that ur life sux, then quickly add JK, for just kidding. U know they really luv u, even though u r an annoying POS (parent over shoulder) with a total SOHF (sense of humor failure) who doesn't have a clue what u r saying b/cuz u seem to be writing in code.

FWIW (for what it's worth), a new idiom has been born. Across the land, every night, teenagers are yakking online in chat rooms with friends and Net acquaintances.

It's fast: Try talking to six people at once. It's brief: three or four words per exchange. It takes wit, concentration and nimble fingers. And it requires tremendous linguistic economy. There's neither time nor space for exposition.

The solution is to abbreviate, contract and condense. Why consume precious keystrokes telling six friends you have to go smack your little brother when BRB (be right back) will do? Want to enter an ongoing conversation? Just type PMFJI (pardon me for jumping in).

Interested in whom you're talking to? Type A/S/L, the nearly universal request to know your correspondent's age, sex and location.

If something cracks you up, say you're OTF (on the floor) or LOL (laughing out loud), or combine the two: ROTFL (rolling on the floor laughing).

And when your POS finally makes you get back to your geometry, it's a snap to type GTG (got to go) or TTYL (talk to you later). C?

Don't think this new lingo is limited to teens. Plenty of adults talk the talk, or type the type, all day at work.

The new argot is the result of computer services that allow users to compile "buddy lists" of friends and family, and construct an exclusive chat network that can be accessed at any time. America Online's Instant Messenger system is the biggest. It has an estimated 75 million users sending more than 700 million real-time messages a day and has given the verb, IMing, to the phenomenon.

But the language is also used in the more public chat venues, where the talk scrolls by like endless movie credits.

While many adults argue that they regularly use the argot for business and pleasure and that a lot of the terms have been rattling around the Net for years, it seems best suited to the rapid-fire lifestyle of youth.

"They want to write as fast as possible, and they want to get their ideas across as quickly as they can," says Jane Mount, co-founder of Manhattan-based Bolt, one of the country's leading Net sites for teens.

Capital letters get left in the dust, except when expressing emotion. "It takes more time to hold down 'shift' and use capitals," Mount says, "Punctuation is going, too."

Many scholars see it as an old phenomenon that can be traced back to rsvp, byob, iyi, and even the hallowed complimentary close in 19th-century letters, yr mst ob svt (your most obedient servant).

"It's natural," says Robert Kraut, professor of social psychology and human-computer interaction at Pittsburgh's Carnegie Mellon University.

Plus, it carries a certain hip exclusivity and can serve as effective code against a prying POS. Donna Jo Napoli, chairman of the linguistics department at Swarthmore College, outside Philadelphia, says: "It shows how up you are, how cool you are: Do you know the latest that people are doing? You feel kind of proud of yourself when you recognize it."

There's already at least one dictionary for netacronyms. Tribal Voice, a Californian company with its own instant messaging system and 6 million users, started it last October with 800 entries. You can find it, and add to it, at www.chatdictionary.com. At last count, it was nearly 1,400 entries and growing.

Well, G2G. C-U-LSR.

---

to keep s.th. short and sweet (fig.) to write or say s.th. in an uncomplicated way

Col. 1:
- 16 **to yak** [jæk] (AE slang) to talk for a long time, often about unimportant things
- 20 **exchange** here: short conversation – **wit** the ability to use words in a funny and clever way
- 21 **nimble** being able to move easily and quickly – **tremendous** a lot of
- 23 **exposition** here: giving a lot of detail about one's ideas
- 24 **contract** [-'-] here: to shorten
- 25 **to condense** to summarize – **precious** ['preʃəs] valuable
- 27 **to smack** to hit or slap
- 37 **to roll on the floor** (fig.) laughing very hard about s.th.
- 40 **it's a snap** (fig.) it's easy
- 43 **lingo** specialized language of a particular field or subject
- 46 **argot** ['ɑ:gəʊ] special language used by a particular group of people
- 47 **to compile** [-'-] to put together
- 50 **to access** BE: ['--], AE: [-'-] here: to be able to use

Col. 2:
- 7 **venue** ['venju:] here: place where people meet to chat
- 8 **movie credits** Abspann
- 12 **to rattle around** (informal) to move around, using a small amount of space in a much larger area
- 13 **to be suited to s.th.** to fit together with
- 25 **to trace back** to look for s.th. in the past
- 26 **hallowed** ['hæləʊd] here: respected – **complimentary close** polite phrase ending a letter (e.g. sincerely)
- 28 **servant** (old use) term used to show one's respect for the person addressed
- 35 **prying** trying to find out about s.th. that is not one's business

From the Guardian Weekly, 27.1.–2.2.2000.
© 2000, The Washington Post.
Reprinted with permission.

Modern t@lking

🎧 Getting Wired: E-mail from Bill

Before you read
- Have you ever contacted any famous people by e-mail?
  If so, who did you contact and what was their response?
  If not, would you ever consider doing so? Who would you contact? Why/Why not?

Sitting at my computer one day, I realized that I could try to communicate with Bill Gates, the chairman and co-founder of the software giant Microsoft, on the information highway. At least, I could send e-mail to his electronic address, which is widely available, not tell anyone at Microsoft I was doing it, and see what happened.
5   I wrote:

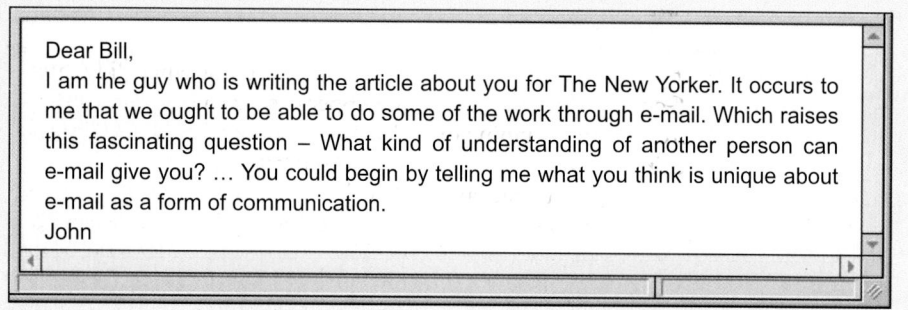

> Dear Bill,
> I am the guy who is writing the article about you for The New Yorker. It occurs to me that we ought to be able to do some of the work through e-mail. Which raises this fascinating question – What kind of understanding of another person can e-mail give you? … You could begin by telling me what you think is unique about e-mail as a form of communication.
> John

I hit "return," and the computer said, "mail sent." I walked out to the kitchen to get a drink of water and played with the cat for a while, then came back and sat at
15   my computer. Thinking that I was probably wasting money, I nevertheless logged on again and entered my password. "You have mail," the computer said.
I typed "get mail," and the computer got the following:

From: Bill Gates <billg@microsoft.com>

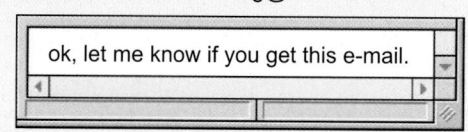

> ok, let me know if you get this e-mail.

20   According to my computer, eighteen minutes had passed between the time I e-mailed Bill and he e-mailed me back. His message said:

> e-mail is a unique communication vehicle for a lot of reasons. however e-mail is not a substitute for direct interaction …
> there are people who I have corresponded with on e-mail for months before actually meeting them – people at work and otherwise. if someone isnt saying something of interest its easier to not respond to their mail than it is not to answer the phone. in fact I give out my home phone number to almost no one but my e-mail address is known very broadly. I am the only person who reads my e-mail so no one has to worry about embarrassing themselves or going around people when they send a message. our e-mail is completely secure …
> e-mail helps out with other types of communication. it allows you to exchange a lot of information in advance of a meeting and make the meeting far far more valuable. e-mail is not a good way to get mad at someone since you can't interact. you can send friendly messages very easily since those are harder to misinterpret.

Margin notes:

7 **guy** (informal) man – **to occur to one** to come to one's mind

10 **unique** [juːˈniːk] extraordinary

23 **substitute** replacement

29 **going around people** here: to be read by a lot of people

33 **to interact** to communicate face to face

We began to e-mail each other three or four times a week. I would have a question about something and say to myself, "I'm going to e-mail Bill about that," and I'd write him a message and get a one- or two-page message back within twenty-four hours, sometimes much sooner. At the beginning of our electronic relationship, I would wake up in the middle of the night and lie in bed wondering if I had e-mail from Bill. Generally, he seemed to write messages at night, sleep (maybe), then send them the next morning. We were intimate in a curious way, in the sense of being wired into each other's minds, but our contact was elaborately stylized, like ballroom dancing.

In some ways, my e-mail relationship with Bill was like an ongoing, monthlong conversation, except that there was a pause after each response to think; it was like football players huddling up after each play. There was no beginning or end to Gates' messages – no time wasted on stuff like "Dear" and "Yours" – and I quickly corrected this etiquette breach in my own messages. Nor were there any fifth-grade-composition book standards like "It may have come to your attention that" and "Looking forward to hearing from you." Social niceties are not what Bill Gates is about, apparently. Good spelling and use of the upper case are not what Bill Gates is about, either. There was no beginning or end to his messages: Thoughts seemed to burst from his head *in medias res* and to end in vapor trails of ellipses. He never signed his mail, but sometimes he put an "&" at the end, which, someone told me, means "Write back" in e-mail language. After a while, he stopped putting the "&", but I wrote back anyway.

[...] After a month of e-mail between Gates and me, my hour in his physical presence arrived. As we shook hands, he said, "Hello, I'm Bill Gates," and emitted a low, vaguely embarrassed chuckle. Is this the sound one e-mailer makes to another when they finally meet in real space? I was aware of a feeling of being discovered. In the front part of Gates' office, we sat down at right angles to each other. Gates had on normal-looking clothes – a green shirt with purple stripes, brown pants, black loafers. He rocked throughout our time together. He did not look at me very often but either looked down as he was talking or lifted his eyes above my head to look out the window in the direction of the campus. The angle of the light caused the purple stripes in his shirt to reflect in his glasses, which, in turn, threw an indigo tinge into the dark circles around his eyes.

The emotional boundaries of our encounter seemed to have been much expanded by the e-mail that preceded it: Gates would be angry one minute, almost goofily happy the next. I wondered if he was consciously using our present form of communication to express feelings that e-mail cannot convey. Maybe this is the way lots of people will communicate in the future: meet on the information highway, exchange messages, get to know the lining of each other's mind, then meet face to face. In each other's physical presence, they will be able to eliminate a lot of the polite formalities that clutter people's encounters now, and say what they really mean. If this happens, it will be a good thing about the information highway: electronic communication won't reduce face-to-face communication; instead, it will focus it.

[...] As we were saying goodbye, Gates said, "Well, you're welcome to keep sending me mail."

I walked out to my car, drove off the Microsoft campus, and headed back over the Evergreen Bridge to Seattle. When I got to my hotel, I logged on and saw I had e-mail from Bill. It had been written about two hours after I left his office. There was no reference to our having just met. He was responding to mail I had sent him several days earlier.

By John Seabrook from Eyewitness to America, David Colbert, ed., New York: Random House, Inc., 1997, pp. 562-565. Originally published in the New Yorker.

---

41 **to be intimate** ['ɪntɪmət] *here:* to be very familiar with s.o.
42 **to be wired into someone's mind** *(fig.)* to understand someone's thoughts – **elaborately** [ɪˈlæbrətlɪ] in a complex way
46 **to huddle up** *(AE) here:* when a football team gets close together to discuss strategy
48 **etiquette breach** [ˈetɪket] act of going against the rules of accepted behaviour
50 **nicety** [ˈnaɪsətɪ] *here:* a polite phrase
53 **to burst** *here:* to come out suddenly – **in medias res** in the middle of an idea – **vapor** (*BE:* vapour) *here:* hardly visible
54 **&** = ampersand, a symbol meaning *and*
58 **to emit** [-ˈ-] to produce
59 **vaguely** [ˈveɪglɪ] *here:* slightly – **chuckle** quiet laughter
61 **at right angles** angle of 90°
63 **loafers** leather shoes without laces – **to rock** to move back and forth slowly and rhythmically
66 **indigo** dark purple blue
67 **tinge** [tɪndʒ] small amount of s.th.
68 **boundary** [ˈbaʊndrɪ] limit
69 **to precede** to come before – **goofily** in a silly way
70 **consciously** knowingly
71 **to convey** to communicate
73 **lining** *(fig.)* thoughts
75 **to clutter** to fill up in a messy way

1 Modern t@lking

After reading: E-mail from Bill

Working with the text
Answer the following questions using information from the text. Write key words only.
The number in brackets indicates the number of points you should find.
1. What is so unique about e-mail? (3)
2. Why is e-mail not an appropriate form of interacting? (1)
3. What is typical about the development of an e-mail relationship? (3)
4. Why is e-mail so convenient? (2)
5. How can e-mailing help prepare for face to face encounters? (3)

Your view
1. a) Summarize the message of the extract and the most important points made in it.
   b) Do you agree with the points made? Give your opinion referring to your personal experience if possible.
2. What kind of person do you think Bill Gates is, judging by this extract?

Style
1. a) Describe the style of the text, including the rhetorical devices used.
   b) Say what you find positive (and/or negative) about the text in terms of the style used.
2. a) Describe Bill Gates' e-mail style and the style of the writer's e-mails during the course of their communication.
   b) Which style is more appropriate in your opinion when writing e-mails in a business or formal context?

A step further
Write to a celebrity whose e-mail address you can find (see *Check the web* box) and find out their views on one or more of the following topics:
a) e-mail as a form of communication
b) how they became successful
c) the pros & cons of being in the public eye
d) their view on a current political/environmental/social issue, which interests you

> **Check the web**
> Find some celebrity e-mail addresses at:
> *http://celebrityemail.hollywood.com*
> *http://www.celebhoo.com*

E-tailing

Analysing statistics
1. Draw bar charts illustrating the figures given in a), b) and c).
2. Write a short text in which you state what the statistics show for Germany, and draw conclusions.

a) Cell phones per 100 inhabitants
Italy: 74
Britain: 68
Spain: 66
Germany: 58
France: 51

b) PCs per 100 inhabitants
Sweden: 63
Britain: 36
Germany: 34
France: 29
Spain: 16
Italy: 16

c) IT spending per capita
Sweden: $4,028
Britain: $3,343
France: $2,838
Germany: $2,737
Italy: $2,083
Spain: $1,904

d) Online connection time, monthly average
Germany: 8 hours 16 minutes
Italy: 7 hours 5 minutes
Spain: 6 hours 33 minutes
France: 6 hours 32 minutes
Sweden: 6 hours 2 minutes
Britain: 5 hours 59 minutes

e) E-commerce revenue in Europe

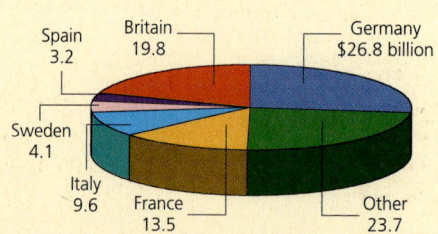

Spain 3.2
Britain 19.8
Germany $26.8 billion
Sweden 4.1
Italy 9.5
France 13.5
Other 23.7

f) Business-to-business online revenue

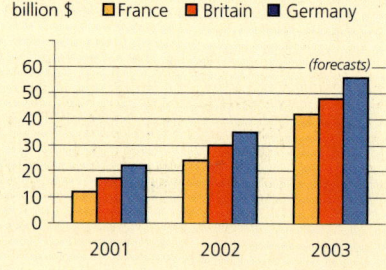

From International Herald Tribune, *March 22, 2001.*

Modern t@lking 1

Before you read: We're off to the online mall
- The following text makes predictions about the future and effects of online consumer trends.
  What would you predict for the next ten years? Make at least three predictions considering possible effects on traditional highstreet retailing and specific retail branches.

After reading

Working with the text
1. Make a table with the following headings and list the features which will be typical in 2010 according to the article.
   Communities • *Families* • *Consumer habits*
2. a) Explain the writer's use of the pseudonym "Ms E. Consumer".
   b) In what ways (if any) would the article have been different if the writer had chosen the pseudonym "Mr E. Consumer"?
3. What is meant by the "pre-Amazon" era? Why did the writer choose "Amazon"?
4. Does the writer feel positive or negative about the trends for the future? Explain your opinion making references to the text.

Creative writing
Write an article in the same style based on your own area or town. Choose your own date in the future, and think of a suitable pseudonym for the character in your article, who can, of course, be male or female. Refer to the predictions you made in the pre-reading task for ideas!

Comment
1. What are the advantages and disadvantages of the way of life described in the article in your opinion? List them in a table of pros and cons.
2. Use your list to write a comment with the title: "Trends and effects of online shopping".

We're off to the online mall

The scene is San Francisco, the date December 2010. In Union Square a few grubby discount stores are open for (thin) trade, but all around them are whole streets of boarded-up shopfronts. There are few pedestrians about, but plenty of delivery vans. In homes and offices all around town, people are staring at their computer screens and chattering into their mobile phones.

Consider Ms E. Consumer, a 45-year-old mother-of-three who works for a public-relations firm. On her screen is a score of messages reminding her exactly what she bought for her three children, her partner (husbands went out in 2005) and her 20-odd relations over the past five years. Each message comes with a suggestion for a gift this year. A few clicks, and she has verified that nobody else is giving the same things. She looks up the lowest prices and best delivery schedules and orders the whole lot in ten minutes. Then she visits the exchange to check the price of the latest WAP-enabled mobile TV-cum-telephone and revises down her $30 bid of yesterday to $25. Before leaving the office she calls up her standing grocery order and adds a dozen oysters and a bottle of champagne. They are waiting for her when she arrives home 45 minutes later. There she uses her mobile phone to order the latest movie and a few tracks from a new music release to listen to while her partner prepares dinner.

Implausible? Worrying? Only five years ago, in the pre-Amazon era, almost nothing was bought online. But extrapolate the past five years' growth, and it is easy to believe that by 2010 close to a fifth of American retail spending could be carried out over the Internet. And for things like books, music, films, toys, white goods and cars, the share seems likely to be much, much bigger.

From The Economist, *February 26, 2000.*

1 **grubby** dirty-looking
2 **discount store** shop with cheap products for sale – **thin** *here:* very little
3 **boarded-up** covered with long, flat pieces of wood – **delivery van** *Lieferwagen*
5 **to chatter** to talk quickly and continuously
7 **score** *here:* a lot
9 **20-odd** approximately 20
10 **to verify** to make sure of s.th.
12 **the whole lot** everything
13 **WAP-enabled** having internet access with 'Wireless Application Protocol' – **-cum-** partly one thing and partly another
14 **standing** *here:* current
19 **implausible** [ɪmˈplɔːzəbl] unlikely
20 **to extrapolate** [ɪkˈstræpəleɪt] to use known facts to make statements about the future

1 Modern t@lking

Before you read: Internet shopping 'could divide British society'
- Think of at least two reasons why you think internet shopping could 'divide society'.
Do you think this is more or less likely to happen? Give reasons.

While reading
- To help you understand the text more easily and deal with the tasks on it, make a brief note of the point made in each paragraph after reading it.

Paragraph	Point made
1 (ll. 1–8)	e-commerce likely to split society

After reading

Working with the text
1. Find examples in the text which describe the consequences of e-tailing:
   a) in general terms (e.g. *"could wreak havoc on the British way of life"* (ll. 12–13)
   b) in specific terms (e.g. *"high street shops may be wiped out"* (ll. 3–4)
2. Summarize the consequences linking causes to effects. Refer to the notes you made while reading and your answer to the previous task.
3. What does the writer mean by the term *"civilised apartheid"* (ll. 15–16 and ll. 77–78).
What does the word *"apartheid"* originally refer to? Do you think it is a suitable word to use in this context? Why/Why not?

Language
1. Rewrite the following sentences replacing the words underlined with your own words:
   a) *"The growth of electronic commerce is threatening <u>to wipe out the familiar row of shops in high streets up and down the country</u>, splitting society into <u>electronic haves and have-nots</u>."* (ll.1–7)
   b) *"Electronic commerce, or e-tailing, involves <u>people buying goods and services via the internet rather than from shops</u>."* (ll. 21–25)
   c) *"… they all agreed that technology <u>had the potential radically to change British society</u>."* (ll. 37–40)
   d) *"He said that although high streets will survive <u>they will do so in a much reduced form</u>."* (ll. 58–61)
2. Write definitions or give synonyms/synonymous phrases for the following words and phrases:
   electronic commerce (ll. 1–2) • to grow unchecked (l. 14) • the launch (l. 26) • expertise (l. 29) • to pose a threat (l. 47) • the well-off (l. 62) • the urban poor (l. 66) • telecommuting (l. 69)

Further activities

Discussion
To what extent do you consider the warnings and predictions in the article to be relevant to German society? Have a discussion in class in which the following groups are represented:
young students (aged 18–20) • young working adults (aged 18–30) • middle-aged people (40–50) • the older generation (60+) • high street retailers • e-tailing companies

> **Having a discussion**
> See *Skills files* on pp. 191 & 192.

Survey
Carry out a survey on online shopping in your class.
1. Work in groups and devise a questionnaire with between 6 and 10 questions. The following ideas may help you:
   have you/your parents/your friends, etc. ever bought things online? • Would you (ever) buy online (again)? Reasons? • What kind of things did you buy? • Method of payment? • Advantages/Disadvantages?
2. Carry out interviews in your class.
3. Analyse the information you gather in your group and draw conclusions.
4. Present your information as a talk with a handout (written summary) to give to your listeners at the end.

Project
You are a high street shop owner and many of your competitors have already gone online. Choose a) or b).
a) You would like to go online because you are afraid of losing customers if you don't. Design an advertisement for a magazine and for a radio spot informing your customers about your online shop and encouraging them to shop there.
b) You are not going to go online! Design an advertisement for a magazine and for a radio spot informing your customers about your shop and encouraging them to shop there rather than shopping online.

Internet shopping 'could divide British society'

THE GROWTH of electronic commerce is threatening to wipe out the familiar row of shops in high streets up and down the country, splitting society into electronic haves and have-nots, according to a report.

A report by The Royal Institute of Chartered Surveyors warns that electronic commerce could wreak havoc on the British way of life if it is left to grow unchecked.

"It could create a civilised British form of apartheid," said Mark Shucksmith, an academic from the University of Aberdeen who contributed to the study.

Electronic commerce, or e-tailing, involves people buying goods and services via the internet rather than from shops.

To mark the launch of the RIC's research foundation teams of researchers were asked to use their expertise to predict what life might be like in 20 years' time.

Although the six reports produced by the teams looked at different aspects of 20th century life – work, transport, housing, shopping, leisure and the countryside – they all agreed that technology had the potential radically to change British society.

Dr Leigh Sparks and Anne Findlay, from the Institute of Retail Studies at the University of Stirling, found that the unchecked growth of electronic commerce was posing a real threat to high street shops in nearly every town up and down the country.

"What we have got in the high street is not sustainable," said Mr Sparks. He believes that many familiar names will disappear as people start to book holidays, order groceries, and buy books and CDs via the internet.

He said that although high streets will survive they will do so in a much reduced form. He added that it was likely that the well-off, who could afford a computer and telephone bills, would avoid the high street, leaving it to the urban poor or the young.

The researchers warned that the growth of e-commerce and "telecommuting" could lead to an exodus of the well-off from the towns to the countryside.

Mark Shucksmith, from the Arkleton Centre for Rural Development Research at the University of Aberdeen, said the result could be a "civilised apartheid" with the wealthy in the countryside and the poor populating towns and cities.

By Mark Ward in The Daily Telegraph, *January 22, 2000.*

1 Modern t@lking

Online issues

> **Listening comprehension**
> You are going to hear about "Young Livin'", a professional help and advice website for young people.

Divorced mother logs on to see children

Before reading
- Have you got a camcorder on your PC at home or have you ever used one?
- When you are on the phone would you like to have a videolink as well? Why/Why not?
- If you had a videolink when/with whom would you make the most use of it?

After reading

Working with the text
1. Make a diagram showing the members of the Nutt family and their family situation and using arrows to indicate how the videolink helps them.
2. a) List all the positive aspects of the videolink that are mentioned in the text under the headings *Children* and *Parents*.
   b) Think of and list possible negative aspects which are not mentioned in the text.
3. a) Describe what you can see in the photos.
   b) Think of a suitable caption to go with each of the photos. Compare your captions with the ones your classmates come up with and choose the best version.
   (The original captions are given on p. 223.)

> **Illustrations & photographs**
> See *Skills file* on p. 190.

Language
1. Collect all the words from the text – either in a list or in a mind map – which belong to the word field 'Family'.
2. Find synonyms/synonymous phrases and opposites for the following words/phrases from the text:
   Col. 1: the working week (l. 3) • to keep in touch (l. 3) • to ensure (l. 19)
   Col. 2: to feel guilty (l. 9) • tough (l. 12)
   Col. 3: invaluable (l. 6) • to sort out (l. 7) • to come to terms with (l. 14)

> **Synonyms & opposites**
> See *Glossary* on pp. 208–210.

A step further
1. "(The videolink) allows us to be a proper family." (Col. 3, ll. 12–13).
   To what extent do you agree or disagree with Mr Nutt's claim? Write a comment of about 250 words giving your opinion.
2. Consider the use of videolinks in other situations:
      private • business • social • other
   In which other situations can/could a videolink be particularly advantageous? Give reasons.

Modern t@lking 1

Divorced mother logs on to see children

A MOTHER who is separated from her children by 150 miles during the working week is keeping in touch with their everyday ups and downs via a computer videolink.

Gill Nutt works in Cambridge while her children, Tom, eight, James, 12, and Gemma, 16, live in Bristol with their father, Tony.

Mr and Mrs Nutt, who are divorced, are taking part in trials of the videolink, which they see as a way in which both can play a role in their children's daily lives.

Through the system, Tom has been able to show his mother his cub badges and his new gerbil, Coco. Mrs Nutt has also been able to ensure that her children are doing their homework.

"It is absolutely fantastic," said Mrs Nutt, 43, a telesales manager. "I can see the children whenever I want to, morning, noon or night, whenever I am at home. We keep in touch more than other separated children. It does not replace being with them, but it takes away the strain and anxiety.

"It has changed my life because I do not feel so guilty all the time. I know I am always there for the children. I can help, whether it's a grazed knee, a tough piece of homework, or boyfriend problems."

The Intel system sends images down an ISDN line between computers in the family's home and Mrs Nutt's flat.

"I can show mum lots of stuff like when I got Coco," said Tom. "I can speak to her whenever I like. It is much better than speaking on the phone because I can see her face."

Gemma added: "I bought some shoes recently and could not wait to see her face. They have five-inch heels and she did look a bit shocked."

James finds the link invaluable when it comes to sorting out problems with his maths homework.

"I can send documents through our computer which mum will look at and check," he said.

Mr Nutt, 63, said: "It allows us to be a proper family. Gill and I have come to terms with our divorce and are good friends but it makes life easier for the children. It has become a major part of all our lives. I do not know how we would manage without it."

By Sean O'Neill, The Weekly Telegraph, 3–6 Dec. 1997, Issue No. 332.

Col. 1: 5 **via** [vaɪə] *here:* by using – 16 **cub** Wölfling, jünger Pfadfinder – 17 **badge** small piece of cloth sewn onto one's clothing – **gerbil** ['dʒɜːbl] Wüstenspringmaus
Col. 2: 7 **strain** state of being worried – 12 **grazed** [greɪzd] scratched

1 Modern t@lking

Internet addiction

- How would you define "internet addiction"?
- How big is the risk of becoming addicted to the net in your opinion? Who do you think is most at risk? Explain your answer.
- Answer the questions below:

Could you be addicted to the internet? See if you recognize any of these warning signs:

1. Do you arrange your daily schedule (e.g. when you sleep) around your internet time?

2. Do you always think about internet sessions (previous sessions or the next ones) when you are involved in other activities?

3. Do you feel that you have to check your e-mail all the time?

4. Do you find yourself accessing the internet more frequently or for increasing periods of time in order to achieve a feeling of happiness?

5. Do you feel depressed or anxious when you are forced to spend less time on the internet and/or have withdrawal symptoms when you aren't online?

6. Do you use the internet to escape from depression, anxiety or anger?

7. Do you lose track of time and stay online much longer than you had originally intended to?

8. Have you tried to limit the time you spend on the internet, but have been unsuccessful in doing so?

9. Have you lied to others about how much time you spend on the internet and/or what activities you participate in when you are online?

10. Have you neglected friends and/or family members, job responsibilities and other commitments because of your time online?

---

1. How many of these symptoms do you think a person has to have to be classified as addicted to the internet? Discuss.
2. What further possible side-effects of internet addiction are not mentioned in the test? Think of two more questions that could be added.
3. a) To what extent could the same questions be asked to identify other addictions such as alcoholism, drugs, etc.?
   b) What parallels and what differences are there between internet addiction and other forms of addiction in your opinion?

Check the web
Get more information about internet addiction at:
http://www.internetaddiction.ca/

Modern t@lking

While reading: Can we get caught in the web?
The following text looks at the question of Internet addiction from a frequent user's point of view.
- Make a note of all the personal information you find out about the writer (background, family, relationships, job, etc.).

Can we get caught in the web?

Psychologists and pundits hype 'Internet addiction.' My own online existence is much more complex.

I've lived and worked on the Internet for nine years now. At first, the online world threatened to engulf me. But now it has made possible a life I love and couldn't sustain any other way.

I have an intense relationship with the Net. Because my boyfriend lives in England, it is our primary means of communicating. And since I work as a freelance journalist, I spend much of my time doing research on the Web and communicating with editors by e-mail. I'm online at least half my day.

When I began my wired life, the Web hadn't been invented. A friend founded a "bulletin board" in New York City in 1990 called Echo, and invited me to help start the conversation. I was immediately hooked by a world where what you write – not how you look or sound – is who you are. It had definite appeal to someone who has always found socializing difficult. And as a writer, I even had an advantage. My style online is conveyed by my sentences and syntax, not my fashion sense or physical appearance.

But there are some serious problems with an online existence. If you aren't careful to limit yourself, you can start to find human contact frightening – even phone calls become scary. Computers do what you want for the most part, but life outside is noisy, unpredictable and crowded. Seeing friends comes to seem a chore; getting groceries an unwanted adventure.

The repetitive nature of online tasks – checking e-mail, searching for data, sending replies – has a soothing, ritualistic quality, somewhat like preparing and using drugs. The Net also offers druglike distractions: engaging in flame-fest arguments with people you will never meet, discussing topics you love but rarely get a chance to share in real life. You write, but don't feel isolated as your words generate near-instant responses. The sense of connection – whether true or false – is compellingly attractive.

Still, I wouldn't call my Internet use an addiction. As a former heroin cocaine addict, I know that experience all too well. Addiction inherently moves you away from love and work. My relationship to the Internet is far more complex.

While heroin and cocaine failed to deliver what I thought they'd promised, the Internet lived up to its billing. For one, I don't know how people sustain long-distance relationships without it. My boyfriend and I use a chat program that allows us to see what the other is writing as we type. We usually spend at least an hour a day communicating this way. Many couples who live together don't spend that much time "listening" to each other.

In today's mobile world, the Net also provides community that geography sometimes can't. While many pundits claimed that the Web helped push the Columbine High School shooters to the edge, I figure that it may have prevented many other such situations. After all, outcast teens can now find friends online – without fear of ridicule or attack. I wish I'd had the Net when I felt there was no one in the world who understood me.

---

1 **pundit** a knowledgeable person – **to hype** to promote a product or idea
4 **to engulf** to surround and close one in
5 **to sustain** to keep up

11 **bulletin board** here: place where you put up notices and reminders in electronic form
12 **to be hooked by s.th.** (informal) to be very fascinated by s.th.
13 **appeal** attraction
15 **to convey** to communicate (e.g. an idea)

20 **chore** difficult task

23 **soothing** comforting
24 **to engage in** (formal) to do s.th. – **flame-fest** (fig.) strange and pointless
27 **compellingly** here: extremely

30 **inherently** fundamentally

33 **billing** here: promise

41 **outcast** not accepted by society or a certain group
42 **ridicule** being made fun of

Modern t@lking

48 profound intense –
postpartum the time right after childbirth
50 to be moved to cause one to feel strong emotions (e.g. happiness about s.th.)
53 to set roots (fig.) to become established
55 vital important

59 methamphetamine drug that acts as a stimulant

64 fear-mongering spreading fear
65 ratings measurement of how popular or good s.th. is

My sister's life has also been bettered by the Net. When Kira conceived her first child in 1995, she joined an online group of mothers around the world who were due to give birth in the same month. Over the years, they've shared the ups and downs of parenting. They've met in person only rarely.

When Kira posted about her profound postpartum depression the other mothers became concerned. Since Kira lives in Florida and most of her family is in New York, the list members offered to fly me down for support. Kira was so moved that she cried when she was told I was coming and how it had been arranged.

Her depression had made her feel that no one cared. Her husband's frequent relocation had given her little chance to set local roots. But online, she found companionship. And it wasn't limited to words on a screen. It was real, practical and vital.

Like anything else that is pleasurable, the Net can be misused. My boyfriend's first few years on the Net included a lot of 18-hour days online.

Such compulsive use can be harmful – but it is probably less so than many other distractions. People can and do use everything from methamphetamine to mountaineering to avoid doing what they should. If you can't face the world, you'll always find somewhere to hide. And even my boyfriend's Net overdose wasn't entirely negative: he now knows UNIX, Linux and other programs I can't even name and has started a Net-related business.

I think psychologists looking to treat "Internet addiction" and fear-mongering pundits hype the bad side of the Net for their own purposes: profits and ratings. What you find in the vast chaos of the Web is mainly what you choose to look for. If you don't look for trouble, chances are, you won't find it.

By Maia Szalavitz, From Newsweek, December 6, 1999.
© 1999 Newsweek, Inc. All rights reserved. Reprinted by permission.

After reading

Devising comprehension questions
1. In your own words note down the most important points made in the text, then note down key words from the text relating to each point.
2. Write a set of 6 questions on the text which refer to the points you identified.
3. Exchange questions with a partner. Answer your partner's questions.
4. Evaluate and (if necessary) correct your partner's solutions to your questions.

Language
Find words in the text which belong in the categories:
- Computers & the internet
- Relationships

Writing a summary
See *Skills file* on p. 185.

Summary
Summarize the text in the form of an article for a college magazine which is running a feature on addiction. Use the third person in your article. Your article should have a maximum of 500 words.

Modern t@lking 1

Style
1. Analyse the text in terms of the style used.
2. To what extent do you think these factors make the message of the text more or less convincing? Explain your opinion.

> **Analysing style**
> See *Skills file* on p. 181.

Your view
1. *"If you can't face the world, you'll always find somewhere to hide."* (ll. 60–61)
   "If you don't look for trouble, chances are, you won't find it." (l. 67)
   Explain the two aspects of internet use which these quotations refer to and give your opinion on both.
2. Do you agree or disagree with Maia Szalavitz's view on internet addiction?
   a) Discuss internet addiction in class or in a group and record the points made in a table or mind map.
   b) Write an argumentative essay of about 500 words considering both a positive and negative view of internet "addiction".
   (Refer to the table/mind map you made during the discussion and the tasks on page 20.)

> **Essay writing**
> See *Skills file* on p. 184.

Project: User's guide

Work in a group of three or four.
Design and produce a user's guide to the internet for people who need to use English at work.
Your guide should include the following:

▶ An A–Z glossary of terms. (An online dictionary, such as at *www.leo.org* may be useful to you in finding translations.)
▶ A description of a search engine which you consider appropriate and relevant. Your description should include key words and phrases which are needed to use the search engine. (Look at the opening page of a good search engine, e.g. *www.google.co.uk* to see which terms appear.)
▶ Choose a chatroom and explain how it works, why people go there, etc. Include points to consider when entering and using a chatroom. You might want to include potential dangers and warnings.

- Decide on details of what to include in your guide (refer to the points above) and divide the tasks amongst the members of your group.
- Decide on a format for your guide and design and produce a cover.
- Decide on the order in which to include the material in your guide and remember to include a contents page.

2 World of work

Why work?

A glossary
While reading the texts in this chapter, compile a glossary on the "World of work" by writing down all the words that belong in the category that you find.
Look up any words you don't know in a dictionary.
Group words which belong together syntactically, e.g.: *manager, to work overtime, highly-qualified* or as a word family, e.g.: *employer (n), to employ (vb), unemployed (adj.)*

Brainstorming
Work in groups and brainstorm ideas on the following:
1. Why do you want to have a job later on? Why do people go to work at all? Think of reasons and try to categorize them.
2. In a book analysing the reasons why people work, Kate Keenan says: "To understand what motivates people, you need to appreciate that people have a number of basic needs that drive them to thrive and to prosper." What do you think these "basic needs" might be?
3. Kate Keenan also talks about 'higher needs'. What would you consider to be higher needs?
4. Look at the the following statements from Kate Keenan's book.
   a) Explain what you think each statement means in your own words.
   b) Discuss the statements then arrange them in the order from most to least important in terms of motivating people to work in your group's opinion.
5. As a group, collect more ideas on how to motivate people at work and at college.

Once the basic drives are satisfied through earning enough money to provide what is essential, it is the higher level needs which begin to make themselves felt.

drive need – **satisfied** fulfilled – **essential** absolutely necessary

The less a particular need is satisfied, the more important it becomes.

The basic needs – food, water and warmth – require to be satisfied if you are to survive. These needs cannot be ignored or wished away.

Once a basic need has been satisfied, there will be an instant desire to satisfy those needs which have yet to be satisfied.

instant immediate – **desire** wish

People need to feel that they belong. They work to acquire a definite place in their society.

to acquire to reach

People want to develop themselves and do better at their chosen occupation.

occupation job

The higher needs are extremely influential, but they are meaningless if the lower needs are not satisfied.

influential powerful, important

The less a higher level need is satisfied, the greater the importance a lower level one will assume.

In most societies, money is the medium through which needs are satisfied.

Essay writing
See *Skills file* on p. 184.

Your opinion
Write an essay with the title "Why work?" Use the ideas you gathered in your group brainstorming sessions as the basis for your essay and include your own opinion.

World of work 2

Before you read: Filling Days

- Will is the main character (protagonist) in Nick Hornby's novel *About a boy*.
  Look at the first three lines of the extract from the novel below:
  "Filling days … time at his disposal … ."
  What reasons could there be for Will having so much time at his disposal? How do you think he might fill his days?

Filling Days

Filling days had never really been a problem for Will. He might not have been proud of his lifelong lack of achievement, but he was proud of his ability to stay afloat in the enormous ocean of time at his disposal; a less resourceful man, he felt, might have gone under and drowned.

The evenings were fine; he knew people. He didn't know how he knew them, because he'd never had colleagues, and he never spoke to girlfriends when they became ex-girlfriends. But he had managed to pick people up along the way – guys who once worked in record shops that he frequented, guys he played football or squash with, guys from a pub quiz team he once belonged to, that kind of thing – and they sort of did the job. They wouldn't be much use in the unlikely event of some kind of suicidal depression, or the even more unlikely event of a broken heart, but they were pretty good for a game of pool, or a drink and a curry.

No, the evenings were OK; it was the days that tested his patience and ingenuity, because all of these people were at work – unless they were on paternity leave, like John, father of Barney and Imogen, and Will didn't want to see them anyway. His way of coping with the days was to think of activities as units of time, each unit consisting of about thirty minutes. Whole hours, he found, were more intimidating, and most things one could do in a day took half an hour. Reading the paper, having a bath, tidying the flat, watching *Home and Away* and *Countdown*, doing a quick crossword on the toilet, eating breakfast and lunch, going to the local shops … That was nine units of a twenty-unit day (the evenings didn't count) filled by just the basic necessities. In fact, he had reached a stage where he wondered how his friends could juggle life *and* a job. Life took up so much time, so how could one work and, say, take a bath on the same day? He suspected that one or two people he knew were making some pretty unsavoury short cuts.

Occasionally, when the mood took him, he applied for jobs advertised in the media pages of the *Guardian*. He liked the media pages, because he felt he was qualified to fill most of the vacancies on offer. How hard could it be to edit the building industry's in-house journal, or run a small arts workshop, or write copy for holiday brochures? Not very hard at all, he imagined, so he doggedly wrote letters explaining to potential employers why he was the man they were looking for. He even enclosed a CV, although it only just ran on to a second page. Rather brilliantly, he thought, he had numbered these two pages 'one' and 'three', thus implying that page two, the page containing the details of his brilliant career, had got lost somewhere. The idea was that people would be so impressed by the letter, so dazzled by his extensive range of interests, that they would invite him in for an interview, where sheer force of personality would carry him through. Actually, he had never heard from anybody, although occasionally he received a standard rejection letter.

The truth was he didn't mind. He applied for these jobs in the same spirit that he had volunteered to work in the soup kitchen, and in the same spirit that he had become the father of Ned: it was all a dreamy alternative reality that didn't touch his real life, whatever that was, at all. He didn't need a job. He was OK as he was.

From **About a Boy** by Nick Hornby, London: Penguin, 1998, pp. 71–72. Annotated edition Klett 573830.

---

2 **lack** not enough of s.th.
3 **enormous** [ɪˈnɔːməs] very large – **at one's disposal** available
7 **to pick people up** (informal) to meet people
8 **to frequent** to go somewhere regularly
13 **ingenuity** [ˌɪndʒɪˈnjuːəti] cleverness
14 **paternity leave** the time off an employer grants a man to take care of a newborn child
16 **to cope with s.th.** to deal with s.th. successfully
17 **intimidating** frightening
22 **to reach a stage** to reach a point in development
23 **to juggle** to do more than one thing at the same time
25 **unsavoury** unpleasant
28 **on offer** (BE) available
30 **doggedly** determinedly
33 **to imply** to indicate indirectly that s.th. is the case
35 **to dazzle** to impress
36 **range** [reɪndʒ] variety
38 **rejection letter** letter stating that one hasn't gotten the job

2 World of work

After reading: Filling days

Working with the text

1. How does Will usually fill his days? Make a list of the things he does.
2. a) When applying for jobs, how does Will sometimes try to hide the fact that his work experience so far has been very limited?
   b) Why do you think he does this?
3. What is meant by the phrase: "… *that they would invite him for an interview, where sheer force of personality would carry him through.*"? (ll. 36–37)
4. Find sentences in the text that characterize his attitude to getting a job and qualifying for various vacancies.
5. Characterize Will Freeman.

Creative writing

How would you spend your time if, like Will, you didn't need to go to work? Write a diary entry for a typical day.

Discussion

a) Work with a partner and make a table of pros and cons of being able to spend your time entirely as you wish.
b) Have a discussion in class on the topic "No work – no fun".

> **Having a discussion**
> See *Skills files* on pp. 191 & 192.

Where next?

> Leiblstraße 10
> 71714 Stuttgart
>
> 10th May 20XX
>
> Dear …
> Thanks for your letter!
> It was interesting to read about your plans for the not too distant future. Where do I see myself in a few years time? Well, …
>
> Bye for now,
> Micha

1. When you leave college what do you expect to do: continue studying or get a job? How concrete are your plans at this stage? Write a short personal letter to a friend in which you write about your thoughts and expectations. (See also *Skills file: Personal letters* on p. 196.)
2. Write a short text in which you analyse and explain the most important tendencies shown by the figures in the table below.
3. a) What do people in your class intend to do when they leave your college: go into employment or continue their education?
   b) What about other school-leavers at your college? Collect statistics and draw conclusions.

first destination *here:* what students do immediately after leaving college or university

higher education university or college attended after finishing school

assumed to be [əˈsjuːm] thought to be, taken to be

FIRST DESTINATIONS OF HIGHER EDUCATION STUDENTS IN THE UNITED KINGDOM FOR THE ACADEMIC YEAR 1999/00.			
	Female	Male	Total
UK employment	67%	62%	65%
Overseas employment	4%	4%	4%
Education & training	20%	21%	20%
Not available for employment, study or training	5%	5%	5%
Assumed to be unemployed	4%	6%	5%
Others	1%	1%	1%

World of work 2

The right choice

Before you read
- Work with a partner. Look at the following personality types. What do you understand by each of them? Write a short definition of each.
- What kind of person do you think you are? And your partner? Why?
  - Realistic
  - Investigative
  - Artistic
  - Social
  - Enterprising
  - Conventional

According to Dr. John Holland most people in the Western world are one of six personality types: Realistic, Investigative, Artistic, Social, Enterprising, or Conventional. People of the same personality tend to "flock together." For example, artistic people are attracted to making friends and working with artistic people. People of the same personality type working together in a job create a work environment that fits their type. For example, when artistic people work together, they create a work environment that rewards creative thinking and behavior – an artistic environment. People who choose to work in an environment similar to their personality type are more likely to be successful and satisfied: For example, artistic people are more likely to be successful and satisfied if they choose a job that has an artistic environment, like choosing to be a dance teacher in a dancing school – an environment "dominated" by artistic type people where creative abilities and expression are highly valued. How you act and feel at work depends to a large extent on your workplace environment. If you are working with people who have a personality type like yours, you will be able to do many of the things they can do, and you will feel most comfortable with them. It means that you probably should choose an occupation whose type is the same as, or similar to, your personality type.

Adapted and reproduced by special permission of the Publisher, Psychological Assessment Resources, Inc., Odessa, FL 33556, from the Self-Directed Search Assessment Booklet by John L. Holland, Ph.D. Copyright 1970, 1977, 1985, 1990, 1994 by PAR, Inc. Further reproduction is prohibited without permission from PAR, Inc.

*2 **investigative** [ɪnˈvestɪɡətɪv] liking to find out about things – **enterprising** showing initiative*

*7 **to reward** to give s.th. positive in return for s.th.*

*13 **extent** [-'-] degree*

Working with the text
1. Make a list of the advantages of choosing a working environment that suits your personality according to Dr Holland.
2. *"How you act and feel at work depends to a large extent on your workplace environment"* (ll. 13–14).
   What factors do you think would help create a good working environment for you? What kind of environment would you find it difficult to work in?

Personality types

Look at the "Personality types" on page 28.
1. Read each description and decide which description most applies to you. You will probably find you are a mixture of up to three types. List them in the order in which they most apply to you.
2. Write a description of your own personality type based on what you have read.
3. a) How useful do you think personality tests are?
   b) Can you think of any disadvantages to them?

> **Check the web**
> For further information on job descriptions, education/training, employment prospects, earnings, related jobs and many other details:
> *http://careerplanning.about.com/careers/careerplanning/*
> Do you want to take an on-line-assessment test? Check the web:
> *http://careerplanning.about.com/careers/careerplanning/cs/selfassessment*

2 World of work

A Realistic
If you have a "realistic" personality these are some of the terms that are likely to describe you:
practical, athletic, straightforward, mechanically inclined, a nature lover, self-controlled, independent, ambitious, systematic.
You are probably good at some of these kinds of things: fixing electrical things, solving electrical problems, putting up a tent, playing a sport, planting a garden, operating tools and machinery.
Your hobbies might include refinishing furniture, growing plants/flowers, playing sports or coaching team sports, hunting/fishing, woodworking, building models, repairing cars, equipment, etc., target shooting, taking exercise classes.

B Investigative
If you have an "investigative" personality these are some terms that are likely to describe you: inquisitive, analytical, scientific, observant, precise, cautious, reserved, broad-minded, independent, logical, curious.
You are probably good at some of these kinds of things: thinking abstractly, solving maths problems, understanding scientific theories, doing complex calculations, using a microscope or computer, interpreting formulas.
Your hobbies might include being a member of a book club, astronomy, doing crossword puzzles/board games, preservation of endangered species, computers, visiting museums, collecting rocks, stamps, coins, etc., amateur radio.

C Artistic
If you have an "artistic" personality these are some terms that are likely to describe you:
creative, imaginative, innovative, unconventional, emotional, independent, expressive, original, impulsive, courageous, open, complicated, idealistic, nonconformist.
You are probably good at some of these kinds of things: sketching, drawing, painting, playing a musical instrument, writing stories/poetry/music, singing, acting, dancing, designing fashions or interiors.
Your hobbies might include photography, performing, writing stories, poems, etc., desktop publishing, taking dance lessons, visiting art museums, designing sets for plays, travel, playing a musical instrument, speaking foreign languages.

D Social
If you have a "social" personality these are some terms that are likely to describe you:
friendly, helpful, idealistic, outgoing, understanding, co-operative, generous, responsible, forgiving, patient, kind, persuasive.
You are probably good at some of these kinds of things: teaching/training others, expressing yourself clearly, leading a group discussion, helping solve arguments, planning and supervising an activity, cooperating with others.
Your hobbies might include volunteering with social action groups, writing letters, joining community organizations, helping others with personal concerns, meeting new friends, attending sporting events, caring for children, religious activities, going to parties, playing team sports.

E Enterprising
If you have an "enterprising" personality these are some terms that are likely to describe you:
self-confident, assertive, sociable, persuasive, enthusiastic, energetic, adventurous, popular, impulsive, ambitious, inquisitive, talkative, extroverted, spontaneous, optimistic.
You are probably good at some of these kinds of things: initiating projects, convincing people to do things your way, selling things or promoting ideas, giving talks or speeches, organizing activities, leading a group, persuading others.
Your hobbies might include discussing politics, reading business journals, watching the Stock Market, attending meetings and conferences, selling products, leading community organizations, operating a home business.

F Conventional
If you have a "conventional" personality these are some terms that are likely to describe you:
well-organized, accurate, numerically inclined, methodical, conscientious, efficient, orderly, practical, thrifty, systematic, structured, polite, ambitious, obedient, persistent.
You are probably good at some of these kinds of things: working well within a system, doing a lot of paper work in a short time, keeping accurate records, using a computer terminal, writing effective business letters.
Your hobbies might include collecting memorabilia, arranging and organizing a household or workshop, etc., playing computer or card games, collecting any related objects, keeping club or family records and files, reading home magazines, writing family history.

Adapted and reproduced by special permission of the Publisher, Psychological Assessment Resources, Inc., Odessa, FL 33556, from the Self-Directed Search Assessment Booklet by John L. Holland, Ph.D. Copyright 1970, 1977, 1985, 1990, 1994 by PAR, Inc. Further reproduction is prohibited without permission from PAR, Inc.

World of work 2

The right job

1. Look up any of the jobs in the list below which you don't know or are unsure of in a dictionary.
2. Group the jobs according to the personality types you think would be best suited to do them.
   (Refer to the Personality types A – F on page 28.) Many jobs can be grouped in more than one category.
   Add any further jobs that you know of including your own preferred career choice if it is not in the list.
3. Say which of the jobs you would most and least like to do giving reasons.
4. Choose one job from each category.
   a) Find out as much as you can about it. Include:
      type of tasks the job involves • qualifications needed • location • pay • career opportunities • job availability.
   b) Find the equivalent jobs in Germany and compare your findings.

Accountant	Computer operator	Illustrator	Probation officer
Air traffic controller	Computer programmer	Journalist	Psychologist
Antiques dealer	Dental technician	Lawyer	Retail Manager
Archaeologist	Dentist	Legal executive	Scientist
Architect	Designer	Librarian	Social worker
Armed forces	Doctor	Manager	Solicitor
Art gallery worker	Engineer	Nature Conservationist	Sports Centre Manager
Bank clerk	Entertainer	Nurse	Surveyor
Bank manager	Farmer	Optician	Teacher
Broadcaster	Fishing industry worker	Paramedic	Technologist
Building Manager	Forensic Scientist	Photographer	Town planner
Careers adviser	Forestry worker	Pilot	Vet
Computer engineer	Hotel Manager	Police officer	

Fair pay

THE TOP FIVE EARNERS IN THE U.S. IN 2000			
	Wealth ($)	age	source of income
1 Gates, William H.	6,300,000,000	44	Microsoft Corp.
2 Ellison, Lawrence	5,800,000,000	56	Oracle Corp.
3 Allen, Paul	3,600,000,000	47	Microsoft
4 Buffett, Warren	2,800,000,000	70	Stock market
5 Moore, Gordon	2,600,000,000	71	Intel Corp.

The average U.S. family had an income of $40,800 in 1999.

1. How many years would it take the average family to earn as much money as Bill Gates had in 2000 based on these figures?
2. How much do you expect to earn/would you like to earn? Which jobs/job categories provide this kind of income?
3. How important is a high salary for you?
4. A high income is a reflection of qualifications and responsibility. Do you agree or disagree with this statement. Explain your view.

Talking about statistics
See *Skills file* on p. 207.

2 World of work

Writing a CV
See *Skills file* on p. 200.

A letter of application
See *Skills file* on p. 197.

Tips for an interview
See *Skills file* on p. 191.

Check the web
Get more information about CV writing at:
http://www.thequalitycv.co.uk/
http://www.bradleycvs.demon.co.uk/

Getting the job

Which job?

1. Look at the job adverts on page 31 and draw up a table with the following headings and fill in information from the ads. (Look up any words you don't know in a dictionary.)
   Personal qualifications needed • Knowledge needed • Information about workplace/job • How to apply
2. Which of the jobs sound most/least attractive to you? Why?
3. Which job do you already feel qualified for?
4. Which of the jobs could you imagine doing in the future?
5. Choose one of the jobs in the adverts on page 31 and apply for it.
   - Prepare your CV.
   - Write a letter of application, addressing it to the person named in the advert.
   - Make a list of questions you might be asked in the job interview. What would your answers be?
   - Work with a partner. One of you is the personnel manager and the other is the applicant. The personnel manager must use the applicant's letter of application and CV to prepare questions for the interview. Role play the interview. If possible ask a third person to watch and assess your performance as applicant and interviewer.

Role play

Work in a group. Decide which of the jobs on page 31 the following people might realistically be interested in. Write a letter of application as if you were the person.
Now exchange your letters with another group. Take on the role of the employer. Read the job advert again and decide in your group if you would invite the person for a job interview. Invite the candidate for an interview or reject them, giving reasons. You can write a formal letter or devise an e-mail or make a mock phone call.

Amanda Sayers, 39, single parent, mother of three children aged 3, 6 & 9; would like to work from home; has word-processing skills, but would also like some training; can work flexible hours

Alan Forrester, 42, married, two children; unemployed for 18 months; very flexible, very good writing skills; has attended several communication seminars; experienced in website design (portfolio included); efficient and friendly

Ian McCartney, 24, single; has just left Wakefield College; applying for first job, is flexible, would consider moving to a different part of the country

Maria MacKenna; 42, mother of three boys aged 14–18; used to work as a secretary 15 years ago, stopped when she was pregnant with her third child; wants to come back into the workplace; would like some training

World of work 2

Be a part of our collegial team! We create publications, websites, and other promotional materials in order to communicate effectively with target audiences. Manage the development of promotional materials such as brochures and newsletters. Requires expert writing, editing, fact checking, and project management skills. Requires excellent marketing skills including analysing and meeting client market needs, marketing departmental services, and fostering client relations. Must work closely with designers to ensure the highest-quality of promotional materials. Must produce accurate, cost-effective products that meet the communications and marketing goals of university clients.
Interested? Please send your resume and cover letter to:
FW Job #J-2345
Nehigh University,
Human Resources,
10 Appletree Hall,
Jefferson City, MO 63048,
FAX: (333) 587-1298
E-mail: job@application.nehigh.edu

Part-time sales staff

PineyOak are seeking Sales Staff. Applicants must be able to work both well in a team and also independently. We are looking for a dynamic person with an outgoing personality. Experience is not essential, training will be given.
Successful candidates would be expected to earn £8,000 to £10,000 p.a. salary basis and commission basis.
Please apply in writing with CV to:
Grant Hughes, PineyOak Ltd., Willis Industrial Park, Cheltenham, TL40 2QB.
www.pineyoak.co.uk

Data entry clerks/typists
vacancies to be filled immediately

Job description: seeking professional self-motivated clerical workers, work in an office environment or from home; skilled and unskilled wanted; training provided; flexible hours. Duties will include creating business documents, typing data entry or various records/data into various database systems.
Qualifications: experience: type 50+wpm, knowledge of standard computer software programs (WORD, WORKS, EXCEL, etc.) is preferred
Job Type: Temporary
Location: Northamptonshire
Salary: Negotiable

For more information and application materials contact e-mail address:
home@atwork.co.uk

Modern Languages
Spanish / Italian
Bellacres School

A teacher with top qualifications in Spanish/Italian is needed for 0.5 of a timetable from October. We are looking for an enthusiastic and talented language instructor to take on the growing numbers of pupils in this popular and successful department.
Send an application, CV and names and addresses of two references to the Headmaster's Assistant, Bellacres School, Midgley Lane, Warwickshire, PV43 8TR from whom further details can be obtained.

Tel 07246 878754
Fax 07246 878732
Email: teacher@bellacres-school.warwickshire.sch.uk

CLERICAL ASSISTANT

Making a sure future.
Landsdown Insurance Company of Boston, a division of the McRider Insurance Group, is an established leader in the property/casualty insurance industry. We are seeking an experienced, dedicated professional to join our team in Greensboro, NC as:

CLERICAL ASSISTANT
PART-TIME POSITION

This part-time position (approximately 15 hours per week) involves typing and keeping a record of correspondence, general filing and handling phones. Superior communication skills are required. Knowledge of WordPerfect or Excel is highly desirable. Please send your resume and a cover letter to:

Landsdown Insurance Company of Boston
P.O. Box 12 Greensboro, NC 22024
Fax: (816) 435-9812
E-mail:
application@mcridergroup.com

Software Designer
£30,000 to £34,000

Our client is seeking a Software Designer to develop and approve software and to review systems and methodologies. The applicant's technical experience should include software development methodologies, enterprise, system architecture, quality processes, client server database systems, graphics, internet technologies, software design and networks.

Contact **Dawes Recruitment** in Hull
Tel.: (03556) 909876
E-mail: bill@dawes-re.com

The Kiral Hotel
PART-TIME RECEPTIONIST

Temporary position to cover maternity leave. The applicant we are seeking is enthusiastic, outgoing, and of neat appearance. Previous experience is not required, as training will be provided on the job. Customer service experience would be an advantage. Previous applicants need not apply. Please apply in writing to the Manager, The Kiral Hotel, Akeley, Bucks, TL44 6HC. 08752 928441. www.kiral.co.uk

2 World of work

The Interview

Before you read

Brainstorm: Write down five adjectives that describe how someone might feel when they are going to a job interview. Write a sentence giving reasons for these feelings.
Example: *Nervous: I can imagine feeling nervous because you never know what you will be asked at the interview.*

---

1 **imposing** impressive	
4 **to expect s.o.** to be waiting for the arrival of s.o.	
7 **one's cup of tea** *(informal)* one's preferred thing or person	
8 **briskly** quickly	
10 **to peruse** [pə'ruːz] *(formal)* to look very carefully at s.th.	
11 **inside** *here:* knowing	
12 **inexorably** [-'----] inescapably	
14 **to mumble** to speak quietly and not clearly	
15 **to pronounce** to state s.th. formally and in public – **sentence** *here:* one's punishment for a crime	
17 **to squint** to look at s.th. with one's eyes partly closed	
20 **deliberately** on purpose	
23 **to condemn** *here:* to show one to be unfit for s.th. – **sabbatical** *Freistellung*	
24 **eventually** finally – **incredulously** very surprised	
28 **to murmur** *syn.* of mumble	
31 **gouache** [gu'ɑːʃ] a method of watercolour painting	
32 **to sail close to the wind** *(fig.)* to do s.th. risky	
37 **reliable** dependable – **to grill s.o.** *(fig.)* to ask s.o. a lot of questions	
39 **to convince s.o.** to make s.o. believe s.th. – **adequacy** ['ædɪkwəsi] *here:* being able to do the job	
44 **to subsist on** to live from	

[...] The door was large and imposing and she had arrived five minutes too early. No time for a coffee opposite. She walked up the stairs that were carpeted in a hairy material and noticed the colourful posters on the walls. She asked to see the director,
5 who she said was expecting her. A receptionist (ash-blonde and as slim as Elizabeth had always longed to be) told her to sit outside in the passageway and wait for him. He arrived. 'Would you come this way, please?' he said.

She knew he was formal in a way that wasn't natural. She knew he wasn't her cup of tea. She knew she wanted to walk briskly out of his office, down those hairy carpeted stairs back into the street. But she knew she wouldn't. She watched the
10 long, thin man peruse her form. How do you hide two years of life that were, in effect, spent in hiding? How do you assume that confident, inside manner when you know only too well that if you don't get some kind of job soon, you'll slip inexorably outside this world that they call the world of living?

The man wasted no time in coming to the point. 'I see,' he mumbled in a manner
15 that reminded her of a judge preparing to pronounce a sentence on the defendant (defendant she certainly felt, defending her very life but with little effect), 'from your CV that you have a gap of ... let's see,' he squinted through his spectacles at the paper on his desk, 'two years.' He sat back and looked at her carefully. She knew she must explain why she had had two years out, and tried to fool him that she was
20 relaxed by swinging her right leg over the knee of her left, leaning deliberately back in her chair. 'I decided I wanted to take time out to ...'

She couldn't finish her sentence. What could she say when the reason would condemn her completely? 'I suppose you could call it a sabbatical', she said eventually. The man looked at her sceptically. 'Two years?' he asked incredulously.
25 By some form of miracle or flash of inspiration, she found herself making up a story about why she'd not worked for so long and said, 'I thought I would try my hand at becoming a ...' (she wasn't sure why she hesitated yet again) '... a painter.' She murmured something about self expression and wanting to 'know herself'.

'I never sold anything,' she added for precaution, 'but I got a few favourable
30 comments on my ... watercolours.' She began to like her story and only wished that she remembered to say gouaches instead of watercolours, then realised she might have been sailing a little close to the wind when she had no idea what gouaches were.

'Most irregular, I'd have thought, to give up the promising career that you had,' was the response.
35 He asked another question, and then several more until she found herself feeling not unlike an onion being peeled right down to its core, that's if onions had cores. He wanted to be sure she was reliable, he said, that's why he was grilling her. After all, after two years of being out of the system she might not be able to teach. She had to convince him of her stamina, reliability and adequacy.
40 How could she show him she was now more adequate than she'd been before? Anyone who had been through and emerged intact had more than enough ability to do what this man required of her. Elizabeth began to wonder if she wanted to be part of his establishment anyway. The money would be pleasant, but money wasn't the only thing she wanted and there was always £36.70 for her to subsist on each week,
45 plus sunshine and walks in the Botanics. Never mind about buying books about

Gwen John. She would be Gwen John, she thought, with wild bravura, then quickly came back to earth, realising she had the talent neither for painting nor for poverty.

The man's face was cold and disinterested. Elizabeth couldn't be bothered to try and win him round – to seduce him with fluttering eyelids, hunched shoulders and coy smiles.

'Well, Miss Tadeuska, thank you very much for coming in,' he said briskly. 'I have enjoyed talking with you. If we need any extra help this summer, we'll let you know.'

She found herself standing outside the door on the hairy carpet. She walked quickly down the steps and didn't care where she went so long as she could be in the street without being noticed. There was a comfort in being unknown.

From "The Interview" by Mary Gladstone, Under Cover: An Anthology of Contemporary Scottish Writing, Colin Nicholson, Ed., Edinburgh: Mainstream Publishing, 1993, pp. 115–117.

46 **bravura** [-'--] confidence

49 **to seduce** to charm – **hunched** gekrümmt
50 **coy** flirtatious

Working with the text
1. Why does the man eventually turn her down?
2. What are Elizabeth's feelings just before the interview starts?
3. Characterize Elizabeth's feeling at the end of the interview.
4. What kind of man is the interviewer?
5. a) Explain lines 9–13 ("She watched the long, thin man peruse her form. … that they call the world of living?") in your own words.
   b) What do you think of this kind of behaviour?
6. "Elizabeth couldn't be bothered to try and win him round – to seduce him with fluttering eyelids, hunched shoulders and coy smiles" (ll. 48–50).
   Do you think Elizabeth behaved in the right way? Give reasons for your answer.
7. What does the phrase "There was a comfort of being unknown" (l. 55) mean for Elizabeth?

Style
What aspects of style does the author use to convey Elizabeth's feelings?

Analysing style
See *Skills file* on p. 181.

Giving advice
"Elizabeth began to wonder if she wanted to be part of his establishment anyway. The money would be pleasant, but money wasn't the only thing she wanted and there was always £36.70 for her to subsist on each week, plus sunshine and walks in the Botanics" (ll. 42–45).
1. Imagine you are Elizabeth and write a letter to an agony aunt asking for advice for future job interviews.
2. You are an agony aunt on a magazine and have received a letter from Elizabeth asking for advice. Write a letter to her in which you give her advice for a future job interview. Make suggestions for the type of jobs you think she could apply for and how she should try to behave at the interview.

Personal letters
See *Skills file* on p. 196.

A step further
- Apart from skills and academic qualifications what other things would you consider important when employing someone?
  a) Make a list of adjectives/characteristics.
  b) Discuss your ideas with a partner and add to your list if necessary.
  c) Collect all your ideas in class, e.g. create a mind map on the board or on a transparency.
  d) Decide on the top five most important items.

Having a discussion
See *Skills files* on pp. 191 & 192.

Mind maps
See *Skills file* on p. 180.

2 World of work

"Do you have any problem being fired by a woman?"

1. Describe the scene in the cartoon.
2. Do you think the man is at an interview or is he being fired?
3. What kind of company do you imagine the woman works for?
4. What point is the cartoonist making?

Talking about statistics

See *Skills file* on p. 207.

6 **regardless of** in spite of –
marital status whether one is married or not

9 **spouse** husband or wife

15 **householder** head of the family
16 **to maintain** to keep intact

http://womensissues.about.com, 2001

Working women: past and present

Before you read: More and more women are working

• Try to guess how these statements are completed:
1. The number of working women in 1900 was … .
   1.7 million • 3.8 million • 5.3 million • 18.4 million
2. The number of working women in 1950 was … .
   10.6 million • 18.4 million • 23.4 million • 29.6 million
3. The number of working women in 1997 was … .
   46.3 million • 59 million • 63 million • 78 million
4. The percentage of divorced women in the labor force in 1997 was … .
   35% • 52% • 74.5% • 97.5%
5. In 1997, the number of families maintained by women was … .
   12.8 million • 20.4 million • 31 million • 79 million
6. In 2001, the percentage of female part-time workers was … .
   17% • 58% • 70% • 83%
7. In 1995, the percentage of multiple jobholders who were female was … .
   12% • 29% • 41% • 47%

Working with the text

1. Read the text and check your solutions to the statements above.
2. Present the statistics in the form of bar or line charts.
3. Explain these words and phrases: a proportion of (l. 2) • the labor force (l. 4) • accounted for (l. 23) • multiple jobholders (l. 24).
4. Find similar statistics relating to the current situation in Germany. Comment and make comparisons.

More and more women are working

Over the past century, women workers have grown steadily in number and as a proportion of the workforce. The number of working women has grown from 5.3 million in 1900 to 18.4 million in 1950 and to 63 million in 1997. Women made up 18.3 percent of the labor force in 1900, 29.6 percent in 1950 and 46.2 percent in
5 1997. In the United States, 99 out of every 100 women will work for pay at some point in their lives. Regardless of their marital status, the majority of women (except widows) – even those with young children – work for pay.
  62.1 percent of married women with spouses present, 65.3 percent of married women with absent spouses, 66.8 percent of never-married women and 74.5 percent
10 of divorced women were in the labor force in March 1997.
  71.9 percent of women with children younger than 18, 77.9 percent of women with 6- to 17-year-olds and 64.8 percent of women with children younger than 6 were in the labor force in 1997. 53.8 percent of women without children younger than 18 were in the labor force in 1997.
15 The number and proportion of families in which a woman is the householder and no spouse is present are growing, too. In 1997, 12.8 million families were maintained by women, representing 18.2 percent of all families, compared with 5.6 million – 10.8 percent of all families – in 1970. 62 percent of women who maintained families were employed in 1997.
20 Most "nonstandard" workers (workers who do not hold regular, full-time jobs) are women. 55 percent of workers paid by temporary help agencies are female. 70 percent of part-time workers are female.
  Women accounted for 85 percent of the total increase between 1989 and 1995 in the number of workers with more than one job. 47 percent of all multiple jobholders
25 in 1995 were women, up from 20 percent in 1973.

World of work 2

Courtauld silk mill workforce

Samuel Courtauld built a silk mill in 1825 in Halstead, Essex (South East England).
Before the Industrial Revolution, Halstead was an agricultural community with a cottage industry producing woollen cloth. In Halstead, as elsewhere in England, unemployment among depressed farming households and former wool workers forced people to find work outside the home. Because their labour was cheap, women more than men were recruited into the textile factories that sprang up all over Britain in the 19th century. Below is a chart of the Courtauld workforce in 1860.

MALES			FEMALES		
Number	Weekly wages*		Number	Weekly wages*	
1	£1000 per year	Mill Manager (+ 3% of profits)	4	10s–11s	Gauze examiners
26	15s–32s	Overseers and clerks	4	9s–10s	Female assisant overseers
6	17s–25s	Mechanics and engine drivers	16	7s–10s	Warpers
3	14s–21s	Carpenters and blacksmiths	9	7s–10s	Twisters
1	15s	Lodgekeeper	4	6s– 9s	Wasters
16	14s–15s	Power loom machinery attendants and steamers	589	5s– 8s	Weavers
			2	6s– 7s	Plugwinders
18	10s–15s	Mill machinery attendants and loom cleaners	83	4s– 6s	Drawers and doublers
			188	2s– 4s	Winders
5	5s–12s	Spindle cleaners, bobbin stampers and packers, messengers, sweepers	899		Total females
–	7s–10s	Watchmen			
–	5s–10s	Coachmen, grooms and van driver	1013 Grand total work force		
38	2s– 4s	Winders			
114		Total males			* Wages are in British shillings

From Under Control: Life in a Nineteenth-Century Silk Factory *by Carol Adams, Paula Bartley, Judy Lown, Cathy Loxton, Cambridge: Cambridge University Press, 1984.*

While you read
Compile your own list of annotations (words with explanations) for terms in the text and table above:
- Before looking in a dictionary try to work out the meaning of new words by:
  1) thinking of related words in English that you know.
  2) thinking of similar words in German or another foreign language you know.
- Look up important words that you still don't know in an English/English dictionary.
- Use the internet to look up specialized terms.

Working with the text
1. a) Which jobs were done by both men and women?
   b) Which job did the highest number of men do?
   c) Which job did the highest number of women do?
2. a) How many men could potentially earn 10 shillings or more a week, and which jobs did they do?
   b) How many women could potentially earn 10 shillings or more a week, and which jobs did they do?
   c) Which was the lowest paid job for men?
   d) Which was the lowest paid job for women?
3. a) What percentage of the total workforce was made up of women? Of men?
   b) Why do you think the labour force was split up in this way?

A step further
Find statistics about employment today: In factories that mainly employ women today, can you find out what percentage of men or women hold the best paying jobs? What kind of jobs do women most often do: career building jobs or dead end jobs? Comment on your findings.

Check the web
Get more information about old occupations at:
http://members.ozemail.com.au/~tonylangham/Occupa.htm

2 World of work

Workers' testimonies

Textile workers, Nottingham, ca. 1860

"I work at Mr. Wilson's mill. I think the youngest child is about 7. I daresay there are 20 under 9 years. It is about half past five by our clock at home when we go in … . We come out at seven by the mill. We never stop to take our meals, except at dinner. William Crookes is overlooker in our room. He is cross-tempered sometimes. He does not beat me; he beats the little children if they do not do their work right … . I have sometimes seen the little children drop asleep or so, but not lately. If they are catched asleep they get the strap. They are always very tired at night … . I can read a little; I can't write. I used to go to school before I went to the mill; I have since I am sixteen."

(Hannah Goode)

"I have three children working in Wilson's mill; one 11, one 13, and the other 14. They work regular hours there. We don't complain. If they go to drop the hours, I don't know what poor people will do. We have hard work to live as it is. … My husband is of the same mind about it … last summer my husband was 6 weeks ill; we pledged almost all our things to live; the things are not all out of pawn yet. … We complain of nothing but short wages … My children have been in the mill three years. I have no complaint to make of their being beaten … I would rather they were beaten than fined."

(Mrs Smith)

From Factory Inquiry Commission (item 83), Great Britain, Parliamentary Papers, 1833.

Mine workers, South Wales mine, ca. 1850

I have been down six weeks and make 10 to 14 rakes a day; I carry a full 56 lbs. of coal in a wooden bucket. I work with sister Jesse and mother. It is dark the time we go."

(6 year old girl)

"I have wrought in the bowels of the earth 33 years. I have been married 23 years and had nine children, six are alive and three died of typhus a few years since. Have had two dead born. Horse-work ruins the women; […] it makes them old women at 40."

(Jane Peacock Watson)

"I hurry for a man with my sister Anne who is going 18. He is good to us. I don't like being in the pit. I am tired and afraid. I go at 4:30 after having porridge for breakfast. I start hurrying at 5. We have dinner at noon. We have dry bread and nothing else. There is water in the pit but we don't sup it."

(Maria Gooder)

"We are door-keepers in the four foot level. We leave the house before six each morning and are in the level until seven o'clock and sometimes later. We get 2p a day and our light costs us 2 1/2 p. a week. […]"

(Mary and Rachell Enock, 11 and 12)

"I have been married 19 years and have had 10 bairns [children]: … My last child was born on Saturday morning, and I was at work on the Friday night … . None of the children read, as the work is not regular. When I go below my lassie 10 years of age keeps house … ."

(Isabel Wilson, 38 years old)

From Children Working Underground, Amgueddfa Genedlaethol Cymru National Museum of Wales, 1979.

Annotations:

- 2 **daresay** guess
- 5 **overlooker** overseer or supervisor – **cross-tempered** in a bad mood
- 8 **to get the strap** (fig.) to get hit with a belt
- 14 **to be of the same mind** (fig.) to agree about s.th.
- 15 **to pledge s.th.** to use s.th. as collateral (Sicherheit) for unpaid debts – **out of pawn** when objects used as collateral are released because debts have been paid
- 18 **to be fined** to have to pay money as a punishment
- 20 **to make a rake** to rake together the coal that's lying on the ground
- 23 **wrought** (old use) past tense form of to work
- 27 **to hurry** here: to move coal from where it was dug out to where it would be brought to the surface
- 30 **to sup** (old use) to drink
- 31 **door-keeper** one who stands at an entryway to make sure traffic moves smoothly
- 32 **level** here: a cave-like tunnel into sloping ground

★ **Listening comprehension**

Listen to Annie McLeod's story about her life as a mill worker.

Working with the text

1. Write a summary of working conditions in the mills and mines based on these statements. Consider the following points: working hours • health problems • education • family life.
2. Why did some workers oppose the imposition of laws restricting women and children's work?

My working life

Tracy Harding, 28, primary response group engineer

by Penny Wark

"I live in a four-bedroom house shared with three other Microsoft people. I'm from Glamorgan and I got this job after someone I knew well at college got in touch. That was 2 years ago.

I have got two alarm clocks because I have been known to sleep through just the one. I work shifts and if I'm on at 9 am, I get up at 8.15. Then it's a 10-minute drive to work in my XR2, followed by a bowl of cornflakes and a cup of tea at my desk.

My job is to provide front-line telephone support to customers. They range from small businesses to large corporations where, if the system is down, they could be losing £1m a minute. You do get people panicking – an engineer under pressure from the manager – or someone who is very angry.

Our job is to solve their problems as quickly as possible. They are pretty complex calls and it is real high-pressure stuff. In an average morning you take four of them.

Lunch varies from going to the canteen for lasagne and chips, to the local pub or shopping – Reading town centre isn't that far. Or you can go for a walk by the Thames. I spend most of my day eating chocolate.

In the afternoon you deal with issues that came up in the morning, research on improving processes in the team or keep up with new products.

The 9am shift finishes at 5.30pm. You're free to go then but quite often before you know where you are it's 7.30pm. I work some weekends and sometimes I'm on call and carry a pager round with me. Outside normal hours we support customers from Europe, Africa, India and the Middle East and have to get translaters on the line.

There are 24 of us in the team, it's hectic and can be stressful, but it's never repetitive. I enjoy being in the team because everybody is really friendly. There are lots of shared houses and lots of social events.

If I have an evening at home I get a video, a takeaway and a bottle of wine. Otherwise it's a meal out or the cinema. I don't spend much time at home, unless it's looking at Teletext for cheap flights. One of our shift patterns is four days on and four days off, so if I'm not working I'm usually planning the next trip. This year I've been to Dubai, Egypt, Thailand, Dublin, Cyprus, Portugal and Brussels.

Microsoft really knows how to hold a good party, which is a big gold star in my book. It hosts three or four a year and everything is free – drink, food and transport.

At parties, I keep going for as long as it lasts. Normal working days are rather more restrained – I crash out at 11pm. As soon as my head hits the pillow, I'm out."

From The Sunday Times, *October 5, 1997.*

Title: **response** answer
Col. 1: *10* **to get in touch** to contact s.o. – *13* **to work shifts** to work during a set period of time – *18* **front-line support** direct help for customers who call with problems – *19* **to range** [reɪndʒ] to vary
Col. 2: *4* **stuff** *(informal) here:* work – *20* **to be on call** to be ready to work immediately when needed – *22* **to support** to help
Col. 3: *1* **repetitive** [-'---] s.th. that is repeated and therefore boring – *23* **restrained** restricted – *24* **to crash out** *(informal)* to fall asleep immediately because one is very tired – *25* **to hit** *here:* to land upon – **to be out** *(informal)* to be asleep

Working with the text
1. What are Tracy's duties?
2. What does Tracy say about the atmosphere at Microsoft?
3. Apart from her work, what else do you find out about Tracy's life? Say what you think about her lifestyle.
4. Would you like to have Tracy's job? Give reasons why or why not.

A *step further*
1. Compare life and work of the mill and mine workers with Tracy Harding. Consider the following:
   Why do the women work? • What are their working hours? • How important is work in their lives?
2. Based on the diffferences you identify, write a text showing some of the most important changes in the world of work then and now.
3. Today women make up the majority of workers in the textile and electronics industries around the world. Why do you think mainly women are employed in these industries?

2 World of work

> **Questionnaires & surveys**
> See *Skills file* on pp. 202 & 203.

Before you read: Working mothers
- Carry out a survey in your class to find out how many of your classmates' mothers work; whether they work full or part-time; what kind of jobs they do; how old their children were when they started work.

Working with the text
1. List the most important findings of the report under the headings:
   Effects on children with stay-at-home mothers • *Effects on children with full-time-working mothers* • *Effects on children with part-time working mothers*
2. What was different about this survey compared to previous surveys and why is this difference considered significant?
3. How do the results of this survey differ from the results of the survey published in 1997?
4. a) According to Professor Ermisch how should the government respond to the most recent findings?
   b) Why is Mary MacLeod concerned about the recent findings?

Language
Show that you have understood the following sentences from the text by rewriting them in your own words. Try to use as few words as possible from the original.
1. "It might be better for policy makers to encourage part-time employment by one parent during a child's pre-school years. The large proportion of employed mothers with young children who are in part-time jobs is evidence that many mothers already prefer this option." (Col. 2, ll. 35–42)
2. "For many mothers full-time work is a necessity, not a lifestyle choice. I hope this research won't be used as another stick to beat them." (Col. 3, ll. 33–36)

Your view
Should mothers stay at home or go to work in your opinion? Write a comment of about 500 words. Give your own opinion and refer to the findings of the surveys in the text.

Creative writing
Read the following story segment and write either a full story or a short play around it.

> **The Secret of a Mother's Success**
> She was busy with her report when he walked in, tossing his baseball up and catching it, over and over again. Then it landed on the desk and rolled towards her, sending papers sliding.
> "You're not coming to the game, are you?" he said. She stared at the ball now lying on the floor and wondered what to say.

Working mothers: Annotations

Col. 1: 23 **to be less likely** to have a smaller chance of happening – 39 **slightly** a little

Col. 2: 8 **to promote** to encourage – 10 **adverse** ['ædvɜːs] negative – 14 **to draw from** to use s.th. as a basis for s.th. else – 15 **sibling** brother or sister – 24 **upbringing** how one's parents raised and educated one during childhood – 31 **consequence** ['---] result – 34 **maternity leave** a woman's time off work to have and take care of a baby

Col. 3: 27 **cast-iron judgement** an unchanging opinion about s.th. – 32 **bearing** effect – **outcome** consequence

Working mothers

by Sarah Cassidy
Education Correspondent

Mothers who return to full-time work before their children start school may be damaging their offspring's future exam results, according to research. Young adults whose mothers worked full-time for most of their early years were less likely to pass A-level exams than children whose mothers stayed at home, claims a study for the Joseph Rowntree Foundation.

A survey of more than 1,200 people born in the 1970s found that children of full-time working mothers were also more likely to be unemployed and to experience psychological problems in early adulthood. However, the daughters of working women were much less likely to become teenage parents than the children of stay-at-home mothers.

The children of part-time working mothers did slightly less well at school than the offspring of mothers who did not work in their earliest

> 7% of all families conform to the tradition of a wage-earning dad, a stay-at-home-mom, and one or more children. In 1969, the figure was 20%.

years. But part-time working had much less effect on children's future A-level results than full-time work, the study found.

The study questioned government policies aimed at encouraging mothers back into full-time work. Ministers should instead promote part-time work because it had few adverse effects on children, said John Ermisch and Marco Francesconi of Essex University's Institute for Social and Economic Research. The findings, drawn from analysis of 516 pairs of siblings taking part in the government-funded British Household Panel Survey, are significant because they measure differences in exam results between siblings whose mothers worked during the childhood of one but not the other. This means the only difference in the children's upbringing is the amount of time their mothers spent with them.

Professor Ermisch said: "The implication of our findings is that if parents have less time to spend with young children before they start school, there may be long-term consequences. This is evidence in support of employment policies such as parental leave and longer maternity leave."

"It might be better for policy makers to encourage part-time employment by one parent during a child's pre-school years. The large proportion of employed mothers with young children who are in part-time jobs is evidence that many mothers already prefer this option."

[...] People whose mothers worked full-time for about 18 months – the average period – before they started school had a 64 per cent chance of passing an

> Over the past 20 years, the time mothers spend with their children has remained about the same despite an increase in the average hours they spend at their jobs.

A-level. This dropped to 52 per cent for those whose mothers worked full-time for an extra year.

These children were also more likely to be out of work as adults, with the chances increasing to 9 per cent from the average of 7 per cent.

If mothers worked part-time for long periods, their children's chance of passing an A-level dropped by 6 percentage points, but they were also less likely to suffer mental problems later in life.

Mary MacLeod, chief executive of the National Family and Parenting Institute, said the survey showed parents should be allowed to return to work part-time. But she added: "We need to be cautious about making cast-iron judgements on working mothers from one study – statistics don't tell you everything. Many aspects of family relationships, and their environment, have a bearing on outcomes for children. "For many mothers full-time work is a necessity, not a lifestyle choice. I hope this research won't be used as another stick to beat them."

The study conflicts with earlier research that found that working mothers did not damage their children's emotional or social development. A comprehensive survey of 40 years' research published in 1997 by London University researchers found no evidence that young children need to be cared for exclusively by their mothers.

From The Independent, *March 14, 2001.*

World of work

Project 1: Decision making

Choosing the right applicant

Work in a group of three or four.

Step 1
You are an interview panel and have just interviewed four applicants for a job. They all have the same skills and all seem to be suitable. As you can't make up your mind, you do some research and find out that:

▶ Dave Hunter, aged 25, lives at home with his parents

▶ Fiona Wilcox, aged 24, is married to a successful architect

▶ John MacFadden, aged 28, is married with one child

▶ Helen Lively, aged 21, is single and lives on her own

Given this new information discuss who to offer the job to. Come to a qualified decision.

Step 2
Now that you have reached a decision you are told that
- Dave Hunter has lied to you about his academic qualifications.
- Fiona Wilcox has been drug tested positively.
- John MacFadden has got epilepsy.
- Helen Lively is pregnant.

a) Discuss your choice again, giving reasons for and against choosing each of the candidates.
b) Compile a letter of acceptance for the successful candidate and letters of refusal for the unsuccessful candidates giving reasons for your decisions.

World of work 2

Project 2: Research & present

The changing world of work

Work on your own or in a group. Choose one of the following topics, carry out research using material available in libraries and on the Internet. Make a formal presentation of your research for your class.

- The Industrial Revolution in Britain and/or America
  http://www.neo-tech.com/businessmen/part6.html
  http://www.kidinfo.com/American_History/Industrial_Revolution.html
- Organized Labour: The Trade Union movement in Britain and/or America
  http://www.tuc.org.uk/tuc/students_history.cfm
  http://www.spartacus.schoolnet.co.uk/USAtu.htm
- Globalization
  http://globalization.about.com/library/weekly/aa080601a.htm
- The future of work and the changing face of the workplace
  http://www.future-at-work.org/
  http://www.eclipse.co.uk/pens/bibby/telework.html

Project 3: Discussion & survey

Drug testing

Choose two of the following tasks.

1. Brainstorm reasons for and against drug-testing. Arrange your arguments in a table under the headings "In favour of drug testing" and "Against drug testing".
2. Find out about drug testing in Britain and the USA. The websites given may help you. Find out what the situation regarding drug testing is in Germany. Compile your information in a file for other students to view.
3. "We want drugs out of the work place, but not the drugs misuser. For example, it costs £35,000 to train a teacher. It makes no sense to dismiss them if a trace of cannabis is found in their urine." Discuss whether you agree or disagree with this statement in your group. Consider other professions as well as teaching. Decide what action should/could be taken in cases like this. Present your arguments and conclusions in the form of a feature article for a newspaper.
4. You want drug testing of teachers and of students to be introduced at your college. Carry out a survey of students' and teachers' opinions on this and present your results to your class. (Consider what drugs you would test for; how often you would test; what the consequences might be if a person was found to have taken drugs; who would test/be tested; etc.)

Check the web

http://www.drugtestingnews.com/
http://www.usdoj.gov/dea/demand/dfmanual/index.html
http://www.drugsprevention.net/default.asp?s=H&d=H7
http://www.drogenscreening.info/

3 Business matters

Entrepreneurs

Getting started
- Would you like to start your own business? Why or why not?
- Say whether you think the character traits below are important for an entrepreneur or not, and give reasons. Think of at least three other traits and add them to the list, e.g.:
  In my opinion, an entrepreneur has to be ambitious in order to become rich and successful.

• adventurous	• energetic	• modest	• shy
• ambitious	• greedy	• organized	• versatile
• caring	• humble	• outgoing	• well-educated
• cautious	• innovative	• patient	• good-looking
• conscientious	• materialistic	• ruthless	• ?

Richard Branson
Founder of …

- Compare Anita Roddick and Richard Branson in terms of their appearance and the impression they make on you as they appear in the photographs.

While you read
1. Complete the captions to the photographs.
2. Note down the similarities and differences between Anita Roddick and Richard Branson.

Anita Roddick
Founder of …

Richard Branson (1950) – capitalist adventurer

From the time that Richard Branson was just a young boy, his mother encouraged him to be enterprising and independent. Thus, at an early age he acquired a skill that would prove invaluable for his future: the ability to stand on his own two feet.

Dyslexic, short-sighted and shy, Branson hated school, yet was enterprising
5 enough to leave school at 16 to publish a national magazine, *Student*.

By 1970 Branson had established a company to sell records by mail order, and he opened his first record store in 1971. The name 'Virgin' was chosen because none of the people involved had any business experience. The Virgin record label was born a short time thereafter, and Virgin Atlantic Airways was launched in 1984. Since then
10 Branson has diversified into a number of areas including radio, railways, hotels, financial services, cinemas, jeans and cola, all with the Virgin brand name.

Apart from financing business ventures, Branson is a record-breaking adventurer. In 1986 he crossed the Atlantic in a speedboat in record time, and was the first to cross both the Atlantic and Pacific in a hot-air balloon. One of his latest plans is to
15 shuttle tourists to a Virgin hotel in outer space for around $100,000 per person.

Branson is also known for his unconventional management style. He has no grand corporate offices and rarely holds board meetings. Instead, he believes that "small is beautiful" and relies on his knack for capitalising on other people's ideas.

Some corporate giants have had to learn the hard way not to underestimate
20 Branson. This flamboyant entrepreneur has won high-profile legal battles against the likes of British Airways and Camelot (organiser of the National Lottery). Despite his reputation as rebel and empire-builder, Branson remains a popular champion of the ordinary consumer against corporate greed and dishonesty.

2 **enterprising** showing initiative – **to acquire** [əˈkwaɪə] to develop
3 **invaluable** very valuable
4 **dyslexic** [dɪˈsleksɪk] *legasthenisch*
10 **to diversify** [-ˈ---] to increase the variety of activities one does or things one makes
15 **to shuttle** to frequently move s.o. or s.th. with transportation
18 **to rely on** [rɪˈlaɪ] to depend on – **knack for s.th.** [næk] (fig.) talent for s.th. – **to capitalise on s.th.** to take advantage of s.th. (in a positive way)
20 **flamboyant** extravagant – **entrepreneur** [ˌɒntrəprəˈnɜː] *Unternehmer* – **high-profile** [ˈprəʊfaɪl] very important
21 **the likes of** such as
22 **empire-builder** *here:* one who keeps increasing the number of companies he/she owns
23 **ordinary** normal – **greed** wanting more of s.th. (e.g. money) than one needs

42

Business matters 3

Working with the text

1. Using the notes you made while reading, write sentences in which you compare the two entrepreneurs. Use the phrases below:
   Branson …, whereas Roddick … *wohingegen*
   Both Branson and Roddick …
   Neither Branson nor Roddick …
   While Branson …, Roddick …
   On the one hand Branson …, but on the other hand Roddick …
2. Which of the two entrepreneurs do you admire the most? Explain why.
3. "Entrepreneurs are born, not made".
   To what extent is this saying true of Branson and Roddick?

A step further

Choose one of the following entrepreneurs – or another of your own choice – and find out as much as you can about them. Use the internet for your research and produce profiles to display in your classroom.

   Bill Gates • Estee Lauder • Sam Walton • Henry Ford

The following websites may help you get started:

Check the web
Bill Gates: *http://www.microsoft.com/billgates/default.asp*
Estee Lauder: *http://www.time.com/time/time100/builder/profile/lauder.html*
Sam Walton: *http://www.time.com/time/time100/builder/profile/walton.html*
Henry Ford: *http://www.time.com/time/time100/builder/profile/ford.html*
Young entrepreneurs: *http://www.youngandsuccessful.com/*

Anita Roddick (1942) – caring capitalist

Anita Roddick, the founder of the Body Shop retail chain, is now one of Britain's wealthiest women. The daughter of immigrant parents who ran a cafe near Brighton, she was instilled with the work ethic from an early age.

After finishing school, Roddick travelled and pursued a number of jobs including teaching and working for the UN. She married Gordon Roddick in 1970, after which they opened a hotel and a restaurant. Then in 1976 Roddick opened the first Body Shop in Brighton with a range of beauty products made exclusively from natural ingredients and packaged in reusable containers.

The Body Shop attracted a growing market of environmentally conscious customers. As it became more successful, the Roddicks set up a system of franchises, and opened further outlets across Britain and Europe. In 1984 the company went public and its shares were floated on the stock market. Today there are more than 1,900 stores located across the world. Roddick has used her fame to promote "caring capitalism" by campaigning for environmental issues, animal rights, human rights and fair trading with the Third World. Body Shop employees have also enjoyed the benefits of this caring, including daycare opportunities and bikes for those who want to leave their cars at home. Roddick's willingness to be different and to make a difference makes her an entrepreneur.

Anita Roddick left the chief executive position in 1998 and resigned her position as company co-chair in 2002, but plans to remain a board member and a consultant. She intends to spend more time concentrating on political and ethical issues that are important to her, such as combating what she considers the unjust politics of the WTO.

---

1 **founder** person who starts a business or an organization
3 **to be instilled with a feeling** to be made to think or feel a certain way
7 **range** [reɪndʒ] variety
10 **franchise** [ˈfræntʃaɪz] smaller company that sells the products and/or services of a larger parent company
11 **to go public** to start to sell shares on the stock market
12 **to float shares** to make shares available for the public to buy
14 **to campaign for** [kæmˈpeɪn] to speak out for
16 **daycare** *Kindertagesstätte*
19 **chief executive** *Generaldirektor(in)* – **to resign** [rɪˈzaɪn] to officially give up one's job
20 **co-chair** *einer von zwei Vorsitzenden* – **board member** *Vorstandsmitglied*
22 **to combat** [ˈ--] to fight
23 **WTO** World Trade Organization

43

3 Business matters

Dot-coms and E-tailing

Before you read: What went wrong at Boo.com?
- Internet companies are often referred to as 'dot.coms'. Why?
- Have you ever bought anything on the internet? Discuss the pros and cons of online shopping, both from the customer's and the retailer's point of view.
- Look at the cartoon on the left and answer the questions below it.

Describe the scene in the cartoon. What does the cartoon tell you about Boo.com?
Think of reasons why things might have gone wrong at Boo.com.

While you read
Match the proper headings to the paragraphs. Be careful! There is one heading too many!

- Who was Miss Boo?
- What else did Boo.com spend its money on?
- How did this business start?
- What caused this dot.com's downfall?
- What was Boo.com?
- Where did the money go?
- What effect has Boo.com's failure had on other dot.coms?

Working with the text
1. Describe the founders of Boo.com and how they became celebrities.
2. Summarise the idea behind Boo.com.
3. Outline the mistakes that led to Boo's collapse.
4. The value of high-tech stocks plummeted and the entire internet industry reacted nervously when Boo.com became the first major internet company to fail. What do you think caused this reaction, and what lessons should other dot.com companies draw from Boo's fate?

Language

! Look up any words you don't know in a dictionary!

1. a) Look at the sets of words below. Find the odd one out and put it in the right set.
   b) Find a heading to go with each set of words.
      i)   to appoint – to slump – to recruit – to fill a post – to employ
      ii) to sack – to fire – to increase – to dismiss – to lay off
      iii) to plummet – to fall – to drop – to decrease – to launch
      iv) to make redundant – to found – to set up – to start – to establish
      v)   to send in the receivers – to go into liquidation – to hire – to go bankrupt – to close down
      vi) to rise – to go bust – to climb – to sky-rocket – to soar

Transitive verbs (e.g. raise) take an object.
Intransitive verbs (e.g. rise) take no object.
Regular: raise – raised – raised
Irregular: rise – rose – risen

2. a) Put in 'raise' or 'rise' in the right form.
   1) Boo.com managed to … capital by attracting big-name investors.
   2) The number of dot.com companies is … rapidly.
   3) The sun … in the east and sets in the west.
   4) I was … in a strict family. We weren't allowed to watch TV or eat sweets.
   5) Great news! Boo.com has decided to … our salaries again!
   6) Unemployment … again last month.
   7) You have … a very important point.
   b) Suggest a German translation for 'raise'/'rise' in each sentence.

to be overdue • to be delayed • to postpone • to be behind schedule • to put s.th. off

3. a) Look at the expressions on the left. Which of them mean 'to change to a later date'?
   b) Which of the other three expressions can be used to describe:
      a late plane? • a project that isn't meeting its deadlines? • a late payment?
   c) Write a short business letter to your teacher explaining why you are late handing in an assignment. Make use of at least three of the expressions.

Business matters 3

What went wrong at Boo.com?

Online retailer Boo.com had ambitions to become the first truly global retailer on the planet. Thus, this 'E-tailer' of high street fashions and sportswear launched its service simultaneously in 18 countries and seven languages, attempting something no other internet start-up had done before. But its real reason for celebrity was its glamorous 30-year-old founders, Kaysa Leander, a former model, and Ernst Malmsten, a former poetry critic – and their amazing ability to spend money.

Leander and Malmsten, who were childhood friends, founded Boo in 1998 with Patrick Hedelin, a fellow Swede. They came to London fresh from the success of their first internet venture, online bookseller Bokus.com, which they had sold for £30m. With that track record, they had little difficulty raising money for their audacious new venture from blue-chip backers such as investment banks J.P. Morgan and Goldman Sachs, the Italian Benetton family and the French billionaire Bernard Arnault, who runs the LVMH luxury goods group. In all, more than $135m was raised in five rounds of financing, making Boo one of the best-funded internet start-ups to date. But by the time the receivers moved in in May 2000, just $500,000 was left.

Much of the money went on salaries. From just seven employees in November 1998, the company grew to more than 400 by mid-1999 – and it still hadn't launched its website. Fashion buyers, marketeers, technology experts, lawyers, designers and writers were recruited to join the "Boo-crew" in offices in London, New York, Stockholm, Amsterdam, Munich and Paris. Boo even had an army of "cool hunters", whose job was to keep the firm abreast of the latest trends in music, fashion and the internet. Indeed, for a long time, the only post unfilled at Boo was that of finance director.

At its peak, Boo was spending a million dollars a week. Senior executives flew first-class and stayed in the finest hotels, taking their assistants with them. Leander and Malmsten lived rent-free at the firm's expense in Notting Hill and Primrose Hill. Many staff were issued with £700 palmtop computers; organic fruit and chocolate biscuits were delivered to the office on a daily basis. Legendary champagne-soaked parties were thrown for the fashionable crowd. Francis Ford Coppola was hired to write Boo's adverts and the world's most expensive copywriter was flown in from New York and paid £3,000 to come up with a script for "Miss Boo".

Miss Boo was the website's 3D animated mannequin who modelled clothes for prospective customers. She was just one of several sophisticated features pioneered on Boo.com. Customers were also able to zoom in on, and rotate, images of items and clothing. […] These gimmicks, however, proved just too ambitious and costly. Technical difficulties forced the company to postpone its planned launch six times. When the site was finally launched in November 1999, six months behind schedule, it could only be accessed by the newest and fastest computers. Even then, it could take anything up to half an hour to download a page.

Sales were more than disappointing. In fact, Boo sold so little of its first range of clothing that it had to dump much of it at a 40% discount at the end of the season. Leander and Malmsten insist that sales had begun to pick up: the company achieved net sales of $1.1m in February to April. But according to one former Boo employee, its call centre was taking only 15 calls a day when it should have been 15 a minute. A respected finance director was finally appointed early in 2000 – Dean Hawkins from Adidas – but he stayed just long enough to make 70 people redundant, then quit. By then, Boo was doomed. Leander and Malmsten were forced to call in receivers KMPG, an accountancy firm, when it became clear that they could not find the $30 million they needed to keep Boo on the road. […] For the Boo-crew, the party was over: the 220 remaining London employees as well as the employees in the US and Europe were made redundant.

Abridged and adapted from the article in The Week, *May 27, 2000.*

---

1 **retailer** a business that sells products (e.g. clothes) to the public
3 **simultaneously** [ˌsɪmlˈteɪniəsli] at the same time
9 **venture** [ˈventʃə] a project which is risky as it is based on new ideas
10 **track record** (fig.) a record of the performance of s.o. or s.th.
11 **audacious** [ɔːˈdeɪʃəs] risky – **blue-chip backers** well-established businesses which financially support business ventures
15 **to date** up until now – **receiver** [rɪˈsiːvə] s.o. appointed by law or a court to manage a business that has gone bankrupt
17 **salary** money earned for work
19 **marketeer** [--ˈ-] s.o. who works in the field of marketing
22 **to keep abreast of s.th.** to keep up to date
24 **peak** high point
30 **advert** (informal) advertisement – **copywriter** person who writes advertisement texts
33 **prospective** potential
34 **to rotate** to turn
35 **gimmick** [ˈgɪmɪk] an extravagant, unnecessary feature
36 **to postpone** to delay
41 **to dump** to get rid of s.th.; *here:* to sell a large quantity of products far below their actual value
46 **to make s.o. redundant** [-ˈ--] (BE) to dismiss s.o. whose services aren't needed or who the company can't afford to employ (AE: to be laid off)
47 **to be doomed** to be certain to fail
48 **accountancy firm** Buchhaltungsfirma
49 **to keep s.th. on the road** (fig.) to keep s.th. going

3 Business matters

The Day the World Turned

Before you read
- A friend of yours is in trouble and needs money. You lend them a substantial amount but they fail to repay you. What action do you take?
- If a person or company fails to make repayments on money they have borrowed what action do you think should be taken?

This text is an extract from the novel In a Land of Plenty *by Tim Pears.*

The Day the World Turned

Charles Freeman, the man-in-charge, had an air of invulnerability about him. There'd never been doubt about whether he'd succeed, in any of his ventures; only to what extent. He gave succour and strength to those around him, however much he also terrorized them. Even his opponents over the years thought less of weak spots he might harbour than of their own he might attack.

Despite rumours, the sheer force of Charles' personality and his confident, - exaggerated forecasts of growth and profit in the Freeman Communications Corporation's annual reports (their figures ratified by City accountants of unimpeachable reputation) had kept Charles' standing intact, share prices inflated and creditors at bay.

When it came, the collapse of Charles' small empire in a town in the middle of England, built up over forty years, happened in a matter of hours. What triggered that collapse was the result of Charles' having made the mistake of borrowing one sum of money from a Swiss bank, and another from an American broking firm to whom he gave FCC shares as collateral. While British banks remained convinced by Charles Freeman's confidence and promises, the foreign ones had a more distant and a cooler perspective. It was they who moved first.

In April the Swiss bank issued its first threat for loan interest repayment that was six months overdue; in May the US brokers gave an ultimatum: repay now or we'll sell the collateral.

Charles was unable to respond. On Thursday, 21 May, the New York firm sold a huge tranche of their FCC shares. Able to delay formal notification of the sale for two business days, they officially informed FCC on Tuesday, 26 May – that Monday was a bank holiday. Twenty-four hours later Charles' company secretary notified the Stock Exchange of the sale. At one o'clock on Wednesday a short announcement streamed across brokers' monitors stating that the American firm's percentage holding of Freemen Communications Corporation had declined. Within an hour FCC's share price began to plummet.

Afterwards, countless people announced to the world that they'd known all along he was heading for a fall, they'd seen it coming, obvious and inevitable, and what's more he was a bullying cheat, a shyster and a fraud; they'd known it all along.

In reality only one man in the town, Harry Singh, had the foresight both to diagnose his father-in-law's imminent demise and to prepare for it. Everyone else in a position to know what was happening had happily thrown more money at Charles when he asked for it. Then came that Wednesday afternoon, and the world turned. The figures that flashed across computer screens were like the whimpers of an animal in distress, and the hunters picked it up and came running; they knew he was in trouble and came for him in a pack; they knew *they* were in trouble. Charles' shield – the illusion of power – fell away. They came, the financiers, bank managers and brokers, scared and ruthless. To find that Harry had only just got there before them.

From In a Land of Plenty *by Tim Pears, London: Black Swan, 1997, pp. 547-548.*

---

1 **to have an air of** to seem – **invulnerability** the state of being impossible to hurt
2 **venture** risky project
3 **to what extent** how much – **succour** ['sʌkə] (formal) help
5 **to harbour** to hide
6 **sheer** pure
7 **forecast** prediction
8 **accountant** Buchhalter(in)
9 **unimpeachable** (formal) honest – **standing** position
10 **creditor** person or institution who lends money to others – **to keep s.th. or s.o. at bay** (fig.) to keep under control
12 **to trigger** to cause
13 **to borrow** here: to take money that must be paid back, often with interest (Zins)
14 **broking firm** Maklergeschäft
15 **collateral** s.th. of value given to a creditor as guarantee of loan repayment
18 **loan** Kredit
19 **overdue** s.th. that should have happened before
22 **tranche of shares** [trɑːnʃ] several shares (Aktie) – **notification** being informed
26 **to stream** to move quickly and continuously
28 **to plummet** to go down very quickly
29 **countless** very many
30 **to head for a fall** (fig.) to be about to fail in s.th. – **obvious** clear – **inevitable** not to be avoided
31 **cheat** Betrüger – **shyster** Gauner – **fraud** Schwindler
32 **to have foresight** to be able to predict s.th.
33 **imminent** sure, certain – **demise** [dɪ'maɪz] (formal) downfall, end
36 **whimper** quiet, scared noise
38 **pack** large group (usually refers to animals, e.g. wolves)
40 **ruthless** having no pity or mercy

46

Business matters 3

Working with the text
1. Put the events in the right order:
   a) The U.S. firm threatened to sell the collateral unless they received immediate payment from FCC.
   b) Brokers learned that the American firm had reduced its shareholding in FCC.
   c) Charles Freeman built up a business empire.
   d) FCC received a demand from the Swiss bank to repay loan interest that was six months overdue.
   e) FCC's shares were overvalued.
   f) The price of FCC shares fell rapidly.
   g) The American firm sold a substantial amount of FCC shares.
   h) Charles took out loans from a Swiss bank and an American broking firm, giving the latter his company's shares as collateral.
2. Compare Charles' reputation before and after his demise.
3. Explain how the following people and institutions contributed to the collapse of FCC. Who, in your view, carries most of the blame:
   the City accountants • the British banks • the Swiss bank • the New York broking firm • Charles Freeman?
4. What action do you think Harry Singh might have taken?

Language
1. Find adjectives in the text that could describe someone who:
   a) … is very sure of him or herself.
   b) … is seen as completely trustworthy and reliable.
   c) … forces his or her way aggressively.
   d) … is cruel and harsh, and who will stop at nothing to get what he or she wants.
2. Find nouns in the text that describe someone who:
   a) … is in a position of leadership.
   b) … is a competitor or enemy.
   c) … lies and behaves dishonestly to get what he or she wants.
   d) … buys and sells shares for other people.
3. a) Group the words below in pairs under the headings *Synonyms* or *Opposites*.
      annual • assistance • collateral • creditors • debtors • demise • downfall • to harbour • imminent • inevitable • to plummet • to prompt • to reveal • security • to soar • succour • to trigger • yearly
   b) Write sentences in which you use one word from each pair.

> Look up any words you don't know in a dictionary!

Similes & metaphors
1. a) Identify the similes and metaphors in the last paragraph.
   b) In the case of language, *synaesthesia* occurs when words which are usually used to describe one sense (e.g. taste) are instead used to describe another. Find an example of this in the answers that you have given for 1. a). Explain your choice.
2. Suggest an appropriate simile or metaphor for Harry Singh's role bearing in mind your answer to task 4 in "Working with the text".

> **Simile and metaphor**
> See *Glossary* on pp. 208–210.

A step further
1. What lessons can be learned from the fate of FCC? Complete the following sentence in as many ways as you can: "FCC might not have collapsed if …"
2. Discuss the pros and cons of the following forms of saving and investment. Consider both the risks and the returns.
      a new business venture • shares (U.S.: stocks) • bonds • buying a lottery ticket • property (U.S.: real estate) • precious stones and metals • works of art (paintings, sculpture, antiques) • savings or high-interest deposit account • storing money under your mattress

3 Business matters

Doing good business

Before you read
- What do you think companies need to do to create a positive public image? Brainstorm ideas with a partner. Give examples of companies that are considered to be 'good corporate citizens'.

Ben & Jerry sell out as hippie ideal is licked

Ben & Jerry's Homemade, the American ice cream maker and symbol of hippie entrepreneurship, sold out to big business in the form of the British company Unilever.

A fierce rearguard action was fought by fans of the company, under the slogan "Multi-Flavours not Multi-nationals" but they have been forced to concede that while small may be beautiful, big has more clout.

Founded in a renovated petrol station in rural Vermont in 1978, Ben & Jerry's swiftly became one of America's great business stories. Ben Cohen and Jerry Greenfield, childhood friends, started their business with just £6,000, a third of which was borrowed.

Using fresh Vermont milk and cream, they gave their ice creams jazzy names like Chunky Monkey, Cherry Garcia, Entangled Mints and Pulp Addiction. In every store there were pictures of Ben and Jerry in tie-dyed T-shirts, peering out from behind glasses and facial hair.

More importantly for those who ate the ice cream, however, was the company's social mission. Ben and Jerry vowed to run their company in line with a manifesto completely at odds with the rest of corporate America. They promised to use only natural ingredients; to help their community by donating 7.5 per cent of all their pre-tax earnings to social action projects; and to create a great working environment for their employees.

The ratio between the salaries of Ben and Jerry themselves and their humblest employee was the lowest in America at a time when other company heads were collecting multi-million dollar pay packages while sacking thousands of workers.

The wholesome image behind the ice cream justified to buyers its high price, higher than its main rival, Haagen-Dazs. Buying Ben & Jerry's, you were not just buying pudding, you were saying something about your own community spirit. The Ben & Jerry's headquarters in Vermont has become a heavily visited tourist attraction.

The decision to sell the company, forced on them by shareholder pressure, was reported to have provoked a rift between the founders. Mr Cohen formed an alliance with a group of investors in an unsuccessful attempt to buy the company, while Mr Greenfield opposed any sale, fearing a sell-out to a standard business. The two men later denied that they had fallen out.

A Save Ben & Jerry's group rallied consumers of the ice cream to purchase shares in the company to block an outside multinational. On its website, the group warned that big companies wanted "to skin the company alive and use its gentle lambskin brand identity to fool unsuspecting consumers into purchasing their soulless profit-driven products".

The issues over which the battle for Ben & Jerry's Homemade was fought raised similar questions to those of the protesters who tried to disrupt meetings of the World Bank and the International Monetary Fund in Washington DC in 2000.

These were the same people who rioted at the Seattle World Trade Organisation meeting in 1999, members of a burgeoning grassroots movement which believes America's soul is being devoured by big business.

In their announcement of the deal with Unilever, one of the world's biggest consumer products companies, Ben & Jerry's promised to maintain its uniqueness. It will operate separately from Unilever and will have an independent board of directors who will focus on the company's social mission.

For millions of Ben & Jerry's fans, however, this old hippie has been shorn of his locks.

By Philip Delves Broughton, The Daily Telegraph, April 13, 2000.

Col. 1: **to be licked** (slang) to be defeated – *3* **to sell out** (slang) *here:* to give up one's principles – *6* **to fight a rearguard action** trying too late to prevent s.th. – *10* **to concede** [kənˈsiːd] to admit – *11* **clout** [klaʊt] power, importance – *22* **entangled** [ɪnˈtæŋgld] *verfangen* – **mint** *Pfefferminz*: word play on *entanglements* (*Verwicklungen*) – **pulp** [pʌlp] *Fruchtfleisch* – *24* **to peer** to look with difficulty – *29* **to vow** to promise – **in line with** according to

Col. 2: *2* **to donate** to give s.th. for a good purpose without expecting payment – *3* **social action projects** projects helping those in need – *6* **ratio** relationship in numbers – *10* **pay package** salary and work benefits – *13* **to justify** to make s.th. seem reasonable – *14* **rival** [ˈraɪvl] competitor – *22* **shareholder** *Aktionär(in)* – *23* **rift** a serious difference in opinion – *27* **to oppose** to not agree with s.th., to keep s.th. from happening – *29* **to deny** to say s.th. is not true – *30* **to fall out** *here:* to have a fight – *31* **to rally** to bring people together to support s.th.

Col. 3: *4* **to skin s.o./s.th. alive** (fig.) *here:* to take a company apart for profitable purposes – *6* **unsuspecting** without suspicion of wrong doing – *12* **to disrupt** [-ˈ-] to interrupt – *13* **International Monetary Fund** (IMF) *Internationaler Währungsfonds* – *19* **burgeoning** (lit.) [ˈbɜːdʒənɪŋ] growing – **grassroots movement** *Volksbewegung* – *21* **to devour** [dɪˈvaʊə] to eat quickly and eagerly – *25* **to maintain** to keep up a certain standard – *31* **to be shorn of ones locks** (fig.) *here:* to no longer be an example of hippie ideals

Working with the text
1. Write down one or two key words for each paragraph as you read the article.
2. Write a summary of the article using your key words you noted down while reading.

Synonyms & opposites
1. a) Find the opposites of these words from the text:
   Col. 1: fierce (l. 6) • rural (l. 13) • swiftly (l. 14) • at odds with (l. 30)
   Col. 2: humble (l. 7) • to sack (l. 11) • wholesome (l. 12) •
   to purchase (l. 32)
   b) Suggest synonyms/synonymous phrases for the words in part a).

The passive
Suggest two ways of putting each of the following sentences into the passive. Start each sentence a different way.
1. Creative people gave Ben and Jerry's ice cream interesting names.
2. Ben and Jerry have sent all shareholders a letter.
3. Recruitment agencies have already offered jobs to Boo's former employees.
4. Boo.com owes its investors a lot of money.

Looking at the issues
1. a) Do you think that this article presents Ben and Jerry's situation objectively or subjectively? Give reasons for your answer.
   b) Do you agree with this article's presentation of Ben and Jerry? Why or why not?
2. a) What example is given of Ben and Jerry's efforts to create a good working environment? Discuss the pros and cons of such a policy.
   b) Give examples of other policies that can help to improve working conditions.
3. a) Describe the view of multinationals that is held by Ben and Jerry's supporters.
   b) Consider how a company such as Unilever might try to counter this view. Write a press release from the Public Relations Department with the aim of winning support for the business deal.

Further activity: brand identity
The expressions "brand identity" and "brand image" refer to the personality of a product, or how the product is perceived by the public.
1. Find key phrases in the text used to describe Ben & Jerry's brand identity (Col. 2, l. 12 – Col. 3, l. 8).
2. Look at the picture of Ben Cohen and Jerry Greenfield. Does this picture convey the image that is described in the article? Why or why not?
3. Describe the "brand image" of a product you know well and present it to the class. If possible, bring along ads for this product and/or for the company that produces it, and say how effective you think these ads put across the company/product's image.

A step further
In the U.S. company heads are expected to pursue business strategies that increase share values. If they don't, it is possible for shareholders to sue* the company. Ben and Jerry found themselves in this position:
"The decision to sell the company, forced on them by shareholder pressure, …"
(Col. 2, l. 21).

- How do you think Ben & Jerry were put under pressure by shareholders?
- Find out what you can about the decision to sell. The following website may be useful:
  http://timesargus.nybor.com/Archive/Articles/Article/7051

Check the web
Get current information about Ben & Jerry's at:
http://www.benjerry.com/co-index.tmpl

A press release
See *Skills file* on p. 205.

* **to sue** to start a legal case to claim money because s.o. has harmed you

3 Business matters

Recipe for success – a role play

The business
GiLa's Diners is a food franchise with a difference: Founded by Ginny Largo in 1992, it has grown rapidly into a nationwide chain of 30 diners specializing in locally flavoured honest-to-goodness cooking and a local atmosphere. Rumours of plans to expand overseas are circulating. The phenomenal success of GiLa's Diners has attracted the attention of the media at home and abroad and has made Ginny Largo a household name.

> **Check the web**
> Get more information about writing mission statements at:
> **http://www.tgci.com/publications/98fall/MissionStatement.html**

The roles
1. A reporter from *Whippersnappers Magazine*, a magazine for entrepreneurs:
   You are going to interview Ginny Largo's publicity officer about Largo's recipe for success. You have prepared a set of questions (see below right) based on the Mission Statement (see below left).
   a) Decide which order to ask the questions in.
   b) Decide on two questions to miss out and replace them with questions of your own.
2. Largo's publicity officer:
   You have agreed to give the interview and have sent the reporter a Mission Statement (see below left) in advance. Write answers to the reporter's questions (see below right) in note form so that you are well prepared for the interview.

The role play
Work in pairs. Write a dialogue between the reporter and Ginny Largo's publicity officer. Use the Mission Statement and questions as a starting point and invent additional questions and answers. Record your interview, or act it out to the class.

Mission Statement

Our goal is to make the name "GiLa's Diners" stand for delicious home-style food and a friendly and unique local dining experience for both our customers and our employees. Here are five ways to achieve this goal:

5 ✓ We respect fellow employees' diversity and recognize that our business benefits from their unique talents and ideas.

✓ We treat customers like friends. We do our best to fulfill their wishes and we specialize in first names and smiles!

10 ✓ All of our diners are unique. Everything from the decor to the daily specials should reflect each diner's distinctive location and local traditions.

✓ We use only the freshest, high-quality ingredients to produce the healthiest, most delicious foods possible. We buy ingredients whenever possible from local growers and 15 producers.

✓ We give a percentage of our yearly profits back to the towns where we are located to support community social programs.

GiLa's Diners Interview

– Why do you think diners are becoming popular in the USA again?
– What's so great about working for GiLa's Diner?
– What qualities do you look for when hiring staff?
– What do you mean by 'diversity'? Why is it so important to you?
– What makes your employees' working environment "motivating"? What kinds of benefits and incentives do you offer them?
– Can you give examples of how you have made use of employees' ideas and talents in your business?
– What kinds of feedback have you had from customers?
– How do each of your diners maintain their uniqueness even though they are part of a franchise?
– How do you ensure that the quality of all of your diners is up to a high standard?
– Which community and social programs do you support?

---

franchise ['fræntʃaɪz] a company or organization that allows smaller companies to sell its products and services independently but in the name and under the supervision of the parent company – **honest-to-goodness** real – **unique** [juːˈniːk] if s.th. is original and one-of-a-kind – **diversity** *here:* where many races are represented – **incentive** [ɪnˈsentɪv] an encouragement (e.g. financial) to do s.th. – **distinctive** if s.th. is clearly unlike some other thing

A step further
1. Compare the websites for two companies in terms of their business, ethical and social aims. Which business would you be more likely to invest in, and why?
2. Write your own mission statement for a company of your invention.

Business matters 3

Investing ethically

- Using a dictionary to help you if necessary, define the terms 'ethical' and 'unethical' in terms of business practice.
- In groups, think of examples of unethical business practices for areas such as pharmaceuticals, advertising, or the treatment of animals. Compare your examples with other groups.
- Are you willing to pay higher prices for 'ethical' products, or have you ever boycotted a company's products for behaving unethically? Give examples.

> **Listening comprehension**
> Listen to Richard Smith, the senior spokesman for a multinational drugs company, giving a presentation to a group of financial analysts, consultants and investment advisors.

Ethical investment
Many people today who buy shares will only invest their money in companies that demonstrate social and ethical responsibility.
Financial analysts and consultants who advise potential shareholders where to place their money are increasingly aware of this trend, and are prepared to make recommendations to clients on this basis.

Communicating in business

Refer to pages 52 & 53 when doing the following tasks.

You work in the Sales Department of Tottytot Ltd., a firm that designs and manufactures children's clothes. The Sales Manager, Jill Evans, is on a business trip and you are standing in for her. Read the mail on your desk this morning (pp. 52 & 53) and do the tasks below.

Dealing with correspondence
1. a) In your notebook, start a checklist of useful business correspondence phrases by matching the 'Useful phrases' below to their proper headings.
   b) Add further examples from pages 52–53 to your checklist.

Business correspondence

Headings	Useful phrases
1. Referring to another letter or call	a) Yours sincerely
2. Giving the reason for writing	b) We hope to hear from you again soon.
3. Giving good news	c) If we can help in any way, please contact us again.
4. Giving bad news	d) With reference to your letter of June 12, …
5. Making a request	e) Please find enclosed …
6. Offering help	f) We apologize for any inconvenience caused.
7. Apologizing	g) Would you like us to …?
8. Referring to enclosed material	h) We would appreciate it if you would …
9. Setting deadlines/making threats	i) I am sorry to have to tell you that …
10. Closing remarks	j) You will be pleased to hear that …
11. Friendly reference to future contact	k) I am writing to enquire about …
12. Signing off	l) If the goods do not reach us by (+ deadline), we will have to (+ threat).

2. Make a list of tasks you need to do in order of priority. Check with a partner that you haven't left anything out, and explain why you chose this order.
3. Do the tasks on your list. Refer to the "Useful phrases" for the writing tasks. Work with a partner for the speaking tasks.

51

3 Business matters

GLAD RAGS PLC
FAX TRANSMISSION

To: Sales Department, Tottytot Ltd.
From: Zandra Westwood,
Purchasing Manager
Subject: Enquiry

Fax: 123 4567
Fax: 0987 654
Phone: 0967652-74
Date: 12 June 2002

Dear Sir or Madam

We saw your new collection at the London Fashion Show and were very impressed by your exciting designs.
Our company is a leading distributor of children's clothing based in Liverpool. We supply retailers all over Europe, and are sure that your collection will sell like hot cakes.
We would therefore be grateful if you could send us an illustrated catalogue, your current price list and details of your terms of delivery and payment.
If your offer meets our requirements, we will be pleased to place a trial order with you.
Many thanks in advance for your attention to our enquiry.

Yours faithfully

Zandra Westwood

Zandra Westwood
Purchasing Manager

From: Excelsior Hotel
Subject: Room reservation

Dear Ms Evans

I am writing to confirm that we have reserved a single room with bath/shower for your client, Max Müller, for the night of Friday, 20th June. If you let us know his flight details in advance, we would be happy to arrange for our limousine to collect him from the airport.
We look forward to hearing from you.

Kind regards

Telephone message

For: Jill Evans
Caller: Max Müller
Time of call: 2.50 pm
Phone number: 0049 7721 5948
Message:

Herr Müller can't come to England for meeting on Friday (has to go into hospital for emergency op). Wants to know whether you can postpone meeting until 27th. Call him back a.s.a.p. to confirm so he can change flight dates.

Dear Sir or Madam

Your invoice No. 492

Having checked your invoice against our records, we regret to inform you that we have been overcharged for the 'Durajean' dungarees.
Your packing list shows that 60 pairs of dungarees were sent, whereas your invoice shows that you have charged us for 70 pairs.
We are returning your invoice enclosed and would kindly ask you to correct it and send it back to us. A copy of the packing list is also enclosed.
Payment will be made as soon as we have received your corrected invoice.

Yours faithfully,

Sarah Rockwell

Sarah Rockwell
Accounts Department
Encl.

INVOICE No. 492

Qty	Description/Model No.	Unit Price	Price
70	'Durajean' dungarees	£30	£2100
20	'Yellow flower' dresses	£40	£800
40	T-shirts (white)	£20	£800
		Sub-total	(£3700)
		+ 16% VAT	(£4292)
		− 10% discount	(£429.20)
		Total:	**£3862.80**

Payment must be effected by cheque or bank transfer within 30 days of receipt of invoice.

Business matters 3

Movers and Shakers Motivational Training

Dear Sir or Madam

Do you want to motivate your staff, build team spirit and increase profits? Then we can help you! We offer a wide range of activities aimed at team-building and developing leadership skills. Some of the key benefits to your staff and thus to your business are:

- Improved Communications
- Greater Motivation
- Problem Solving Techniques
- Increased Confidence
- Development of Planning Skills

Our activities can be tailor-made to meet your company's needs and objectives. Choose from sumo wrestling, potholing, abseiling, orienteering, raft building, learning how to pilot a helicopter and other contests and challenges. Full details about our activities and prices can be found in the enclosed brochure.

If you are interested in finding out more about our services, please do not hesitate to contact us.

Yours faithfully
John Smith
Marketing Director
Enclosure

I can't stand canteen food any longer! Fancy joining me for lunch at La Pergola? We'll need to book a table, so call or e-mail me as soon as you get in.
Jo XXX
P.S. Jill's pot plants look thirsty

KIDDYWINKS CLOTHES

21 High St.
Taplow
Bucks, SL2 2DD
Tel. 0189 9879

Ms J. Evans (Sales Manager)
Sales Department
Tottytot Ltd.
Marlow Trading Estate

Our ref. CN/PD   Your ref.   15 June 2002

Dear Ms Evans

Your offer of 21 May

Thank you for the above-mentioned offer for your line of 'Yellow flower' dresses. We would like to order 50 in all children's sizes. If they sell well, we would be in a position to place larger orders on a regular basis.

Please ensure that the dresses reach us by the end of August. As agreed, payment will be made on receipt of the goods.

We hope that this will be the beginning of a long and pleasant business relationship.

Yours sincerely,
Clive Norris
Clive Norris
Store Manager

Dear Jill
Please send out press releases and invitations to all the fashion mags. It'll give us some free advertising!
Yours,
Graham

MEMORANDUM

To: *All staff*
From: *Graham Watson, PR Dept.*
Subject: *Celebration*

I am delighted to tell you that we have won the Children's Design Award this year. We will celebrate our success on 27 June at 11am in the Conference Room. Please let me know a.s.a.p. whether you are able to attend.

Listening comprehension

There is also a message for you on the telephone answering machine. Listen and take notes.

3 Business matters

They do things differently round here

Do cultural differences matter?

It might seem surprising that cultural differences still matter in this age of globalization. After all, common music, fashion and food trends show up all around the world. In fact, however, our own cultural backgrounds still greatly influence the way we communicate, work and spend our free time. Culture not only influences more obvious things such as clothing and eating habits, but also more subtle aspects that are integral parts of our personalities and belief systems – from the physical distance we keep between each other, from the way we criticize or praise to how we deal with conflicts.

We are often not aware of how much we are shaped by our own culture until we find ourselves living and working with people with a different set of influences, which is increasingly the case in this age of international migration and diversity. Once we are in this situation, finding out that others do things in ways that we don't, or that they have a completely different idea of what is "right" sometimes proves unsettling, and even threatening; after all, such experiences challenge many of our own methods, habits and beliefs – things which we have never had to think twice about before. The major purpose and challenge of intercultural competence is to help us to learn to deal with such situations constructively in our everyday lives.

It is not only important to take cultural differences into consideration if you are dealing with Asian or African cultures, where you might expect them to arise. Many Germans are surprised to find out how many differences exist between cultures that, at least outwardly, appear very similar to theirs. Consider just a few examples of Americans, who we think we know well from the media or from our vacations. In the US, it is important to be outgoing and friendly – even upon the first encounter with someone; this aspect of American societal behavior helps to maintain harmony within a group of very diverse people. However, for Americans, just like Germans, it takes more time to build up a deeper relationship with someone. Germans, however, often misinterpret this initial friendliness as something deeper, and then accuse Americans of hypocrisy when they find out that they have not immediately won a lifelong friend. Small talk during business hours, which may seem like a waste of precious work time for Germans, is for Americans an important way to establish a positive and motivating work environment. Germans may consider a heated discussion to be an interesting exchange of ideas, and it is a question of honesty for many to state their opinions clearly, even if this may cause hurt feelings: Americans – in their opinion out of respect for the other "side" – often try to avoid conflicts if possible, or to solve them through more indirect means. The result? Americans are frequently shocked by German directness, which they often perceive as rudeness, and Germans think that Americans are either indecisive or even dishonest. These misinterpretations on both sides can lead to misunderstandings, conflicts and prejudices.

How does one learn to build the "bridges" between cultures that are proof of one's intercultural competence? It is crucial to recognize that this is a lifelong learning process which requires our patience and willingness to find out about other cultures as well as about ourselves. It also requires us to recognize how much we are influenced by our own culture and its underlying values. Most importantly, it requires us to accept the fact that things can and will be done differently from the ways that we are used to. We need to bring ourselves to withhold judgement about other cultures while we are learning about them, and to recognize that this learning experience in no way threatens our own cultural basis, but rather enriches it.

Michael Rössler, Institut für Auslandsbeziehungen e.V.,
Intercultural Training and Consulting, Stuttgart, 2001.

---

3 **to influence** to have an effect on
5 **obvious** easy to see or notice – **subtle** ['sʌtl] *opp. of* obvious
6 **integral** ['---] essential
7 **to praise** to say good things about s.o. or s.th.
9 **to be shaped by s.th.** to be influenced by

14 **threatening** making s.o. feel like they are in danger of being harmed – **to challenge** to put s.th. into question
15 **to think twice about s.th.** to think carefully about s.th.
18 **to take s.th. into consideration** to think about s.th.

27 **initial** [ɪˈnɪʃl] beginning
28 **hypocrisy** [hɪˈpɒkrəsi] saying or doing s.th. that one doesn't believe in
30 **precious** [ˈpreʃəs] valuable
31 **heated** *here:* intense

37 **indecisive** not able to make decisions

44 **underlying** basic

46 **to withhold judgement** to wait before deciding whether you like or dislike s.th.

Business matters 3

Working with the text
1. For whom is intercultural competence an important aspect of everyday life, and why?
2. a) Our culture influences many aspects of our everyday lives. Give examples of these aspects from the text.
   b) Some of these aspects are more difficult to recognize than others. Explain why this is the case.
3. In order to become interculturally competent, do you only have to become an expert about other cultures? Explain.
4. a) In two columns, summarize the examples of American and German behavior that you have found in the text.
   b) Describe the misunderstandings that arose from these differences.

Using symbols
In this text, the process of learning to understand other cultures is referred to as "building 'bridges'" (ll. 40–41). Do you find this symbol suitable? Can you think of another symbol?

Language
Find words in the text which mean the following:
1. the act of moving from one location to another
2. discomforting
3. meeting
4. to keep away from s.th.
5. very important
6. to add to s.th. in a positive way

A step further
In groups, come up with aspects of what you consider to be 'typically American'. Remember to consult friends, films, TV, newspapers and magazines for additional ideas. As a class, compare your lists and come up with a class list. Then, establish contact with a partner American school and ask them to do the same for Germans. Exchange your lists. Identify and talk about reasons for cultural misunderstandings.

> **Tip**
> Generalizations about cultural differences can sometimes be useful, but beware of stereotypes!
> There are always exceptions, and cultural habits can change, too!

> **Listening comprehension**
> *Felix Hilger is on a two-month internship in an American company. He hopes to gain some insight into American business practices.*

> **Check the web**
> Get more information about setting up an e-mail project with an American school at:
> **http://www.stolaf.edu/network/iecc/**

Project: International e-tailing

Work in a group of three or four.
You are young entrepreneurs interested in e-tailing.
1. Decide on a product or service you think will sell well internationally.
2. Work out and produce a profile for your business including the following points:
   ▶ A brief introduction of yourselves and the product/service you plan to sell.
   ▶ Details about the product/service (name, features, etc.)
   ▶ The target group
   ▶ Your plans for marketing the product
   ▶ Capital requirements (how much money you think you will need for your start-up and what you need it for)
3. a) Either present your product profile to your class, who will act as venture capitalists interested in financing a dot.com business, or write a letter to a venture capitalist (your teacher/other members of your class) asking for financial backing for your business.
   b) As a venture capitalist, decide which of the products or services you would like to support and write a letter inviting the group to come for a meeting to discuss the matter further.

4 Energy & the environment

Global warming

Understanding the cartoon

1. Describe the cartoon in as much detail as possible.
2. What point is the cartoonist making?
3. Who does Uncle Sam represent?
4. How is Uncle Sam presented in the cartoon? Concentrate on his behaviour and appearance.
5. Which U.S. president is caricatured here? Describe how this president is presented.

Further activities

1. Act out the scene concentrating on the body language of the president and Uncle Sam.
2. What other arguments can you think of that might make Uncle Sam actually do something?

From International Herald Tribune, *November 21, 1997.*

★ Listening comprehension

Listen to how the volunteers of the UK Phrenology Network help scientists record climate changes during the seasons.

Climate change: scientific certainties and uncertainties (pp. 58 & 59)

Before you read

- What do you think the world will be like in fifty years' time? Make a list of ideas and compare your predictions with those of other students in your class. Discuss any differences.
- What do you know about climate change? Make a list of the facts you know and their possible consequences. Present them in class. Compare and discuss your results.

After reading

Working with the text/note taking

Collect information from the text in note form under the following headings:
- Climate change
- Human activities
- Geographical changes
- Changes in temperature
- Changes in atmosphere

Energy & the environment 4

Language

Style: euphemisms
1. The terms "human conflict" (l. 53) and "health problems" (l. 59) are used euphemistically in the text. Why do you think these euphemisms were chosen? Find 'non-euphemistic' alternatives.
2. Think of euphemisms used in other situations and explain why they are used.

Paraphrasing (Work with a partner.)
Often when you are speaking in a foreign language you can't remember or don't know the exact term you need and so you have to paraphrase. Take turns to choose one of the German terms given in the box on the right and paraphrase it in English without saying which term you have chosen. See if your partner can give you the English equivalent, which can be found in the text.

Vocabulary
a) Find words and phrases in the text which are used to show that an outcome is probable but not certain.
   Example: *to appear to be* – "The earth <u>appears to be</u> warming." (l. 7)
b) Make further statements about your view of how the world may be in 2050 using the phrases you have found. (You can refer back to the task you did before reading the text for ideas.)

> **Euphemism**
> See *Glossary* on pp. 208–210.

> - globale Erwärmung (l. 19/ ll. 25–26)
> - Durchschnittstemperatur (l. 9)
> - Treibhausgas (l. 14)
> - Energiegewinnung (l. 18)
> - negative/positive Auswirkungen (ll. 27–28)
> - mit dem Klima zusammenhängende Faktoren (ll. 37–38)
> - Strahlung der Sonne (l. 50)

A step further

Top five discussion (Work in groups.)
1. Have a discussion in your group and come to an agreement on the five most important causes and consequences of global warming. Make a list giving reasons for your choices.
2. Present your group's choices to the other groups in your class using if-clauses and phrases from the vocabulary task above whenever possible.
   Example: *We think that gas emissions are the most important cause of global warming because if gas emissions continue on a "business as usual" basis, carbon dioxide levels will probably double from pre-industrial levels by the end of this century.* (See lines 32–34 of the text.)
3. Compare and discuss your results and find the "Top five" for your class.

> **Having a discussion**
> See *Skills files* on pp. 191 & 192.

Further activities
- Find out more about the causes and effects of climate change. The websites below may be useful.
- Choose one aspect of climate change and find as much information as possible. You could write a letter or e-mail to organizations asking for more information or you could do an internet search.
- Use the material you find (or are sent) to design a leaflet or poster for an environmental organization and display it in your classroom.

> **Letter writing**
> See *Skills files* on pp. 196–199.

Check the web

Get more information about global warming at:
- *http://www.epa.gov/globalwarming/kids/gw.html*
- *http://www.unfccc.int/resource/iuckit/index.html*
- *http://www.wildweather.com/features/global_warming.htm*
- *http://community.middlebury.edu/~rosenber/DR-personal-homepage/ globalwarming/gwact2.html*

Use a search engine, e.g. *www.google.com* and enter the key words **global warming**.

4 Energy & the environment

Climate change: scientific certainties and uncertainties

The earth's systems of air, water and land have always been dynamic. Studies of ancient climates show that there have been alternating periods of global warmth and global chill at various times. Sometimes the transitions from one state to another have been abrupt, at other times the rate of change has been slow, but in all cases change has been driven by natural processes.

But now evidence is gathering that human activities are changing or perhaps accelerating climate change. The earth appears to be warming.

Widely accepted facts

- Average global temperature has risen by 0.6 °C in the last 130 years.
- Carbon dioxide levels in the atmosphere have risen by about 25% in the last 200 years, increasing from about 280 parts per million to 356 parts per million today.
- Methane levels in the atmosphere have doubled over the last 100 years.
- Nitrous oxide levels are rising at about 0.25% each year.
- Carbon dioxide, methane and nitrous oxide are all greenhouse gases which trap radiation emitted from the earth's surface, keeping the earth warmer than it otherwise would be.
- Carbon dioxide, methane and nitrous oxide levels are rising mainly as a result of human activities connected with energy generation, transport and agriculture.
- The order of importance in contributing to human-induced global warming is carbon dioxide (70%), methane (20%), nitrous oxide plus other gases (10%).
- Temperature has not increased as much as you would expect from the observed carbon dioxide increase. It is thought that tiny particles in the atmosphere from, for instance, industrial activities or volcanic eruptions, reflect sunlight and produce a cooling effect.
- A doubling of carbon dioxide levels would theoretically lead to an average global temperature rise of 1–2 °C if all other factors remained the same. But in reality other factors will also change in response to rising temperature and may produce feedbacks, some negative, some positive. For example, water vapour in the atmosphere increases as temperature rises and is itself a potent greenhouse gas.

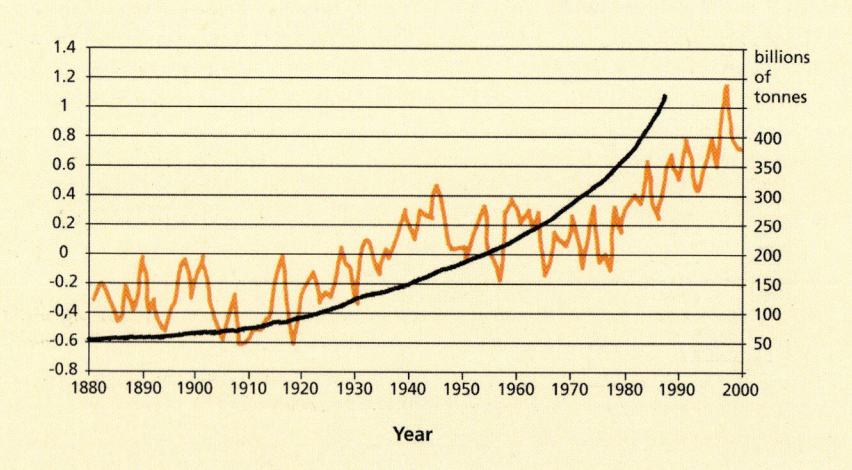

Source: U.S. National Climatic Data Center, 2001

---

2 **alternating** [ˈɔːltəneɪtɪŋ] going back and forth between two things
3 **transition** the process of changing from one state into another
4 **abrupt** [əˈbrʌpt] sudden
6 **to gather** to collect
7 **to accelerate** [əkˈseləreɪt] to get faster

10 **carbon dioxide** [ˈkɑːbn daɪˈɒksaɪd] Kohlendioxyd
12 **methane** [ˈmiːθeɪn] Methan
13 **nitrous oxide** [ˈnaɪtrəs ˈɒksaɪd] Distickstoffoxid
15 **to emit** [ɪˈmɪt] to release

19 **to contribute to** [kənˈtrɪbjuːt] to cause a result – **induced** [ɪnˈdjuːst] caused by

23 **volcanic eruption** when lava, hot ash and steam break through the volcano's surface

28 **vapour** [ˈveɪpə] Dampf
29 **potent** [ˈ--] strong, powerful

Global temperature changes (left hand scale)
Carbon emissions (right hand scale)

Energy & the environment 4

What is likely to happen?

Global consequences:
- If greenhouse gas emissions continue on a "business as usual" basis, models predict that carbon dioxide levels will double from pre-industrial levels within the next few years. When the effect of other factors such as increased water vapour is added, the estimated average global temperature rise will be between 1.5 and 4.5°C, the most likely value being 2.5°C.
- The rise in temperature will produce an impact on a wide range of climate-related factors.
- Global sea levels are likely to rise by about 50 cm over the next century, and will continue to rise further in the future. Low-lying coasts will flood and some habitats such as saltmarshes will be lost unless they can be protected from flooding.
- We might expect more extreme weather events – heatwaves, floods, droughts, storms – but it is impossible to predict where these are likely to occur with the present generation of models.
- The world's vegetation zones will undergo major changes, in particular boundary shifts between grasslands, forests and shrublands.
- Deserts will become hotter, desertification will extend and is more likely to become irreversible.
- Half the world's glaciers could melt and Arctic ice would be reduced in extent. When ice melts, the amount of solar radiation which can be absorbed by the exposed land increases so warming will be amplified further.
- Freshwater systems will experience changes in temperature, flows and levels, affecting biodiversity, water supplies and probably water quality. Human conflict over access to water resources may increase.
- Agricultural productivity is likely to vary across regions. Although global productivity may stay about the same, there may be increased risk of famine in arid and semi-arid regions.
- Mass movements of people away from flooded or arid regions would cause conflicts and health problems.
- Human and animal diseases may spread to new areas.

1998 Greenhouse Gas Emissions Per Capita (Metric Tons of CO2 Equivalent per Person)

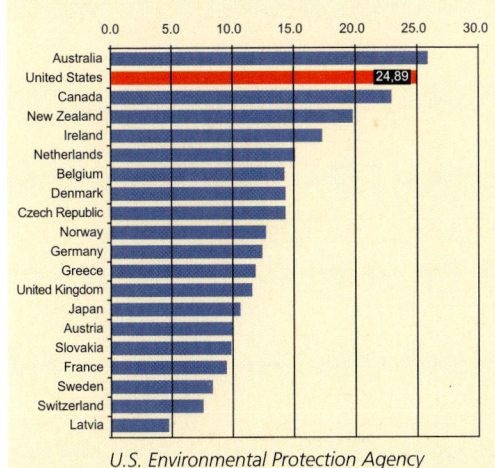

U.S. Environmental Protection Agency

UK consequences:
The UK will be directly or indirectly affected by most of the expected global impacts of climate change. The specific effects will depend upon regional changes which are impossible to predict accurately at present. A general northwards shift by 50–80 km per decade of natural habitats and agricultural zones is likely. Forestry and some forms of farming are likely to benefit, but significant impacts are likely on soils, wildlife, water resources and agriculture in the south.

From the Natural Environment Research Council brochure, October 2000.

---

32 **"business as usual"** the same procedure as always

37 **impact** ['--] effect
40 **habitat** a natural and unique plant or animal environment
41 **saltmarsh** a flat area of ground which is soaked with salt water
42 **drought** [draʊt] an unusually long period without rainfall
45 **to undergo** to experience, to go through – **boundary** borders between two zones
46 **shrub** small woody plant
47 **desertification** [dɪˌzɜːtɪfɪˈkeɪʃn] the process of land turning into desert
48 **irreversible** [ˌ--'---] impossible to change back to a previous state
51 **to amplify** to increase greatly
53 **biodiversity** a wide variety of plants and animals that live in particular natural environments, in this case in water
56 **famine** ['fæmɪn] state of extreme food shortage causing starvation – **arid** ['ærɪd] so dry that no plants can grow
73 **wildlife** referring to animals and living things that live in the wild

---

Analysing data & diagrams

1. Look at the graph and the bar chart. Describe the facts presented in them as briefly and precisely as possible.
2. What is striking about the data shown?
3. Suggest solutions and write a report, letter, or essay using the information given. Consider the implications for industrialised and developing countries. Find a suitable title. Remember to use the *Skills files*.

4 Energy & the environment

Forms of energy

While you read: Kicking the carbon habit

Annotations
Compile your own list of annotations (new words with explanations) to go with this text.
- Before looking in a dictionary try to work out the meaning of new words by:
    1) considering the word you don't know carefully in the context as a whole.
    2) thinking of related words in English that you know.
    3) thinking of similar words in German or another foreign language you know.
- Look up important words that you still don't know in an English/English dictionary.
- Note down the meaning of the words in English as well as the German equivalent.

> Surviving without a dictionary / Using an English-English dictionary
> See *Skills files* on pp. 194 & 195.

After reading

Working with the text
1. Which of the energy forms described do you find most attractive? Give reasons.
2. You work in the PR department of an energy producing company. Devise a slogan for at least three of the types of energy mentioned in the text.

    Example: "Taking the heat out of global warming – S☀lar p☀wer!"

3. Describe in your own words the differences between the four ways of using solar energy.
4. a) What are the advantages of solar energy according to the text? List them in note form in a table.
   b) Complete your table with counter-arguments of your own. Use other sources of information that are available to you (e.g. libraries, internet, science textbooks, etc.).
   c) Use your notes to have a discussion in class about the pros and cons of solar energy.

Language
1. Rewrite these sentences using synonyms/synonymous phrases for the words underlined:
   a) *Scientists advising climate negotiators say the world needs to cut emissions of greenhouse gases by 50 per cent or more <u>within the next century</u>.*
      (Col. 1, ll. 17–21)
   b) <u>More efficient</u> *power stations would help. So would <u>switching</u> from coal, the dirtiest of the fossil fuels, to natural gas, which <u>emits</u> less carbon dioxide.*
      (Col. 1, ll. 25–29)
   c) *"Biomass" burning <u>stands equal</u> with solar power in Shell's recently announced $500 million investment in renewable energy.*
      (Col. 1, l. 53–Col. 2, l. 2)
   d) *In Britain, <u>there are proposals</u> to convert set-aside farmland for willow and poplar crops <u>to burn in</u> power stations.*
      (Col. 2, ll. 4–7)
   e) *But <u>opponents</u> say nuclear power <u>consumes so much money and technical expertise</u> that it <u>crowds out other, cheaper, safer and more acceptable</u> forms of energy.*
      (Col. 2, ll. 36–40)
2. Find opposites for these words from the text:
   Col. 1: to raise (l. 24) • energy-saving (l. 31) • public (l. 33) • to manage (l. 44)
   Col. 2: renewable (l. 1) • increasingly (l. 16)

Style
The style of the text is informal.
1. What does this tell you about the readership the article is aimed at?
2. Find at least five examples of sentences in which informal language is used and rewrite them in formal English.

> Analysing style
> See *Skills file* on p.181.

KICKING THE CARBON HABIT

Scientists advising climate negotiators say the world needs to cut emissions of greenhouse gases by 50 per cent or more within the next century. That is a hard task, especially with world population set to almost double, and with developing countries aspiring to raise their emissions to Western levels. More efficient power stations would help. So would switching from coal, the dirtiest of the fossil fuels, to natural gas, which emits less carbon dioxide. (That is how Britain cut its emissions during the 1990s.) Numerous energy-saving measures from lagging the loft and fuel-efficient light bulbs to better public transport and "smart" systems to run factories could make big inroads. But ultimately, we have to find new ways of generating electricity. Along with solar power, here are the other main runners:

Wind If Britain is a bit climatically challenged in the solar stakes, it is the best spot in Europe for wind power – 40 per cent of the continent's potential according to one study. Sad then that it managed to contribute only 1 per cent of the 6,000 megawatts added to the world's wind generating capacity last year. Worldwide the big four in windmills are Germany, the US, Denmark and India.

Biomass burning Away from electricity grids, wood is the main fuel for the world's poor. Now it is making a comeback in power stations. "Biomass" burning stands equal with solar power in Shell's recently announced $500 million investment in renewable energy. It plans large forest plantations in developing countries to feed town power plants. In Britain, there are proposals to convert set-aside farmland for willow and poplar crops to burn in power stations. Of course, burning wood produces carbon dioxide. But the cleared land can be used to grow more trees, which will absorb the same amount of carbon dioxide.

Hydroelectricity Apart from biomass, hydroelectricity is the biggest current source of "renewable" electricity worldwide. But large hydroelectric dams are increasingly stigmatised as anti-social. Their power turns out not to be very renewable, either. Many reservoirs will silt up and become useless within 40 years. But the future could well lie with millions of small hydroplants supplying villages from local streams.

Geothermal "Hot rocks" provide a million Americans with their electricity. The Philippines and Mexico are other big users. But big generating plants tapping geysers or hot underground rocks often create big local problems.

Nuclear Fears of another Chernobyl and concerns about disposal of waste haunt the industry. Even so, installed capacity is at a record. South Korea is the current world leader in reactor construction. Nuclear power generation does not emit greenhouse gases. But opponents say nuclear power consumes so much money and technical expertise that it crowds out other, cheaper, safer and more acceptable forms of energy.

Fuel cells Many renewable sources of electricity are intermittent, depending on the sun or wind. Better storage of energy is urgently needed. The hydrogen fuel cell could be the answer. As the electricity is generated it is used to separate hydrogen from water. The hydrogen is then stored in fuel cells, like batteries, which can be transported round the world or attached to a car engine. The energy is released by recombining the hydrogen with oxygen to make water. The first commercial fuel-cell factory only opened in 1995. But some see the emergence by the end of the next century of a worldwide "solar-hydrogen" energy economy.

Solar energy Solar has several advantages over other forms of energy. Most important is the sheer amount of energy that the sun pours forth: 2.5 million quintillion joules a year, which is 6,000 times as much as the entire human race uses annually. Sunshine is also the most widely available non-exhaustable energy source. Relatively few places have access to hydropower, geothermal energy or wave energy, or have the right weather and geography to make use of wind power. But nearly every place gets enough sunlight to make some solar power generation feasible. Solar energy is totally without pollution or risk of hazardous waste, and is therefore preferable compared to conventional energy sources such as fossil fuels and nuclear power. Moreover, because solar technology works on both small and large scales, it can be pursued by individuals, small communities and large power-generating utilities. Most other energy sources, by contrast, only work on a large scale.

Types of solar heating

Photovoltaic Devices convert sunlight directly into electricity. Sunlight falls on panels made of certain materials (e.g. silicon), causing electrons to break loose and flow as electric current. Photovoltaic cells can produce electricity for everything from wristwatches to houses.

Solar Thermal Devices indirectly produce electricity. Sunlight heats water or another fluid, which then turns a turbine to produce electricity.

Passive Solar Heating refers to constructing a building so that the sun keeps it warm. Typically, most windows face south and as few as possible face west. Sun-warmed air circulates throughout the building through vents.

Active Solar Heating relies on solar collectors, often on a building's roof, to heat water or air, which then circulates through the building to heat it. Typically, these collectors also provide the building's hot water.

From The Guardian, *November 27, 1997.*

4 Energy & the environment

Nuclear energy

Before you read: Putting waste in its place
- Are you in favour or against the use and production of nuclear power? Give reasons.
- What are the main arguments used by supporters and opposers of nuclear power? Brainstorm ideas with a partner and draw up a list.

Analysing the advert
Working with the text
1. In your own words explain the difference between 'Low Level Waste', 'Intermediate Level Waste' and 'High Level Waste'.
2. Explain the following methods of treating nuclear waste:
   incineration • secure containment • vitrification

Layout & style
1. Analyse layout, illustrations and language employed.
2. Do you think BNFL's PR-department did a good job? Why/Why not?
3. Suggest alternatives as if you were a competing advertising company.

A step further
1. Write a short formal letter or e-mail to BNFL asking for further information on the treatment of nuclear waste.
2. BNFL wants to build a nuclear waste disposal site in your area. Not everyone is in favour so there is to be a public hearing.
   Form the following groups:
   - a pressure group of unemployed people from the region you live in
   - representatives of BNFL who need to build a disposal site and have chosen your region
   - representatives of the ruling party of your city council who have not been successful in creating new jobs so far
   - representatives of the opposition party of your city council who are strictly against the site
   - members of a Greenpeace group
   - owners of a huge recreation park in the immediate neighbourhood of the planned site
   - members of an initiative of farmers whose land surrounds the area.

   In your groups collect arguments in preparation for an open discussion of the plans to build the nuclear waste disposal site. Choose one person to represent your group at the discussion.

> **Letter writing**
> See *Skills files* on pp. 196–199.

> **Check the web**
> Get more information about BNFL at:
> http://www.bnflinc.com

Using energy: saving energy

1. Look at the illustration showing where energy is used in a typical household. Identify which form of energy is used (gas, electricity, or petrol) for items a)–i) and write a short summary of the information referring to the following percentages of energy used in a typical household:
   - heating 45%
   - hot water 16%
   - lighting 1%
   - TV, etc. 0.5%
   - cooking, etc. 3%
   - dishwasher 2%
   - car 30%
   - fridge/freezer 2%
   - washer/drier 0.5%

2. Work with a partner and make five proposals of how and where energy can be saved in the home.
3. Compare your ideas with others in your course and decide on the five best energy saving ideas.
4. Write an essay of about 500 words pointing out where energy is wasted and suggesting ways in which energy could be saved at your school.

Energy & the environment 4

This glass disc simulates the amount of vitrified waste that would be produced in serving one person's lifetime electricity needs by nuclear energy.

PUTTING WASTE IN ITS PLACE

All manufacturing processes produce waste.

Some of the waste products from Oldbury, as with all nuclear power
5 stations, are radioactive which means that they must be disposed of under Government supervision and regulation. They fall into two categories:

Low Level Waste (LLW) comprising
10 material such as rubber gloves, paper towels and packaging. It is incinerated, compacted and sealed in drums, and placed in engineered stores at Drigg in Cumbria. About 90% of
15 all radioactive waste is classified as LLW, and also includes routine material from hospitals and laboratories. It can be safely handled by workers without radiation shielding.

20 **Intermediate Level Waste** (ILW) comprises fuel cladding, reactor components and chemical process residues. It is handled using remote tools and can retain its radioactivity
25 for many centuries; it is therefore kept in secure containment, usually using concrete or steel, at power stations or at the BNFL reprocessing plant at Sellafield.

There is a third category, **High**
30 **Level Waste**, although none is stored at nuclear power stations. HLW is the material left behind in the reprocessing of spent nuclear fuel, and is stored in shielded,
35 stainless steel tanks at the British Nuclear Fuels' plant at Sellafield.

It is then converted into solid glass blocks for long term storage, in a process known as vitrification.
40 Very little HLW actually exists, however. Its total volume after 30 years of electricity production would fit inside 4 double decker buses.

As with all nuclear operations, safety
45 margins err on the side of extreme caution. A cup of coffee (a naturally radioactive substance) made inside a nuclear site could, technically, be classified as nuclear waste if
50 brought outside.

Low Level Waste

From the brochure Oldbury a power in your life. © *Magnox Electric plc.*

(caption): **vitrified** having been melted down and turned into glass blocks

Col. 1: 6 **to dispose of s.th.** [-'-] to get rid of s.th. – 7 **supervision** the act of watching to see that s.th. is done properly – 9 **to comprise** [-'-] to be made up of – 11 **to incinerate** [ɪnˈsɪnreɪt] to burn – 12 **to compact** [-'-] to press s.th. together to make it smaller – **to seal** [siː l] to close very tightly – 19 **shielding** protection – 21 **fuel cladding** protective barrier between radioactive materials and the environment – 23 **residue** [ˈrezɪdjuː] a small amount of s.th. left after most is gone – **remote tool** device that keeps users from coming into direct contact with s.th.

Col. 2: 26 **secure** [-'-] well-protected, strong – 28 **BNFL** British Nuclear Fuels plc – 34 **spent** used up – 36 **stainless steel** *Edelstahl* – 46 **to err on the side of caution** to rather be overcautious in a case of doubt

4 Energy & the environment

Energy & conservation

• This text was written in 1977. What does that tell you about the question of energy conservation?

"Let our kids find their own oil."

WASHINGTON – The argument that President Carter gives for energy conservation is that if we keep using up the petroleum reserves we have now, there won't be any left for our children.

It's probably strong logic with many people, but Clemstone, my gas-guzzling friend, isn't buying it.

"Let the kids find their own oil," he said after the President's address on television.

"How can you say that?"

"We found it, didn't we? We dug in the ground and we brought the stuff up with our own hands. Why should we give the kids our oil on a silver platter?"

"We have to think of future generations who may suffer because of our waste and abuse."

"Why?" Clemstone asked me.

"Because," I said weakly.

"Look, do you think they'll appreciate the oil and gas if we just leave it to them? I know kids. The only things that have any meaning for them are those they worked for themselves. What we should say to them is, 'We're using up whatever petroleum we've found in the ground. You want some for yourselves, go out and find it.' That's the kind of challenge that will grab them."

"But you can't use up all our reserves in ONE generation."

"Sure we can. It's OUR oil and gas. Why should we freeze so some rotten kids can have gas to fool around in their cars 20 years from today?"

"There's something wrong with your argument," I told Clemstone, "but I can't put my finger on it."

"There is nothing wrong with it. Each generation should fend for itself. Do you think we'd be where we are today if we depended on handouts of oil from our parents? No sir, we worked to get that petroleum. We drilled holes in Texas and Oklahoma. We sweated for it in the Gulf of Mexico and froze our tails off on the northern slopes of Alaska. We kissed the feet of desert sheiks to get our oil. And, by heaven, when we got it we appreciated it." […]

"You make a strong argument against conservation," I told my friend, "but you forget one thing. You can't take it with you."

"I'm not taking it with me," he yelled. "I'm going to use it up right here, today, tomorrow, next week, next year. When I go there won't be a quart of the stuff left."

"What will your kids think of you? What will they say about a father who doesn't leave his kids a quart of oil after he's gone to that big Exxon station in the sky?"

"They'll bless me. They will eventually say, 'Thanks, Dad, for not making it easy on us. Thanks for having the faith in us so we could find our own Alaskan slope. You found your oil and we found ours, and our kids can find their own.'"

"I'm not sure that was the message the President was trying to get over to the American people," I said. "Of course, it wasn't," Clemstone said. "But he doesn't have the confidence in the next generation that I do. He doesn't think they have the moral fiber and the pioneer spirit to go out and drill for their own fuel."

"But suppose it's true that there aren't any more reserves of gas and oil left?"

"If my son came to me and said, 'Dad, I can't find any oil,' do you know what I'd do? I'd hand him a shovel and say, 'Okay, go out and dig for coal'."

By Art Buchwald, Washington Post, April 28, 1977. Reprinted with permission of the author.

---

4 **guzzling** ['gʌzlɪŋ] consuming a lot of s.th.
5 **to buy s.th.** (informal) here: to believe s.th.
9 **to give on a silver platter** (fig.) s.th. given to one for nothing in return
11 **abuse** [ə'bju:s] the act of misusing s.o. or s.th.
18 **to grab s.o.** (informal) here: to catch the attention of s.o.
20 **rotten** worthless, no-good
21 **to fool around** (informal) to act in a silly way
24 **to fend for oneself** to take care of oneself
25 **handout** s.th. got for free
27 **to freeze one's tail off** (slang) to become very cold
28 **slope** steep side of a hill – **sheik** Scheich
29 **by heaven** expression used for emphasis
31 **You can't take it with you** (humorous saying) one can't bring anything along once one is dead
37 **to have faith in s.o.** to believe in s.o.
39 **to get s.th. over to s.o.** to communicate an idea to s.o.
42 **fiber** here: character
45 **shovel** tool used for digging holes in the ground

Energy & the environment 4

Working with the text
1. Summarise the arguments for and against saving energy which are given in the text.
2. Look at the way Clemstone uses personal pronouns: what is the effect on the listener and reader?
3. What characteristic elements of a satire can you find in this text?

Your view
The text was written in the late seventies. Do you think it is still relevant today? Give reasons for your opinion.

Further activities
1. In lines 22–23 the narrator is lost for words:
    "There is something wrong with your argument … but I can't put my finger on it."
    a) Think of arguments which the narrator could have used.
    b) Write a new dialogue between Clemstone and the narrator starting from line 6 in which the narrator argues back convincingly.
2. Comment on Clemstone's proposals and his attitude towards the younger generation. Say whether you think he could be referring to your generation and whether you agree or disagree with his views, giving reasons.

> **Narrator**
> See *Glossary* on pp. 208–210.

Energy user no. 1: the car

> "What if we were inventing the automobile today rather than a century ago? What might we do differently?"
>
> Rick Wagoner, President and CEO of General Motors Corp.

- With a partner or in a group answer Rick Wagoner's question and discuss what you think the car of the future will be like: Think about forms of fuel, size, customer requirements, etc. Present your ideas to your class.
- Read the quotes below and then combine the points made in each of them to create a short text with the title "The car in the 21st century". Add further points which you raised in your initial discussion above.

> "AUTOnomy is more than just a new concept car; it's potentially the start of a revolution in how automobiles are designed, built and used. […] AUTOnomy is not simply a new chapter in automotive history. It is volume two, with the first hundred years of the automobile being volume one. The 20th century was the century of the internal combustion engine. The 21st century will be the century of the fuel cell."
>
> Rick Wagoner, President and CEO of General Motors Corp., January 2002

combustion engine engine that works by burning gasoline

> "What if there were a form of energy that could solve our air pollution problems, would eliminate our dependence on foreign oil, could solve our balance of payments woes, would eliminate oil spills, would create domestic jobs, and could be made from unlimited, renewable, and sustainable resources? Well, there is – it's hydrogen!"
>
> Rick Smith, President, Hydrogen Energy Center, September, 1997

woe s.th. that causes worries – **renewable** that which can be replaced – **sustainable** when amounts of s.th. can be kept at a constant level

> "With a hydrogen economy, we have a major opportunity for sustainable economic development, which respects the environment and creates the path to non-petroleum and renewable energy sources without constraining economic growth."
>
> Larry Burns, General Motors Vice President of Research & Development and Planning, January 2002

to constrain to restrict

Evolution of Energy

FUEL CELLS are the future and the future and the future is now, sort of.

As the most likely alternative to fossil fuels, fuel cells power all sorts of prototype vehicles, as well as the space shuttles and various power cogeneration facilities around the world.

But it's going to be awhile before consumers are able to purchase fuel-cell cars from their local dealerships, and even longer before gasoline fades into history.

"We don't expect to see them in commercial use or mass production for 10 to 20 years," said John Wallace, Ford Motor Co.'s director of fuel cell programs. "But we're doing this work in anticipation of something happening that would require us to replace our existing motor vehicle technologies."

The gulf between promise and fulfillment – and how to bridge it – was a key topic Thursday during the G8 Energy Ministers conference at the Detroit Marriott Renaissance Center Hotel.

Fuel cells, which operate like batteries, use stored hydrogen and oxygen to produce electricity. In vehicles, hydrogen fuel cells are virtually pollution free because they release water vapor instead of carbon dioxide.

Indeed, former space shuttle astronaut Kenneth Cameron, now program executive for General Motors' fuel-cell effort, drew surprise and chuckles Thursday when he told a panel that he and other astronauts used to drink the water that was the only residue of the shuttle's fuel-cell power generation.

"The infrastructure remains the greatest challenge," he said, referring to the thousands of gasoline stations that would have to be converted to hydrogen facilities. Without that, he said, vehicles powered by fuel cells would become just so many lawn ornaments.

Cost is another problem. William Miller, president of United Technologies Corp.'s fuel cells unit, estimated the power created by fuel cells on the shuttle costs $600,000 per kilowatt. His company is working on a fuel cell product for use in power plants that will cost $1,500 per kilowatt. But putting fuel cells in cars and homes requires getting the cost down to $25 to $50 per kilowatt, Miller said.

Technical standards are yet another hurdle. There are multiple types of fuel cells in development using different chemicals as a source of hydrogen. Miller and other speakers suggested the government can play a role in harmonizing standards, both among domestic manufacturers and across international borders.

Because of the difficulties, it's likely that the first fuel cells to come into wide use will power buses and fleet cars rather than private cars or homes.

Miller noted that buses can store a day's hydrogen supply on their roofs, returning to depots at night for a refill. In the same way, fleet cars like vans operated by United Parcel Service and similar firms all return to a home base, where hydrogen facilities can be built.

But beyond that, Ford's Wallace cited four things that must happen for the technology to become more widely available: Consumers must see a clear advantage in fuel-cell cars, the new technology must be reliable, it must be compatible with current systems and it must be easy to understand.

"Right now," he said, "fuel cells fail on all those four steps."

Despite that dash of reality, all the speakers at Thursday's discussions were optimistic.

Christine Farkas, an analyst with Merrill Lynch Equity Research who follows fuel-cell companies, told a panel that many of those firms are finding profits elusive. Nonetheless, she said, "we're convinced there's a terrific long-term future" for the industry.

Currently, all three Detroit automakers – General Motors, Ford and DaimlerChrysler AG's Chrysler Group – plan to introduce fuel-cell vehicles to the market by the middle of the decade.

GM introduced its next-generation fuel-cell vehicle, called the Autonomy, at the North American International Auto Show in January. The Autonomy is a prototype vehicle that GM says will get the equivalent of more than 100 miles per gallon.

Chrysler Group showed a fuel-cell-powered minivan concept called the Natrium at the auto show. The Natrium extracts hydrogen from sodium borohydride, the active ingredient in many detergents, to power a Town and Country minivan up to 300 miles at a top speed of 85 m.p.h.

Ford introduced the Focus FCV fuel-cell prototype in 2000.

U.S. automakers are investing in fuel-cell technology because they believe alternative-fuel vehicles will create new revenue streams. The challenge for car companies will be to build vehicles that make good business sense.

Gov. John Engler is counting on the so-called hydrogen economy to establish Michigan as the hub of fuel-technology research and development through his proposed NextEnergy program.

NextEnergy is a plan to make Michigan a world leader in the research, commercialization and manufacturing of alternative energy technologies such as hydrogen fuel cells.

The program will be based in a facility to be built near Ann Arbor over the next three to four years.

Some environmental groups are in favor of the NextEnergy project. Lana Pollack, president of the Michigan Environmental Council in Lansing, says Engler is on the right track. Pollack, who also sits on the advisory council for NextEnergy, said Michigan is making a case for becoming the world center for the next generation of energy research.

"America can't meet today's energy needs by using yesterday's technologies," Engler said Thursday during the G8 meetings.

By John Gallagher and Alejandro Bodipo-Memba, Detroit Free Press, May 3, 2002.

Energy & the environment 4

Annotations: Evolution of Energy

Col. 1: 13 **cogeneration facility** [fə'sɪləti] place where energy (e.g. electric and thermal) is produced – 18 **fade** [feɪd] to disappear 26 **to replace** to get rid of s.th. and put s.th. else in its place – 28 **gulf** wide distance – **fulfillment** making s.th. happen that is wished for or promised – 36 **virtually** almost – 37 **to release** [-'-] to set free – 38 **vapor** ['veɪpə] *Dampf* – 42 **to draw** *here:* to cause – **chuckles** quiet laughter – 43 **panel** small group of people who meet for a purpose – 45 **residue** ['resɪdju:] that which is left over, extra – 53 **just so many** *here:* only – **lawn** a piece of land covered with grass

Col. 2: 13 **hurdle** difficulty – 23 **to power** to cause s.th. to function – **fleet cars** a group of cars that belong to a business – 25 **to note** *here:* to pay specific attention to s.th. – 28 **van** *Lieferwagen* – 33 **to cite** [saɪt] to name – 37 **reliable** s.th. or s.o. that can be depended upon – 40 **to fail** to not meet expectations – 47 **to follow** *here:* to keep up with developments in e.g. a field or topic – 49 **elusive** [ɪ'lu:sɪv] *here:* difficult to achieve

Col. 3: 16 **detergent** chemical substance used for cleaning things – – 24 **revenue stream** ['revnju:] steady source of income – 27 **to count on** to depend on – 29 **hub** centre – 31 **proposed** s.th. which is planned and is being discussed – 45 **on the right track** *(fig.)* doing s.th. in a way that will probably be successful – 47 **to make a case for s.th.** *(fig.)* to argue in favour of s.th.

Working with the text
1. According to the text when can customers expect to be able to buy fuel-cell cars?
2. What point was Kenneth Cameron making which made his listeners laugh?
3. Explain in your own words the problem described by Cameron in Col. 1, ll. 47–53:
   "The infrastructure … lawn ornaments."
4. Why is cost a major problem?
5. What role should/could the government play?
6. According to the information in the article do you think the speakers at the congress are justified in feeling optimistic?
7. What has been achieved to date in this field?
8. "The challenge for car companies will be to build vehicles that make good business sense." (Col. 3, ll. 24–26) What do you suggest?

Language
1. Explain these terms from the text in your own words:
   a) commercial use (Col. 1, l. 21)
   b) mass production (Col. 1, l. 21)
   c) to harmonize standards (Col. 2, ll. 17–18)
   d) domestic manufacturers (Col. 2, ll. 18–19)
   e) long-term future (Col. 2, ll. 50–51)
   f) good business sense (Col. 3, l. 26)
2. Rewrite these sentences using synonyms/synonymous phrases for the words underlined:
   a) "But it's going <u>to be awhile</u> before consumers are able <u>to purchase</u> fuel-cell cars from <u>their local dealerships…</u>". (Col. 1, ll. 15–17)
   b) "But we're doing this work <u>in anticipation of</u> something happening that would <u>require</u> us to replace our <u>existing motor vehicle technologies</u>." (Col. 1, ll. 24–27)
   c) "The infrastructure remains <u>the greatest challenge</u>, he said …". (Col. 1, ll. 47–48)
   d) "<u>Despite that dash of reality,</u> all the speakers at Thursday's discussions were optimistic." (Col. 2, ll. 42–44)

Below: The AUTOnomy. What does "autonomy" mean? Do you think the name is well chosen?

Further activity
Describe how a fuel cell works using information from the text and referring to the diagram on the right.

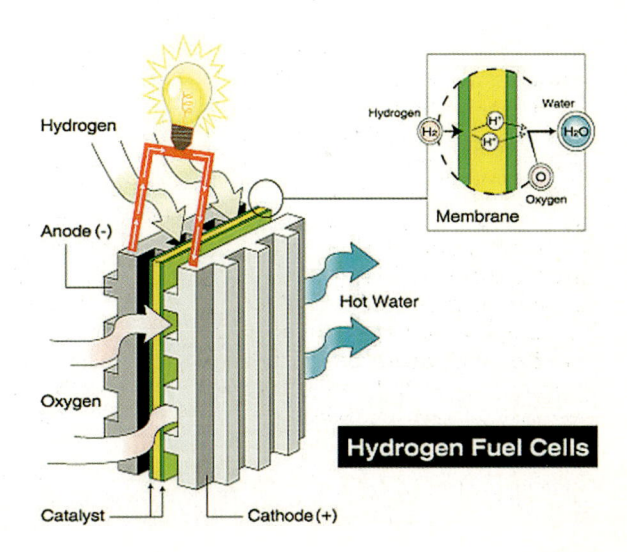

4 Energy & the environment

Car-sharing clubs

Before you read: How CityCarClub improves city life ...
- What do you know about car-sharing?
- Where do you think car-sharing clubs might have the most/least chances of success? What kind of services do you think car-sharing clubs need to offer in order to attract members?

After reading

Working with the text
1. If CityCarClub was successful in a big way, what major changes could we expect to see in our towns and cities according to the text?
2. What further advantages would there be for the environment?
3. Find examples of improvements mentioned in the text which belong in the following categories, and list them in key words under the appropriate headings:
   - *Local environment*
   - *Global environment*
   - *Personal environment*

Style
The text is part of a CityCarClub advertising brochure.
1. Find examples of persuasive language and rhetorical devices used in the text which show that this is the case.
2. a) Make notes on the ideas expressed in the following section:
   "A better life with less consumption ... finding a new urban lifestyle"
   (Col. 1, ll. 24–34).
   b) Use your notes to rewrite the text in your own words and in factual style.

> **Analysing style**
> See *Skills file* on p. 181.

Further activity
Make complete sentences using the phrases below, then put your sentences in a logical order to show how a car club works.
- check condition of car
- fill in receipt with mileage
- find car in special reserved parking space
- keep copy of receipt to check against monthly bill
- make reservations on phone any time, any day
- pay deposit and receive personal key
- return car to parking space
- return keys to safe with receipt
- take car key from safe at car park

Comment
Would you be prepared to take part in a car-sharing scheme? Write an essay in the form of a formal comment saying why or why not.

> **Essay writing**
> See *Skills file* on p. 184.

Creative writing: Family drama
The 10 year old Fisher family car has broken down again! Having the car repaired will be very expensive. They are sitting at the dinner table discussing the possibilities of either repairing the car, buying a new one or joining a car club.
Write a short scene with the following characters:
- Herman Fisher, 45 years old
- Elizabeth Fisher, 44 years old
- Ruth, 18
- Thomas, 16
- Michael, 11

Try to make your scene as lively and dramatic as possible.

Energy & the environment 4

How CityCarClub *improves city life and our environment*

Green Parks instead of Car Parks

City space is scarce and valuable. In the inner areas especially, there are many better uses for it than for car parking. Land can be better used for housing, business or public amenities. On the roads themselves we need more space for buses, bikes and for people to walk or just to pass the time. Since each CityCarClub car replaces 5 to 6 private cars, in the longer term it reduces the number of cars on the road. Therefore we shall be better able to build more green parks instead of more car parks. In this way CityCarClub helps gain the space needed to make cities vibrant and successful.

Better air and less noise through less traffic

Since participants in CityCarClub tend also to use other means of transport, they drive less: a survey for the Swiss office for energy affairs showed that former car owners decrease their energy consumption for transport by 50% when they join CityCarClub. The effect of CityCarClub is to reduce pollution, energy consumption, noise and traffic accidents. Since cars are a major source of the CO_2 emissions that cause global warming, CityCarClub contributes to reducing this at source.

A better life with less consumption – finding a new urban lifestyle

Imagine the whole population of the globe adopting the energy-consuming way of life we have. One can't reproach anybody for aspiring to the example set by the richer countries. We therefore have a responsibility to develop a way of life that is both comfortable and enjoyable and which can be sustained even when the whole world follows. CityCarClub is an example of this combination: it can provide a high quality of life with less use of resources.

CityCarClub reduces housing costs

New houses usually need to have large areas set aside for parking. By reducing these, more houses can be built on the same site. Alternatively, more space can be made available for gardens, play areas or other amenities. Higher quality housing can be provided at lower cost.

Saving money on shared cars

You will clearly save a lot of money if you combine City-CarClub with more frequent use of your bike or public transport and so travel less by car. But even if you drive as much as you did before (9000 km or 6,000 miles in our example) you are still better off with CityCarClub:

Let us assume that in one year you take a City-Club car for a 2 week holiday trip and use the car for two more weeks. During the rest of the year you make one weekend trip (2 days) every 4th week, and use the car for 5 single hours each week for any other trips, such as shopping or leisure. During the year you still drive 9000 km (6,000 miles). By using CityCarClub you save a significant amount of money compared to the cost of using your own private car. For a medium range car, you could save as much as £1,400!

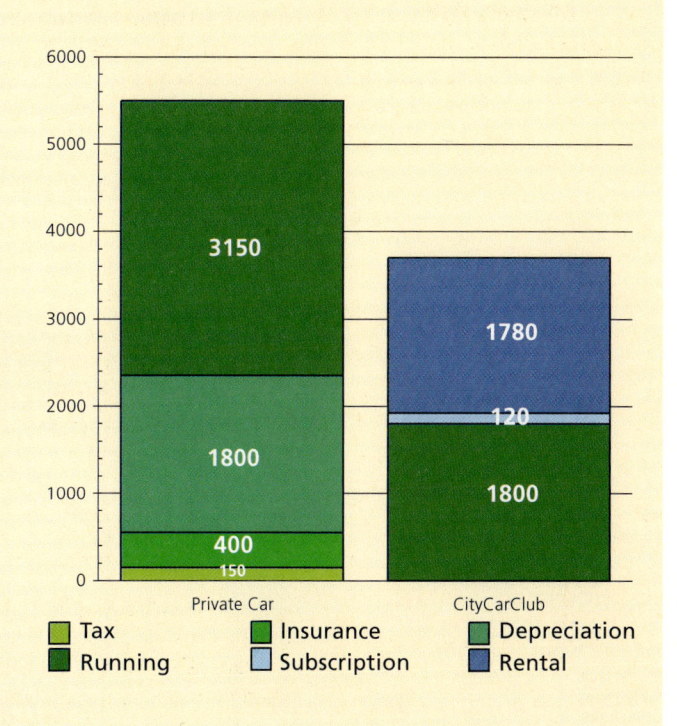

From the "CityCarClub" brochure, Car Free Cities Network

---

2 **scarce** [skeəs] very limited in amount – *5* **public amenity** [əˈmiːnətɪ] public facility, e.g. a shopping centre – *12* **vibrant** [ˈvaɪbrənt] full of life and energy – *23* **at source** *here:* from the beginning – *28* **to reproach s.o.** to find fault with s.o. for his/her actions – **to aspire to** [əˈspaɪə] to have the ambition to achieve s.th. – *47* **to be better off** to be in a better situation – *53* **leisure** [ˈleʒə] free time

4 Energy & the environment

Ecology & the economy

Before you read: Should you recycle ...
Copy and complete the mind map on recycling.

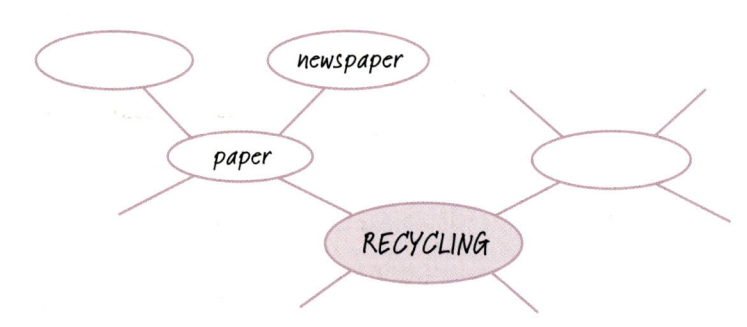

Mind maps
See *Skills file* on p. 180.

After reading

Working with the text
1. Why is Matthew Leach against the recycling of paper?
2. What is Marianne Grieg-gran's and Amelia Craighill's standpoint on recycling?
3. In what way does the author criticise the European Commission?

Style
How do the author's language and choice of words show that the article has been taken from a quality newspaper?

Further activities / correspondence
1. Find out whether the 1994 directive on waste management has been fulfilled.
   http://europa.eu.int/comm/environment/waste/packaging_index.htm
2. Contact environmental groups to find out their attitudes towards recycling.
   (See *Check the web* box.)

Looking at the cartoon
Decribe the cartoon in detail considering:
- location
- characters
- text
- point made
- your opinion

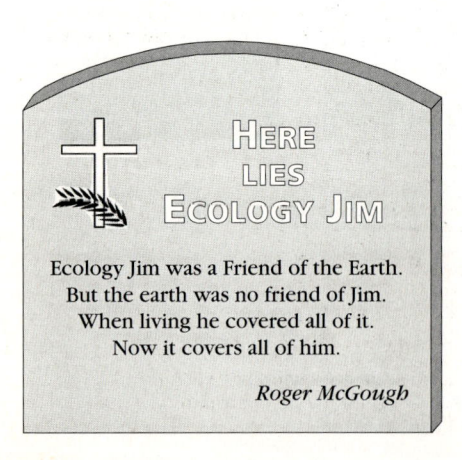

Check the web
Get more information about organisations concerned with the protection of the environment at:
Greenpeace:
http://www.greenpeace.org/homepage/
Friends of the Earth:
http://www.foe.co.uk/

HERE
LIES
ECOLOGY JIM

Ecology Jim was a Friend of the Earth.
But the earth was no friend of Jim.
When living he covered all of it.
Now it covers all of him.

Roger McGough

YO! AMIGO!!
WE NEED THAT TREE TO PROTECT US FROM THE GREENHOUSE EFFECT!

DEVELOPED COUNTRIES

Should you recycle this paper? Maybe not!

When you've finished with this newspaper, will you, a little smugly, take it to be recycled? Charles Arthur, Science Editor, discovers that some environmentalists now think you would be better to burn it instead.

A growing number of environmentalists who have carried out detailed economic studies of the costs of recycling – a practice that has an almost religious place in the greener lifestyle – believe it may be environmentally unfriendly.

"The higher you value the environment, the better incineration comes out," according to Matthew Leach, an energy policy analyst at Imperial College's Centre for Environmental Technology.

That's a startling thought, given that used paper is rapidly becoming a raw material: in western Europe more than half of newsprint is recycled, and the paper disposal business in Europe handles 130 kilograms (286 pounds) per head annually. Now Leach says: burn it – for instance in your fireplace. You don't speed up global warming, since 99 per cent of virgin paper comes from sustainable forests, not rainforest. And you can use the heat to save electricity.

This is not the sort of answer that consumers, who for years have been trained to obediently collect their newspapers and dump them at the local collection site, expect to hear. But it gets worse. Those local collection sites, and the few companies which in this country pulp the papers, are the worst model of recycling you can dream up. Instead, we should have kerbside collection, and recycling (or incineration) at as many locations as possible. Why? Because the fuel used by the lorries transporting it adds more to global warming than the process of making fresh paper.

"This debate seems to have become fashionable recently," said Marianne Grieg-gran of the International Institute for Environment and Development yesterday. "There have been scientific papers in the past four years arguing that recycling might not be the best solution."

There are some glimmers of reassurance. It is always good to recycle aluminium cans, because so much electricity is needed to extract the metal from its ore, bauxite. Saving electricity means saving fossil fuel. Recycling aluminium "saves about 95 per cent of the energy", said Amelia Craighill, of the environment department at the University of East Anglia. Glass recycling is less clear-cut – but recycling can make significant energy savings. So yes, recycle that wine bottle.

But paper recycling is less simple. Maybe it should be composted on a landfill – where the methane gas produced could be burnt for energy. Or it should be burnt outright. Or it might be recycled. The environmentalists are still arguing.

The European Commission though seems to have made its mind up already. Its 1994 directive on waste management insisted that by 2001, 50 per cent of paper waste should have been recovered and recycled. Perhaps someone should have told them about the debate.

By Charles Arthur, The Independent, *December 6, 1997.*

---

3 **smugly** selbstgefällig

18 **incineration** [ɪnˌsɪnrˈeɪʃn] the process of burning s.th.

29 **disposal** the process of getting rid of s.th.

35 **virgin paper** paper that has not been recycled before
36 **sustainable** when amounts of s.th. can be kept at a constant level

43 **to dump** to get rid of s.th. quickly

47 **to pulp** to crush s.th. until it is a smooth mixture
49 **to dream up** to think of

50 **kerbside collection** when s.th. no longer wanted is put out next to the kerb (*Randstein*) and is then taken away

67 **glimmer** *here:* a small indication
68 **reassurance** statement(s) that makes s.o. feel confident about s.th. again
71 **ore** *Erz*

79 **clear-cut** obvious

84 **landfill** *Deponiegelände*

87 **outright** immediately

4 Energy & the environment

Before you read: How to make lots of money, …
- The title of the following text is "How to make lots of money and save the planet too". What solutions do you think the text might offer? Think of ideas with a partner.

After reading

Working with the text
1. According to the article what is the traditional relationship between many companies and environmentalists?
2. How do environmental pressure groups and/or firms in Europe and the USA fight for tougher legislation?
3. Make a list of all the advantages of tough legislation mentioned in the article.

Presentation
Prepare a presentation of the attitudes of political parties towards environmental regulations.
a) Write a letter to the major political parties in Britain and America asking for information on their policies.
b) Present the results in class.

Looking at the cartoon
1. What does the cartoon tell you about the way we treat our planet?
2. Do you think this opinion is valid? Why/Why not?
3. Imagine the cartoon depicts a scene from a science fiction film. Outline a possible film plot.

Giving a talk or presentation
See *Skills file* on p. 189.

Letter writing
See *Skills files* on pp. 196–199.

Cartoons
See *Skills file* on p. 190.

Energy & the environment 4

How to make lots of money, and save the planet too

In principle, you might expect "greens" and businessfolk to be at one another's throats. [...]

Yet a strange love affair is growing between some firms and some parts of the green movement. In places such as Washington and Brussels a fast-growing army of business lobbyists is working for tougher laws. Many firms have discovered that green laws can be good for profits – either by creating new markets or by protecting old ones against competitors.

Whenever a green law forces a company to change its machinery, clean up some manufacturing process, decontaminate a site or even just "consider" the environmental impact of something it is doing, it adds to the clean-up industry. [...]

The driving force behind this industry's growth is government regulation. In America its godfather was California's Jerry Brown, who as governor pushed through clean-air rules that led indirectly to Los Angeles' "Smog Valley", where many clean-up firms started. America, Japan and Germany – the three countries with the largest share of the world environmental market – all have particularly stringent environmental laws. "It is an industry uniquely dependent on government policy," says Adrian Wilkes, director of the Environmental Industries Commission (EIC).

The EIC argues for tougher environmental standards, more rigorous enforcement, and investment subsidies. Its impressive list of supporters includes 25 green campaigners and parliamentarians. But its money comes from the clean-up firms. British firms that manufacture pollution-control equipment have been complaining that the National Rivers Authority makes it too easy to discharge pollutants into rivers, and that air-quality standards are too weak. [...]

Even on global environmental issues some businesses are beginning to lobby for tougher agreements. The main opponents of international targets to reduce greenhouse-gas emissions are coal producers and oil-producing countries. Yet other businesses are siding with the greens. The Business Council for a Sustainable Energy Future, a group of American clean-energy firms formed in 1992, has been calling for international targets on greenhouse gases, which would boost demand for clean energy. Earlier this year it launched a European offshoot.

Insurance firms, worried by a spate of natural disasters, have begun to campaign on climate change. Even big oil firms are thinking twice about their stance. Tough targets would hurt demand for oil, but could help their natural-gas businesses. [...]

Protect me, I'm green

Environmental regulation can also raise barriers to entry in established markets. This is most stark when green rules protect domestic producers from imports. In 1994 the European Union complained unsuccessfully about American standards on car fuel-efficiency. Ostensibly aimed at conserving energy, these happened to protect American car makers from imports of large, upmarket European cars. Another dispute involves Germany's packaging ordinance, which forces brewers to use refillable bottles. Apart from its green merits, the rule also protects Germany's small brewers which, unlike foreign competitors, already have local distribution systems in place.

Green laws can split domestic industries too. American greens are urging the full EPA to toughen limits on chlorine emitted by the paper-making industry. Though some big paper companies are opposing tougher standards, others, who have already invested in chlorine-free technologies, are siding with the greens. [...]

In other words, even greenery's most vigorous opponents now direct a lot of their energy towards trying to influence how laws are written rather than whether they are written at all. For the mainstream green movement, this is splendid; environmentalists now have rich allies in smart suits. Whether the emergence of the green business lobby is good news for environmental policy-making, however, is another question. Governments should forever be wary of lobbyists, even those in suits.

From The Economist, *June 3, 1995.*

---

1 **to be at one another's throats** *(fig.)* to be fighting against each other

12 **godfather** *here:* the person who is the driving force behind s.th.

15 **stringent** ['strɪndʒənt] strict

18 **rigorous** ['rɪgrəs] strict – **enforcement** [-'--] act of making sure that a rule is obeyed
19 **subsidy** [sʌbsɪdɪ] Subvention – **impressive** beeindruckend
22 **to discharge** [-'-] to let s.th. out of one place and into another

25 **target** ['--] goal
27 **to side with s.o.** to support s.o.'s point of view, usually with words and/or actions – **sustainable** when amounts of s.th. can be kept at a constant level
30 **offshoot** s.th. developed from s.th. else
31 **spate** [speɪt] large number (usually of unpleasant things)
32 **stance** [stænts] point of view on s.th.

36 **stark** extreme

38 **ostensibly** [ɒs'tentsɪblɪ] *(formal)* apparently
39 **upmarket** expensive, high quality
40 **ordinance** ['---] official rule – **brewer** Brauer(ei)
41 **merit** worth, value
43 **to split** to divide
44 **EPA** Environmental Protection Agency *(U.S. governmental organization)*
47 **vigorous** ['vɪgrəs] active
49 **mainstream** most representative part of a group
50 **emergence** coming into being
52 **to be wary of s.th.** ['weərɪ] to be cautious about s.th.

4 Energy & the environment

🎧 Earth Song

What about sunrise
What about rain
What about all the things
That you said we were to gain …
5 What about killing fields
Is there a time
What about all the things
That you said was yours and mine …
Did you ever stop to notice
10 All the blood we've shed before
Did you ever stop to notice
The crying Earth the weeping shores?

Aaaaaaaaah Aaaaaaaah

15
What have we done to the world
Look what we've done
What about all the peace
That you pledge your only son …
20 What about flowering fields
Is there a time
What about all the dreams
That you said was yours and mine …
Did you ever stop to notice
25 All the children dead from war
Did you ever stop to notice
The crying Earth the weeping shores?

Aaaaaaaaah Aaaaaaaah
30
I used to dream
I used to glance beyond the stars
Now I don't know where we are
Although I know we've drifted far
35
Aaaaaaaaah Aaaaaaaah
Aaaaaaaaah Aaaaaaaah

Hey, what about yesterday
(What about us)
What about the seas
(What about us)
The heavens are falling down
(What about us)
I can't even breathe
(What about us)
What about the bleeding Earth
(What about us)
Can't we feel its wounds
(What about us)
What about nature's worth
(ooo,ooo)
It's our planet's womb
(What about us)
What about animals
(What about it)
We've turned kingdoms to dust
(What about us)
What about elephants
(What about us)
Have we lost their trust
(What about us)
What about crying whales
(What about us)
We're ravaging the seas
(What about us)
What about forest trails
(ooo,ooo)
Burnt despite our pleas
(What about us)
What about the holy land
(What about it)
Torn apart by creed
(What about us)
What about the common man
(What about us)

Can't we set him free
(What about us)
What about children dying
(What about us)
Can't your hear them cry
(What about us)
Where did we go wrong
(ooo,ooo)
Someone tell me why
(What about us)
What about babies
(What about it)
What about the days
(What about us)
What about all their joy
(What about us)
What about the man
(What about us)
What about the crying man
(What about us)
What about Abraham
(What about us)
What about death again
(ooo,ooo)
Do we give a damn

Aaaaaaaaah Aaaaaaaah

Col. 1: 10 **to shed blood** to kill people – 12 **weeping** (*fig.*) crying – 19 **to pledge** to promise – 32 **to glance** to look quickly at s.th.

Col. 2: 15 **womb** [wu:m] *Mutterleib* – 35 **creed** a person's beliefs, opinions and principles

Col. 3: 21 **Abraham** the original descendant of the Jewish people

Written and composed by Michael Jackson (Joe). © 1995 by Mijac Music, für D/CH/GUS/Osteuropäische Länder: NEUE WELT MUSIKVERLAG GMBH, München.

Energy & the environment 4

Working with the song
1. Do you like the song? Why/Why not?
2. Have a close look at the first two verses (ll. 1–27). Summarize what Michael Jackson is singing about in your own words.
3. Who do you think "you" and "we" are in the first two verses?
4. Now look at the rest of the song. Put the problems mentioned into different categories and find an appropriate heading for each.
5. Which other environmental problems could have been mentioned in the song? Write at least ten more lines as a continuation of the song.

> **Writing a summary**
> See *Skills file* on p. 185.

A step further
1. Do you think a pop song is a good way of making people aware of problems like these? Give reasons.
2. a) What other ways can you think of for increasing awareness of environmental issues?
   b) Which methods – if any – do you think should be avoided at all costs? Why?

Further activity
Find other songs dealing with environmental problems or other serious political or social issues and present them in class. Compare each of them with "Earth Song" discussing similarities and differences.

Project: Research and report – local action

Work in a group of three or four.
Choose one of the areas dealt with in this chapter and research and prepare a report on how this topic is dealt with (or not) in the area in which you live.
The ideas below may help you.
- Global warming & climate change
  heating systems used in your area • changing weather phenomenon: flooding, heatwaves, etc.
- Forms of energy
  types of electricity produced in your area: nuclear, solar, wind, fossil fuel, etc. • recent changes • problems, dangers
- Energy & conservation
  Environmental groups and activists in your area • local environmental problems and solutions • measures taken, planned and/or necessary at local level
- Cars & fuel
  traffic and infrastructure in your area • public transport systems • car clubs
- Ecology & the economy
  businesses in your area involved in recycling • businesses involved in producing ecological goods (e.g. solar panels)

5 Science & technology

Futurology

- Imagine you had the subject 'Futurology' at school. What would it cover?
- Write a definition of 'futurology'. Compare your definition with a partner's. Finally look the term up in a dictionary and amend your definition if necessary.

Oops! They got it horribly wrong

"But what is it good for?" asked an engineer at the advanced computing systems division of IBM, 1968, when shown an early version of the microchip.

Scientists from the 1960s to the mid-1980s predicted that every home would have a robot servant by now.

In 1969, just after the Moon landings, US vice-president Spiro Agnew predicted a man on Mars by 2000.

"Drill for oil? You mean drill into the ground to try and find oil? You're crazy," drillers told Edwin L. Drake after he had tried to enlist them for the first project to drill for oil in 1859.

to enlist to hire

"This telephone has too many shortcomings to be seriously considered as a means of communication. The device is inherently of no value to us." So said a Western Union Internal memo, 1876.

"Heavier-than-air flying machines are impossible," said Lord Kelvin, president of the Royal Society, in 1895. It was he who also announced in 1897: "Radio has no future."

shortcoming fault – **device** [dɪˈvaɪs] object used for a particular purpose – **inherently** by its nature

Fifteen predictions which will change our world

First commercial application	earliest	most likely	latest
Computers which write most of their own software	2003	2005	2007
Full voice interaction with machine	2003	2005	2007
Totally automated factories	2004	2007	2010
National UK decisions influenced by electronic referendums	2007	2010	2014
Artificial brains with 10,000 or more cells	2007	2010	2014
Prevention of cancer	2009	2013	2017
Robotic exercise companion	2015	2020	2025
Cities built deep underground in Japan because of high land prices	2015	2020	2025
Extension of average life span to 100+	2015	2020	2025
Human knowledge exceeded by machine knowledge	2012	2017	2022
Artificial intelligence imitating thinking processes of the brain	2013	2018	2023
Intelligence enhancement by external means	2025	2030	2035
Artificial brains	2030	2035	2040
Use of unlimited nuclear fusion as power source	2035	2040	2045

From the articles by Simon Reeve, The European, *23 February – 1 March 1998*.

Science & technology 5

Ten advances that have already arrived

- Electrolux has invented a robotic vacuum cleaner which will clean your house. Expect it in the shops soon.
- Computers and programmes have been developed to recognize human speech with varying results.
- BT is experimenting with "augmented reality" – glasses linked to a computer which project images and text in front of the wearer's eyes.
- Some computer games can be operated just by human thought using SQUID technology.
- Professor Igor Alexsander of Imperial College, London, says he has developed the world's first thinking computer.
- Eye-scanners and machines that can recognise a person by their fingertips and voice have been developed to replace PIN numbers in the banks' cash dispensing machines.
- Scientists have developed a computer which can tell whether a person is happy or sad and recognises 'yes' or 'no' by a person's head nodding or shaking.
- A 3-D talking head which can show emotions has already been developed.
- Doctors have said they can already use artificial muscles for heart surgery.
- Scientists are using nanotechnology, where tiny objects are built from atoms to make micro-machines with gears smaller in diameter than a human hair.

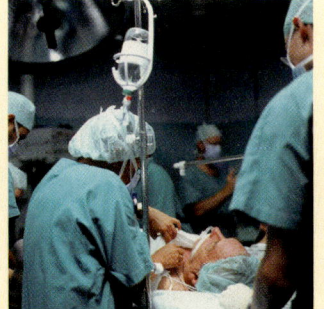

By Simon Reeve, The European, *23 February – 1 March 1998.*

11 **augmented** *here:* expanded – 12 **to project** [-'-] to make s.th. appear – 15 **SQUID** *short for* Superconducting Quantum Interference Device – 37 **gear** ['gɪə] *Zahnrad*

Oops! They got it horribly wrong
1. What do the "things they got wrong" tell you about futurology?
2. Which of the "things they got wrong" do you consider to be the least and most important "mistakes"? Why?

Fifteen predictions which will change our world
1. Look at the predictions. What do you understand by:
    electronic referendum • artificial brain • robotic exercise companion • nuclear fusion
2. Group the predictions in four categories. Give each category a heading.
3. Choose the prediction which you find most fascinating and explain your choice.
4. Work in groups. Rank the predictions from the most desirable to the least desirable. Compare results in class, and try to agree on a common ranking.

Advances that have already arrived
1. Try to find any of the products mentioned under "advances" on the internet and find out more about them, e.g. where and at what price they are being offered.
2. Choose two of the ten "advances", and describe ways in which a) they can be used positively and b) they could be used negatively.
3. As a business person looking to invest a substantial amount of money, which of the products would you choose? Why?

Creative writing: science fiction play
It's 2010. You are at home. Full voice interaction with a machine of your choice is possible. Write a dialogue between the machine and yourself as an opening scene for a science fiction play. Think of a good title for your play.

5 Science & technology

Before reading: We can beam you up …
- If you saw this article's headline in a newspaper would you read the article? Why/Why not?
- In the TV series and film *Star Trek* people are teleported from one place to another. How does teleportation work in *Star Trek*? Describe it to someone who has never seen the series.

Working with the text
1. Describe Anton Zeilinger's experiment in your own words.
2. How does the author view the possibility of humans being beamed up?
3. Explain in which other field teleportation can be applied.

Style
- Most texts are mixtures of several text types: descriptive, expository, narrative, instructive, argumentative. Identify the dominant text type in the article and give reasons and examples to support your choice.

> **Analysing style**
> See *Skills file* on p. 181.

Your view
1. Teleportation of human beings: fact for the future – or fiction forever? Discuss.
2. Would you let yourself be teleported if you had the chance? Give reasons.
3. In your opinion should research work in this field be financed privately or out of public funds and taxes?

We can beam you up, as long as you're a photon

Teleportation – just like in *Star Trek* – has been achieved in a laboratory. That's the good news, or part of it. The bad news? It has only been achieved with a photon, a single wave packet of light, and it would be incredibly difficult to repeat it with any object that had mass.

However, the work by a team at the Institute for Experimental Physics in Innsbruck could lead to super-fast computers which perform calculations using photons, and work faster than anything our present technologies can manage.

In the experiment, run by Anton Zeilinger, professor of experimental physics, certain physical properties of a photon were transferred instantly to another photon, without any connection or communication between the two.

The experiment requires three photons – the original, and a pair of "entangled" photons, whose quantum properties (known as "spin") are complementary.

When the spin of the original photon and one of the others is measured, the third photon takes on the spin of the first. This means that "information" about the first photon has effectively been transmitted without any signal passing.

Though it seems to violate Einstein's finding that no information can travel faster than light, it is a consequence of quantum mechanics: the "entangled" photons could be a galaxy apart, but measuring one would still mean the other displayed the complementary spin to its partner.

However, it is highly unlikely that teleportation and "beaming down" to planets, as Captain James T. Kirk and the crew of the Starship Enterprise did each week in the television series, will be a reality in the future.

"People are much too large," said Professor Zeilinger.

But the work, reported in the science journal *Nature*, may lead to "quantum super-computers" which could process information faster than the speed of light. The next step is to create a cluster of entangled particles in which "superpositions" of information could be stored.

A computer bit is either zero or one. A quantum bit could be in the superposition of zero and one – both at the same time.

By Charles Arthur, The Independent, *January 16, 1998.*

---

3 **photon** a particle, or packet, of energy that e.g. light waves are made of – 22 **entangled photons** photons whose physical properties are linked – **quantum property** *Quanteneigenschaft* – 23 **complementary** *entgegengesetzt und gleichzeitig ergänzend* – 29 **to violate** to go against s.th., e.g. an idea – 49 **cluster** a group of things – 50 **superposition of information** quantum theory: for computers, a single quantum bit, (smallest unit of information), could simultaneously exist in two states and have two values.

Science & technology 5

Computers and Robotics

Before you read
- Write a definition of the word 'transistor' using these key words:
  electronic device • amplification/increasing loudness • to switch/turn on and off.
- What devices do you know that contain transistors? Draw up a list with a partner.

After reading

Working with the text
1. How has transistor technology developed since 1947?
2. How has the power gained by faster computers been used up to now?
3. What are the predictions as to how increased processing power will be used in the future?

Language
1. What do you understand by:
   "the dawn of the PC era" (Col. 1, l. 17–18) • "standard stuff" (Col. 2, l. 7/8) • "natural interface" (Col. 3, l. 6)?
   Explain the terms in your own words.
2. Rewrite the following lines: *"While ever more realistic games … the future of computing itself."* (Col. 2, l. 13 – Col. 3, l. 16) replacing the following terms:
   software giants • natural interface • speech recognition • processor speed.

Your view
Bill Gates talks about "speech recognition and synthesis" as the way forward for computers. What other developments do you think there might be in the near and more distant future? What, in your opinion, could/should be done to make computers more user-friendly and accessible for the public at large?

> **Check the web**
> Find out about the history of the transistor at:
> http://www.pbs.org/transistor/index.html

Where next for the transistor?

On December 16, 1947, the first transistor – the size of a cigarette packet and comprising a slab of germanium, a thin plastic wedge and some gold foil held together by a paperclip – was cobbled together at Bell Laboratories, New Jersey, by John Bardeen and Walter Brattain.

More than fifty years on, we are surrounded by millions of transistors – in radios, televisions, telephones and hifis. But by far the highest density can be found inside our computers. Today a standard microprocessor … typically contains several million transistors within a square inch. […]

In the early Eighties, at the dawn of the PC era, the clock speed of a PC's processor was 5MHz, and the first Macintosh ran at 8MHz. Since then, the power provided by faster processors has pretty much gone on one thing: graphical interfaces. Colour displays capable of displaying thousands of colours are now standard stuff, together with desktop photographs, pseudo-3D toolbars and buttons, and dinky animations during operations like copying files and collecting email.

While ever more realistic games will no doubt be able to consume as much processing power as becomes available over the next few years, it's less obvious what the productivity software that makes us buy computers in the first place is going to do with it. But the software giants, it turns out, have already decided.

Bill Gates is betting on speech recognition and the emergence of a more "natural interface" to computers – something he has described as "the next big wave".

"Speech recognition and synthesis will be the next big advance. We're just now getting enough processor speed to start bringing this into the mainstream interface," he said during a visit to Cambridge University. "We think that is not only the future of Windows, but the future of computing itself."

From The Daily Telegraph, *December 16, 1997.*

Col. 1: *3* **comprising** *(formal)* made of – **slab** a wide, flat piece of s.th. – **germanium** [dʒəˈmeɪniəm] an element often used as a semiconductor – *6* **to cobble together** to put together quickly – *10* **to surround** to encircle s.th. – *18* **clock speed** the frequency with which a computer processes data or carries out a command
Col. 2: *4* **to go on one thing** *here:* to be used for one purpose – *5* **interface** *Schnittstelle* – *10* **dinky** [ˈdɪŋkɪ] small and cute
Col. 3: *4* **to bet on s.th.** *(fig.)* to hope for or expect s.th. – *5* **emergence** [-'--] the coming into existence of s.th. – *12* **mainstream** standard

5 Science & technology

Before you read: *House 'brain' develops helping habit*
- If you had a robot at home which jobs would you like it to do for you?

After reading

Language & Working with the text
1. a) Find synonyms in the text for these verbs:
   to find out about • to watch carefully • to know or guess what is going to happen in the future (*two examples*) • to do • to save
   b) Write a brief description of how the house 'brain' works using each of the verbs you have found.
2. Conflicts between what Dr Mozer wants and what his computer decides for him are mentioned at the end of the text.
   a) What is the source of these conflicts according to the text?
   b) Think of three specific things they might disagree on.
3. Would you like to have a house "brain"? Give your opinion.

Creative writing
Write a text in the form of a diary from the point of view of a house 'brain' which is installed in your home. You can invent facts relating to your family's habits to make your text more interesting or amusing, if you want.

Col. 1:
- 12 **occupant** ['ɒkjəpənt] person who lives in a house
- 13 **dwelling** *(formal)* place where s.o. lives

Col. 2:
- 3 **twist** *here:* a surprising, unexpected aspect
- 7 **device** [dɪ'vaɪs] tool, instrument
- 12 **to interact** *here:* to exchange information
- 16 **wiring** electricity cable
- 17 **actuator** ['æktʃueɪtə] an electrical device that switches s.th. on or off
- 20 **conflict** ['--] disagreement

HOUSE 'BRAIN' DEVELOPS HELPING HABIT

by Roger Highfield
Science Editor

A HOUSE has been given an electronic "brain" so that it can learn the habits of its occupants in an experiment to develop more efficient dwellings.

The house in Boulder, Colorado, was bought in 1991 by Dr Michael Mozer of the computer science department at Colorado University.

The computer observes his habits, eventually learning to anticipate his needs, including which rooms will be occupied at what times, when he leaves and returns, and when hot water will be needed.

Many homes can be programmed to perform tasks but it is a complex process. "The twist is that this house programs itself by observing inhabitants," said Dr Mozer. "It is based on neural networks, which are learning devices inspired by the human brain."

In Dr Mozer's house, artificial neural networks consisting of hundreds of simple, neuron-like processing units interact to predict and control the environment.

To provide the brain with information, Dr Mozer has installed 75 sensors and five miles of wiring in the home, as well as actuators to control lighting, ventilation and air and water heating.

However there are sometimes conflicts between what the occupant wants and the computer's mission to conserve energy.

From The Saturday Telegraph, *November 15, 1997.*

Science & technology 5

Robonurse takes care of elderly (pp. 82 & 83)

Before you read
- Which jobs in hospitals do you think could be done by robots? Which jobs do you think should always be done by people? Give reasons for your choices.

Working with the text
1. The central computer is called "Robonurse". Why is this name appropriate?
2. Make a list of the tasks that can be done by the computer system in the robotic room paying special attention to their medical functions.
3. What non-medical uses of the system are suggested in the text? Think of at least two more and compare with a partner. Decide which of your ideas are most likely to become reality giving reasons.
4. Why has this system been developed in a country like Japan? To what extent is the development of the system also relevant to Europe?

> **Listening comprehension**
> Listen to the article "Humanoid helpers".

Language
1. "Robonurse" is a portmanteau expression.
    a) Explain the term 'portmanteau' in your own words. (Look it up in a dictionary if necessary.)
    b) Think of two (or more) other portmanteau expressions which you know in English and explain them.
2. a) Find words/phrases in the text which mean:
    - s.o. who sits around all day watching TV
    - to be very lazy and never do any work
    - s.th. that has been done in the same way for hundreds of years
    - a fairly new way of doing things
    - to make you think critically about s.th.
    - to look after
    - the most important factor
    - to give warning of a problem or danger
    - irrespective of
    b) Write a text with the title "Roboteacher gives students a hard time". Use each of the words/phrases you found in part a).

Style
- The author personifies robots. Find examples and explain their effects on the reader.

Your view
Your local hospital is considering setting up robotic rooms. Consider how you would feel about being taken care of by a robot if you were a hospital patient. Write a formal letter to the local hospital management expressing your opinion.

Giving a speech
Write a speech arguing either for or against the development of robotic rooms in hospitals as if you were the government minister of health.

> **Personification**
> See *Glossary* on pp. 208–210.
>
> **Letter writing**
> See *Skills files* on pp. 196 & 199.
>
> **Giving a talk or presentation**
> See *Skills file* on p. 189.

Science & technology

Robonurse takes care of elderly

HEALTHCARE. – Robotic rooms that can monitor people's breathing patterns and fetch things are being built in Japan.

by Sean Hargrave

It is a couch potato's dream come true – the robotic room that does everything for you.

Japanese researchers are building the world's first room whose occupants need never lift a finger. Although initially aimed at automating the care of the sick and elderly, the technology is likely to be used one day to build bedsits for the lethargic. All the occupant need do is point at an object and an obedient robot fetches it or turns it on.

The concept involves building a single robot around the bed. Although many devices wait on the occupant, they are all controlled by a central computer that allows them to interact with one another.

The scientists from the University of Tokyo were prompted to begin work on the concept room by the realisation that, as in many other countries, the average age of their population is rising.

In Japan there is a strong tradition of children looking after their elderly parents. There is also, however, a recent trend for women not to give up work when they marry, raising the question of how busy individuals can look after relations without needing to be there. The room would also be used by hospitals to keep an eye on the elderly and sick without the continual attention of a nurse.

The key to the room is a clever bed where the elderly or ill person would reside most of the time. To keep a record of his or her movements, the mattress incorporates 221 small pressure sensors. These have an electric signal passing through them that is altered if the person applies pressure on them. The change in current is signalled to a computer that continuously monitors each sensor. It is programmed to analyse the signals and establish what position the person in bed has assumed.

This will enable carers to look at a record of the bed occupant's movements to ensure he has been relatively mobile and so reduce the risk of bed sores. It could also raise the alarm if the person assumes an unhealthy position – lying on a stitched wound, for example.

Further pressure sensors are placed under floor tiles so the room can track a person out of bed. These sensors are not as

---

elderly ['eldəlı] (n.) old people

to monitor ['mɒnɪtə] to check s.th. on a regular basis
pattern way in which s.th. is usually done; *here:* rhythm of one's breathing

9 **initially** [ɪ'nɪʃlɪ] at first

13 **bedsit** (BE) small one-roomed flat

16 **obedient** [əʊbi:dɪənt] willing to do what one is told to do

28 **to be prompted** to be encouraged to do s.th.

51 **to reside** [rɪ'zaɪd] *(formal)* to stay in, to live in

54 **to incorporate** [ɪn'kɔ:preɪt] to contain
55 **pressure** Druck

58 **to alter** to change

60 **current** the flow of electricity

67 **to assume a position** [ə'sju:m] to move one's body into a certain position

73 **bed sore** an infection resulting from lying for too long in the same position

77 **stitched** [stɪtʃt] sewn up – **wound** [wu:nd] injury

81 **to track** to follow or keep informed about s.o. or s.th.

sophisticated as those in the bed because they do not need to monitor the position of the person, merely let the central computer know where the person is. If the computer detects the occupant has not moved for an unusual amount of time, it will raise the alarm. Similarly, if several sensors detect pressure at the same time, carers will be alerted that the patient has fallen over and needs attention.

The bed has a second bank of sensors to monitor the occupant's well-being. Above the bed, five video cameras are constantly trained on the patient to ensure he or she is moving and, more important, to pick up the chest motion of breathing. The cameras enable the central computer to look at the elderly person from several angles to ensure he or she is always monitored, no matter which position is assumed.

The central computer keeps a count of how many times the chest rises and falls, giving a continuously updated figure of how many times a minute the patient is breathing.

The researchers envisage nursing staff checking vital statistics for patients remotely on a computer screen, although it is also likely that concerned children could check up on their parents over the Internet. By keying in a password they could download a history of mum or dad's movements and details of their vital signs.

The cameras that monitor a patient's breathing from above also function as movement monitors. Due to the wrap-around view the five lenses give, the central computer can build up a three-dimensional image of the patient.

Patients can point at objects they would like fetched or turned on. An elderly patient wanting to shave, for example, could point at the sink and start the hot water running in advance, reducing the amount of time they have to spend standing. If they want to watch television, they need only point at it and it will turn itself on.

The Tokyo researchers are developing a robotic arm that can pick up objects the patient is pointing at and bring them to his bedside. Similarly, small "pet" robots are being developed to carry smaller items and keep the patient company. A medium-sized robot is also being researched that could use two "hands" to hold and manipulate items for the person, such as turning the pages of a book or showing him well-wishers' cards.

The team warns that several years of research are needed before the robotic room could be trusted to guard our loved ones, though a prototype of the room is under construction in Tokyo.

From The Sunday Times, *January 4, 1998.*

---

90 **to detect** to discover

100 **bank** *here:* row, line

104 **to be trained on** to be programmed to point at

122 **to envisage** [ɪnˈvɪzɪdʒ] to consider an idea as possible future reality
124 **remotely** from a distance

129 **to key in** to type information into a computer

133 **vital signs** [ˈvaɪtl] signs of life, e.g. breathing, pulse

138 **wrap-around** from all angles

149 **in advance** before s.th. else

168 **to manipulate** [məˈnɪpjəleɪt] *here:* to operate, to move

5 Science & technology

Scientist's responsibility

Before you read: Send in the clones
What do you know about clones and cloning? Have a brainstorming session in class and put all your ideas in a mind map. Your mind map can also show the possible effects of cloning.

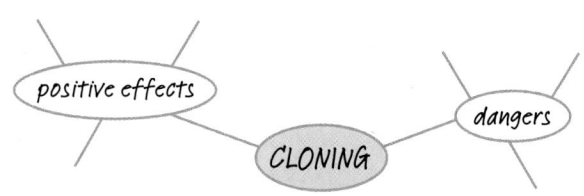

> **Mind maps**
> See *Skills file* on p. 180.

positive effects — CLONING — *dangers*

While reading
Read the text a section at a time. Do the "Working with the text" tasks in the boxes next to the text after you have read each section. (Annotations are on p. 87.)

After reading

1. **Working with the text:** Write a heading for each of the sections (see "While reading" task).
2. **Vocabulary:** The title is a play on words referring to a well-known song *Send in the clowns*.
   a) Do you think this was a good choice for a title? Give reasons for your opinion.
   b) Invent a new title using a different play on words.
      You can find out more about the song and the lyrics at the following website:
      http://home.istar.ca/~townsend/pop_standards/send_in_the_clowns.htm
   c) Explain what Professor Silver means by the term "Gen-Rich" in line 85.
3. **Style:** How does the author, Anne Treneman, attract and keep the reader's attention? Examine her choice of words, use of rhetorical devices, sentence structure, etc.

> **Analysing style**
> See *Skills file* on p. 181.

4. **Points of reference:** Find out about and interpret the significance of the author's use of the term "brave new world" used in lines 9–10. The following websites may be useful:
   http://www.huxley.net/studyaid/index.html
   http://home.concepts.nl/~corn_856/bravereview.html
   http://www.huxley.net/studyaid/bnwbarron.html
5. **Comment:** In lines 22–24 Anne Treneman asks four rhetorical questions:
   - "Is it immoral to mess around with life in this way?"
   - "Can the mystery of life be contained in a Petri dish?"
   - "Is it a sin?"
   - "Should it be illegal?"
   Answer one of the questions in a comment.

> **Essay writing**
> See *Skills file* on p. 184.

A step further
(Work with a partner or in a group for this project.)
a) Find out as much as you can about cloning and genetic engineering in general on the internet. Some useful websites are given in the box on page 87.
b) Examine the different ways and methods in which genetic engineering is treated in your school in different subjects such as English, Chemistry, Religion/Ethics, Biology, etc.
c) Present your findings to your class in a suitable way (e.g. talk/brochure/poster/report/etc.).

> **Projects & group work**
> See *Skills file* on p. 201.

Science & technology 5

Send in the clones

The prospect of cloning human beings sends a shiver down many spines, but not Lee Silver's. An eminent scientist, he says 'let the market take its course, it will anyway', though there are things, as Ann Treneman discovers, that disturb even him.

The first thing I notice about Lee Silver is that he is short. You may think it is unfair to mention this. After all, he is a molecular biologist at Princeton University, a renowned fertility scientist, the author of a new book about "cloning and beyond". So why do I have to go and mention his height? Because of genes, that's why. Genes are Professor Silver's subject and he points out that he has a few that could be improved on. He has asthma, for instance. And then there is the matter of 5ft 4in. "It is a fact in America that every inch of height increases your salary," he says. "It's incredible but true."

Dr Silver believes that we are not that far from being on the brink of a brave new world of reproductive genetics – or reprogenetics as he calls it – where parents will have the choice to pass such things on to their children. "If I could have fixed it so my children didn't have asthma, I would have thought very seriously about that," he says.

He asks me what my family disease is and I say cancer. So, he asks, would I use genetic manipulation to reduce the risk of my children getting cancer? Yes, I say without thinking. "Well," he says, "if you can imagine it, it is going to be done. It is a basic instinct for parents to want their children to have all possible advantages. I'm suggesting that our technologies will allow us to get children with, at first, simple traits such as being taller or who are resistent to cancer, or diabetes, or heart disease."

I shiver. Dr Silver makes it sound so simple. Too simple perhaps. Things get much more complicated if you think about this for even one more second. Is it immoral to mess around with life in this way? Can the mystery of life be contained in a Petri dish? Is it a sin? Should it be illegal? Dr Silver says that these questions may be very interesting but that they miss an essential point – which is that it *will* be done.

The ethicists are not going to decide this. Nor are governments. "Instead," he says, "the marketplace will. There are going to be people who want to use the technology, and it will be available, and the people who want to use it will find others who will take their money. After all, the first basic instinct is to have biological children. The second is to provide your children with all possible advantages."

Dr Silver is a scientist who is not afraid of being a science fantasist. He says this is because he has tenure and so can say what he likes. He does not necessarily approve of his brave new world, but he does think it is feasible.

He believes, for instance, that there will be human clones, and probably sooner rather than later. He also believes that genetic selection and engineering will be available to parents with enough money to afford it. They will be able to review a selection of their embryos and decide which they want to be their child. And, perhaps scariest of all, they will be able to genetically manipulate embryos. Not only can we lessen the threat of cancer, but we can add a bit of musical ability too.

Cloning is going to be better than sex – but only for a few. "The first instance I can think of is a man and a woman who are both sterile," says Dr Silver. "They want a biological child. Anybody who denies the power of this instinct doesn't understand human nature. In America the average amount spent to have a child by *in vitro* fertilisation is $50,000 to $60,000. In the case where both are sterile, cloning will be a way to have a biological child."

Section 1 (ll. 1–13)
Make a table of details about Professor Silver. Include the following information:
- job
- place of work
- height
- family status
- family illnesses

Section 2 (ll. 9–20)
What will parents be able to do in the future?

Section 3 (ll. 21–41)
True or false?
- Governments will decide on the use of genetic manipulation.
- If the technology is there, people with money will use it.
- Human cloning will happen in the near future.
- People will be able to reduce the risk of illness in their children but they won't be able to choose other abilities such as skill in sports or music.

5 Science & technology

> **Section 4 (ll. 42–63)**
> What three kinds of groups are most likely to make use of cloning?

Dr Silver doesn't have a problem with this. He thinks it is amoral not to love a child and isn't that bothered if it's a clone or not. In fact he thinks clones have had a bit of a bad press. I agree. We've all been watching too many movies. "Most people get upset about cloning because they think you can replicate an entire person. People still think this!" This is not true, he says, because a cloned child will be growing up in a different time and place than their parent. Not to mention a different personality and soul. "What I try and tell people is all you are doing is creating a later-born identical twin."

The other people who will use cloning are women who would prefer to avoid men and their sperm altogether. This includes lesbian couples and some single women too. "I have a friend. She's 40 and has a seven-year-old from a previous marriage. She wants to have another child but doesn't see why she should use a sperm donor," he says. "She says a sperm donor can bring in all sorts of genetic disease. If cloning becomes available, she would prefer to use that." I ask if his friend is sane. He says that she is perfectly sane, a little negative about men perhaps, but certainly sane.

> **Section 5 (ll. 64–72)**
> How many people are most likely to make use of cloning?
> How will you be able to recognize a cloned child?

"You know I don't think cloning is so bad. I think it is irrelevant actually. I think it is going to become available some place and I think it will be used by a small percentage of people." I ask when it will happen, if 15 years is reasonable, and he nods. "There will be cloning clinics and people will have children by this technique and nobody would know. The children might just look like them by chance anyway. You might whisper: I wonder if that's a cloned child. Nobody would know."

He shakes his head. "Cloning is a sideshow. It doesn't do anything to society. The main theme of my book is reprogenetics. Forget cloning. What will have an effect on society is genetics and making genetic changes in the embryo."

> **Section 6 (ll. 73–81)**
> What is the difference between a Virtual Child and a Designer Child?

So we are back to talking about asthma and height, and Dr Silver starts to talk even faster. He foresees a future where parents with enough money will be able to purchase two types of procedures. The first – which he calls The Virtual Child – involves analysing a batch of your own embryos to decide which one has the best genetic profile. This is an extension of genetic screening which is already done for some diseases. The second type of procedure uses genetic engineering to create a Designer Child. The parents choose which genes to add to their embryo and then it is implanted. "This is the most significant thing that is going to happen to the human race, ever," says Dr Silver.

> **Section 7 (ll. 82–96)**
> List the main dangers of cloning as seen by Professor Silver.

For the first time in our conversation, Dr Silver says that he finds this frightening. He does not know where to draw the line. Which genetic advantages should parents use and how many of them? In the long-term, he says, genetic engineering would do nothing less than split society between the "naturals" and the "Gen-Rich". "I'm ambivalent on this," he says. "On the one hand it's hard to stop parents from giving their children things and so individual use of the technology cannot be condemned and yet the logical outcome of this is a society that is torn apart. I don't have a solution though. My purpose in writing the book is to make people think about it."

And so then Dr Silver and I go back to thinking about ourselves and genetic manipulation and our own lives. So, I say as I look down on him, what about the height thing? "In my own case I do think that being short is a disadvantage in life," he says. "I guess if I was selecting embryos for some other reason, I would, but I wouldn't do it just for that."

It's a tough call but, aged 45 and with children already, he won't have to make it for real. His children might.

By Ann Treneman, The Independent, *January 22, 1998.*

Science & technology 5

Send in the clones: Annotations

	prospect ['--] idea
	shiver shaking because you are cold or frightened
	spine bones going down the middle of your back
	to send a shiver down one's spine *(fig.)* to scare s.o.
	eminent ['---] well-known, respected
	to take (its) course to be allowed to develop without outside interference
	to disturb to upset
l. 3	**renowned** [rɪˈnaʊnd] well-known
	fertility [fəˈtɪləti] *Fruchtbarkeit*
l. 9	**to be on the brink of s.th.** *(fig.)* to be about to begin
l. 19	**trait** [treɪt] characteristic
l. 23	**to mess around with** *(informal)* to change, to manipulate
l. 24	**Petri dish** *Petrischale*
l. 34	**tenure** [ˈtenjə] job status in which employees have the right to keep their positions until they retire
l. 35	**feasible** [ˈfiːzəbl] possible
l. 38	**to afford s. th.** [-ˈ-] to have the money to pay for s.th.
l. 40	**scary** [ˈskeəri] frightening
l. 44	**to deny** [-ˈ-] to say s.th. isn't true
ll. 45/46	*in vitro* **fertilisation** *künstliche Befruchtung*
l. 49	**to be bothered** to care about s.th., to be worried about s.th.
l. 49/50	**to have a bad press** *(fig.)* to be treated badly and unfairly in public
l. 51	**to replicate** [ˈreplɪkeɪt] to make an exact copy of
l. 60	**donor** *Spender*
l. 62	**sane** [seɪn] sensible, rational
l. 70	**sideshow** *here:* a secondary issue
l. 76	**batch** [bætʃ] set
l. 77	**extension** *here:* use
	genetic screening tests done to see if a person will get certain 'family' diseases
l. 83	**to draw the line** *(fig.)* to stop
l. 87	**to condemn** [kənˈdem] to say that s.th. or s.o. is very bad
l. 95	**a tough call** [tʌf] *(fig.)* a difficult choice

Check the web

To get more information about genetic engineering and cloning, use a search engine such as **google.com** and enter the search words '*genetic engineering*' or '*cloning*'.
Here are some website suggestions:

http://www.ri.bbsrc.ac.uk/library/research/cloning/ (Dolly the sheep; cloning)
http://www.anth.org/ifgene/beginner.htm (beginner's guide to genetic engineering including diagrams, history and many links)
http://www.greenpeace.org/~geneng/ (Greenpeace information on genetic engineering)

5 Science & technology

> No tasks have been set on this short story. It is up to you to decide how you would like to deal with it. When you have read it work on your own or in pairs or groups and devise tasks. Be as creative as you can!

🎧 **The Weapon**

The room was quiet in the dimness of early evening. Dr. James Graham, key scientist of a very important project, sat in his favorite chair, thinking. It was so still that he could hear the turning of pages in the next room as his son leafed through a picture book.

5 Often Graham did his best work, his most creative thinking, under these circumstances, sitting alone in an unlighted room in his own apartment after the day's regular work. But tonight his mind would not work constructively. Mostly he thought about his mentally arrested son – his only son – in the next room. The thoughts were loving thoughts, not the bitter anguish he had felt years ago when he 10 had first learned of the boy's condition. The boy was happy: wasn't that the main thing? And to how many men is given a child who will always be a child, who will not grow up to leave him? Certainly that was rationalization, but what is wrong with rationalization when – The doorbell rang.

Graham rose and turned on lights in the almost-dark room before he went 15 through the hallway to the door. He was not annoyed: tonight, at this moment, almost any interruption to his thoughts was welcome.

He opened the door. A stranger stood there. He said, "Dr. Graham? My name is Niemand; I'd like to talk to you. May I come in a moment?"

Graham looked at him. He was a small man, nondescript, obviously harmless – 20 possibly a reporter or an insurance agent.

But it didn't matter what he was. Graham found himself saying: "Of course. Come in, Mr. Niemand." A few minutes of conversation, he justified himself by thinking, might divert his thoughts and clear his mind.

"Sit down," he said, in the living room. "Care for a drink?"

25 Niemand said, "No, thank you." He sat in the chair; Graham sat on the sofa.

The small man interlocked his fingers; he leaned forward. He said, "Dr. Graham, you are the man whose scientific work is more likely than that of any other man to end the human race's chance for survival."

A crackpot, Graham thought. Too late now he realized that he should have asked 30 the man's business before admitting him. It would be an embarrassing interview – he disliked being rude, yet only rudeness was effective.

"Dr. Graham, the weapon on which you are working."

The visitor stopped and turned his head as the door that led to a bedroom opened and a boy of fifteen came in. The boy didn't notice Niemand; he ran to Graham.

35 "Daddy, will you read to me now?" The boy of fifteen laughed the sweet laughter of a child of four.

Graham put an arm around the boy. He looked at his visitor, wondering whether he had known about the boy. From the lack of surprise on Niemand's face, Graham felt sure he had known.

40 "Harry" – Graham's voice was warm with affection – "Daddy's busy. Just for a little while. Go back to your room; I'll come and read to you soon."

"Chicken Little? You'll read me Chicken Little?"

"If you wish. Now run along. Wait, Harry, this is Mr. Niemand."

The boy smiled bashfully at the visitor. Niemand said, "Hi, Harry," and smiled back 45 at him, holding out his hand. Graham, watching, was sure now that Niemand had known: the smile and the gesture were for the boy's mental age, not his physical one.

The boy took Niemand's hand. For a moment it seemed that he was going to climb into Niemand's lap, and Graham pulled him back gently. He said, "Go to your room now, Harry."

50 The boy skipped back into his bedroom, not closing the door.

Niemand's eyes met Graham's and he said, "I like him," with obvious sincerity. He added, "I hope that what you're going to read to him will always be true."

---

1 **dimness** darkness
3 **to leaf through** to turn pages of e.g. book without paying close attention
8 **mentally arrested** *zurückgeblieben*
9 **anguish** [ˈæŋgwɪʃ] great unhappiness
19 **nondescript** [ˈ---] uninteresting
20 **insurance agent** [ɪnˈʃʊərns ˌeɪdʒnt] (AE) (BE: broker) person who sells insurance
22 **to justify** to make s.th. sound right or reasonable
23 **to divert one's thoughts** [daɪˈvɜːt] to cause oneself to think about s.th. else
26 **to interlock** to weave together
29 **crackpot** (informal) crazy person
30 **to admit s.o.** to let s.o. in
42 **Chicken Little** (mid-19th century fable) term used e.g. in reference to people who needlessly spread panic
44 **bashfully** shyly
51 **sincerity** [sɪnˈserəti] honesty

88

Science & technology 5

Graham didn't understand. Niemand said, "*Chicken Little*, I mean. It's a fine story – but may *Chicken Little* always be wrong about the sky falling down."

Graham suddenly had liked Niemand when Niemand had shown liking for the boy. Now he remembered that he must close the interview quickly. He rose, in dismissal.

He said, "I fear you're wasting your time and mine, Mr. Niemand. I know all the arguments, everything, you can say I've heard a thousand times. Possibly there is truth in what you believe, but it does not concern me. I'm a scientist, and only a scientist. Yes, it is public knowledge that I am working on a weapon, a rather ultimate one. But, for me personally, that is only a by-product of the fact that I am advancing science. I have thought it through, and I have found that that is my only concern."

"But, Dr. Graham, is humanity *ready* for an ultimate weapon?"

Graham frowned. "I have told you my point of view, Mr. Niemand."

Niemand rose slowly from the chair. He said, "Very well, if you do not choose to discuss it, I'll say no more." He passed a hand across his forehead. "I'll leave, Dr. Graham. I wonder, though … may I change my mind about the drink you offered me?"

Graham's irritation faded. He said, "Certainly. Will whisky and water do?"

"Admirably."

Graham excused himself and went into the kitchen. He got the decanter of whisky, another of water, ice cubes, glasses. When he returned to the living room, Niemand was just leaving the boy's bedroom. He heard Niemand's "Good night, Harry," and Harry's happy "'Night, Mr. Niemand."

Graham made drinks. A little later, Niemand declined a second one and started to leave.

Niemand said, "I took the liberty of bringing a small gift to your son, doctor. I gave it to him while you were getting the drinks for us. I hope you'll forgive me."

"Of course. Thank you. Good night."

Graham closed the door; he walked through the living room into Harry's room. He said, "All right, Harry. Now I'll read to –"

There was sudden sweat on his forehead, but he forced his face and his voice to be calm as he stepped to the side of the bed. "May I see that, Harry?" When he had it safely, his hands shook as he examined it.

He thought, *only a madman would give a loaded revolver to an idiot*.

---

57 **in dismissal** giving a signal that s.o. should leave

62 **by-product** s.th. which is an additional and unintended result of doing s.th.

65 *runzeln – frowned*

67 **to pass** *here:* to move s.th. lightly

70 **to fade** [feɪd] to disappear

72 **decanter** [-'--] glass bottle

76 **to decline** to say no to s.th.

78 **to take the liberty of doing s.th.** to do s.th. without asking permission beforehand

86 **madman** crazy person – **loaded** *geladen*

Schweiss – sweat

By Fredric Brown from And The Gods Laughed, *West Bloomfield; MI: Phantasia Press, 1987.*

Project: Instruction manual

Choose one of the devices listed below or any other modern device of your own choice.

Design and produce an instruction leaflet or manual explaining:
▶ the purpose of the device;
▶ how it works;
▶ how to operate it.

Devices
- coffeemaker
- mobile phone
- CD player
- TV
- digital camera
- high class ball point pen
- solar heating/photovoltaic cell
- microwave oven

6 Space – the final frontier?

APOLLO HOUSTON SKYLAB
STAR WARS
STAR TREK COSMONAUT
COLUMBIA, 1ST FEBRUARY 2003 UFOs

20TH JULY 1969

- The dates, words and illustrations above are all significant in terms of the history of space travel. What do you know about them or associate with them?

Space travel

Before reading/listening to the song 'Space Oddity'
- If you had the chance to go on a journey into space either as an astronaut or a tourist would you consider going? Why/Why not?

After reading/listening

Working with the text
1. Describe what happens in the song in a few sentences using the following phrases:
   At the beginning/end • then • at first • suddenly
2. In your own words describe how Major Tom feels about being in space physically and emotionally.

Language
1. Explain line 9: "You've really made the grade".
2. Find the metaphor used by Major Tom to describe his spaceship. Think of metaphors to describe a car, your house, your school, your classroom, etc.
3. Find words in the text which belong to the field of space travel and explain them. Add more examples to your list as you work on the other texts in this chapter.

Comment
- Comment on the melody, the instrumentation and the text:
  – Describe how David Bowie differentiates between "Ground Control" and "Major Tom" in the song.
  – Say whether or not you like the song, giving reasons.

Creative writing
1. Write another verse to the song breaking the news to Major Tom's wife of what has happened.
2. You work at Ground Control and have to break the news to Major Tom's wife. What would you say/do? Write the scene in the form of a screenplay. (The extracts from the screenplay of *Independence Day* on pp. 102–104 may help you.)
3. Write a newspaper article about the events described in the song. Give your article a suitable headline. You could include "quotes" from Ground Control, Major Tom's wife and family, ex-astronauts, a space travel expert, person opposed to space travel, etc.

Metaphor
See *Glossary* on pp. 208–210.

Listening comprehension
Listen to excerpts of the live recording of the Apollo 11 moon landing.

Space Oddity

Ground Control to Major Tom
Ground Control to Major Tom
Take your protein pills and put your helmet on

Ground Control to Major Tom
5 Commencing countdown, engines on
Check ignition and may God's love be with you

Ten, Nine, Eight, Seven, Six, Five, Four, Three, Two, One, Lift-off

This is Ground Control to Major Tom
You've really made the grade
10 And the papers want to know whose shirts you wear
Now it's time to leave the capsule if you dare

"This is Major Tom to Ground Control
I'm stepping through the door
And I'm floating in a most peculiar way
15 And the stars look very different today

For here
Am I sitting in a tin can
Far above the world
Planet Earth is blue
20 And there's nothing I can do.

Though I'm past one hundred thousand miles
I'm feeling very still
And I think my spaceship knows which way to go
Tell my wife I love her very much she knows"
25 Ground Control to Major Tom
Your circuit's dead, there's something wrong
Can you hear me, Major Tom?
Can you hear me, Major Tom?
Can you hear me, Major Tom?
30 Can you …

"Here am I floating round my tin can
Far above the Moon
Planet Earth is blue
And there's nothing I can do."

Space Oddity: *words and music: David Bowie*
© Westminster Music Ltd., für D. Essex
Musikvertrieb GmbH, Hamburg.

6 Space – the final frontier?

The International Space Station

Before you read
- The International Space Station (ISS) is probably one of the most important contemporary space projects. What use will the Space Station be?
  - Look at the suggestions below from the ISS brochure and rank them in your own order of importance.
  - Compare your order of importance with a partner and discuss any differences. Rearrange your order if necessary.
  - Add any more ideas of your own if you can.

To give private industry the opportunity to develop products in space for use on earth

To perform long-term observations of earth and space

To study the long-term effects of weightlessness on the human body and to use that knowledge in the exploration of space and to better the health of humans on earth

To bring together the world community through governmental, academic, and industrial cooperation

To develop new processes and products to benefit life on earth

As a laboratory for carrying out experiments in the absence of gravity's effects

To test new technologies for the next step in the human exploration of the solar system

Adapted from the brochure International Space Station: Improving Life on Earth and in Space: The NASA Research Plan, An Overview © *NASA 1998.*

After reading

Working with the text
1. Draw a table with four columns with the headings:
   Paragraph • People & organisations • What can be done on the ISS • Terms used to describe the ISS
   Complete the table with information from the text. You may not always be able to complete every column for each paragraph.
2. Refer to your table and to the list you generated in the pre-reading task and write your own text with the title: "The ISS: city in space"

Language & Style
1. a) Elaborate or sophisticated language is frequently used in the text. Replace the phrases underlined with more informal everyday language:
   "<u>In the world of human endeavor,</u> the International Space Station (ISS) will break new ground. The ISS <u>will afford</u> scientists, engineers, and entrepreneurs <u>an unprecedented platform</u> on which to perform complex, long-duration, and replicable experiments <u>in the unique environment of space</u>. The station <u>will maximize its particular assets</u>: prolonged exposure to microgravity and the presence of human experimenters in the research process." (ll. 1–8)
   b) Find at least one more similar example in each paragraph and replace each one in the same way.
2. a) Identify two particular adjectives which are used very frequently by the writer.
   b) Note down all the expressions in which they are used.
   c) What does the frequent use of these particular adjectives tell you about the writer's motives?

Comment & criticism
Evaluate the text in the form of a criticism.
- Consider who the text was written by, for whom and with what aim.
- Comment on whether you find the text convincing.
- Say whether or not you think the text is successful in achieving its aim and suggest improvements if necessary.

A step further
1. You are in charge of the publication of a new NASA brochure. Would you include this article? Give reasons for your decision.
2. Choose two aspects of the future use of the ISS and write an article informing your readership about them. (You will need to find further information before you write your article!)

Space – the final frontier? 6

The International Space Station

In the world of human endeavor, the International Space Station (ISS) will break new ground. The ISS will afford scientists, engineers, and entrepreneurs an unprecedented platform on which to perform complex, long-duration, and replicable experiments in the unique environment of space. The station will maximize its particular assets: prolonged exposure to microgravity and the presence of human experimenters in the research process. Yet the ISS is much more than just a world-class laboratory in a novel environment; it is an international human experiment – an exciting "city in space" – a place where we will learn how to live and work "off planet" alongside our international partners.

As an international crew of astronauts lives and works in space, the ISS community will expand here on Earth as researchers use the technologies of "telescience" to control and manipulate experiments from the ground. Advancing communications and information technologies will allow Earth-bound investigators to enjoy a "virtual presence" on board the ISS as they take their place in a world community that will use and benefit from an orbiting laboratory. Our city in space will include as its citizens the international cadre of astronauts and the researchers whose virtual presence will make the incredible breadth of ISS research possible.

This ambitious human experiment in our city in space will play out as the ISS executes its concurrent roles as:
• An advanced testbed for technology and human exploration
• A world-class research facility
• A commercial platform for space research and development

The governments of the United States, Canada, Europe, Japan, and Russia are collaborating with their commercial, academic, and other international affiliates in the design, operation, and utilization of the ISS. As our astronauts and Earth-bound researchers act as space operators and investigators, they will generate a wealth of knowledge that we will apply in the fields of commerce, science, engineering, education, and space exploration.

NASA is committed to using the ISS program to enhance math and science education in our Nation's classrooms. Student projects will fly on the ISS, while interactive videoconferencing and telescience technologies will involve students and teachers in ISS experiments from the ground. The ISS will be a virtual classroom in space, as the excitement of space research and development is used to engage the interest of our next generation of scientists, engineers, and space entrepreneurs.

Future missions of human exploration will require crew members to live and work productively for extended periods in space and on other planets. Key biomedical, life support, and human-factor questions must be answered to ensure crew health, well-being, and productivity. To address these challenges, NASA will work with its industrial partners to apply innovative technology to the challenges of human space exploration, ranging from advances in telemedicine, robotic control, and life support to onsite raw material utilization, miniaturized technology, and bionics. In the coming decades on board the ISS, fundamental and applied research on gravity's effects will build the necessary knowledge base for long-duration missions beyond Earth orbit, enabling us to fulfill our quest for human exploration of the solar system.

From the brochure International Space Station: Improving Life on Earth and in Space: The NASA Research Plan, An Overview © NASA 1998.

---

2 **to break new ground** *(fig.)* to do s.th. that has never been done before – 4 **long-duration** [djʊəˈreɪʃn] lasting a long time. – 5 **replicable** [ˈrepliəbl] which can be exactly repeated – 7 **prolonged exposure** [-,- -ˈ---] a situation where one experiences the effects of s.th. for a long time – 10 **novel** new, unusual – 12 **off planet** not on earth – 16 **telescience** where scientists in one place perform experiments with resources and instruments in another place – 22 **orbiting** moving around a planet or star (*here:* the earth) – 23 **cadre** [ˈkɑːdə] small group of trained people – 25 **breadth** variety – 26 **ambitious** [æmˈbɪʃəs] challenging – 27 **to play out** to continue – **concurrent** happening at the same time – 34 **affiliate** organization which has official connections with another – 35 **utilization** [juːtlaɪˈzeɪʃn] *(formal)* usage – 38 **to apply** to make use of – 42 **to enhance** [ɪnˈhɑːns] to improve – 53 **extended** longer – 55 **to ensure** [-ˈ-] to make certain that s.th. will become reality – 56 **to address** [-ˈ-] *here:* to deal with – 59 **to range** to vary – 60 **onsite ... utilization** *here:* use of material in space – 61 **bionics** *here:* where biological principles are used in the study and production of e.g. electronic systems – 65 **to enable** to make it possible for s.o. to do s.th. – **to fulfill** to carry out – **quest** mission

6 Space – the final frontier?

The ultimate thrill ride

Before you read
1. What risks/dangers do you think may be involved in the building of a space station?
2. What (if anything) justifies building a space station?

While reading
Note down the risks and dangers mentioned in the text. (Make notes, don't write full sentences.)

After reading

Working with the text
1. a) Divide the text into two parts. (Give the line numbers for each part.)
   b) Choose a key word or phrase from each section as a subtitle and explain your choice.
2. (The notes you made while reading will help you answer some of these questions.)
   a) What preceded the ISS in terms of space travel and how is this perceived by the writer in comparison?
   b) What is the function of the spacesuit? How does it protect the astronaut?
   c) What makes docking particularly dangerous?
   d) What dangers do astronauts face on space walks?
   e) Explain the safety problems of the airlocks in your own words.
   f) According to the article, what was the original purpose of the ISS, how has this changed and why?

Style
1. Define the style of the text giving examples from the text to support your choice.
2. Find examples of various rhetorical devices including similes and metaphors in the text and explain their effect on the reader.

Comment
Write a short comment saying whether or not the writer of the article is pro or contra the ISS in your opinion and giving your personal opinion on the building of a space station.

A step further
Check the web and if possible other sources and make a file of information about the development of the ISS from its outset to the present day. Don't copy from the material you find. Include illustrations and diagrams.

> **Similes, metaphors imagery**
> See *Glossary* on pp. 208–210.

> **Check the web**
> Get more information about the ISS at:
> http://www.nasa.gov

---

thrill exciting
1 **ho-hum** boring – **to epitomize** [-'---] to be a perfect example of s.th.
2 **18-wheeler** very large lorry
4 **white-knuckle maneuver** [ˈwaɪtˌnʌkld məˈnuːvə] (*BE manoeuvre; knuckle = Knöchel*) very risky movement – **nail-biting** nerve-racking – **jinx** bad luck
5 **on sabbatical** not working – **snafu** [snæfˈuː] (*AE: slang*) chaotic situation
7 **The Perils of Pauline** (*fig.*) 1914 weekly silent film series showing dangerous situations
12 **high-wire act** *Drahtseilakt*
14 **nickel** (*AE*) five-cent piece **saliva** [səˈlaɪvə] the liquid in one's mouth

The ultimate thrill ride

The era of ho-hum space missions, epitomized by space-shuttle flights about as exciting as an 18-wheeler cruising Interstate 80, is over. This is the age of the space station. The most expensive and complicated construction job ever, it will be full of white-knuckle maneuvers, nail-biting spacewalks and, unless the space-jinx gods are
5 on sabbatical, life-threatening snafus. "It's not going to be pretty," says NASA chief Daniel Goldin. "We're going to have some unbelievably tough problems. You're going to see the perils of Pauline."

The risks start on the launch pad. A study ordered by NASA concluded that there is a 74 percent chance that one of Russia's 12 missions, or one of NASA's 33, will
10 be lost. "Lost" could mean fatalities; all of NASA's missions carry crews, and some of Russia's do. Even if no one dies on the launch pad, assembling the space station will be an orbital version of a high-wire act without a net. Think of it as building, by hand, a fleet of 747s – while the pieces are flying 250 miles above solid ground. A nickel-sized tear in a spacesuit will make saliva boil off the astronaut's

94

Space – the final frontier?

tongue, dry up her eyeballs and leave her with about 10 seconds of consciousness to realize that, in a vacuum, screaming is pointless.

If this were a circus, the first time the ringmaster would ask for silence would be during a docking maneuver. Russia's supply vehicles come in hot – engineer-speak for fast. Docking at any speed will make the station vibrate; a fast docking could squash a component and even knock out life support. For although the station can withstand "soft, nudging dockings," says NASA's Victor Cooley, it can't take "contact velocities higher than [a half mile per hour]." There is virtually no room for error. On Earth, U.S. civil engineers require safety factors of 1.5 to 8; an elevator, say, must be able to lift at least triple the weight posted on the little white card. Due to cost constraints, however, the station's components have a safety factor of 1.1 – just 10 percent wiggle room before they crack or crumple.

Assembly will require 160 spacewalks totaling at least 960 hours. [...] Making the dozens of requisite cable and duct connections will be like installing desktop computers in the dark, in subzero temperatures, wearing moonsuits. When two astronauts lift a 23,000-pound, 40-foot solar array to the end of the truss that runs along the station like a giant backbone, for example, "It will be at least a six-hour job," says former shuttle astronaut Brewster Shaw, an executive at Boeing. The longer a crew is out, the greater the chance of getting hit by a micrometeorite (leading to the boiling-saliva-off-your-tongue thing). Even more fun will be spacewalks that find astronauts at the end of a 30-foot robot arm, in foot restraints. Engineers have pleaded with the crews' trainers to emphasize that they can't rock back and forth. "You can literally break off that platform if you lie back and rock forward just twice," says Cooley. How do the astronauts feel about the risks? "I wouldn't say 'scared'," says astronaut Joe Tanner. [...] "'Highly motivated' is a better term."

Staying inside should be safer, but not by much, says space consultant James Oberg. Among his concerns: airlocks open out, not in. That means you can't use air pressure to keep them closed. Why does that matter? Orbiting in and out of sunlight will expose the station to temperatures from 250 degrees to minus 100 degrees Fahrenheit. That could cause metal fatigue and warping, which are good ways to ruin a tight seal around the door that keeps you from getting sucked toward Pluto. NASA doesn't think the airlocks pose any risk but Oberg also critizises the station's paucity of windows. If the crew can't see, there are more chances of nasty surprises like collisions with supply ships.

What makes these dangers even more problematic is that they are not in the service of anything, well, worthy. After President Reagan proposed an $8 billion station in his 1984 State of the Union address, NASA envisioned it as an orbiting lab, factory and staging platform for missions to Mars. But money problems – the station, many years behind schedule, is billions over budget – have scrubbed most of the science, and industry has shown little interest in renting space. Its sole purpose has come down to this: it fosters cooperation among the 16 nations involved (the United States, Russia, Canada, Japan, Italy and 11 in Europe). And it keeps Russian scientists, who are building one third of the station, too busy to sell their ballistic-missile-making services to, say, Iran. [...]

If the station is ever finished, the sparkling behemoth will look bigger and brighter than anything in the night sky except the moon and Venus. It will pass overhead every 90 minutes at 17,500 miles an hour. And if it doesn't actually do anything useful, then perhaps, in a funny way, that is just as well. In return for the risks and heroics, we shouldn't reap anything so prosaic as perfect protein crystals. The space station should, instead, release us from the bounds of Earth, offering humankind the first stepping stone off our natal planet. Until it does, though, putting it together is going to be one heck of a thrill ride.

By Sharon Begley and Adam Rogers, From Newsweek, November 30, 1998, © 1998 Newsweek Inc. All rights reserved. Reprinted by permission.

---

18 **docking maneuver** when one spacecraft positions itself close to another to establish a connection
20 **to squash** [skwɒʃ] to crush – **to knock out** here: to make s.th. unable to function
21 **nudging** pushing gently
22 **velocity** [vɪˈlɒsətɪ] speed
23 **civil engineer** Bauingenieur(in)
24 **triple** three times s.th.
25 **constraint** [-ˈ-] limit, control
26 **wiggle room** (fig.) margin of error – **to crumple** to collapse
28 **requisite** [ˈrekwɪzɪt] necessary – **duct** Luftschacht
30 **solar array** Solaranlage – **truss** Gerüst
35 **foot restraint** s.th. that keeps one's feet in one place
36 **to plead** [pliːd] to beg – **to emphasize** [ˈemfəsaɪz] to make very clear
41 **airlock** Luftschleuse
44 **fatigue** [fəˈtiːg] here: the weakening or breakage of metal as a result of stress – **warping** bending that results in the damage of a material
45 **seal** Siegel – **to be sucked toward s.th.** to be pulled with great force toward s.th.
47 **paucity** [ˈpɔːsətɪ] (formal) lack – **nasty** very unpleasant
50 **worthy** having an important purpose
51 **to envision** to imagine s.th. as possible future reality
53 **to scrub** here: (informal) to cancel or give up
54 **sole** only
55 **to foster** to encourage
57 **ballistic missile** Raketengeschoss
59 **behemoth** [bɪˈhiːmɒθ] s.th. that is extremely big
62 **funny** here: strange
63 **to reap** [riːp] to get s.th. in return for one's efforts – **prosaic** [prəʊˈzeɪɪk] (formal) dull, boring
64 **the bounds of s.th.** the limits of s.th.
65 **stepping stone** Sprungbrett – **natal** [ˈneɪtl] relating to the place and/or time of birth
66 **one heck of** (slang) ein irrsinniger

6 Space – the final frontier?

> **Role play: talk show**
> You are guests on a talk show, discussing the question whether the money invested in the ISS is well invested.
> Work in groups each representing one of the following participants of the talk show.
> - a NASA astronaut
> - a politician, who wants to cut public spending
> - a politician, who wants to promote science
> - a politician, who believes that we should solve problems on Earth first
> - a member of a charity organisation
> - a private investor (e.g. in space tourism)
> - a Russian cosmonaut
> - a European space scientist
>
> Before you hold the discussion…
> … prepare arguments to support 'your' point of view. • … try to anticipate the arguments your opponents will use.
> • … think of counter-arguments.

"If I Forget Thee, Oh Earth …"

While you read the following short story you may find it helpful to do the following:
- Write down one or two key words per paragraph as a record of the storyline.
- After every two or three paragraphs write a question which you think might be answered in the next part of the story.
- After every two or three paragraphs try to predict what is going to happen next in the story (and see how often you are right/wrong!).
- Keep a note of the different characters including their names, relationship to each other, etc. and adding to it as you read.
- Note down words that you don't understand with the line numbers so that you can look them up later.

Arthur C. Clarke (born in 1917) is regarded as a space-age visionary, who predicted space travel in 1945, long before rockets were tested.
One of the best known science fiction authors, Sir Arthur has written more than 80 books, including the classic *2001: A Space Odyssey*.
He has made Sri Lanka his home and has lived on the island since 1956.
Find out more at:
http://www.kirjasto.sci.fi/aclarke.htm

4 **slender** thin
5 **to creep** to move very slowly
7 **longing** a deep wish for s.th.
8 **to purge** to get rid of – **tang** *here:* a sharp odor
16 **airlock** *Luftschleuse* – **tense** *here:* excited
17 **cramped** without much space
18 **roar** a very loud noise
19 **to fade away** to disappear

When Marvin was ten years old, his father took him through the long, echoing corridors that led up through Administration and Power, until at last they came to the uppermost levels of all and were among the swiftly growing vegetation of the Farmlands. Marvin liked it here: it was fun watching the great, slender plants creeping with almost visible eagerness toward the sunlight as it filtered down through the plastic domes to meet them. The smell of life was everywhere, awakening inexpressible longings in his heart: no longer was he breathing the dry, cool air of the residential levels, purged of all smells but the faint tang of ozone. He wished he could stay here for a little while, but Father would not let him. They went onward until they had reached the entrance to the Observatory, which he had never visited: but they did not stop, and Marvin knew with a sense of rising excitement that there could be only one goal left. For the first time in his life, he was going Outside.

There were a dozen of the surface vehicles, with their wide balloon tires and pressurized cabins, in the great servicing chamber. His father must have been expected, for they were led at once to the little scout car waiting by the huge circular door of the airlock. Tense with expectancy, Marvin settled himself down in the cramped cabin while his father started the motor and checked the controls. The inner door of the lock slid open and then closed behind them: he heard the roar of the great air pumps fade slowly away as the pressure dropped to zero. Then the "Vacuum" sign flashed on, the outer door parted, and before Marvin lay the land which he had never yet entered.

Space – the final frontier?

He had seen it in photographs, of course: he had watched it imaged on television screens a hundred times. But now it was lying all around him, burning beneath the fierce sun that crawled so slowly across the jet-black sky. He stared into the west, away from the blinding splendour of the sun – and there were the stars, as he had been told but had never quite believed. He gazed at them for a long time, marvelling that anything could be so bright and yet so tiny. They were intense, unscintillating points, and suddenly he remembered a rhyme he had once read in one of his father's books:

Twinkle, twinkle, little star,
How I wonder what you are.

Well, he knew what the stars were. Whoever asked that question must have been very stupid. And what did they mean by "twinkle"? You could see at a glance that all the stars shone with the same steady, unwavering light. He abandoned the puzzle and turned his attention to the landscape around him.

They were racing across a level plain at almost a hundred miles an hour, the great balloon tires sending up little spurts of dust behind them. There was no sign of the Colony: in the few minutes while he had been gazing at the stars, its domes and radio towers had fallen below the horizon. Yet there were other indications of man's presence, for about a mile ahead Marvin could see the curiously shaped structures clustering round the head of a mine. Now and then a puff of vapour would emerge from a squat smokestack and would instantly disperse.

They were past the mine in a moment: Father was driving with a reckless and exhilarating skill as if – it was a strange thought to come into a child's mind – he were trying to escape from something. In a few minutes they had reached the edge of the plateau on which the Colony had been built. The ground fell sharply away beneath them in a dizzying slope whose lower stretches were lost in shadow. Ahead, as far as the eye could reach, was a jumbled wasteland of craters, mountain ranges, and ravines. The crests of the mountains, catching the low sun, burned like islands of fire in a sea of darkness: and above them the stars still shone as steadfastly as ever.

There could be no way forward – yet there was. Marvin clenched his fists as the car edged over the slope and started the long descent. Then he saw the barely visible track leading down the mountainside, and relaxed a little. Other men, it seemed, had gone this way before.

Night fell with a shocking abruptness as they crossed the shadow line and the sun dropped below the crest of the plateau. The twin searchlights sprang into life, casting blue-white bands on the rocks ahead, so that there was scarcely need to check their speed. For hours they drove through valleys and past the foot of mountains whose peaks seemed to comb the stars, and sometimes they emerged for a moment into the sunlight as they climbed over higher ground.

And now on the right was a wrinkled, dusty plain, and on the left, its ramparts and terraces rising mile after mile into the sky, was a wall of mountains that marched into the distance until its peaks sank from sight below the rim of the world. There was no sign that men had ever explored this land, but once they passed the skeleton of a crashed rocket, and beside it a stone cairn surmounted by a metal cross.

It seemed to Marvin that the mountains stretched on forever; but at last, many hours later, the range ended in a towering, precipitous headland that rose steeply from a cluster of little hills. They drove down into a shallow valley that curved in a great arc toward the far side of the mountains: and as they did so, Marvin slowly realized that something very strange was happening in the land ahead.

The sun was now low behind the hills on the right: the valley before them should be in total darkness. Yet it was awash with a cold white radiance that came spilling over the crags beneath which they were driving. Then, suddenly, they were out in the open plain, and the source of the light lay before them in all its glory.

---

22 **imaged** *here:* to be presented in visible electronic form
24 **fierce** [fɪəs] *here:* bright
25 **splendour** ['splendə] beautiful appearance
26 **to gaze** [geɪz] to look steadily at s.o. or s.th. for a long time – **to marvel** ['--] to think about s.th. with surprised admiration
27 **unscintillating** [ʌn'sɪntɪleɪtɪŋ] shining with a steady light, not sparkling
30 **twinkle** sparkle

34 **to abandon** [ə'bændən] to give up

36 **plain** flat land without trees
37 **spurt of dust** a cloud of dust that shoots out suddenly

41 **to cluster** to group around s.th. – **vapour** *Dampf*
42 **squat** [skwɒt] short – **smokestack** tall factory chimney – **to disperse** [-'-] to become less concentrated
43 **reckless** without care
44 **exhilarating** [ɪɡ'zɪləreɪtɪŋ] exciting
47 **slope** the side of a hill
48 **jumbled** mixed up
49 **ravine** [rə'viːn] deep, narrow valley
50 **steadfastly** steadily
51 **to clench one's fists** to curl one's fingers up tightly e.g. out of anger

57 **scarcely** ['skeəsli] hardly

59 **to comb** [kəʊm] *here:* to brush up against – **to emerge** to appear
61 **rampart** a wall made of earth

63 **rim** edge
65 **cairn** [keən] a pile of stones that is a memorial or marker – **to surmount** to put s.th. on top of s.th. else
67 **precipitous** [prɪ'sɪpɪtəs] very steep – **headland** a piece of land that comes to a point and extends into water
68 **shallow** *opp. of* deep
69 **arc** curved line
73 **awash** filled with – **radiance** ['reɪdɪəns] bright light
74 **crag** steep rocky cliff or part of a mountain

6 Space – the final frontier?

It was very quiet in the little cabin now that the motors had stopped. The only sound was the faint whisper of the oxygen feed and an occasional metallic crepitation as the outer walls of the vehicle radiated away their heat. For no warmth at all came from the great silver crescent that floated low above the far horizon and flooded all this land with pearly light. It was so brilliant that minutes passed before Marvin could accept its challenge and look steadfastly into its glare, but at last he could discern the outlines of continents, the hazy border of the atmosphere, and the white islands of cloud. And even at this distance, he could see the glitter of sunlight on the polar ice.

It was beautiful, and it called to his heart across the abyss of space. There in that shining crescent were all the wonders that he had never known – the hues of sunset skies, the moaning of the sea on pebbled shores, the patter of falling rain, the unhurried benison of snow. These and a thousand others should have been his rightful heritage, but he knew them only from the books and ancient records, and the thought filled him with the anguish of exile.

Why could they not return? It seemed so peaceful beneath those lines of marching cloud. Then Marvin, his eyes no longer blinded by the glare, saw that the portion of the disc that should have been in darkness was gleaming faintly with an evil phosphorescence: and he remembered. He was looking upon the funeral pyre of a world – upon the radioactive aftermath of Armageddon. Across a quarter of a million miles of space, the glow of dying atoms was still visible, a perennial reminder of the ruinous past. It would be centuries yet before that deadly glow died from the rocks and life could return again to fill that silent, empty world.

And now Father began to speak, telling Marvin the story which until this moment had meant no more to him than the fairy tales he had once been told. There were many things he could not understand: it was impossible for him to picture the glowing, multicolored pattern of life on the planet he had never seen. Nor could he comprehend the forces that had destroyed it in the end, leaving the Colony, preserved by its isolation, as the sole survivor. Yet he could share the agony of those final days, when the Colony had learned at last that never again would the supply ships come flaming down through the stars with gifts from home. One by one the radio stations had ceased to call: on the shadowed globe the lights of the cities had dimmed and died, and they were alone at last, as no men had ever been alone before, carrying in their hands the future of the race.

---

77 **oxygen feed** device that supplies oxygen
78 **crepitation** [ˌkrepɪˈteɪʃn] popping sounds
79 **crescent** [ˈkresnt] curved shape, like a quarter moon
81 **glare** [gleə] too powerful brightness
82 **to discern** [dɪˈsɜːn] to barely recognize s.th. from far away – **hazy** [ˈheɪzɪ] *here:* blurred
83 **glitter** shininess
85 **abyss** [əˈbɪs] *here:* a very great distance
86 **hue** colour
87 **moaning** [məʊn] long, soft and sad sound – **pebbled** filled with small stones – **patter** soft, tapping sounds
88 **benison** *(formal)* blessing
89 **heritage** s.th. that is inherited
90 **anguish** intense sadness
93 **to gleam** to shine – **faintly** weakly
94 **funeral pyre** [paɪə] *Scheiterhaufen*
95 **aftermath** the result of s.th. that happened before – **Armageddon** the terrible war that ends in the destruction of the world
96 **perennial** constant
104 **sole** only – **agony** [ˈægənɪ] terrible physical or psychological pain
106 **to come flaming down** *(fig.)* to shine so brightly while moving that s.th. looks as if it is on fire
107 **to cease** [siːs] to stop
108 **to dim** to gradually become less bright

Imagine being Marvin and seeing the Earth like this for the first time ever. How do you think you would have reacted? What do you think you would have said?

Space – the final frontier? 6

Then had followed the years of despair, and the longdrawn battle for survival in this fierce and hostile world. That battle had been won, though barely: this little oasis of life was safe against the worst that Nature could do. But unless there was a goal, a future toward which it could work, the Colony would lose the will to live, and neither machines nor skill nor science could save it then.

So, at last, Marvin understood the purpose of this pilgrimage. He would never walk beside the rivers of that lost and legendary world, or listen to the thunder raging above its softly rounded hills. Yet one day – how far ahead? – his children's children would return to claim their heritage. The winds and the rains would scour the poisons from the burning lands and carry them to the sea, and in the depths of the sea they would waste their venom until they could harm no living things. Then the great ships that were still waiting here on the silent, dusty plains could lift once more into space, along the road that led to home.

That was the dream: and one day, Marvin knew with a sudden flash of insight, he would pass it on to his own son, here at this same spot with the mountains behind him and the silver light from the sky streaming into his face.

He did not look back as they began the homeward journey. He could not bear to see the cold glory of the crescent Earth fade from the rocks around him, as he went to rejoin his people in their long exile.

From Across the Sea of Stars *by Sir Arthur C. Clarke,* New York: Harcourt, Brace and World, 1959. Reprinted by permission of the author and the author's agents, Scovil Chichak Galen Literary Agency, Inc.

110 **despair** hopelessness – **longdrawn** long-lasting
111 **fierce** cruel, terrible – **hostile** ['hɒstaɪl] very unfriendly
115 **pilgrimage** journey that has a deep symbolic importance
117 **to rage** *here:* to make a sound that is very loud
118 **to scour** to clean s.th. with great intensity
120 **to waste** *here:* to get rid of – **venom** ['--] poison
123 **insight** intuition

Working with the text
1. Where and when does the story take place?
2. a) Describe what has happened to the human race according to the story.
   b) Describe the currrent situation for the remaining human beings.
3. Characterise the relationship between Marvin and his father.

Style
1. Light imagery is often combined with religious allusions in the story. Find examples and describe the atmosphere created.
2. Marvin remembers an old nursery rhyme:
   "Twinkle, twinkle, little star, How I wonder what you are." (ll. 30–31).
   a) Why does Marvin consider the question stupid?
   b) *"And what did they mean by 'twinkle'?"* (l. 33). Explain "twinkle" for Marvin.
3. What are the typical features of science fiction literature? Which of these features can you identify in the story?

> **Science fiction**
> See *Glossary* on pp. 208–210.

Creative Writing/Comment
1. Do you think it is a good idea to set up a manned colony in outer space? Give reasons for your opinion.
2. Write a short scene in which the crew of the last supply ship from Earth arrive at the colony and have to break the news to the colonists of what has happened.
3. Write a sequel to the story with the title "End of Exile" set at a future point in time when the colonists first return to Earth.
4. Your government is planning on setting up a manned colony in space. Design either:
     a) a leaflet describing the new colony and saying why it is necessary.
   or b) a leaflet from a pressure group opposing the setting up of the colony which points out problems, difficulties, etc.
5. To what extent do you think the scenarios described (a manned space colony/a nuclear Armageddon) are realistic? Write a comment.
6. Write a script for a film version of the story concentrating on casting, camera positions and music and sound effects.

6 Space – the final frontier?

Satellites

Science fiction writer Arthur C. Clarke (author of the short story *If I Forget Thee, oh Earth...* on pp. 96–99) first proposed geosynchronous orbits* for communications satellites in 1945 – 25 years before the first communications satellite was placed in geosynchronous orbit!

For many years satellites were exotic, top-secret devices. They were used primarily in a military capacity, for activities such as navigation and espionage. Now they are an essential part of our daily lives.

Work with a partner (or in a group) and find out more about satellite use in at least one of the following areas. You can find useful information at the websites given. Present your findings in a suitable form to your class:

- weather reports
- television transmission
- telephone calls and the internet
- newspapers and magazine printing & distribution
- navigation via Global Positioning System (GPS)

*__Geosynchronous Equatorial Orbit__ – *from* 'geo' = Earth + 'synchronous' = moving at the same rate

What are the advantages of geo-synchronous orbit? The illustration may give you some ideas.

Check the web
Get more information about satellites at:
http://octopus.gma.org/surfing/satellites/
http://www.thetech.org/exhibits_events/online/satellite/

Get more information about the military use of satellites at:
http://www.stopstarwars.org/html/intro.html
http://www.nasa.gov

NOAA Satellites help rescue 166 people in U.S. in 2001

Before you read
What kind of accidents/rescues do you think might have taken place in which satellites helped?

After reading

Working with the text
1. Make a table with the headings *Sea*, *Land* and *Air* and list the types of accidents/rescues mentioned in the text.
2. Describe the kinds of satellites mentioned, how they work and how rescue forces are alerted as a result.
3. What other uses do the NOAA satellites have apart from detecting emergencies? Explain the technical terms given in the last paragraph in your own words.

Language
Find words/phrases in the text that belong to each of the categories below. Choose at least two words per category. Choose words which are new to you and which you think will be useful to you in the future! Write an English definition to go with each word and a sentence of your own using each word.
   Words with suffixes and/or prefixes • the gerund (-ing forms used as nouns) • verbs • other

Creative writing
Write either a short story or a newspaper report based on one of the rescues mentioned in the text.

Research & report: Star wars – the military use of satellites and space technology
Under the Bush administration the U.S. military space program has increased in importance. Some factions believe that more should be done to develop a technology which could protect U.S. satellites (and attack enemy satellites) in space, some speak of establishing a Space Force similar to the Air Force. Other groups, such as Greenpeace, are vehemently against an extended arms race in space.
Find out more about the U.S. military space program (past and present).
Write a report giving your opinion on the pros and cons of an extended arms race in space.

Space – the final frontier? 6

NOAA SATELLITES HELP RESCUE 166 PEOPLE IN U.S. IN 2001

February 1, 2002 – Thanks to environmental satellites with rescue tracking capability, NOAA and the Russian government saved 166 lives in the U.S. waters and wilderness in 2001. The NOAA satellites are part of an international Search and Rescue Satellite-Aided Tracking Program known as Cospas-Sarsat. The system uses a constellation of satellites in geostationary and polar orbits to detect and locate emergency beacons on vessels and aircraft in distress.

Of the 166 rescues last year, 112 people were saved on the seas; 39 in the Alaska wilderness, and 15 on downed aircraft in states around the country. A variety of rescues took place on the seas. Engine fires, flooding, rough seas and water spouts all caused emergencies resulting in distress calls and rescues. In Alaska, stranded hunters and lost persons were among those rescued. Downed aircraft incidents included those making emergency landings and those that crashed in bad weather.

"Our business is saving lives," said Ajay Mehta, manager of NOAA's Sarsat program. "We are an international humanitarian program whose goals and rewards are saving lives. More than 13,000 lives have been saved worldwide since the system became operational in 1982 and more than 4,500 in the United States alone. September of this year marks the 20th anniversary of the first Sarsat rescue."

NOAA's National Environmental Satellite, Data, and Information Service operates the U.S. Mission Control Center in Suitland, Md, and represents the United States in this program by providing satellites and ground equipment.

"We had an unusual rescue last year with a bear circling a private plane that had crashed in Alaska with two people on board," said Mehta. "These folks were in a dangerous predicament. Yet, because there was an emergency locator transmitter on board the aircraft that activated upon impact, rescue authorities were able to respond to the distress quickly. On arrival the search and rescue aircraft saw the situation unfolding and dispatched a helicopter to retrieve the occupants and bring them to safety. […]

NOAA's Geostationary Operational Environmental Satellites (GOES) can instantly detect emergency signals. The polar-orbiting satellites in the system detect emergency signals as they circle the Earth from pole to pole. Emergency signals are sent to the U.S. Mission Control Center in Suitland, Md., then automatically sent to rescue forces around the world. Today there are 35 countries participating in the system.

NOAA's National Environmental Satellite, Data, and Information Service (NOAA Satellite and Data Service) is the nation's primary source of operational space-based meteorological and climate data. In addition to search and rescue, NOAA's environmental satellites are used for weather forecasting, climate monitoring, and other environmental applications such as volcanic eruptions, ozone monitoring, sea surface temperature measurements, and wild fire detection. NOAA Satellite and Data Service also operates three data centers, which house global data bases in climatology, oceanography, solid earth geophysics, marine geology and geophysics, solar-terrestrial physics, and paleoclimatology.

National Oceanic and Atmospheric Administration (NOAA),
http://www.noaanews.noaa.gov/stories/s858.htm

---

1 command antenna **2** communication antenna **3** solar cells **4** batteries **5** radio receivers & transmitters **6** rocket fuel **7** main rocket motor **8** rocket thrusters **9** camera

Can you explain how a satellite works?

NOAA *short for* National Oceanic and Atmospheric Administration

Col. 1:
- 2 **rescue tracking** using devices to locate people needing help
- 10 **orbit** the continuous path of s.th. moving around a planet or star – **geostationary orbit** [ˌdʒiːəˈsteɪʃnrɪ] geosynchronous orbit – **polar orbit** when a satellite crosses both polar regions once during each orbit
- 11 **beacon** [ˈbiːkn] a light (e.g. fire) used to signal danger or emergency
- 12 **vessel** *(formal)* ship or boat – **in distress** in trouble or danger
- 18 **water spout** weather event similar to a tornado that occurs over water
- 21 **stranded** unable to get out of a place
- 23 **incident** [ˈɪnsɪdnt] s.th. (usually unpleasant) that happens

Col. 2:
- 5 **predicament** [prɪˈdɪkəmənt] difficult or unpleasant situation
- 8 **impact** [ˈ--] when s.th. hits s.th. else (here, the ground)
- 11 **to unfold** *here:* to happen
- 12 **to retrieve** to bring back
- 33 **application** use of s.th. for a specific purpose
- 35 **surface** [ˈsɜːfɪs] the topmost layer of an object
- 42 **paleoclimatology** [ˌpælɪəklaɪməˈtɒlədʒɪ] the study of climate developments and changes over time

6 Space – the final frontier?

UFOs

Independence Day – extracts from the screenplay

While-reading
While reading the following extracts from the screenplay of the film *Independence Day* note down what the following abbreviations and words mean:
  INT. • EXT. • CONTINUOUS • widen • super up • super • cut to • same

Extract 1
AN AMERICAN FLAG
Oddly still, posted in gray dusty sand.
WIDEN TO REVEAL:
5   EXT. LUNAR SURFACE – THE MOON
One small step for man, one large pile of garbage for moon-kind. Untouched for years, the flag stands next to the cast off remains of the Apollo mission. Slowly the discarded equipment begins to RATTLE and SHAKE.
AN ENORMOUS SHADOW creeps towards us blotting out the horizon, a loud
10 RUMBLE is heard.
Suddenly we are covered in DARKNESS as the SHADOW engulfs us.
Only the lonely image of our EARTH hangs in the air, until a huge silhouetted OBJECT suddenly blocks our view.
CUT TO:
15 EXT. NEW MEXICO – RADIO TELESCOPE VALLEY – NIGHT
A field of large satellite dishes scan the skies.
Super up: S.E.T.I. INSTITUTE, NEW MEXICO
INT. INSTITUTE – MONITORING CONTROL CENTER – SAME
A lone TECHNICIAN works on his putting skills. Behind him, wall to wall technical
20 equipment quietly sifts through data. A RED LIGHT begins to flash.
The Technician turns and slowly walks towards the source. One by one a series of LIGHTS turn on. The Technician (TECH ONE) grabs a pair of headphones. His eyes widen.
INT. SLEEPING QUARTERS – SAME
25 Sleepily a SUPERVISOR picks up the phone.
SUPERVISOR: *If this isn't an insanely beautiful woman, I'm hanging up.*
INT. CONTROL CENTER – SAME
TECH ONE: *Shut up and listen.*
He holds the phone up to a speaker, increases the volume. A strange FLUCTUATING
30 TONE plays out in sequential patterns.
INT. SLEEPING QUARTERS – SAME
HEARING it, the Supervisor BOLTS UP, banging his head on the bunk above him.
INT. CONTROL CENTER – MOMENTS LATER
A pajama party on acid. Five other technicians, in various states of undress, hover
35 anxiously around the main console. The Supervisor enters, tying his robe.
SUPERVISOR: *God, I hope it's not just another damned Russian spy job.*
TECH THREE: (overlapping) *Negative. Computer affirms the signal is unidentified.*
TECH TWO: (hanging up the phone) *The boy from Air Res Traffic says the skies are clear. No terrestrial launches.*
40 TECH ONE: *It's the real thing. A radio signal from another world.*
The room becomes quiet as they realize that after years of searching the heavens, they might have finally found something.

---

5 **lunar surface** the topmost layer of the moon
7 **cast off** that which is no longer wanted – **remains** *Überreste*
8 **discarded** s.th. that has been gotten rid of
9 **enormous** [ɪˈnɔːməs] very, very large – **to creep** to move very slowly – **to blot out** to hide
11 **to engulf** [-ˈ-] to surround and cover completely
16 **to scan** to search
17 **S.E.T.I. Institute** (short for Search for Extra-Terrestrial Intelligence) Institute for research relating to the study of life in the universe
19 **to put** [pʌt] *here:* to hit a golf ball with a golf club
20 **to sift through** to sort through carefully
29 **fluctuating** [ˈflʌktʃueɪtɪŋ] rising and falling
30 **sequential** characterized by a sequence
32 **to bolt up** to stand or sit up very suddenly – **bunk** *Etagenbett*
34 **acid** (slang) LSD – **to hover** [ˈhɒvə] to stand in one place while making small nervous movements
37 **to affirm** to show that s.th. is true
38 **Air Res Traffic** (short for Naval Air Reserve Traffic Control) armed forces members who monitor flight activity

Space – the final frontier? 6

Extract 2

INT. SPACE COMMAND – THE PENTAGON – CONTINUOUS
Banks of computers, Technicians and assistants working feverishly through the 45
night. The Officers cross the room.
Super: SPACE COMMAND – THE PENTAGON
COMMANDING OFFICER: *Satellite reception has been impaired but we were able to get these.*
They arrive at a glass table. The surrounding officers snap to attention as a SECOND 50
OFFICER quickly brings over a large transparency. We SEE a grainy image of a large vague OBJECT.
GENERAL GREY: *Looks like a big turd.*
The two officers exchange a glance.
COMMANDING OFFICER: *We estimate it has a diameter of over five hundred and* 55
fifty kilometers and a mass roughly one fourth the size of our moon.
The General turns to the Second Officer, concerned.
GENERAL GREY: *A meteor?*
SECOND OFFICER: *No Sir. Definitely not.*
GENERAL GREY: *How do you know?* 60
SECOND OFFICER: *Well, er… it's slowing down.*
GENERAL GREY: *It's doing what?*
SECOND OFFICER: *It's… slowing down, Sir.*
The General walks over to a phone, picks it up.
GENERAL GREY: *Get me the Secretary of Defense.* (pause) *Then wake him up.* 65

Extract 3

INT. AIR FORCE ONE – SAME
Back in the passenger section, the President sits with General Grey and Chief of Staff Nimziki. The Technician from the command module is briefing them.
TECHNICIAN: *They must be targeting our satellites. We've lost all satellite* 70 *communication, tracking and mapping.*
GENERAL GREY: *Have NORAD relayed intelligence to our on board computers?*
The Technician nods and exits. Defeated, the President slumps sullenly.
GENERAL GREY: *We've moved as many of our forces away from the bases as possible but we've already sustained heavy losses.* 75
The President nods his approval absently. Coming out of the bathroom, David overhears.
NIMZIKI: *I spoke with the Joint Chiefs when they arrived at NORAD. They agree, we must launch a counter offensive with a full nuclear strike. Hit 'em with everything we've got.* 80
PRESIDENT: *Above American soil?*
NIMZIKI: *If we don't strike soon, there may not be much of an America left to defend.*
The Technician returns, his face is white with fear.
GENERAL GREY: *What's the latest from NORAD?* 85
OFFICER: *It's gone, sir. They've taken out NORAD.*
NIMZIKI: *That's impossible …*
GENERAL GREY: *My God, the Vice President and the Joint Chiefs …*
NIMZIKI: *Mr. President, we must launch. A delay now would be more costly than when you waited to evacuate the cities!* 90
That stings the President. He considers the option. David is shocked.
DAVID: *You can't be seriously considering firing nuclear weapons?*
CONSTANCE: *David, don't …*
David pushes past her.

---

45 **feverishly** with a lot of activity and agitation
48 **to impair** to keep s.th. from functioning optimally
50 **to snap to attention** to stand up suddenly and salute
51 **transparency** *Folie* – **grainy** unclear
53 **turd** *(vulgar) Scheißhaufen*
54 **to exchange a glance** (fig.) to look at each other meaningfully
69 **to brief s.o.** to tell s.o. the details of s.th.
72 **NORAD** North American Aerospace Defense Command
73 **to slump** to sit down heavily **sullenly** in a bad mood
75 **to sustain** to experience – **heavy** *here:* a lot of s.th.
76 **absently** doing one thing while thinking about s.th. else
77 **to overhear** to hear a conversation by chance
78 **Joint Chiefs of Staff** the officers with the highest rank in the armed forces
91 **to sting** *here:* to make s.o. feel bad about s.th.

6 Space – the final frontier?

96 **fallout** shower of radioactive particles after an explosion	95 **DAVID:** *If you fire nukes, so will the rest of the world. Do you know what that kind of fallout will do? How many innocent people …*
97 **to run interference** *(fig.) here:* to try to block an objection or opposing idea	The General gets up running interference. Constance tries to pull David back.
98 **stern** very serious, strict	**GENERAL GREY:** (stern) *Sir, I remind you that you are just a guest here …*
100 **insanity** craziness	**CONSTANCE:** (overlapping) *David, please …*
	100 **DAVID:** *This is insanity! You'll kill us and them at the same time. There'll be nothing left!*
	NIMZIKI: (interrupting) *Sit down and shut up!*
	Suddenly Moishe is on his feet, interrupting.
	MOISHE: *Don't tell him to shut up! You'd all be dead, were it not for my David.*
106 **to besiege** [bɪˈsiːdʒ] to surround	105 *You didn't do anything to prevent this!*
	As everyone is about to besiege Moishe, the President tries to calm him down.
	PRESIDENT: *Sir, there wasn't much more we could have done. We were totally unprepared for this.*
	MOISHE: *Don't give me unprepared! Since nineteen fifty whatever you guys have*
	110 *had that space ship, the thing you found in New Mexico.*
	DAVID: (embarrassed) *Dad, please …*
	MOISHE: *What was it, Roswell? You had the space ship, the bodies, everything locked up in a bunker, the what is it, Area fifty one. That's it! Area fifty one. You knew and you didn't do nothing!*
116 **tabloid** small-sized newspaper with short, often sensational articles and many pictures	115 For the first time in a long time, President Whitmore smiles.
	PRESIDENT: *Regardless of what the tabloids have said, there were never any space crafts recovered by the government. Take my word for it, there is no Area 51 and no recovered space ship.*
	Chief of Staff Nimziki suddenly clears his throat.
From the screenplay Independence Day *by Dean Devlin and Roland Emmerich.*	120 **NIMZIKI:** *Uh, excuse me, Mr. President, but that's not entirely accurate.*
	The President and General Grey turn to Nimziki, shocked.

Working with the text

1. Find out as much as you can about the spacecraft in each of the extracts and write as detailed a description of it as possible.
2. *(Extract 1)*
   a) What is the original version of the line *"One small step for man, one large pile of garbage for moon-kind."* (l. 6)? When and where was it used and by whom?
   b) Write a narrative version of the extract as if you were turning the screenplay into a science fiction novel.
3. *(Extract 2)* Decribe the relationship between the General and the officers.
4. *(Extract 3)*
   a) What problem is the President facing and what are the options available to him according to the text?
   b) Where and what is Area 51?
   c) At the end of the extract why is David embarrassed and the President shocked?

Style
Choose one of the extracts. Consider the stage directions, choice of words, sentence structure and behaviour of the characters, and describe the atmosphere they create.

A *step further*: Your opinion
1. **NIMZIKI:** *"Mr. President, we must launch. A delay now would be more costly than when you waited to evacuate the cities!"* (ll. 89–90)
   DAVID: *"If you fire nukes, so will the rest of the world. Do you know what that kind of fall out will do? How many innocent people …"* (ll. 95–96)
   Consider these two points of view. Who do you think is right? What should the President do? Can you think of any other options?
2. In the film the President has not been fully informed about the state of affairs regarding Area 51. How believable or unbelievable do you think this is in a real-life context?

Space – the final frontier? 6

LIFE UFO POLL

1. Do you think there is intelligent life somewhere in the universe, other than on Earth?

   ❏ Yes   ❏ No   ❏ Not sure

2. Do you think intelligent beings from other planets have ever visited Earth?

   ❏ Yes   ❏ No   ❏ Not sure

3. Do you think the US government is withholding information from the public about the existence of UFOs?

   ❏ Yes   ❏ No   ❏ Not sure

4. In your opinion, are UFOs real or just the product of people's imagination?

   ❏ Real   ❏ Imaginary
   ❏ Not sure

5. Have you or anyone you know ever seen a UFO?

   ❏ Yes, personally   ❏ Yes, someone I know
   ❏ No   ❏ Not sure

6. Have you or anyone you know ever had an encounter with beings from another planet?

   ❏ Yes, personally   ❏ Yes, someone I know
   ❏ No   ❏ Not sure

7. If beings from another planet asked you to come aboard their spacecraft, would you go?

   ❏ Yes   ❏ No   ❏ Not sure

8. In your opinion, should the US government support scientific observation in search of intelligent life on other planets?

   ❏ Yes   ❏ No   ❏ Not sure

Survey of 1554 adults age 18 and older, condicuted January 12–13, 2000. Margin of error: plus or minus 2.5 percent.
From LIFE UFO Poll by Yankelovich Partners, LIFE, March 2000, pp. 46–56 © 2000 TIME Inc. Reprinted by permission.

Life UFO poll

1. Answer the questions in the Life UFO poll on the left, collect the results of all the students in your class and and present them as percentages.
2. Estimate the results found in the U.S.
   Compare your estimates with the actual results at the bottom of the page.
   Discuss similarities and/or differences between your estimates and the actual results and between the results for your class and the U.S. results.

Fishbowl discussion: Project Blue Book

From 1947 to 1969, the U.S. Air Force investigated Unidentified Flying Objects in a project called Project Blue Book. Of a total of 12,618 sightings reported to Project Blue Book, 701 remained "unidentified". In 1969 after an investigation by the University of Colorado it was decided to stop the project for the following reasons:

1. *No UFO reported, investigated and evaluated by the Air Force was ever an indication of a threat to national security.*
2. *There was no evidence submitted to or discovered by the Air Force that sightings categorized as "unidentified" represented technological developments or principles beyond the range of modern scientific knowledge.*
3. *There was no evidence indicating that sightings categorized as "unidentified" were extraterrestrial vehicles.*

Since the termination of Project Blue Book, nothing has occurred that would support a resumption of UFO investigations by the Air Force.

Work in groups.
1. In your group think of arguments for and against the termination or continuation of "Project Blue Book".
2. Elect one person from your group to represent your group in the discussion. The person elected must represent the opinion of the group, not their own opinion!
3. Elected representatives sit in a circle. One extra empty chair is added to the circle.
4. The elected representatives discuss the issue. At any time during the discussion other members of the class can join in and make a statement by sitting down on the extra chair. In this case, they make their point and then leave the group again.

1. Yes: 54%; No: 32%; Not sure: 14% **2.** Yes: 30%; No: 54%; Not sure: 16% **3.** Yes: 49%; No: 40%; Not sure: 11% **4.** Real: 43%; Imaginary: 42%; Not sure: 15% **5.** Yes, personally: 6%; Yes, someone I know: 13%; No: 79%; Not sure: 2% **6.** Yes, personally: 1%; Yes, someone I know: 6%; No: 92%; Not sure: 1% **7.** Yes: 21%; No: 74%; Not sure: 5% **8.** Yes: 54%; No: 41%; Not sure: 5%

7 ¡Hola, USA!

In search of the American Dream

Getting started
• What pictures and associations come to your mind when you hear the phrase 'Hispanics in the USA'? Make a table with the following categories and fill them in as you brainstorm:

Economic situation • Education • Language • Media and film portrayal • Famous people • Political power • Cultural influence • Assimilation • ...

Compare your answers with a partner. Discuss the similarities and differences in your lists. Add to the table as you work through the chapter.

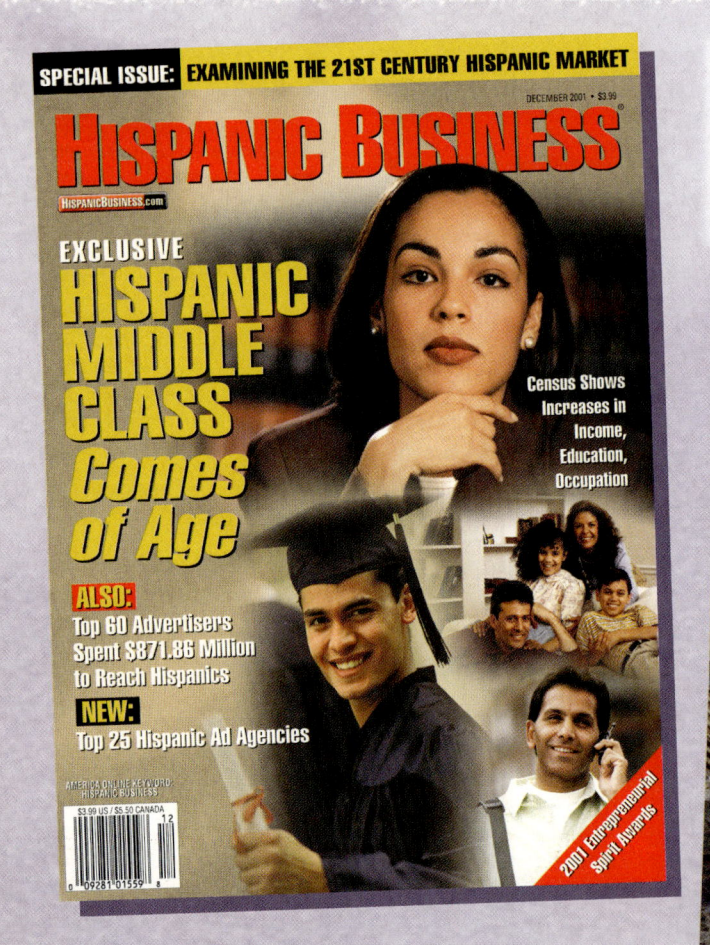

Working with the pictures
1. Compare both illustrations. Write down words and phrases contrasting the people in them.
2. Use the words and phrases to describe the different images of Hispanics shown here.

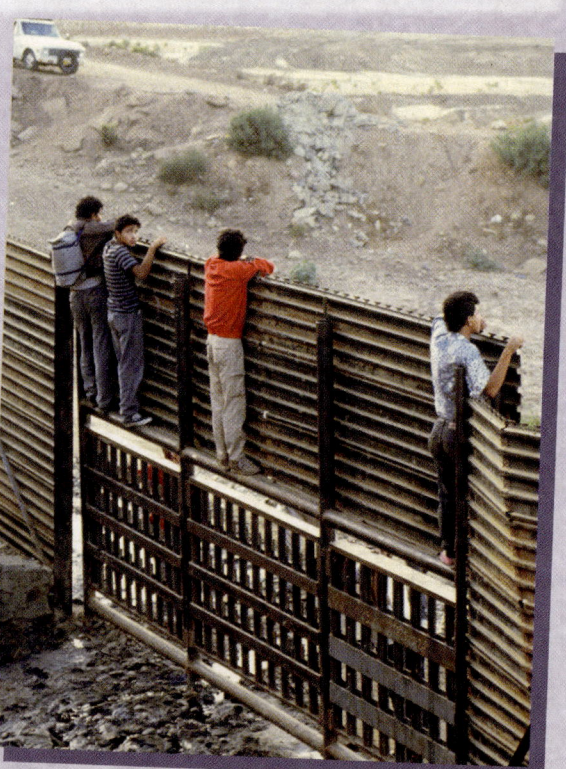

to come of age *here:* to reach a position of power and influence

Coyote's Game

Before you read
• Write a list of reasons why people leave their homes behind and risk their entire savings and even their lives to enter another country illegally.
• Estimates vary, but there could be as many as 12 million illegal aliens living in the USA. The majority of these aliens come from Mexico. Why do you think that this is the case?

Check the web
For more from HISPANIC BUSINESS Magazine:
http://www.hispanic business.com/magazine/

¡Hola, USA! 7

The Coyote's Game

Border-patrol agent Nate Lagasse is sitting quietly in his Toyota Land Cruiser about three miles west of a small Arizona town on the Mexican border, following a group of 12 immigrants through his night-vision goggles. He radios directions to three colleagues, who are out in the mesquite on foot and closing in on the aliens. "They don't even know we are here yet," whispers Lagasse, who has turned off his headlights and allowed his truck to roll to a halt without hitting the brakes. "It's just like hunting."

Something alerts the aliens, and they hit the dirt, probably at the order of the coyote, or guide, they have paid to get them across. But Lagasse has marked their location and talks his three agents in on top of them. After a few minutes, a voice comes over his radio: "We have them now." The immigrants make no attempt to escape. The sight of a few agents in uniform is often enough to pacify a large group; some agents have singlehandedly detained 100 people at once.

Between 6 million and 12 million illegal aliens live in the U.S., the majority are from Mexico and most move through Arizona. It draws more than a third of the illegals […]. But the busiest place in the state is the tiny border town of Naco, a place so anonymous that its name derives from the last two letters of Arizona and Mexico. Naco (pop. 800) is little more than a bar, a school, a couple of streets and 220 border-patrol agents. Across the line in Mexico is a town with the same name, 10 times the population and all the makings of a first-class staging area – guest houses, grocery stores and an army of local guides, or coyotes, to show the way.

As soon as the sun goes down, hundreds of men, women and children, armed with water bottles, toothbrushes, toilet paper and perhaps phone numbers in Phoenix, or Denver or Los Angeles, come walking, running and crawling north across the border. Each night border-patrol agents round up roughly 500 and next morning return them to Mexico, only to have them start all over again the following evening. It's a never-ending drill, often with life-and-death stakes. The border patrol says 383 people died last year attempting to cross the border from Mexico. "Is this problem solvable?" asks Victor Manjarrez, 37, top agent in the Naco station. "I think we in the border patrol are getting better at what we are doing. But with a Third World economy to the south and a First World economic power to the north, you will always have this problem."

---

1 **border-patrol agent** person who controls activity on the border
3 **night-vision goggles** ['gɒglz] *Nachtsichtgerät*
4 **mesquite** [mes'ki:t] hot, dry land with small shrubs (*Busch*)
6 **to hit the brakes** (informal) to activate the brakes (*Bremse*)
8 **to alert** to catch one's attention – **alien** foreigner – **to hit the dirt** (informal) to lie down very quickly
9 **guide** [gaɪd] *Führer(in)* – **to mark a location** to draw e.g. a circle around a place on a map to make it easy to find
10 **to talk s.o. in on top of s.o.** to give another person directions for how to find s.o.
12 **to pacify** ['pæsɪfaɪ] to calm s.o. down
13 **to detain** [-'-] (formal) to keep s.o. under one's control
17 **to derive from** [dɪ'raɪv] (formal) to come from
20 **with all the makings of** fully prepared to be – **staging area** *here:* place where a journey is prepared for and begun
22 **armed with** *here:* carrying
25 **to round up** to catch and hold together in a group

By Terry McCarthy, TIME Magazine, June 11, 2001. © 2001 Time Inc. Reprinted by permission

---

After reading

Working with the text

1. Why do you think that this article is titled "Coyote's Game"?
2. Summarize the main points of the article in 4–5 sentences.
3. How do the illegal aliens react when they are caught and sent back to Mexico?
4. What makes this 'game' so dangerous for the aliens?
5. Write a comment: *"But with a Third World economy to the south and a First World economic power to the north, you will always have this problem"* (ll. 30–32).

Language

1. Lagasse comments that the process of catching illegal aliens is "just like hunting". Find examples of other language used in the text which illustrate this idea of hunting.
2. Find synonyms/synonymous phrases for the following words and phrases:
   to close in (l. 4) • to make no attempt (l. 11) • singlehandedly (l. 13)
   • to draw (l. 15) • roughly (l. 25) • never-ending (l. 27)

Working with the cartoon

What do you think the artist is saying about illegal immigration with this cartoon? Would you describe this cartoon as funny, serious or both? Give reasons for your answer.

NO EXIT © Andy Singer
THE FIRST ILLEGAL IMMIGRANTS

7 ¡Hola, USA!

Before you read: Sweat of their brows reshapes economy
- This text is about a Mexican immigrant who works at various day jobs. What kind of jobs do you think these people end up doing, and why? Under which conditions?

While reading

Surviving without a dictionary

In the text, try to work out the meanings of undefined words you don't know without using a dictionary. We have marked some words you may not know with numbers corresponding to techniques in the *Skills file: Surviving without a dictionary* on p. 194.

> **Surviving without a dictionary**
> See *Skills file* on p. 194.

After reading

Working with the text
1. Who is "Santa Claus"? Why has he been given this name?
2. What did Barrera mean when he said *"I was ashamed to fight for pennies"* (Col. 1, l. 18)?
3. How does Barrera feel about his life in the USA and about Americans?
4. Is Barrera working legally in the States? Quote from the text to support your answer.
5. a) In your own words, describe the current job market in America.
   b) What role do education and skills play in this job market?

Language
1. a) Find words in the text that belong to the word field "employment".
   b) Add at least three other words of your own to this word field.
2. Which words (Col. 1, l. 30 – Col. 2, l. 22) do these definitions and translations belong to?
   a) chance
   b) to look like s.th.
   c) *Sprosse*
   d) here: *Intensität*
   e) limited
   f) *Weiterentwicklung*
   g) very
   h) expensive
   i) not changing
   j) with the effects of inflation also calculated
   k) *Vermittler*
   l) to inspire
   m) *Dienstleistungen*
   n) money one is paid for work
   o) *Sanduhr*
   p) to keep putting s.th. into different order
3. Phrasal verbs are often verb + adverb combinations that together have a single meaning, e.g. "held together" (Col. 1, l. 6). Find four other examples of these types of phrasal verbs in the text. Write new sentences using each of the phrasal verbs you find.

Creative writing
Imagine that you are Manuel Barrera. You arrive home and your wife asks you about your day. Write a dialogue between the two.

- Write a dialogue between two of the workers.
- Write a poem based on this picture.

"Memorial of the Fields" by Sergio Hernandez

> **Check the web**
> Get more information about Sergio Hernandez at:
> http://www.americanlynching.com/sergio.html

Sweat of their brows reshapes economy

[...] The early morning sky is beginning to glow² with heat when a van comes into the day-labor yard. The boss behind the wheel is an elderly³ man, with deep ebony skin and a long snowy white beard, his eyeglasses held together with tape and rubber bands. He is looking for three movers. Cespedes asks the laborers in Spanish who wants to work for the man he dubs "Santa Claus".

Manuel Barrera steps forward from behind the fence. Moving¹ is hard, heavy lifting, but there may be shade, even air conditioning. The man with the beard offers him too little. Barrera holds out. He wants $7 an hour but settles for $6.50. Two other men agree to go too.

Later, Barrera confesses, "I was ashamed² to fight for pennies."

Now 48, Barrera crossed the Rio Grande while in his twenties on his long journey from Guatemala City to Houston for one single purpose: to work for U.S. dollars. He says that he has neither been welcomed with open arms² nor been turned away. He, too, is ambivalent² about Americans. His life, he believes, is better in Houston, but also very hard. He hopes his children will do better.

Immigrants like Barrera have taken over entire sectors of the labor market, creating new wealth and offering¹ services³ that were unavailable or too costly¹. They have made money for themselves and for the middlemen³. But they have also competed, with a ferocity² fired³ by a will² to survive, with the native-born Americans who lack³ the skills required for advancement¹ in the new post-industrial¹ economy.

The job market this current wave of immigrants enter is vastly³ different from the one that absorbed the last great wave of immigrants earlier this century.

Today, the factories are gone, and the economy resembles² an hourglass³. At the top, the elevator class works in tall buildings shuffling⁴ papers and typing on keypads. At the bottom, immigrants paint the walls and clean the carpets. There are fewer and fewer jobs requiring medium-level skills for average pay. It is as if someone has cut the rungs³ from the middle of the ladder.

Because many immigrants have only modest³ educations, their ability to move from the lower rungs of the ladder to the higher has grown more difficult. At the top of the economy, the opportunity² for advancement is great and salaries³ are climbing; at the bottom, wages are stagnant² or falling. For the lowest-paid workers, a recent Rand Corp. study shows, inflation-adjusted³ wages are about one-third lower than they were in the 1970s. [...]

Barrera opens the first truck, which is filled to the ceiling with a jumble of garage-sale junk, refrigerators and art from Africa – carved masks and ceremonial spears and huge³ pieces of mahogany² furniture, the heaviest furniture ever made.

Barrera sighs. There will be no air conditioning today. The metal-sided vans are ovens, and as the day wears on³, the heat becomes something a man physically recoils from and the loads to lift so heavy that Barrera and his co-workers almost fear them, as if the weight could break³ a man.

There is no lunch break³. No toilets. That is assumed. After a few hours, the men grow dizzy, weave on their feet and demand² something to drink. It is so hot that not only is Barrera's shirt soaked³ with sweat, but so are his bluejeans, lathered in a white froth, like a horse.

Barrera is a man with a happy face but, he says, he has a heavy heart. He believes he should not be here, surrounded by younger men, offering his body for day labor. He has worked here as a baker, a shoemaker. He is a married man and a father of three who owns a simple home and a little white truck. After years of living in the shadows as an illegal alien, his papers are now in order.

"This is work, and I will do it because it puts food on the table," Barrera says. "But I did not foresee¹ that it would turn out like this."

This is how it is in America. This is the kind of work that many of the record-breaking² number of new immigrants do. This is the fine print of the deal between the newcomers and the native-born that is overlooked¹ in the thick reports of numbers compiled by the Bureau of Labor Statistics and in the research of think-tanks examining the immigrants' impact.

After eight hours of work, Santa Claus pays the men, including the "bonus"² he has been promising all day. The two younger workers get $50. Barrera is given $60 because he knew how to drive the van, a skill worth a bit more. "You all sure got me out of a jam," Santa Claus says. "You all are hard workers, hard."

Moving his possessions, including the art and furniture he says is worth hundreds of thousands of dollars, cost Santa Claus $217.88, rental van included. A professional moving company in Houston bid the same job for $980.

After his hours in the sun, loading and unloading the vans, Manuel Barrera is about to head³ home to his wife and children. His last words to a reporter who has spent the day with him: "If you hear about a better job, will you call me?"

By William Booth, The Washington Post, July 13, 1998. © 1998 The Washington Post. Reprinted with permission.

Title: brow *Stirn*

Col. 1: 2 **van** *Lieferwagen* – 3 **day-labor yard** place where people wait to be hired for the day – 5 **ebony** ['ebnɪ] black – 8 **mover** person who moves furniture – 10 **to dub** to call – 15 **to hold out** to not give up – 16 **to settle for** to agree to s.th. that isn't ideal – 18 **to confess** to admit

Col. 2: 19 **Corp.** short for corporation – 24 **jumble** ['dʒʌmbl] mixture of things – 25 **garage sale** event where one sells unwanted possessions in one's garage – **junk** worthless things – 30 **to sigh** [saɪ] to let out a breath loudly because of sadness or frustration – 34 **to recoil from** [-'-] to pull back quickly – 39 **to assume** [ə'sju:m] to think s.th. is a certain way without having asked s.o. else about it – 40 **to weave on one's feet** [wi:v] to walk unsteadily – 44 **lathered in a white froth** ['lɑ:ðə, frɒθ] covered in white, soapy-looking bubbles

Col. 3: 2 **to have a heavy heart** *(fig.)* to be sad – 9 **to live in the shadows** to live in hiding, in fear of being caught – 13 **to turn out** to develop – 18 **fine print** here: details – 21 **to compile** [-'-] to collect and put together information – **Bureau of Labor Statistics** ['bjʊərəʊ] U.S. government organization that collects information and statistics about the labor market – 23 **think-tank** *Expertenkommission* – 24 **impact** effect – 31 **to get s.o. out of a jam** *(fig.)* to help s.o. get out of a difficult situation – 38 **to bid** to make an offer of how much one will pay or charge for s.th.

7 ¡Hola, USA!

Hispanic influences

Projected U.S. Racial and Ethnic Composition: 1999–2050 (fig. 1)

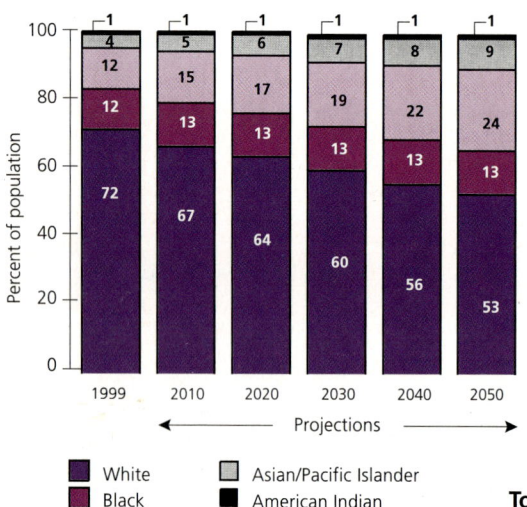

Year	White	Black	Hispanic	Asian/Pacific Islander	American Indian
1999	72	12	12	4	1
2010	67	13	15	5	1
2020	64	13	17	6	1
2030	60	13	19	7	1
2040	56	13	22	8	1
2050	53	13	24	9	1

U.S. population figures

★ Between 1990 and 2000, the total U.S. population increased by 32.7 million to a population of 281.4 million. Therefore, in 10 years, the population grew by approx. 13 %, the largest population increase in U.S. history.

★ In 2000, 75.1 % of the population identified their race as "White", followed by 12.3 % as "Black or African American", 0.9 % as "American Indian and Alaska Native", 3.6 % as Asian, and 0.1 % as "Native Hawaiian and Other Pacific Islander".

★ In 2000, approx. 35.3 million or 13 % of the population identified themselves as having a "Hispanic" or "Latino" origin. This population group has increased by approx. 58 % in the last 10 years. "Hispanic" or "Latino" is a term for an ethnic and not a racial group, so people of different races may also say that they are of either origin. "Origin" indicates either where a person was born or where e.g. that person's parents were born.

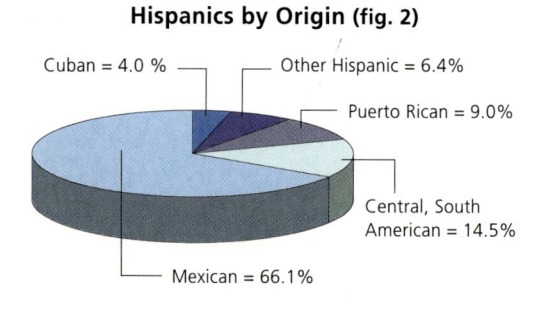

Hispanics by Origin (fig. 2)
- Cuban = 4.0 %
- Other Hispanic = 6.4 %
- Puerto Rican = 9.0 %
- Central, South American = 14.5 %
- Mexican = 66.1 %

Top 10 Hispanic States by Percent of Total Hispanic Population (fig. 3)
- California = 31.1 %
- Texas = 18.9 %
- New York = 8.1 %
- Florida = 7.6 %
- Illinois = 4.3 %
- Arizona = 3.7 %
- New Jersey = 3.2 %
- New Mexico = 2.2 %
- Colorado = 2.1 %
- Washington = 1.3 %

Working with statistics

1. According to the projections in figure 1, which group will experience the greatest population loss by the year 2050? Which one will experience the greatest population gain? For which group are the numbers predicted to remain constant?
2. Describe which information from the fact box you found to be particularly interesting and/or surprising, and why.
3. Look at figures 2 and 3. Compare the percentages of the different Hispanic groups in the U.S., as well as where they live. What explanations can you give as to why certain groups have come in greater numbers, and where they have settled?

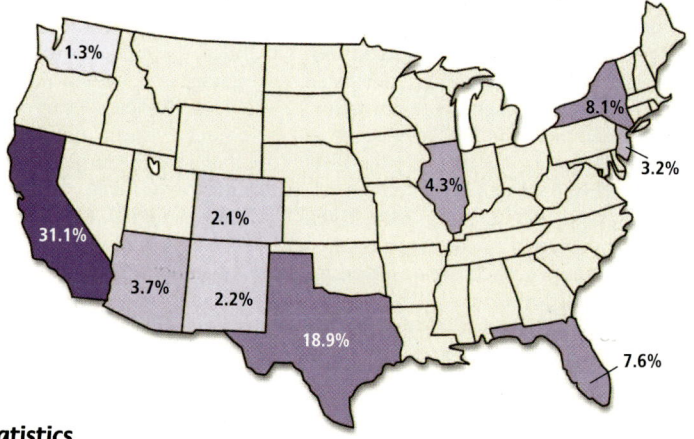

Talking about statistics
See *Skills file* on p. 207.

Giving a presentation
See *Skills file* on p. 189.

A step further

Prepare and give a 10-minute presentation about Hispanics in the U.S. using the information above as a basis. As you prepare, think about the following points:
- the order in which you plan to present the information
- which information you plan to emphasize and/or leave out
- which point(s) you would like to go into more detail about using additional information that you have found on the internet
- what conclusions you would like to make based upon the information you present

Check the web
Get more information about racial and ethnic groups in the U.S. at:
http://www.census.gov

¡Hola, USA! 7

Hispanics abound, hard to pin down (p. 112)

Before you read
- With a partner, write a list of German words related to statistics and statistical research. Then find the correct equivalents in a German/English dictionary.
- Increasing numbers of Hispanics are entering the American middle class. Can you think of reasons why this is happening?

Working with the text
1. Think up a subtitle for the first section of the article.
2. In what ways do native and immigrant Hispanics differ from each other in terms of income and education?
3. Why have increasing numbers of native-born Hispanics entered the middle class?
4. What kinds of jobs are educated Hispanics more likely to fill?
5. a) Why are advertisers beginning to focus more attention on the Hispanic population?
   b) What kinds of challenges will they face in targeting this market?

Translation & style
1. a) How would you describe the style of writing of this article? Give examples to support your answer.
   b) Does this style of writing successfully bring across the important points in the article, or would you have preferred a different style of writing? Give reasons.
2. Translate the following section of the article:
   "It's old news that Hispanics … insists he isn't white." (Col. 1, ll. 4–32)
   Try to use the author's style of writing in your translation.

> **Analysing style**
> See *Skills file* on p. 181.
>
> **Translating**
> See *Skills file* on pp. 182 & 183.

Language
1. Make a table with three columns marked *gerund*, *participle* and *progressive tense*, and write down examples in the text in the correct columns. Be prepared to explain your answers.
2. a) Explain the following examples of figurative language in your own words:
   - to range all over the lot (Col. 1, l. 25)
   - to go hand in hand (Col. 2, ll. 27–28)
   b) Write sentences of your own using these phrases.

Hispanics abound, hard to pin down: Annotations (p. 112)

Title: **to abound** to be present in large numbers – **to pin down** to keep s.o. from accomplishing s.th.

Col. 1: *5* **demographic** relating to population facts and statistics – *10* **to surpass** [-'-] to reach a higher level than s.o./s.th. else – **Anglo** ['æŋgləʊ] *(informal)* short for Anglo-American, s.o. who speaks English and has English ancestors – *12* **to seek** to try to do s.th. – **to market to** to sell things to – *15* **boundary** ['baʊndrɪ] border – *16* **Caucasian** [kɔː'keɪʒn] racial grouping (no longer in scientific use) common term for a white person – *27* **recent** ['riːsnt] s.th. that happened shortly before – **mayoral race** ['meərl] when candidates compete to be elected mayor (Bürgermeister) – *37* **pitch** *(informal) here:* talking in a certain way to convince s.o. to do s.th. – *38* **target audience** the group one is trying to attract – *39* **native-born** ['neɪtɪv] *opp. of* immigrant – *42* **gap** *here:* difference – *44* **income** the money one earns for work

Col. 2: *2* **to confound** [-'-] *here:* to do better or worse than – *18* **to triple** increase three times over – *21* **influx** ['ɪnflʌks] large increase – *24* **to graduate** ['grædjueɪt] einen (Schul-)abschluss machen – *25* **as opposed to** in contrast to – *28* **particularly** [pə'tɪkjələlɪ] especially – *44* **to pool** to put s.th. (e.g. resources) together – *45* **wage earner** person who makes an income

Col. 3: *4* **some** *here:* approximately – *6* **degree** Abschluss – *12* **service job** low-paid jobs in the service sector – *14* **blue-collar worker** Arbeiter(in) – *15* **mid-level** short for middle level – *21* **associate professor** professor of the second highest rank (C3-Professor) – *24* **to prefer** to like s.th. more than s.th. else – *26* **proficiency** [prə'fɪʃnsɪ] how good s.o. is at doing s.th. – *30* **to contribute** [-'--] to add to s.th – *33* **to predict** to make a statement about the future based on present information – *35* **purchasing power** ['pɜːtʃəsɪŋ] buying – *39* **indelible** [-'---] permanent – *44* **clout** power

Hispanics abound, hard to pin down

by Jim Barlow

It's old news that Hispanics will dominate the demographic future of Houston, Texas and much of the United States.

Here in Houston, Hispanics are the largest ethnic group, according to the 2000 census, surpassing Anglos for the first time.

But those seeking to market to Hispanics have a real problem. First of all, this is a culture that cuts across racial and national boundaries. Hispanics might be black, Caucasian or Asian; from Cuba, Puerto Rico or Argentina. While Mexican-Americans dominate in Houston, the percentage of Hispanics from Central and South America in the city grew from 10 percent to 24 percent from 1990 to 2000.

How Hispanics identify themselves also ranges all over the lot. Orlando Sanchez, who came close to winning the recent Houston mayoral race, told a conference on race a couple of weeks ago in Baton Rouge that he is white. And then there's my son-in-law, born in Mexico, also a Caucasian, who insists he isn't white.

Fortunately, businesses don't have to psychoanalyze Hispanics. They just have to sell to them. And for those in business, the best way to determine the pitch is to look at the target Hispanic audience and determine one fact. Is it a native-born one? Or an immigrant one?

Gap in income levels

Why? Because there is a big difference between income levels of Hispanic immigrants and the native-born. That's on average, of course. Individuals can always confound the averages.

Hispanic Business, a California-based magazine, took a closer look at census information in its December issue and came up with some interesting demographic differences between native-born and immigrant Hispanics.

Up until 1989, incomes for both native-born and immigrant Hispanics were climbing. They are still rising for the natives. But starting around 1989, immigrant household incomes started dropping – from around $39,000 a year in 1989 to $35,000 in 1999.

That came as the number of foreign-born U.S. Hispanics more than tripled in the last two decades – most coming from Mexico and Central America.

This influx of Hispanic immigrants has less education than the native-born. For example, 55 percent of immigrants had not graduated from high school as opposed to 25 percent of the native-born. And in this country, income and education go hand in hand, particularly during hard times.

More in the middle class

Among the native-born, Hispanics are moving into the middle class. Between 1979 and 1999 the number of Hispanic middle-income households almost doubled, from 1.4 million to 2.5 million.

Income per adult among middle-income Hispanics grew 9 percent over that same period.

One of the chief reasons why so many Hispanic households have entered the middle class is that members of these families tend to pool their incomes. These households have on average 2.26 wage earners, one more than Hispanics in lower-income groups.

And the other reason is – of course – education. Some 20 years ago, only 9 percent of native-born Hispanics had college degrees and 47 percent had high school degrees. By 1999, 13 percent of Hispanics were college grads and 62 percent had high school degrees.

With more education, Hispanics are moving out of service jobs. Among middle-class Hispanics, about half are blue-collar workers, a fourth are mid-level professionals, and another quarter are administrators and professionals.

Those trying to market to the Hispanic middle class must also look beyond Spanish. Stephen Trejo, an associate professor of economics at the University of Texas at Austin, says U.S.-born Hispanics strongly prefer communicating in English.

"Hispanics experience dramatic improvements in English proficiency as we move from first-generation immigrants to their second-generation children. And these language improvements contribute in important ways to earnings progress," Trejo adds.

The magazine *Hispanic Business* - predicts this movement to the middle class by Hispanics will bring $76 billion in new purchasing power in the next decade to add to their present $278 billion.

"Just as the baby-boom generation put its indelible mark on American culture and became the focus of Madison Avenue and corporate marketing, so will the Hispanic generation as it continues to grow and gain economic clout," the magazine predicts.

By Jim Barlow, Houston Chronicle, February 10, 2002. Copyright 2002 Houston Chronicle Publishing Company. Reprinted with permission. All rights reserved.

¡Hola, USA! 7

Legal Alien

Bi-lingual, Bi-cultural,
  able to slip from "How's life?"
  to "Me'stan volviendo loca,"
  able to sit in a paneled office
5 drafting memos in smooth English,
  able to order in fluent Spanish
  at a Mexican restaurant,
  American but hyphenated,
  viewed by Anglos as perhaps exotic,
10 perhaps inferior, definitely different,
  viewed by Mexicans as alien,
  (their eyes say, "You may speak
  Spanish but you're not like me")
  an American to Mexicans
15 a Mexican to Americans
  a handy token
  sliding back and forth
  between the fringes of both worlds
  by smiling
20 by masking the discomfort
  of being pre-judged
  Bi-laterally.

"Legal Alien" by Pat Mora is reprinted with permission from the publisher of Chants, (Houston: Arte Público Press – University of Houston, 1985).

Pat Mora

– born Jan. 19, 1942, El Paso, Texas
– living in the Southwest and the Cincinnati area
– bilingual (English, Spanish)
– writes poetry, children's books, nonfiction
– winner of many awards: National Endowment for the Arts Creative Writing Fellowship in poetry
– topics: include Mexican-American culture, family, being bilingual and bi-cultural in the U.S.
– writing language: English and Spanish (e.g.: "Legal Alien")
– "Legal Alien" from the poetry collection "Chants"

3 **Me'stan volviendo loca** *(Spanish)* They're driving me crazy – *4* **paneled** *getäfelt* – *5* **to draft** to write – **smooth** *here:* fluent – *8* **hyphenated** *here:* having two cultural backgrounds (Mexican-American) – *16* **handy** convenient – **token** s.th. that represents a group – *18* **fringe** edge – *20* **to mask** to hide

Working with the poem
1. a) What do you understand by the term "legal alien"?
   b) What connotations does the term have for you?
   c) Is there a German equivalent for this term? If so, what is it and what connotations does it have? If not, think of one, and give reasons for your choice.
2. Do you think that she feels comfortable living in several worlds? Give reasons.

Style
1. The author speaks of *"sliding back and forth between the fringes of both worlds"* (ll. 17–18). How does she emphasize this concept through the structure of her poem?
2. Describe the tone of this poem in as much detail as possible.
3. What is the effect of Mora's use of Spanish in the poem, in your opinion?

A step further
1. Should minority cultures acculturate to the majority culture of the land in which they live, or should the majority culture become more varied by picking up aspects from minority cultures? Discuss.
2. Complete one of the following:
   - If you are bi-cultural/bilingual, write a poem about your own experiences in a predominantly monocultural society.
   - If you are mono-cultural/monolingual, write a poem about your experiences in a society that is becoming more bi-cultural.

Check the web
Write a mini biography for Pat Mora using the information listed above as well as information that you find on the internet (for example at http://www.patmora.com). Try to vary your sentence structures, and use connectives where appropriate.

Listening comprehension
In Believe in Who You Are, *Mario talks about his experiences as a Mexican-American in the USA.*

7 ¡Hola, USA!

Before you read: Courting a Sleeping Giant
- Do you think it is important to be politically active? Why or why not?
- Look at the title of this article. What do you think this article will say about Hispanic political involvement and about how politicians view the Hispanic voting population?

Working with the text
1. In what ways are the Census 2000 results significant for Hispanics?
2. What does Rodolfo de la Garza mean in reference to Hispanic political participation when he says that they only *"help shape things. … They don't lead things. They don't define things."* (ll. 14–15)?
3. How has the rise in Hispanic population affected this group's relationship with the African American population?
4. a) Why hasn't the increase in the Hispanic population meant an equal increase in Hispanic political influence?
   b) What are some possible causes for Hispanics not wanting to vote?
5. In your own words, explain Charles Gonzalez' comment: *"My fear is that we have not only isolated ourselves, but we have handicapped ourselves"* (ll. 44–45).

Language
1. Copy and complete the table below with the following words from the text:
   huge (l. 7) • far (l. 12) • legal (l. 30) • to maximize (l. 32) • assimilation (l. 40) • increasingly (l. 48)
   a) Put a check mark in the correct box to indicate if the given word is a verb, noun, adjective or adverb. Pay attention to the context!
   b) Fill in the other boxes where possible. Be careful! Not every box can always be filled in!

	opposite	synonym	noun	verb	adjective	adverb
growth	decrease	increase	✓	to grow	growing	—

2. a) Work with a partner. Make a word field for the word 'politics' using words from the text.
   b) Choose five words from the word field and write a definition for them (if a definition has been provided for a word you have chosen, rewrite it in your own words).
   c) Read a definition to your partner and ask him/her to guess the word that you have defined.
   d) If you have both defined the same word(s), compare your definitions and write a combined version.

A step further
Write a comment on one or more of the following:
1. Considering current Hispanic voter participation problems, do you think that politicians will target this group less in the future? Give reasons.
2. According to U.S. Census information for the November 2000 election, a large number of Hispanics did not vote because of conflicting work or school schedules or because they were too busy. Are these legitimate reasons not to go and vote, in your opinion?
3. Find out about trends in voter turnouts in recent elections in Germany and comment on these. Do you think that the aspects listed in question 2. have any effect on voter turnout in Germany, or are there other more important factors?

> **Essay writing**
> See *Skills file* on p. 184.

> **Check the web**
> Get more information about U.S. population voting patterns at:
> *http://www.census.gov/population/*
> *www/socdemo/voting.html*

This picture shows U.S. President George W. Bush and Mexican President Vicente Fox. What do you think the two could be saying to each other?

Courting a Sleeping Giant

The biggest political news of the 2000 Census was that Hispanics – more than half of them tracing their roots to Mexico – have become the largest minority group in the U.S., surpassing African Americans at least six years sooner than expected. Where that's happening is turning out to be as surprising as how fast. Of the congressional districts that saw the biggest increases in their Latino populations over the past decade, not a single one is in a state along the Mexican border. Rural areas saw huge growth in Hispanic populations, but so did cities and suburbs. [...] "It's the only part of the electorate that's growing," says Antonio Gonzalez, president of the Southwest Voter Registration Education Project.

But while that means that politicians in places as diverse as Las Vegas and Jasper County, S.C., are courting these constituents as never before, Hispanic political clout still lags far behind the numbers – and will for perhaps a generation to come, Latino leaders fear. Even in parts of the country where Latinos have long been the largest ethnic group, they only "help shape things," says University of Texas political scientist Rodolfo de la Garza. "They don't lead things. They don't define things."

Where Hispanics have just arrived, they've only just begun to crack the city councils, the school boards and the county commissions. Though Hispanics account for one-fifth of Nevada's population, there are only two Latinos in the 63-member state legislature, and virtually none hold local office in the cities and counties where they are the most highly concentrated. "We're on the ground floor of political empowerment," says Gonzalez.

The once-a-decade-exercise of redistricting now under way in every state will help mobilize Latino voters and encourage them to seek elected office. But no one expects Latinos to show the kind of huge gains that the Congressional Black Caucus made after the 1992 election. Indeed, the boom in the Hispanic population has fostered political tension between the two minority groups. "On issues, we're very close," Gonzalez says, "but power is power." [...]

There are many reasons that Latino political influence has not kept pace with the Census, the most obvious being that many of those counted are neither citizens nor even legal residents of the U.S. Hispanics are more dispersed than, say, African Americans, which means legislators have to work harder to draw districts to maximize their voting power. And those enormous Census numbers do not translate at the polls, at least not yet. More than a third of Latinos are under the voting age; and those who are eligible to vote often don't. Though the Latino and African American populations in the U.S. are roughly the same size, 6 million more blacks are registered to vote. Turnout rates are lower than average even among more educated and affluent Hispanics.

But what really worries Hispanic leaders is that many newcomers don't seem to want to participate. For whatever reason – longer waits, higher application fees, cultural factors that work against assimilation – a smaller and smaller portion of new immigrants are even trying to become citizens. Some Latino politicians blame bilingualism, the cause for which they fought in the 1970s and 1980s, for discouraging assimilation. "A Latino can exist in their own community and never have to learn English to survive," says Texas Congressman Charles Gonzalez. "My fear is that we have not only isolated ourselves, but we have handicapped ourselves."

And yet, if all these factors make it more difficult for Latino politicians to play traditional ethnic politics, they have also forced the most successful among them to adapt to the realities of an increasingly multicultural electorate. [...] George W. Bush, for his part, intends to stay ahead of the curve. The day before Cinco de Mayo, he invited 200 guests to the South Lawn for mariachi music and Mexican food. "Mi Casa Blanca," he declared, "es su Casa Blanca."

By Karen Tumulty, TIME Magazine, June 11, 2001.
© 2001 Time Inc. Reprinted by permission.

7 ¡Hola, USA!

Before you read: The legacy of generation Ñ
- Can you think of any examples of the influence of the Spanish-speaking world here in Germany?

Working with the text
1. What does Haubegger mean when she uses the term "Manifest Destino" (l. 7) to describe the 21st century?
2. How has the aspect of assimilation changed for Hispanics in the U.S.?
3. Why, according to Haubegger, is the Hispanic community attractive for politicians?
4. Why will advertisers increasingly target the Hispanic population?
5. What is Haubegger's point of view about bilingualism?
6. Explain why Haubegger believes that the "re-Latinization" (l. 42) of the U.S. is a good thing for everyone.

Language
1. a) Find synonyms/synonymous phrases for the following words:
    to be nearing (l. 2) • eventually (l. 4) • undeniably (l. 6) • ultimately (l. 11) • numerous (l. 12)
    • preceding (l. 16) • simultaneously (l. 18) • median (l. 35) • to be headed (l. 40) • pivotal (l. 43)
   b) Write sentences in which you use these words correctly.
2. Many Hispanics speak 'Spanglish', a mixture of English and Spanish. Look at the magazine cover on p. 117 and give examples of the Spanglish used there.

Style
1. Give examples of aspects of style that Haubegger has used to make this a persuasive text.
2. In your opinion, has Haubegger stated her case convincingly? Why or why not? Give reasons for your response.

A step further
1. Compare the points made about Hispanic political influence in this article (ll. 26–33) and in the text "Courting a sleeping giant". Discuss.
2. What do you think Christy Haubegger would say about the poem "Legal Alien" (p. 113), or Pat Mora about this article?
3. Make any final changes or additions to the table that you started at the beginning of this chapter (see "Getting started" activity on p. 106). Discuss what you have learned about Hispanic Americans while working through this chapter.

> **Having a discussion**
> See *Skills files* on pp. 191 & 192.

The Legacy of Generation Ñ

About 20 years ago, some mainstream observers declared the 1980s the "decade of the Hispanic." The Latino population was nearing 15 million! (It's since doubled.) However, our decade was postponed – a managerial oversight, no doubt – and eventually rescheduled for the '90s. What happens to a decade deferred? It earns
5 compounded interest and becomes the next hundred years. The United States of the 21st century will be undeniably ours. Again.

It's Manifest *Destino*. After all, Latinos are true Americans, some of the original residents of the *Américas*. Spanish was the first European language spoken on this continent. Which is why we live in places like *Los Angeles, Colorado* and *Florida*
10 rather than The Angels, Colored and Flowered. Now my generation is about to put a Latin stamp on the rest of the culture – and that will ultimately be the Ñ legacy.

We are not only numerous, we are also growing at a rate seven times that of the general population. Conservative political ads notwithstanding, this growth is driven by natural increase (births over deaths) rather than immigration. At 30, I may
15 be the oldest childless Latina in the United States. More important, however, while our preceding generation felt pressure to assimilate, America has now generously agreed to meet us in the middle. Just as we become more American, America is simultaneously becoming more Latino.

This quiet *revolución* can perhaps be traced back to the bloodless coup of 1992,
20 when salsa outsold ketchup for the first time. Having toppled the leadership in the condiment category, we set our sights even higher. Fairly soon, there was a

---

1 **mainstream** typical

3 **to postpone** to cause s.th. to happen at a later time. – **managerial** [ˌmænəˈdʒɪəriəl] s.th. relating to managers – **oversight** s.th. that one has forgotten to do
4 **to defer** to postpone
7 **Manifest Destino** the Spanish translation of *Manifest Destiny*, a 19th century idea describing the U.S. "mission" to settle North America
11 **legacy** [ˈlegəsi] direct result
13 **notwithstanding** in spite of

16 **generously** here: kindly

20 **to topple** here: to achieve better results than s.th. else
21 **condiment** [---] Soße – **to set one's sights higher** (fig.) to aim for a higher goal

congresswoman named Sanchez representing Orange County, a taco-shilling Chihuahua became a national icon and now everyone is *loca* for Ricky Martin.

We are just getting started. Our geographic concentration and reputation for family values are making us every politician's dream constituency. How long can New Hampshire, with just four Electoral College votes – and probably an equal number of Hispanic residents – continue to get so much attention from presidential candidates? Advertisers will also soon be begging for our attention. With a median age of 26 (eight years younger than the general market) Latinos hardly exist outside their coveted 18 – 34 demographic. […]

Face it: this is going to be a bilingual country. Back in 1849, the California Constitution was written in both Spanish and English, and we're headed that way again. If our children speak two languages instead of just one, how can that not be a benefit to us all? The re-Latinization of this country will pay off in other ways as well. I, for one, look forward to that pivotal moment in our history when all American men finally know how to dance. Latin music will no longer be found in record stores under FOREIGN and romance will bloom again. Our children will ask us what it was like to dance without a partner.

"American food" will mean low-fat enchiladas and hamburgers served with rice and beans. As a result, the American standard of beauty will necessarily expand to include a female size 12, and anorexia will be found only in medical-history books. Finally, just in time for the baby boomers' senescence, living with extended family will become hip again. "Simpsons" fans of the next decade will see Grandpa moving back home. We'll all go back to church together.

At the dawn of a new millennium, America knows Latinos as entertainers and athletes. But, someday very soon, all American children can dream of growing up to be writers like Sandra Cisneros, astronauts like Ellen Ochoa, or judges like José Cabranes of the Second Circuit Court of Appeals. To put a Latin spin on a famous Anglo phrase: It is truly *mañana* in America. For those of you who don't know it (yet), that word doesn't just mean tomorrow; *mañana* also means morning.

By Christy Haubegger, from Newsweek, July 12, 1999. © 1999 Newsweek, Inc. All rights reserved. Reprinted by permission.

23 **taco-shilling Chihuahua** [tʃɪˈwɑːwɑː] reference to the Mexican beer brand with a bottle cap that looks like a coin
25 **loca** (Spanish) crazy
27 **reputation** Ruf
29 **constituency** [kənˈstɪtjuənsɪ] group of potential voters
30 **Electoral College** elected representatives who cast votes to elect the President and Vice President
34 **to beg for** to ask for s.th. either eagerly or urgently
37 **coveted** [ˈkʌvɪtɪd] highly valued
38 **demographic** here: age group
39 **face it** (informal) acknowledge and accept s.th.
42 **benefit** advantage – **to pay off** to have positive results
45 **to bloom** here: to become more widespread
49 **anorexia** [ˈænrˈksɪə] Magersucht
50 **senescence** [sɪˈnesns] growing old – **extended family** nuclear family plus grandparents, etc.
51 **hip** (informal) popular
57 **Anglo** [ˈæŋɡləʊ] (informal) here: English

Project: Immigrants in Germany

A class in the United States wants to find out more about the situation of immigrants in Germany. Prepare a presentation for them in English in which you deal with aspects such as the following:
▶ the variety of racial/ethnic groups living in Germany (also population figures)
▶ description of populations (e.g. population numbers, age groups)
▶ Fields of employment/unemployment numbers
▶ political and cultural issues (e.g. integration, political rights, asylum seekers)
You will find useful information on the website for the *Bundesregierung Deutschland*: http://www.bundesregierung.de/frameset/index.jsp.
(Look under A–Z > *Innenpolitik*.)

Giving a presentation
See *Skills file* on p. 189.

8 Changing lifestyles

Families

socially excluded see box on p.126

nuclear family traditional family consisting of mother, father and their children

Talking about families

Work with a partner. Look at the different types of families in the cartoon and discuss the questions below.

1. a) In your opinion, which types of family are becoming more common? Less common? Suggest reasons for these trends.
   b) What could be the reasons for a "single-parent" family?
   c) Which types of family are not shown? Describe them.
2. Which of the ten families is closest to, and which furthest from, your idea of the 'ideal family'? Explain why.
3. Only the "long term family" has a caption. Write captions to go with at least two of the other families.
4. Explain what the cartoon "Then … and now" tells us about changing attitudes to the family.

Changing lifestyles 8

Strange but true

- The number of new fathers over 50 has risen by a third over the past 10 years.
- Two-thirds of families do not eat a regular meal together.
- The UK birth rate has declined. In 1911 the average UK family had 3.5 children. Today it is 1.7.
- England has the highest divorce rate in the European Union: By 2010, half of all marriages are expected to end in divorce.
- A third of births are outside marriage.
- There will soon be more step families than traditional nuclear families.
- 7% of the population think friends are more important than family.
- Mothers in Yemen who survive their child-bearing years typically have eight children. In Afghanistan the figure is seven, in Italy and Spain one.
- Only 10 per cent of girls are clinically overweight, but 60 per cent want to lose weight.
- More women in their thirties are deciding against motherhood.
- Fifty-eight per cent of marriages are civil, rather than religious ceremonies.
- The number of working women is increasing. They will soon make up half the workforce.
- The number of couples who live together before they get married is rising.
- By 2020 one in three of us will be living alone.
- One in 25 children do not know who their father is.

Causes & effects
1. The statistics above describe current aspects of lifestyle. Which of these are also relevant for your country? Suggest possible causes.
2. In groups, come up with a list of at least five predictions for the year 2050 based on these trends and statistics.

> **Explaining causes**
> This is because (of) …
> It could be a result of …
> This is largely due to …
> This may be caused by …
> One reason might be …
> A possible cause is …

Looking at tenses
List the statements above under the following headings. Say which tenses are used to refer to each type of statement:
- *Current trends and developments*
- *Predictions*
- *The result of a trend*
- *Something that happened in a time now past*

Describing trends
1. Brainstorm current trends in each of these areas:
   - eating habits
   - holidays and travel
   - shopping
   - sport and leisure
   - work and career
   - fashion and design
2. Choose one of the trends from each area. Write a statement about each one, giving a possible cause and saying what you think the trend will lead to. Use the phrases in the boxes to the right to help you.
   Example: People are eating less meat. This is largely due to recent health scares. As a result, the demand for fruit and vegetables will rise.

> **Describing effects**
> This may lead to …
> This could result in …
> As a result, there will be …
> A possible effect will be …
> A (likely) result is that …

8 Changing lifestyles

The modern family

Before you read: We're mixed up and very happy
- Look at the title of the newspaper article on p. 121. Check the meanings of "mixed up" in your dictionary and suggest what the article might be about.

Working with the text
1. Compare the type of family the writer assumed she would have with one she has now.
2. a) Describe how the writer's children feel about their family.
   b) What surprises her about their attitude towards 'the family'?
3. According to the writer, which famous thinkers were against the family, and why?
4. Compare the writer's understanding of the family with that of the "people on high". Support your answers with evidence from the text.

> **Translating**
> See *Skills file* on pp. 182 & 183.

Translation & vocabulary
1. Translate the following lines from the text: Col. 2, l. 26 – Col. 3, l. 6.
2. Write your own sentences in which you use at least 6 words or phrases that have been annotated in the text.

Grammar practice

1. Superlatives
Decide whether you need 'of' or 'in' to complete these examples. Then identify and write a 'rule' about how to use 'in' or 'of' with superlatives.
a) the cleverest … the children
b) the nicest classroom … the school
c) the lowest birthrate … Europe
d) the highest percentage … single mothers
e) the cruellest hours … the morning
f) the fastest runner … the team

> Families can be the safest and the most oppressive places **in the world**, the happiest and most miserable. (BUT … We're the happiest family **of all**.)

2. Infinitives after question words
Complete the sentence with further examples of what a parent needs to think about:
"When you're there at the coalface, what you think about is how to …, what to …, whether to …, who to …, where to …." (Col. 3, ll. 20–27)

Language
1. Reread the sentences in which the following examples of figurative language occur:
   - "strung between past and future like a bead" (Col. 1, ll. 25–26)
   - "buoyant as boats in a harbour" (Col. 2, ll. 13–14)
   - "rootedness" (Col. 2, l. 24)
   - "at the coalface" (Col. 3, ll. 20–21)
2. Decide which of the definitions below fit with the words and phrases above.
   - being firmly based, in the way that a tree is attached to the ground
   - being a part of something continuous
   - doing the difficult, day-to-day work
   - not being pulled down by difficult situations
3. Write sentences in which you use each of the figures of speech in 1. to talk about other situations and/or people.

> **Essay writing**
> See *Skills file* on p. 184.

Creative writing
"Growing up with one parent is just as good as growing up with two."
Do you agree or disagree with this statement? Write an essay in which you discuss the arguments for and against the statement, and give your opinion.

Changing lifestyles 8

The Family

We're mixed up and very happy

By Nicci Gerrard

THIS is not how I'd planned it. This is not the way it was ever going to be when I was a complacent middle-class girl looking ahead to my future, and so certain that what I wanted I could get.

I had a mother, who mostly stayed at home and baked cakes for when we returned from school, wore perfume and pink lipstick and long earrings when she went out in the evening; a father who left for work in the morning wearing a soft grey suit with a shirt that smelt of the iron; brothers and sisters whom I played with, quarreled with, took utterly for granted.

Happy families: Sunday lunch, books at bedtime, photographs on the sideboard of the wedding day; annual holidays, a settled chronology of a family life strung between past and future like a bead. I knew I too would have a husband like that, children like that, a life with that consoling sense of order.

Thirty years later, and I have two children by my first marriage and two by my second. My first husband also has two more children, and occasionally my younger daughters ask me what exactly is their relationship to them: are they kind-of sisters, or more like cousins?

My brother lives down the road and he too has biological children and a stepson. My sister lives in Angola in an untraditional family arrangement. Our children tack between families and lives, negotiating diverse relationships, buoyant as boats in a harbour. A lot of people love them.

But sometimes – usually late at night or in the cruel early hours of morning – my 11-year-old son or my nine-year-old daughter ask me why it is they have two families, two homes; why they can feel so homesick in either. For them the nuclear family represents unity and wholeness, rootedness and a sense of belonging.

What is this thing, 'the family' that holds such power over them? For my four children, a traditional family is not their norm, and yet they still regard it as the desired state (in the same way as against their experience, they still think fathers go out to work and mothers stay at home). Marriages can be good, and they can be hell. Families can be the safest and the most oppressive places in the world, the happiest and most miserable. […]

In a way, those who understood the family best wanted to destroy it. Plato, Jesus, Marx all saw that when people were enmeshed in family life it diluted their commitment to other crucial things such as the state, God, the revolution, getting out at night, doing the garden, sorting out the attic.

People on high talk down to us about the beauty of the nuclear family, the moral rightness of it, with chilly, abstract certainty.

When you're there at the coal-face, what you think about is how to get them to school on time, what to put in their lunch boxes, […] whether to get strawberry or spearmint toothpaste, who to call in to mend the window broken by a football.

Family isn't just a place, a noun. It's an activity, it should be a verb. To family is to love unconditionally and muddle along the best you can, whatever the policy makers say.

From The Observer, *October 25, 1998.*

Col. 1: *6* **complacent** [kəmˈpleɪsnt] happy with one's situation – *19* **to quarrel** [ˈ--] to argue – **to take s.th. for granted** to consider s.th. normal and not special – *20* **utterly** completely – *26* **bead** Perle – *29* **consoling** [-ˈ--] comforting

Col. 2: *11* **to tack** [tæk] *here:* to move – *12* **to negotiate** [nɪˈɡəʊʃɪeɪt] *here:* to deal with (s.th. difficult) – *13* **buoyant** [ˈbɔɪənt] able to float – *30* **desired** [dɪˈzaɪəd] strongly wished for

Col. 3: *5* **oppressive** [-ˈ--] *here:* miserable – *10* **to be enmeshed** to be involved in s.th. that you can't easily get away from – *11* **to dilute** *here:* to weaken – **commitment** dedication – *12* **crucial** very important – *16* **people on high** people with an official status (e.g. politicians) – *19* **chilly** without emotion – *20* **coalface** an exposed section of coal in a mine – *30* **unconditionally** given freely without expecting anything in return – *31* **to muddle along** weiterwursteln, sich durchwursteln – *32* **policy maker** s.o. who makes political decisions

8 Changing lifestyles

Relationships

Before you read: To marry or not to marry?
- Make a list of arguments for and against marriage. Compare your list with your classmates'. Which are the five most common arguments given for and against the issue?

While you read
Summarise Darwin's arguments for and against marriage. (Don't copy them word for word.)

Comparing notes
1. Compare Darwin's list with yours and comment on the differences. Are any of them a result of changes in lifestyle and values since 1838?
2. In this excerpt, Darwin lists several reasons for not getting married. Why do you think that he still decided to get married in the end?

Debate
Hold a class debate on the motion: "This house believes that the institution of marriage is dead and should be buried."

> **Having a discussion**
> See *Skills files* on pp. 191 & 192.

Writing
1. Darwin has written to you, an advice column editor, about whether he should marry Emma Wedgewood. Based on what you know from this article, write a column responding to him.

Lifestyles questionnaire
1. In groups, come up with questions in which you deal with issues related to family life and relationships. The following topics may help you:
   - living together before marriage/remaining unmarried but living together
   - long-distance relationships (unmarried and married)
   - marrying before the age of 30/in your 30s/40s and upwards
   - gay/lesbian marriages
   - having children or not/how many
   - single parents/two unmarried persons living together as parents
   - children as a factor in the decision of whether to get divorced or not
   - making the divorce process less/more difficult
   - the government's role in family life (e.g. tax benefits, legislation)
   - who to consult in the case of family problems (e.g. friends, extended family, psychologists or psychiatrists, clergy)
2. As a class, organize your questions into a questionnaire.
3. Answer the questionnaire individually, and compare and discuss answers as a class.

> **Questionnaires & surveys**
> See *Skills file* on pp. 202 & 203.

> **Cartoons**
> See *Skills file* on p. 190.

Working with the cartoon
1. Explain the caption in your own words.
2. Which child is talking in the cartoon? Give reasons for your answer.
3. Look at the mothers in the picture. How would you describe them?
4. Write captions for this cartoon from both the single and from the double mothers' points of view.

'Single mums are so passé my dear, what you need is a double mum.'

Changing lifestyles 8

To marry or not to marry?

In July 1838, Charles Darwin was 29 and at a crossroads. He was attracted to his cousin, Emma Wedgewood, but should he marry her? He did what young men reputedly still do when faced with an emotional crisis: he drew up a list. In fact, he drew up two lists in parallel columns. One was headed "Not marry". He began with "Freedom to go where one liked". Then there were the benefits of conversation in gentlemen's clubs. He wouldn't be forced to visit relatives and have all the expense and anxiety of children. And "perhaps quarrelling", he added apprehensively. The next problem with marriage was underlined twice: "Loss of time". [...]

Darwin worried about not having time to read in the evenings, and the worry and the responsibility, not enough money to buy books and if there were very many children, then he would have to work hard to feed them and "it is very bad for one's health to work too much".

The other column was headed "Marry". [...] He wrote "Children (if it please God)" and then "Constant companion". He obviously needed to imagine what this would amount to because he added a series of explanatory clauses: "& friend in old age who will feel interested in one, object to be beloved and played with. Better than a dog anyhow." He added that it would mean having someone to look after the house, and there would be "the charms of music and female chit chat" and it would probably be good for his health – Darwin always worried about his health – and yet, he worried, a "terrible loss of time!"

But then he gave in. He stopped writing a list and wrote what was almost a poem on the misery of bachelor life: "My God, it is intolerable to think of spending one's whole working life, like a neuter bee, working, working, and nothing after all. – No, no, won't do. – Imagine living all one's day solitary in smoky dirty London House."

That was it. He carried on in this vein until the "Marry" column was safely longer than the "Not Marry" column and then wrote across the bottom. "Marry – Marry – Marry QED." Obviously, there would be things to give up. [...] "I never should know French – or see the Continent – or go to America – or go up in a Balloon."

But what the hell? Charles and Emma were married the following year. It is not recorded whether he ever showed her his list.

From "Icing on the Cake?", by Sean French, The Guardian, March 21, 1998.

---

1 **to be at a crossroads** to have to make an important decision
3 **reputedly** [rə'pju:tɪdlɪ] *(formal)* supposedly true
7 **anxiety** [æŋ'zaɪətɪ] worries – **apprehensively** nervously
14 **constant** ['--] **companion** person who is always present (e.g. husband or wife)
15 **to amount to** to be like
18 **chit chat** talking of things that aren't serious or important
21 **to give in** to agree to s.th. you did not originally want
22 **bachelor** a man who is not married – **intolerable** [-'----] not acceptable
23 **neuter bee** [nju:tə] *here:* worker bee
25 **in this vein** in this way
27 **QED** *(Latin)* Quod erat demonstrandum *(was zu beweisen war)*

Working with the cartoon
1. What do you think is meant by the term "Immediate Family"?
2. What point is the cartoonist making about this "Immediate Family"?
3. Which of the following terms would you use to describe the message of this cartoon, and why?
   funny • critical • old-fashioned • satirical • realistic • sad • surprising • unclear • ironic
   Why didn't you choose the other term(s)? Are there any other terms that you would have included?
4. What might Charles Darwin have said about this cartoon? Be creative!

8 Changing lifestyles

Birthrate trends

Before you read: Zero population
- What are the advantages and disadvantages of having children?
- How do you think your reasons for and against having children are different from those of your parents? Your grandparents?

Working with the text
1. Why is Art Buchwald disturbed about declining birthrates?
2. Summarize the young people's arguments as to why they don't want to have children.
3. How do the attitudes of the older and younger generation differ in this article?

> **Satire**
> See *Glossary* on pp. 208–210.

Style
1. Why do you think the author wrote most of this text in dialogue form?
2. Look up the meaning of 'satire' in the glossary. Would you call this article satirical? Explain why/why not.

Language
1. Suggest opposites for the following words and phrases in context:
   even (l. 3) • to be disturbed by s.th. (l. 4) • to continue (l. 9) • law-abiding (l. 16) • productive (l. 17) • to protest (l. 27) • to not be able to stand s.th. (l. 28)
2. Explain the phrases "to go up the wall" (ll. 40/41) and "to go down the drain." (ll. 43/44)

A step further
According to U.S. Census figures, the U.S. population was approx. 203 million in 1970 and approx. 281 million in 2000. Look at the graph below illustrating the fertility rate and the actual birth rate during this time.

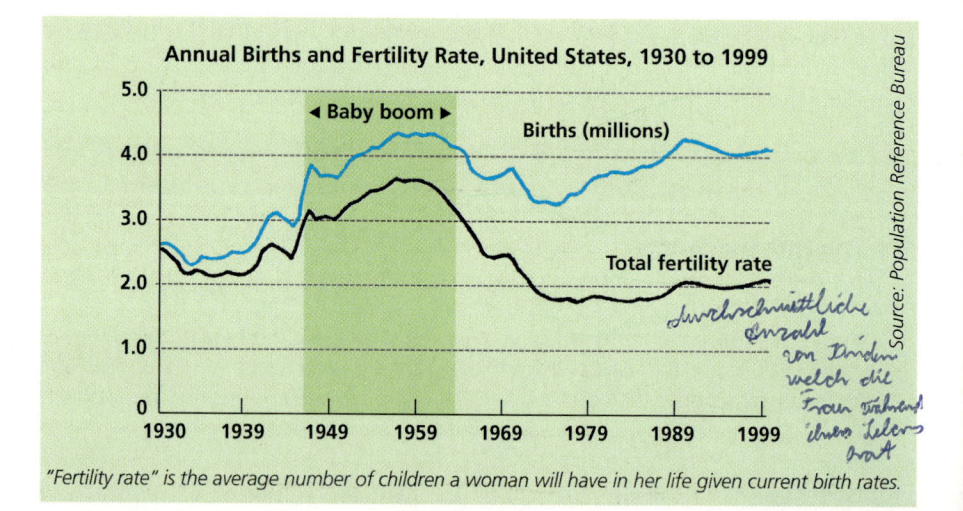

Annual Births and Fertility Rate, United States, 1930 to 1999

◄ Baby boom ► Births (millions) — Total fertility rate
Source: Population Reference Bureau

"Fertility rate" is the average number of children a woman will have in her life given current birth rates.

> **Check the web**
> Get more information about American family trends at:
> *http://www.prb.org/Template.cfm?Section=PRB&template=/Content Management/Content Display.cfm&ContentID=5885#blending*

1. a) What has happened to the fertility rate since 1971, when this article was written?
   b) How do the total number of births compare with the fertility rate in this time period?
   c) What factor(s) do you think have caused the change in population as is described above?
2. Does this information prove or disprove Art Buchwald's fears about the U.S. population?
3. When did the baby boom take place in the USA? When did it take place in Germany?
4. Would you agree or disagree with the arguments in this article for not having children? Give reasons.

Changing lifestyles 8

Zero population

The latest news from the Census Bureau is that younger women are refusing to have children, and the United States is fast approaching a "zero population growth" rate. This means that the death rate and birthrate figures in the country will soon be even.

Disturbed by this information, I sought out three young ladies in a coffeehouse to find out what had gone wrong. Their names were Fern, Clara, and Mary Jane, and they were sitting with three boys – Harry, Fred, and Claude.

"Ladies," I said, "I have just read in the newspapers that women in this country only had an average of 2.4 children in 1971 as opposed to 2.9 children in 1967, and if the trend continues, they will be down to 2.1 in a few years, which could mean zero population growth. How can you explain it?" I asked.

"Who wants kids?" Fern asked.

"But," I said, "that is the role of women – to reproduce their own kind."

"That's the point," Clara said. "Who wants to reproduce people like us?"

"I don't understand," I said.

Clara said, "It's a generation problem. Your generation had a high opinion of yourselves. You thought you were wonderful people – brave, strong, honest, law-abiding, productive, and God-fearing. Therefore, you wanted to reproduce more of the same."

"You assumed that your offspring would be just like you, and you wanted to flood the country with little copies of yourself."

"Well, it didn't work out that way," Clara concluded. "You produced an entirely different breed, and we've decided we don't want any more like us because we can't stand each other."

"Why should we make babies who are as unhappy and miserable as we are?" Mary Jane asked.

"I don't want any kids like Harry," Fern said.

"But," Harry protested, "you're my girlfriend."

"I don't mind you as my boyfriend," Fern said, "But I couldn't stand you as my son."

"It's true. I could never think of raising a Claude or a Fred. I wouldn't have the stomach for it," said Clara.

"That isn't a nice thing to say," Fred said defensively.

"Well," Clara replied, "would you like to be the father of Fern or Mary Jane or Harry or Claude?"

"I wouldn't even want to be the father of me," Fred said.

"If I understand you," I said, "the reason why you don't want to have babies is that you're afraid they'll all turn out like you."

"You got it, Pops," Fern said. "We know what we've done to our parents, and we're not going to let our kids do that to us."

Clara said, "I couldn't hassle with my kids the way I hassle with my mother. I'd go up the wall."

"But," I protested, "if all of you feel that way, the American people – the greatest, most magnificent and wondrous people the world has ever seen – could go down the drain."

"It's not our fault," Mary Jane said. "We're physically but not mentally equipped for it."

Fern said, "Once the country gets down to zero population growth, I might reconsider the whole proposition. But at the moment, I'd rather take the money it costs to raise a child and go to Europe."

"Even buying a Honda motorcycle," Harry said, "would be more fun than having a kid like me."

By Art Buchwald from I Never Danced at the White House, Greenwich, Conn.: Fawcett Crest, 1971, pp. 105–107. Reprinted with permission of the author.

---

1 **Census Bureau** government organization in charge of population counts – **to refuse** [rɪˈfjuːz] to not do s.th.
4 **to seek out** to look for
19 **offspring** descendant, child
20 **to flood** here: to fill
40 **to hassle with s.o.** [ˈhæsl] to argue with someone
45 **equipped** [ɪˈkwɪpt] prepared
48 **proposition** [ˌ--ˈ--] here: idea

125

8 Changing lifestyles

Future lifestyles

Before you read: Future scenarios
- What improvements, if any, would you like to see in the future for the following categories: changes in employment • education • health and medicine?

While you read
1. Read the article about predictions for the year 2010 and make notes under the following headings:
   - *Changes in employment*
   - *Retailing**
   - *Education*
   - *Health and medicine*
   - *Inner-cities*
   - *Social problems*
2. Mark the trends you see as positive with a plus (+) and those you see as negative with a minus (-).

Discussing the predictions
1. Working in groups, compare your notes. Explain your choices of plus and minus signs. Who do you think will have the most successful future life? The least successful life? Give reasons.
2. Which (if any) of the predictions listed in this text have already come true?
3. How likely do you think it is that the other predictions will come true? Come up with at least two positive and two negative predictions that you think will/won't come true in the future. Explain why.
4. Read the definition of social exclusion. Discuss the view that "the socially excluded have only themselves to blame."

Language
1. Explain the words by giving synonyms/synonymous phrases, definitions or opposites.
   - a) prestigious (l. 3)
   - b) previous (l. 16)
   - c) to eliminate (l. 20)
   - d) burden (l. 22)
   - e) deprived (l. 37)
   - f) convenient (l. 43)
2. Write sentences with the words. Try to use two or more words in one sentence.

Role play: An interview
Work in pairs or groups of three. Make a radio or TV interview that takes place in the year 2020.
1. Choose one of the people described on the following page (or a couple if you are working as a group of three). Write a list of questions you would like to ask this person/this couple.
2. Decide who will be the interviewer, and who will be the interviewee(s).
3. Depending on your roles, prepare prompt cards with answers and questions for the interview.
4. Record your interview as a radio broadcast or TV talk show. Other pupils can take part by 'phoning in' to express opinions and ask questions, or by being active members of the talk show audience.

> **Listening comprehension**
> *Take notes as you listen: you are going to hear part of a radio programme in which an expert on social exclusion, Nick Larson, is being interviewed.*

---

* **retailing** the selling of goods (usually in small numbers) directly to the public

Having a discussion
See *Skills files* on pp. 191 & 192.

Social exclusion
"A short hand term for what can happen when people or areas suffer from a combination of linked problems such as unemployment, poor skills, low incomes, poor housing, high crime environments, bad health, poverty and family breakdown."
(Social Exclusion Unit, 1999)

Changing lifestyles 8

Future scenarios

Rachel

Meet Rachel. She's single, self-employed and successful. She studied for her degree on the internet, taking a portfolio of courses from the world's most prestigious universities. After working as an advertising executive in New York, Sydney and Toronto, she has set up her own business in London. Rachel knows she wants a child sometime, but does she want a girl or a boy? And should she wait until her early 50s to give birth? After all, given her genetic background and healthy lifestyle, she expects to live until her late 80s. Life isn't that stressful. She lives in one of the crime-free, wealthy, inner city areas of London; works from home; checks her health regularly using a self-monitoring device; shops on-line and takes regular holidays visiting a few of the 2000 friends she has made on the internet. She likes living alone and enjoys the variety and mobility of her life. But sometimes she wonders is this all. Perhaps religion or philosophy offer the answer?

Craig and Maria

Life's not so great for Craig and Maria. They are 34 years old and live in Rochdale with Maria's two children from a previous relationship. Craig has two children of his own but rarely sees either of them.

Craig has no qualifications, is unemployed, has a criminal record and, like many of his friends, deals in drugs. Drugs are a huge problem: much too big for the police to eliminate. Maria works part-time in a low paid job at the local supermarket. Life is much the same for Maria as for her mother: she looks after the children but has the additional burden of her elderly parents who are in poor health and didn't make enough pension contributions when working. Maria's children are a worry. They don't have access to a PC at home and are not doing well at school. Like many children, medication has been prescribed to help with their hyper-activity and poor concentration. Maria can see no future for them except a life of insecure, low paid jobs, petty crime and unstable relationships. Perhaps she should leave Craig? Everyone seems to be splitting up these days.

Duncan and Kim

Duncan and Kim have lived together for 12 years. Duncan became a self-employed tax adviser when his firm closed its large, high rental offices in the centre of London. It's easier to work from home and meetings can be held using interactive PDA's. But he still travels a great deal to Europe, because the harmonisation of tax laws has led to a huge expansion of business there. Kim, as a government employee, enjoys part-time flexi-work. She is also studying for a higher degree with Harvard University.

Their ten-year-old son, like all children, is expected to have his own PC, which is at the core of the learning process. Unlike the more deprived areas of the country, his school has become a learning resource centre and teachers work with pupils on an individual basis. The family home is full of modern technology which has replaced many traditional household tasks. But they still employ a cleaner on a weekly basis and a live-in au pair. Their health monitoring equipment checks on the health condition of Kim's mother who lives in Scotland. Kim orders on-line all her mother's shopping needs. It's so much more convenient than having her live with them.

---

3 **portfolio** *here:* selection

10 **self-monitoring device** [dɪˈvaɪs] an object that makes it possible for s.o. to check s.th. oneself

18 **to have a criminal record** vorbestraft sein

23 **pension contributions** the monthly sum one pays toward retirement
25 **hyper-activity** [ˌhaɪprækˈtɪvətɪ] Hyperaktivität
27 **petty crime** a less serious crime
28 **to split up** (informal) to end a relationship

32 **PDA** (personal digital assistant) palm computer
33 **harmonisation** making two or more separate systems similar enough to work together
35 **flexi-work** a job in which the time one works is flexible
37 **to be at the core of s.th.** to be the most important part of s.th.

From Britain Towards 2010: the Changing Business Environment *by Professor Richard Scase, Swindon: Economic and Social Research Council (ESRC), 1999.*

8 Changing lifestyles

Write a short dialogue between one of these characters and his mother.

Leaving home

While you read
Two people are describing their experiences of leaving home. Decide whether they are male or female, and note down examples in the text to support your point of view.

Working with the text
1. What reasons do C. Smith and B. Jones give for wanting to leave home?
2. a) What are the positive aspects for them about being away from home?
   b) What do they miss or find difficult once they have left home?
3. In your own words, describe how both C. Smith and B. Jones react as a result of leaving home. Compare their reactions, and come up with reasons as to why they reacted in the ways that they did.

Translation & language
1. Translate lines 16–22 of the C. Smith text. Beware of false friends!
2. Make a table with the columns **gerunds** and **present participles**, and list the -ing forms that you find in the B. Jones text in the correct column. Remember: Gerunds are used like nouns in a sentence (e.g. as a subject, object, or after a preposition)!

Style & creative writing
1. B. Jones makes use of hyperbole in lines 8–12. Give examples of this and explain what effect this technique has on the text.
2. Pick a place (your classroom, a room at home, etc.) and write a description of it using the technique of hyperbole.

Hyperbole
See *Glossary* on pp. 208–210.

---

1 **to dread** opp. of to look forward to s.th.
2 **digestion** *Verdauung*
3 **to quiz** [kwɪz] to ask
5 **annoying** irritating
8 **vet** [abbrev. for veterinarian [ˌvetrɪˈneəriən]) *Tierarzt, Tierärztin*
10 **adjustment pains** [əˈdʒʌstmənt] discomfort when starting s.th. new and/or difficult
12 **wee hour** early hour
16 **to take s.th. for granted** to think s.th. isn't special or worth taking notice of
19 **quid** [kwɪd] (*informal*) British pound
22 **hall** (*here*) university or college housing
25 **amazed** [-'-] very surprised

C. Smith: "As a teenager, I dreaded the dinnertime ritual, where the entire family sat down to "have good food and a good laugh to help the digestion", to quote my parents. I hated the way Mum would quiz me about school. I was fed up with always having to help with the cleaning and cooking, and with taking care of my little sister
5 when I just wanted to go out with friends. Then there were my father's annoying jokes that he told all the time. I thought I'd go mad. I dreamt of my day of escape, when I could go to university and do what I wanted.

Now I'm living on my own and studying to be a vet. The freedom is great, probably because I've prepared myself for it, both mentally and practically. I haven't
10 really gone through many of the adjustment pains that a lot of my mates have – some of them have never washed their own clothes or cooked their own meals before! I love doing what I want, how I want, until any wee hour of the morning. If I want to, I live on things like bread rolls, biscuits, chocolate and TV dinners. Sometimes I clean my room daily at 3am, and other times I don't clean it for three weeks. I can
15 choose who to be with, or when I want to be alone.

Still, sometimes I miss the familiar things I've always taken for granted. Lately I've tried to cook decent meals for myself, but the food never tastes like Mum's, no matter what I do. I definitely miss being able to beg for more pocket money when it's suddenly gone – did I ever need a few quid the other night! I actually miss Dad's
20 stupid jokes, and my little sister running after me and copying everything I do. I've also wondered what happened to all of those friends who used to ring up. It's a good thing I've got new friends in the hall who are interested in who I am now.

Embarrassing as it is to admit it, I tend to call home more often these days. Yesterday Dad answered the phone: 'Hello love! I hope those animals know how
25 lucky they are!' He told me that he was amazed when I laughed."

Changing lifestyles 8

A step further

1. a) Make a "Declaration of Independence" poster for young people leaving home. Start like this:

   > Being independent means:
   > – being able to cook your own meals.
   > – not having to …

   b) What do you most look forward to about leaving home? What will you miss when you leave home?

2. In groups, compare what you have written for the *While you read* section.

3. a) What kinds of work do the males in your home do? The females? Describe.
   b) Come up with a list of 'typical' male and female tasks.
   c) Do you think that such tasks should be divided according to sex? If so, why? If not, suggest other alternatives. Explain your answer.

Working with the cartoon

1. Is the trend shown in the cartoon common in your country, too? Why or why not?
2. Discuss the pros and cons of grown-up children moving back home.
3. How much rent (as a proportion of earnings) do you think 'adult children' should pay if they stay at home or return home to live?
4. Create a thought bubble for Mum and/or the removal men in this cartoon.

B. Jones: "My parents used to tell me it was a good thing I was leaving home while I still thought I knew everything. The day couldn't come soon enough when I could pack my things into my old banger and move into a room in digs. It didn't matter that it was no bigger than a wardrobe. I was so happy to move out that I couldn't think of anything else. Even if the heating seldom worked, it was all mine! No more parents telling me when to be home or to tidy up my room, and no more of their ridiculous advice!

But soon I also had no more real food (unless you count crisps and beer), no more clean dishes, and no more car (it had broken down). Instead I had lots of other things, like mountains of unwashed clothes, a fridge full of the hairy experiment that was once veg, and enough balls of dust the size of tumbleweed to make my room look like something out of a western.

One morning as I was staring at the piles of smelly laundry and mouldy dishes, feeling sorry for myself, I made a shocking discovery: I realised I'd either have to starve and be buried in the muck or change my lifestyle – radically.

I decided that I'd better start acting more sensible like the grown ups – at least when it helped to make my life more comfortable. I learned to separate my washing so that I didn't turn all of my white T-shirts and socks pink, how to scrub the dishes and the floor back to their original color, how to make pasta that didn't still crunch and toast that wasn't scorched black. I even found a reasonable garage that repaired my car. Now I'm working on how to get the heating fixed. Funnily enough, this makes me proud that I've actually succeeded in running my own life. I also secretly admit that I've learned to appreciate what my parents have done for me a lot more. Have I told them this? Of course not. Even if I wanted to, there's no point in scaring them to death. They'd think I'd gone absolutely barmy."

3 **old banger** (BE: informal) old car – **in digs** (BE: informal) in a rented room in a house
5 **seldom** opp. of often
7 **ridiculous** [rɪˈdɪkjələs] silly, foolish
10 **fridge** [frɪdʒ] abbrev. for refrigerator
11 **veg** [vedʒ] abbrev. for vegetable(s) – **tumbleweed** ball-shaped prairie plant rolled about by the wind
13 **laundry** [ˈlɔːndrɪ] dirty clothes – **mouldy** [ˈməʊldɪ] *schimmelig*
15 **to starve** to suffer from hunger – **muck** (informal) s.th. unpleasant
19 **to crunch** to make a crackly sound
20 **scorched** slightly burned – **reasonable** opp. of expensive
25 **barmy** [ˈbɑːmɪ] (BE: informal) crazy

8 Changing lifestyles

Living well

Before you read: *Advice, like youth, probably just wasted on the young*
- What aspects are important for living your life well?

Working with the text
1. Why do young people need to be reminded to enjoy the *"power and beauty of (their) youth"* (l. 7)?
2. Why is it useless to worry about the future, according to Schmich?
3. Is it a mistake not to know early in your life what you would like to do with it? Why/why not?
4. Explain why it is important to value the following people:
   a) parents   b) brothers and sisters   c) good friends
5. In your own words explain the double meaning of "run out" (l. 57).
6. In your own words explain why we need to be careful about the advice we are given (ll. 59–62).

Language
Rewrite lines 44–48 replacing the following words with synonyms/synonymous phrases:
for good (l. 44) • link (l. 45) • to stick with (l. 46) • a precious few (l. 47)
• to hold on (l. 47)

Style
1. Describe the register used in this text. Include the following in your description: vocabulary • sentence structure • tone
2. What types of rhetorical devices are used in this text?

Creative writing
Mary Schmich's title for this column is "Advice, like youth, probably just wasted on the young". Write approx. 200 words in which you explain if you agree or disagree with this point of view.

A step further
1. Someone posted Mary Schmich's text on the internet as a graduation speech by the author Kurt Vonnegut (which Vonnegut himself denied)! To this day it has not been found out who did this. Is this purely an innocent and funny joke or a more serious action, in your opinion? Discuss.
2. Do you believe that material online should be free for everyone to use as they wish, or that there should be some restrictions put on usage? Discuss.

Check the web
For more information about the whole sunscreen issue:
http://www.washingtonpost.com/wp-srv/style/features/daily/march99/sunscreen0318.htm

Analysing style
See *Skills file* on p. 181.

Advice, like youth, probably just wasted on the young

Ladies and gentlemen of the class of '97:
Wear sunscreen.
If I could offer you only one tip for the future, sunscreen would be it. The long-term benefits of sunscreen have been proved by scientists, whereas the rest of my
5 advice has no basis more reliable than my own meandering experience. I will dispense this advice now.
Enjoy the power and beauty of your youth. Oh, never mind. You will not understand the power and beauty of your youth until they've faded. But trust me, in 20 years, you'll look back at photos of yourself and recall in a way you can't grasp
10 now how much possibility lay before you and how fabulous you really looked. You are not as fat as you imagine.

---

2 **sunscreen** cream that protects the skin from the sun
5 **reliable** dependable – **meandering** [mɪˈændrɪŋ] *here:* widely varying
6 **to dispense** [-ˈ-] *(formal)* to give s.th.
8 **to fade** [feɪd] to disappear
9 **to grasp** *(fig.)* to understand
10 **fabulous** [ˈfæbjələs] great

Don't worry about the future. Or worry, but know that worrying is as effective as trying to solve an algebra equation by chewing bubble gum. The real troubles in your life are apt to be things that never crossed your worried mind, the kind that blindside you at 4 p.m. on some idle Tuesday.

Do one thing every day that scares you.

Sing.

Don't be reckless with other people's hearts. Don't put up with people who are reckless with yours.

Floss.

Don't waste your time on jealousy. Sometimes you're ahead, sometimes you're behind. The race is long and, in the end, it's only with yourself.

Remember compliments you receive. Forget the insults. If you succeed in doing this, tell me how.

Keep your old love letters. Throw away your old bank statements.

Stretch.

Don't feel guilty if you don't know what you want to do with your life. The most interesting people I know didn't know at 22 what they wanted to do with their lives. Some of the most interesting 40-year-olds I know still don't.

Get plenty of calcium. Be kind to your knees. You'll miss them when they're gone.

Maybe you'll marry, maybe you won't. Maybe you'll have children, maybe you won't. Maybe you'll divorce at 40, maybe you'll dance the funky chicken on your 75th wedding anniversary. Whatever you do, don't congratulate yourself too much, or berate yourself either. Your choices are half chance. So are everybody else's.

Enjoy your body. Use it every way you can. Don't be afraid of it or of what other people think of it. It's the greatest instrument you'll ever own. Dance, even if you have nowhere to do it but your living room.

Read the directions, even if you don't follow them.

Do not read beauty magazines. They will only make you feel ugly.

Get to know your parents. You never know when they'll be gone for good. Be nice to your siblings. They're your best link to your past and the people most likely to stick with you in the future.

Understand that friends come and go, but with a precious few you should hold on. Work hard to bridge the gaps in geography and lifestyle, because the older you get, the more you need the people who knew you when you were young.

Live in New York City once, but leave before it makes you hard. Live in Northern California once, but leave before it makes you soft. Travel.

Accept certain inalienable truths: Prices will rise. Politicians will philander. You, too, will get old. And when you do, you'll fantasize that when you were young, prices were reasonable, politicians were noble and children respected their elders.

Respect your elders.

Don't expect anyone else to support you. Maybe you have a trust fund. Maybe you'll have a wealthy spouse. But you never know when either one might run out.

Don't mess too much with your hair or by the time you're 40 it will look 85.

Be careful whose advice you buy, but be patient with those who supply it. Advice is a form of nostalgia. Dispensing it is a way of fishing the past from the disposal, wiping it off, painting over the ugly parts and recycling it for more than it's worth.

But trust me on the sunscreen.

By Mary Schmich, The Chicago Tribune, June 1, 1997.

---

15 **to be apt to be** to be likely to be
16 **to be blindsided** (AE) to be suddenly confronted by s.th. (usually negative)
17 **idle** ['aɪdl] lazy
20 **to put up with** to accept s.th. that is not what you like
21 **reckless** careless
22 **to floss** to clean between one's teeth with silk string
23 **jealousy** ['dʒeləsɪ] Eifersucht
26 **insult** ['--] negative statement about s.o.
28 **bank statement** Kontoauszug
36 **the funky chicken** Ententanz
38 **to berate** [bɪ'reɪt] (formal) to scold
45 **siblings** ['--] brothers, sisters
48 **to bridge a gap** (fig.) to overcome differences
52 **inalienable** [ɪ'neɪlɪənəbl] (formal) undeniable – **to philander** [fɪ'lændə] to have a love affair
54 **to be noble** here: to be honest
56 **to support** to help – **trust fund** Treuhandfonds
57 **spouse** husband or wife
59 **advice** [-'-] Rat
60 **to fish s.th. from s.th.** to take s.th. out of s.th. – **disposal** [dɪ'spəʊzl] Müllschlucker
62 **to trust s.o. on s.th.** to believe s.o. about s.th.

8 Changing lifestyles

Before you read
- How does society expect old people to behave? Make a list of characteristics.
- Look at the pictures below. Which older people are "typical" and which aren't typical in your opinion? Give reasons for your answers.

Warning

When I am an old woman I shall wear purple
With a red hat that doesn't go, and doesn't suit me,
And I shall spend my pension on brandy and summer gloves
And satin sandals, and say we've no money for butter.
5 I shall sit down on the pavement when I'm tired
And gobble up samples in shops and press alarm bells
And run my stick along the public railings
and make up for the sobriety of my youth.
I shall go out in my slippers in the rain
10 And pick the flowers in other people's gardens
And learn to spit.
You can wear terrible shirts and grow more fat
And eat three pounds of sausages at a go
Or only bread and pickle for a week
15 And hoard pens and pencils and beermats and things in boxes.
But now we must have clothes that keep us dry
And pay our rent and not swear in the street
And set a good example for the children.
We must have friends to dinner and read the papers.
20 But maybe I ought to practise a little now?
So people who know me are not too shocked and surprised
When suddenly I am old, and start to wear purple.

2 **to not suit s.o.** to not look good on s.o.
3 **pension** [ˈpɛnʃn] monthly sum one receives after retiring
5 **pavement** *Gehsteig*
6 **to gobble** [ˈɡɒbl] to eat a lot quickly – **sample** *Kostprobe*
7 **railings** *Geländer*
8 **sobriety** [səʊˈbraɪəti] *here:* being serious, sensible (*Nüchternheit*)
11 **to spit** *spucken*
13 **at a go** at once
14 **pickle** *saure Gurke*
15 **to hoard** to collect in large numbers – **beermat** *Bierdeckel*
17 **to swear** to say bad words

From *Selected Poems* by Jenny Joseph, London: Bloodaxe Books Ltd. 1992.

Changing lifestyles 8

Working with the text
1. Paraphrase this poem in no more than two sentences.
2. Describe the woman who is speaking in this poem. How old would you say she is? How would you describe her personality?
3. The content of this poem can be divided into three parts. Give line examples to show where each of these parts starts and ends, and explain your choices.
4. How would you describe the tone of this poem?

A step further
1. Refer back to the list you made about society's expectations for old people's behaviour. Do you think that the speaker in this poem intends to follow these expectations? Why or why not?
2. Give examples of eccentric habits that you have noticed in old people you know well. How do you feel about these habits?
3. Look at the pictures again on p. 132. Which picture do you think could most likely be of the speaker in the poem? Give reasons for your answers.
4. In many Western societies, the process of growing old is viewed negatively. Yet, in the coming years, older people will make up the majority of most Western populations. What do you think can be done to improve the image of growing old?

> **Illustrations & Photographs**
> See *Skills file* on pp. 190.

Creative writing
1. Write a poem along similar lines to this one, but from a man's point of view.
2. Write a poem of your own, using plenty of specific objects and experiences. Be sure to think up a suitable title. Start out like this:
   When I pass the Abitur, I shall ...

> **Memos**
> See *Skills file* on p. 204.

MEMORANDUM   **HarbourHouse Publications**

To: Editorial Team
From: Max Rupert, Director of Publications
Subject: Lifestyle magazine launch

Please come up with suggestions for the content and layout of a magazine to be launched by the end of this year. Bear in mind the following points:
→ TARGET MARKET: The Marketing Department has revealed two gaps in the market: The "free 'n' easies" (18–30 age group), and the "golden oldies" (60–80 age group).
→ FEATURES: Suggestions for special features dealing with topical issues.
→ DESIGN: Outline ideas for the overall design (glossy/matt, colour, no. of pages, advertising, etc.)

Please send your report as soon as possible or present it to me at our next meeting.

I look forward to your creative ideas!

Max Rupert

Project: Lifestyle magazine launch

It is the year 2050. You are a team of magazines editors and have just received this memo from your boss. Carry out the tasks below. Read the memo on the left, then prepare the report and presentation for your boss.

▶ TARGET MARKET: Choose one of these groups and write a lifestyle profile of the typical reader.
▶ FEATURES: Decide on regular features. Present your ideas in the form of a contents page.
▶ DESIGN: Come up with a name and slogan expressing the magazine's philosophy and design an eye-catching cover for the first issue.

9 Mad for ads

134

Mad for ads 9

Analysing adverts
Look at the adverts on the opposite page.
1. What product is being advertised in each?
2. a) What message does each advert convey?
    (If you buy ..., you will ...)
   b) Which of the adverts do you consider to be the most/the least effective? Why?
3. Choose *one* of the adverts on p.134. Which parts of the AIDCA formula did advertisers consider in designing their advert?
4. a) Match the strategies below with the appropriate part(s) of the AIDCA formula.
    - include a list of stockists who have the product
    - D use a headline telling readers to buy (e.g. "Go and check this out today")
    - A use creative devices such as colours, a slogan and illustrations
    - place the ad in a publication whose readers are likely to use the product
    - A C use full-page and half-page ads
    - C show how money can be saved by using the product
    - A place at the front of a magazine and if possible on a righthand page
    - I include special offers
    - identify a particular need which the product fulfils
    - C show that the product is good value for money
    - I include a coupon or invitation to sample or test the product
    - A show the benefits of the product
    - D show that the product will give satisfaction
   b) Add further ideas of your own.

> **The AIDCA formula**
> Advertisers often use the AIDCA formula to plan adverts. AIDCA stands for:
>
> **A**ttention: How can we grab your attention?
>
> **I**nterest: How do we get you interested in the product?
>
> **D**esire: What arguments would make you desire (want) this product?
>
> **C**onviction: How can we convince you that this product is worth buying?
>
> **A**ction: How can we make you take action and buy the product?

1. **It's good to talk.**
2. **Be the first to know.**
3. **Taste. Not waist.**
4. **Surely the best tactic.**
5. **Don't dream it. Drive it.**
6. **Just do it!**
7. **Every time a good time.**
8. **Plink, plink. Fizz, fizz, oh what a relief it is.**

5. a) Look at the slogans above and guess what type of product is being advertised. (Some of them you may know!) Find the correct answers on p. 223.
   b) What do the slogans promise the customer?
   c) What rhetorical devices do the slogans use?
6. Think of slogans for the following products using similar rhetorical devices:
    a packet of crisps • a pair of shoes • a new deodorant • chewing gum

Group work/Presentation
- Work in groups. Design an advert for a product of your choice. Include a sketch showing the layout of the advert. Think of a catchy slogan and include some copy text describing the product. Present your advert in class.

9 Mad for ads

Advertising is …

> "Advertising is of the very essence of democracy. An election goes on every minute of the business day across the counters of hundreds of thousands of stores and shops where the customers state their preferences and determine which manufacturer and which product shall be the leader today, and which shall lead tomorrow."
> *Bruce Barton (1955), chairman of BBDO*

> "Advertising is legalized lying."
> *H.G. Wells*

> "Advertising is what you do when you can't go see somebody. That's all it is."
> *Fairfax Cone (1963), ad agency partner*

> "Advertising is the modern substitute for argument; its function is to make the worse appear the better."
> *George Santayana*

> "Advertising is the greatest art form of the twentieth century."
> *Marshall McLuhan (1976), Canadian social scientist*

Your view

1. Explain what you understand by each of the quotations above and then give your opinion on how true you think each statement is.
2. Choose one of the quotations and write an essay discussing the point made. Use real examples from the world of advertising to support your viewpoint, if possible. Write about 250 words.
3. What is advertising in your opinion? Collect statements of your own in class which begin "Advertising is…"

> **Essay writing**
> See *Skills file* on p. 184.

Language & translation

1. Translate the quotations into German paying attention to style.
2. Write a dictionary style definition for the word "advertising".
3. Collect as many words as you can related to the field of advertising. Group the words you collect in suitable categories. The categories below may help you get started. (Add to your collection as you work on this chapter.)
   Synonyms for "advertisement" • People in advertising • …

> **Translating**
> See *Skills file* on p. 182 & 183.

Advert Oscars

Find out which types of advertising have been really successful in grabbing your attention by taking part in your own 'Advert Oscars'.
- Nominate an advert in each of the categories listed below.
- Discuss the nominations in pairs or groups giving reasons for your choices.
- Agree on one advert for each category in your group and then in your class.
- Award the winning ads the 'Advert Oscar'! You could even have an Oscar Award-giving ceremony, complete with nominations and winners' speeches!

> **Having a discussion**
> See *Skills files* on pp. 191 & 192.

Categories
a) Best advert of all time
b) Most shocking advert
c) Most offensive advert
d) Most original advert
e) Most effective advert

Draw conclusions about what makes adverts effective based on the types of adverts that win the "Oscars".

Mad for ads 9

Celebrities in advertising

Michael Schumacher's Choice

Speedmaster Automatic
Model in 18 k red gold.
Day-Date, AM/PM.
OMEGA – Swiss made since 1848.

Ω OMEGA
The sign of excellence

http://www.omega.ch

> **Check the web**
> Find out more about Michael Schuhmacher at:
> *http://www.schumacher-fanclub.com/*
> *http://www.formula1.com/drivers/bio.html*
> Visit Omega's homepage and find out which famous personalities are currently promoting their products at:
> *http://www.omega.ch/*

Analysing the advert
Describe this advert in detail referring to style, layout, choice of graphics and illustrations, copy (text), information, etc. Give your opinion on the advert.

Working with the advert
1. Look at the advert. What do you know about Michael Schumacher? Why do you think Omega chose him to endorse one of their products?
2. a) Name three other products which are endorsed by a famous person on television or in print.
   b) What image do they convey of the particular product?
3. What do you consider to be the advantages of using celebrities to advertise products? What are the potential problems or dangers of using celebrities?
4. Which celebrities would you employ to advertise the following? Give reasons.
    anti-drug campaign • a serious newspaper • a skateboard • a low-fat yoghurt • a mobile phone

Your view
Why are some celebrities paid enormous amounts for advertising whereas others earn nothing? What justification, if any, is there for this phenomenon? Discuss.

9 Mad for ads

Reaching the audience

Before you read: Nascar's new campaign
- What do you normally do when there is a commercial break on TV?
- Make a list of the advantages of advertising on TV.

The review on p. 139 was published by the website 'Advertising Age' (see Check the web box).

Working with the text
1. a) How does the writer portray the people who work for advertising agencies?
   b) How does he characterize the "Early American crowd"?
   c) From what you know about the U.S. what other groups can you identify?
2. What mistake do advertising agencies often make in TV adverts according to the text?
3. Explain the meaning and significance of the "tagline" (l. 55).
4. According to the writer, what makes the Nascar adverts so effective?

Language
1. Find opposites for the following adjectives from the text. Wherever possible use a suitable prefix.
   highly educated (l. 10) • urban (l. 11) • well-to-do (l. 11) • confident (l. 13) • aware (l. 15) • foreign (l. 20) • ordinary (l. 64) • quiet (l. 73) • understated (l. 73)
2. Find synonyms in the text for the following words:
   hardly • highly interesting • stupidly • keen • on purpose • partly • known
3. Write your own statement on the effectiveness of advertising using at least **five** of the words you found in task 1 and **three** of those given in task 2.

Further activities: Analysing TV advertising
1. Think of a television advert or spot which particularly appeals to you. Describe the spot to a partner and say why you like it.
2. Find out what type of TV adverts are most and least popular in your class. Try to identify what kind of adverts appeal to different kinds of people (male/female/interest related/etc.).
3. What do you consider to be most important if an advert is to reach its audience? Draw up a list of between 5 and 10 items. Choose a type of product that you are interested in. Concentrate on three examples of TV spots for your chosen product. Then answer the following questions.
   - How is the product presented?
   - What is the message of the spot?
   - Who do you think the target audience is? Is it represented in the spot, or not?
   - What makes the spot effective? (e.g. celebrity endorsement, a memorable tagline, humour, good looking actors …)

Summarize your findings in your own spot review (refer to *adage.com* for help) and present your ideas in class.

Check the web
Read current ad reviews on the *Advertising Age* website:
http://www.adage.com/
At Y & R's website (the company who produced the NASRA adverts), find out about the people who work for the agency, and view their current print and TV avertisements:
http://www.yandr.com/

Writing a summary
See *Skills file* on p. 185.

★ Listening comprehension
Listen to this excerpt from the novel *What's Eating Gilbert Grape* by Peter Hedges.

Mad for ads 9

Nascar's new campaign

Before we start talking Nascar, we should discuss the biggest problem in this country's advertising: the absence of Early American furniture.

You can search all the reception areas of all the (advertising) agencies in all the cities and you will never, ever see a big sofa with maple-trimmed arms and brown, tweed fabric [...]. Why is this? Well, first, as anyone dressed all in black will tell you, these things are ugly – objectively ugly, according to science and nature and the immutable laws of the cosmos. Highly educated, urban, coastal and generally well-to-do ad people simply are not an Early American crowd. They are so not an Early American crowd, in fact, so confident in their rarified tastes and smug in their aesthetic superiority, that they are scarcely aware of an Early American crowd. [...]

But there's the problem: Most of the country is an Early American crowd. There is a whole big population out there, and it isn't reading *Architectural Digest*, watching foreign films and sipping chai. It is reading *Parade*, watching Stallone and swilling Bud. You don't have to go to Iowa to find Middle America. It is in Pasadena and Miami and Queens, New York. It eats macaroni and cheese, it reads romance novels, and it smokes.

It doesn't know who Robert Mapplethorpe was, it doesn't understand that Early American sofas [...] are mockeries of God's plan, but it sure has most of the money for buying the products that advertising people stupidly persist in advertising hiply to their own elitist selves.

To cite one tiny example, think of that Philips spot for the flat TV, filled with funky, edgy, lower-Manhattan young dot-commers. Very cool – except the people who buy $2,000 TVs are mainly sitting in Barcaloungers watching *Cops* or *Touched by an Angel* or *Nascar*. [...]

Which, with 63 million extremely ardent fans, is the No. 2 TV sport, after football. Put aside for the moment that watching auto racing on TV is like watching the *Traffic Channel*. And ignore the propensity for Nascar's marquee personalities to die in horrific crashes [...]. The fact is that Middle America loves it. Not just trailer-park America. Not just snuff-dipping America. Not just wallet-chained-to-the-belt America. More of America than, for instance, golf.

So it is extremely fascinating to see what Nascar is up to now. Unlike so many advertisers who foolishly craft messages as if they were targeting a more sophisticated audience, Nascar – which already owns a solid chunk of Middle America – is intentionally aiming somewhat above its core demographic to cultivate a wider audience still. [...]

A charming and funny campaign from Y&R Advertising and Impiric, Chicago, uses TV and print to portray Nascar enthusiasm as a magnificent obsession. The tagline: "How bad have you got it?"

One spot shows a young wife telling her pointedly non-redneck husband she is pregnant. He immediately conjures a fantasy about screeching through the streets on the way to the hospital, zooming in and out of traffic at high speed. Only after that reverie does he embrace her. "Oh, honey, I love you." [...]

In another spot, the whole family pulls into a donut joint and climbs out of the car ... through the windows, Nascar-style. In another, junior videotapes an ordinary drive with Dad. At home, they slap it in the VCR in fast-forward and just imagine. And the best spot of all shows a couple in bed trying to sleep while through the partially open window they listen to someone gunning an engine outside. The wife gets up – and opens the window all the way. Fabulous.

Nobody in these spots is dressed all in black. The families depicted here are quite ordinary. The sophistication lies in the approach: quiet, understated, knowing. The ads assiduously avoid the clichés of the sport – and even the famous drivers – to find the essence: the thrill that (allegedly) never goes away.

From AdAge.com by Bob Garfield from NASCAR'S NEW CAMPAIGN IS IN WINNER'S CIRCLE, March, 2001.

Nascar *(also written NASCAR) abbrev. for* National Association for Stock Car Racing (**stock car** standard car modified for racing)
6 **maple-trimmed** with parts made of wood *(Ahorn)* – 10 **immutable** *(formal)* unchanging – 20 **chai** *(Indian)* mixture of tea, spices and milk – **Parade** *(US)* popular magazine – 21 **to swill** *(informal, negative)* to drink in large quantities – 22 **Middle America** middle class America – 25 **Robert Mapplethorpe** (1946–1989) American photographer famous for his studies of nudes – 27 **mockery** laughing at s.th. disrespectfully – 29 **to persist** *here:* to keep on doing – 32 **edgy** nervous, irritable – 34 **Barcalounger** *(brandname)* comfortable armchair with a built-in leg rest – 36 **ardent** very enthusiastic – 37 **put aside** not taking s.th. into account – 39 **propensity** *(formal)* tendency – 40 **marquee personality** star – 41 **trailer-park** *(AE)* low-income communities living in mobile homes – 42 **snuff** tobacco which is inhaled – 46 **to craft** to make skillfully – 48 **chunk** big piece – 50 **core demographic** *here:* main target audience – 54 **to portray** to characterize – 57 **redneck** *(negative, informal)* belonging to the uneducated white working class – 58 **to screech** *here:* to drive fast and noisily – 60 **reverie** daydream – 63 **joint** *here:* a cheap café – 68 **to gun an engine** to make an engine work loudly – 72 **to depict** to show – 74 **assiduously** carefully – 76 **allegedly** supposedly

9 Mad for ads

Leading advertisers

Fig. 1 **TOP TEN LEADERS RANKED BY US ADVERTISING SPENDING IN US IN 2001**
*Dollars are in millions.

RANK 2001	RANK 2000	Advertiser	Headquarters	TOTAL U.S. ADVERTISING SPENDING 2001	2000	%CHG	U.S. MEASURED MEDIA SPENDING 2001	2000	%CHG
1	1	General Motors Corp.	Detroit, MI	*$3,374	*$3,945	-14.5	*$2,207	*$2,959	-25.4
2	2	Procter & Gamble Co.	Cincinnati, OH	2,541	2,614	-2.8	1,702	1,660	-2.6
3	3	Ford Motor Co.	Dearborn, MI	2,408	2,345	2.7	1,270	1,198	5.9
4	6	Pepsi Co	Purchase, NY	2,210	2,114	4.5	674	677	-0.4
5	4	Pfizer	New York, NY	2,189	2,258	-3.0	805	800	0.5
6	5	Daimler Chrysler	Auburn Hills, MI/ Stuttgart, Germany	1,985	2,162	-8.2	1,400	1,687	-17.0
7	9	AOL Time Warner	New York, NY	1,885	1,776	6.2	1,565	1,474	6.2
8	7	Philip Morris Cos.	New York, NY	1,816	1,966	-7.7	1,325	1,770	-25.1
9	8	Walt Disney Co.	Burbank, CA	1,757	1,819	-3.4	1,054	1,091	-3.4
10	10	Johnson & Johnson	New Brunswick, NJ	1,618	1,601	1.0	882	924	-4.6

Fig. 2 Note: Dollars are in millions.

TOP ADVERTISERS IN 12 MEDIA

MAGAZINE
1. Procter & Gamble Co. $477.3
2. Philip Morris Cos. 448.3
3. General Motors Corp. 391.4
4. AOL Time Warner 305.5
5. Ford Motor Co. 303.3
6. DaimlerChrysler 258.3
7. L'Oreal 236.0
8. Johnson & Johnson 211.3
9. Toyota Motor Corp. 199.3
10. Pfizer 163.5

SUNDAY MAGAZINE
1. National Syndications $138.3
2. Bradford Exchange 52.1
3. Bose Corp. 46.2
4. Procter & Gamble Co. 44.7
5. Dell Computer Corp. 37.6
6. Roll International 28.1
7. Bristol-Myers Squibb Co. 27.8
8. U.S. Government 23.5
9. Walt Disney Co. 20.9
10. Campbell Soup Co. 19.0

NEWSPAPER
1. Federated Dept Stores $485.7
2. May Department Stores Co. 431.9
3. Verizon Communications 322.2
4. AT&T Wireless 311.8
5. AOL Time Warner 212.6
6. SBC Communications 211.5
7. Dillard's 204.3
8. Target Corp. 190.6
9. Sprint Corp. 182.8
10. General Motors Corp. 178.8

NATIONAL NEWSPAPER
1. Ford Motor Co. $67.5
2. AOL Time Warner 53.7
3. IBM Corp. 49.2
4. General Motors Corp. 46.8
5. Dell Computer Corp. 45.5
6. Hewlett-Packard Co. 43.3
7. Federated Dept Stores 40.9
8. Walt Disney Co. 39.1
9. Merrill Lynch & Co. 35.6
10. Sprint Corp. 34.5

NETWORK TV
1. General Motors Corp. $661.8
2. Procter & Gamble Co. 596.5
3. Johnson & Johnson 430.4
4. Philip Morris Cos. 416.7
5. AOL Time Warner 359.4
6. Pfizer 343.8
7. GlaxoSmithKline 335.4
8. PepsiCo 334.8
9. Walt Disney Co. 311.4
10. Ford Motor Co. 305.1

SPOT TV
1. DaimlerChrysler $559.5
2. General Motors Corp. 475.1
3. Honda Motor Co. 275.9
4. Ford Motor Co. 250.1
5. Verizon Communications 226.2
6. Toyota Motor Corp. 201.6
7. Yum Brands 186.5
8. McDonald's Corp. 179.5
9. Nissan Motor Co. 172.1
10. General Mills 163.8

SYNDICATED TV
1. Procter & Gamble Co. $189.1
2. GlaxoSmithKline 127.7
3. AOL Time Warner 97.8
4. Pfizer 76.5
5. Berkshire Hathaway 71.5
6. General Motors Corp. 66.7
7. McDonald's Corp. 66.4
8. Unilever 65.7
9. Johnson & Johnson 63.7
10. Philip Morris Cos. 62.8

CABLE TV NETWORKS
1. AOL Time Warner $294.1
2. Procter & Gamble Co. 271.6
3. General Motors Corp. 249.3
4. Philip Morris Cos. 222.7
5. AT&T Corp. 158.0
6. General Mills 150.4
7. Pfizer 145.6
8. Johnson & Johnson 130.0
9. GlaxoSmithKline 124.3
10. Walt Disney Co. 122.9

NETWORK/NATIONAL SPOT RADIO
1. SBC Communications $73.2
2. Verizon Communications 69.1
3. Viacom 47.9
4. AT&T Wireless 44.3
5. Walt Disney Co. 43.8
6. AOL Time Warner 41.6
7. Home Depot 39.9
8. News Corp. 36.5
9. General Motors Corp. 35.8
10. Sears, Roebuck & Co. 33.1

OUTDOOR
1. Anheuser-Busch Cos. $44.7
2. Philip Morris Cos. 41.5
3. McDonald's Corp. 35.5
4. AOL Time Warner 27.4
5. Diageo 27.2
6. General Motors Corp. 25.7
7. Walt Disney Co. 25.5
8. Cendant Corp. 24.7
9. Gap Inc. 23.0
10. Nextel Communications 22.6

INTERNET
1. Ebay $45.4
2. General Motors Corp. 44.3
3. Providian Corp. 29.3
4. Amazon.com 27.7
5. AOL Time Warner 27.2
6. Barnes & Noble 26.0
7. Bank One Corp. 25.9
8. Classmates Online 24.3
9. Vivendi Universal 22.2
10. Dell Computer 21.0

YELLOW PAGES
1. ServiceMaster Co. $48.5
2. U-Haul 37.0
3. BGI 27.2
4. State Farm Mutual Auto Ins. 26.0
5. Ford Motor Co. 24.7
6. Allstate Insurance Group 22.0
7. General Motors Corp. 20.0
8. Unigroup 19.0
9. Sirva 17.9
10. Qwest Communications Int'l 17.7

Mad for ads 9

The Top 100 US Advertisers

Reviewing the 47 years *Advertising Age* magazine has produced its 100 Leading National Advertisers report, not since that other recession year of 1991, when the nation's top advertisers recorded a 3.9% decline in ad spending, has negative ad growth been recorded.

Recession and war

Both years were scarred by the dual theme of recession and war: Recession-plagued 1991 was marked by the Persian Gulf War; the war on terrorism began in 2001, also a year of recession. The overall decline by the 100 Leaders in 1991 was marked by reductions in total advertising by 59 of the companies; 46 did so in 2001 [...].

The top 100 as usual proved more dedicated to at least maintenance-level spending in 2001. Their 1.3% decline in all forms of advertising bettered the 6.5% drop by all advertisers [...] The 100 Leaders claimed 39.4% of total U.S. media expenditures in 2001 vs. 38.3% in 2000. Their media outlays hit $42.99 billion, down 5.2%, vs. $118.45 billion for all advertisers, down 7.8%, according to Taylor Nelson Sofres' CMR.

Unmeasured media up

Unmeasured forms of advertising and marketing – a cornucopia that includes direct marketing, sales promotion, tele-marketing and event marketing, to name a few – rose 3.6% to $37.95 billion for these elite 100, thus appropriating the marketing wisdom that calls for less brand-building through media when a cost-conscious mentality pervades.

There were signs of a turnaround in 2002, albeit for marginal ad growth. Several media kingpins showed strong gains in the first quarter of the year: Newspapers rose 9.3% and network TV 6.6%, according to CMR.

There was evidence, though somewhat thin, of the 100 Leaders pushing up spending levels, in the first quarter of 2002. The top 10 Leaders in this report, a group accounting for 30% of the media total of the 100 and 11.8% of all advertiser measured media in 2001, raised their collective consumer media 1.1%. That's a start.

From AdAge.com by R. Craig Endicott, AD AGE LEADING NATIONAL ADVERTISERS REPORT, June 28, 2002.

Col. 1:
- 6 **decline** decrease
- 10 **to be scarred** [skɑːd] to be affected by s.th. in a negative way
- 12 **plagued** [pleɪgd] being continually bothered by s.th.
- 16 **reduction** decrease
- 19 **to prove to be** to show evidence of being s.th.
- 20 **dedicated** fully supportive of s.th. – **maintenance level spending** spending enough money to keep s.th. at a certain level
- 25 **expenditure** money spent
- 26 **outlay** expenditure
- 27 **to hit** (informal) to reach

Col. 2:
- 2 **CMR** provider of marketing information
- 6 **cornucopia** [ˌkɔːnjʊˈkəʊpɪə] a lot of different things
- 8 **event marketing** when companies organize an event to sell a product
- 10 **to appropriate** [əˈprəʊprɪeɪt] to make use of s.th. for one's own purposes
- 13 **cost-conscious** being careful about expenses – **to pervade** to be present everywhere
- 15 **albeit** [ɔːlˈbiːɪt] although – **marginal** minimal
- 16 **kingpin** (informal) the most important person in a certain area

Looking at statistics

1. Look at the statistics in Fig. 1 showing the top ten advertisers in the U.S. in 2001.
   a) Consider similarities and differences in the amounts that they spent on advertising in 2001 compared to 2000.
   b) Give reasons for similarities, differences and trends which you can identify.
2. a) Find the top ten advertisers in the statistics in Fig. 2 and comment on the types of media preferred by them.
   b) Identify trends in the statistics in Fig. 2 and try to explain them. For example, which type of companies advertise in which type(s) of media? Why?

Working with the text

Read the text and answer the following questions:
1. Why was 2001 similar to 1991?
2. How did the advertising spending of the top 100 compare with advertising spending as a whole?
3. Explain the term "unmeasured media" (Col. 2, l. 4) in your own words.
4. What positive news is there for the advertising world at the end of the article?
5. Why do you think that world events (recession, wars, etc.) affect advertising spending? Think of other phenomena that might affect advertising spending positively and negatively. Explain your choices.

> **Talking about statistics**
> See *Skills file* on p. 207.

9 Mad for ads

Advertising standards

Advertisements should be:
- legal, decent, honest and truthful
- prepared with a sense of responsibility to consumers and to society
- in line with the principles of fair competition generally accepted in business

Before you read: Pot Noodle has learnt …

1. a) Look at three of the codes for print advertising in Britain in the box to the left. Explain in your own words what you think each point means. If possible use examples.
   b) Think of cases in which adverts might break these codes and write sentences to show what you mean.
   For example: An advert would be illegal if it encouraged people to buy stolen goods.
2. What other principle(s) do you think should be added to the list?
3. Check out the websites of the Ad Council (U.S.) and the Advertising Standards Authority (Britain). Make a table in which you compare the functions of the two bodies.

Working with the text

1. On what grounds has the new Pot Noodle ad been banned?
2. What were Pot Noodle trying to say with their new slogan?
3. What have been the effects of the latest Hula Hoops ad?
4. Apart from banning ads, what can the ITC order the companies to do with them?
5. What changes have been going on in the world of charity advertisements?
6. What does the writer mean when she says we have "grown cynical" about certain ads?
7. Where do you think advertising will have to go next to shock us?
8. What do some of these banned adverts have in common?

Further activities

1. Look on the internet and/or in magazines and newspapers and find at least three examples of adverts which shock you or which you think shouldn't be allowed. Explain what you find offensive about the adverts.
2. a) Try and find at least three examples of adverts which have caused public anger in Britain. Use some of the weblinks given as a starting point or go to an online newspaper and type relevant words into their search engine.
   b) For each of the adverts, consider whether you would recommend a ban on it, then write a paragraph on each explaining your decision. You should write this in the form of a report, stating the following:
   why people would complain about the advert • arguments for banning it • arguments against banning it • your decision on the advert • why you feel, on balance, that your decision is right • advice for that company or similar companies for the future
3. Work in a group. Imagine that you have been asked to draw up some rules and guidelines for people who wish to advertise in your school paper. Your group has been asked to come up with details of how these regulations would work in practice. Copy the following table leaving enough space for your answers and complete it with examples of adverts that you would find unacceptable, and reasons why you would not want to see these ads published.

Category	Type of ads you would ban	Reason for these bans
Illegal	ads showing cigarettes	pupils might buy them
Misleading		
Offensive		
Irresponsible		

Check the web

www.asa.org.uk
Advertising Standards Authority: find out about recent decisions they have made in their archive; look at their mission statement to see how they interpret their role

www.adcouncil.org
The Ad Council in the U.S.: find out what their main activities are and look at their mission statement

www.bbfc.co.uk
British Board of Film Classification – responsible for giving ratings to all films released in the UK

www.itc.org.uk
Independent Television Commission: checks all TV ads before they are allowed on air

www.tradingstandards.gov.uk
Trading Standards website: If you are sold a faulty or dangerous product you can find out how to take action against shops and suppliers

www.subvertise.org
"subverts" (subverted adverts): a group of people who are unhappy with the inaccuracies of modern ads – change, delete or add words and pictures to existing posters to make something new

Pot Noodle has learnt that it is just trash cuisine

OVER the past few years, Pot Noodle has come to accept its role in the culinary world. No longer does it aim to be some kind of gourmet noodle plat du jour in an exquisitely crafted plastic cup. It has learnt that it is lazy, post-pub fodder, up there with the kebab in the higher echelons of trash cuisine.

Its latest advertising campaign proudly announces that Pot Noodle is "the slag of snacks". However, it is this very campaign that has landed Pot Noodle in hot water (and stir). After 130 complaints, the Broadcasting Standards Commission has labelled the slogan (not the snack) "disgusting" and the advert has been banned from television before the 9pm watershed.

Pot Noodle is not alone. In recent weeks, several advertisements have found themselves on the wrong side of the censors. The latest Hula Hoops ad for SHOKS, showing electric eels slithering out of taps, emerging from toilets and gliding up people's legs, received 106 complaints in its first week. Although some came from animal lovers concerned for eel welfare, the vast majority were made by parents. Young children believed that Hula Hoops really had tipped thousands of electric eels into Britain's water supply. The ad now cannot be shown before 7.30pm.

Complaints have also been filed for the Carling ad featuring a man licking his home clean as his girlfriend sprinkles lager around the house, and the X-Box games console, showing a man crashing into his grave. After 136 complaints, the Independent Television Commission (ITC) declared the X-Box advertisement "offensive, shocking and in bad taste". They reminded the Broadcast Advertising Clearance Centre that they must be aware of people's sensitivities to subjects such as death before they give an advert the green light to be shown on television.

Shock advertising is becoming increasingly popular. We're seeing more naked flesh, more expletives, more sexual innuendo than ever before. Confrontational, overtly sexual advertising campaigns owe much to lads' mags, which desensitised us not only to the sight of naked female flesh and soft-porn imagery, but also propounded a kind of aggressive, irreverent lingo.

The issue is whether the public arena is an appropriate venue for such images and language. Writ large on billboards, or broadcast throughout the day, the images are there to be seen by young children.

At the other end of the scale, we are also being exposed to more harrowing images of abuse, poverty and illness, courtesy of charitable organisations. Having learnt the tricks the advertising industry uses to flog soft drinks, underwear and perfume, they too are turning to shock tactics to convey their message.

Charities, however, have a more emotive card to play. The adverts for Barnardo's – "Battered as a child, it was always possible that John would turn to drugs …" – plunge the viewer into a murky world of pimps, drug abuse and suicide.

What they say

In 2000, the Advertising Standards Authority received 13,199 complaints. The most complained-about advertiser was Yves St Laurent, with 948 complaints. YSL came under attack for its adverts for Opium perfume, starring a naked Sophie Dahl.

A constant bombardment of such images is numbing our response. When the first images of starving children in Ethiopia were broadcast by the BBC, we could not tear our eyes away. But, over the years, we have seen these pictures again and again. We no longer feel that sudden lurch of compassion. Similarly we have grown cynical about the tear-jerking charity appeals showing vulnerable and abused children. They have consequently been forced to adopt increasingly graphic approaches.

Quite where advertising goes next is anyone's guess. Perhaps the most shocking thing would be to see an advert that didn't use expletives or naked flesh to sell its product.

By Laura Barton, Education Guardian, July 2, 2002.

Col. 1: *5* **plat du jour** *(French)* dish of the day – **exquisitely** [ɪk'skwɪzɪtlɪ] finely – *7* **fodder** usually refers to animal food – *8* **echelon** ['eʃəlɒn] level – *12* **slag** *(BE rude)* Schlampe – *18* **to ban** to forbid s.th. – *19* **watershed** *(BE) here:* the time before which material unsuitable for children may not be broadcasted – *24* **SHOKS** savoury snacks shaped like Hula Hoops – *25* **tap** Wasserhahn – *32* **to tip** *here:* to pour – *36* **to file a complaint** to make an official complaint

Col. 2: *2* **to sprinkle** to spread – *11* **sensitivity** especially strong feeling about s.th. – *13* **to give s.th. the green light** to declare s.th. alright to do – *17* **expletive** ['---] bad language – *18* **innuendo** [ˌɪnjuˈendəʊ] negative indirect reference – *19* **overtly** [-'--] obviously – *20* **to owe** *here:* to have gotten s.th. from another source – *24* **to propound** to promote – *25* **irreverent** disrespectful – **lingo** language – *27* **appropriate** proper – **venue** ['venjuː] where s.th. takes place – *28* **writ large** *(lit.)* very obvious – *33* **to be exposed to** to be put in a situation where experiences s.th., usu. unpleasant or harmful – **harrowing** very upsetting – *35* **courtesy of** thanks to – *37* **to flog** *(informal)* to sell

Col. 3: *2* **to convey** to communicate – *5* **emotive** emotional – *6* **battered** hit – *8* **to plunge s.o.** *here:* to put s.o. suddenly into a situation – *9* **murky** dark and dirty – **pimp** Zuhälter – *20* **to numb** to reduce or cut off feeling – *23* **to tear one's eyes away** [teə] *(fig.)* to look away – *27* **lurch** *here:* a strong feeling – **compassion** the feeling of wanting to relieve others' suffering – *28* **tear-jerking** [tɪə] causing tears – *34* **anyone's guess** s.th. that no one knows

9 Mad for ads

"I think the dosage needs adjusting. I'm not nearly as happy as the people in the ads."

Looking at the cartoon
1. Who are the two people and where are they?
2. What do you think is wrong with the woman and what kind of medicine is she taking?
3. What kind of magazine and advertisements do you think they are referring to?
4. The woman says she is "not nearly as happy as the people in the ads". Would you therefore consider the ads to be out of line with the advertising code? Why/Why not?
5. Write a spoof* letter to the Advertising Standards Authority complaining about the adverts from the woman's point of view.

*spoof = seemingly serious but in fact meant as a joke

> **Cartoons**
> See *Skills file* on p. 190.

Advertising is everywhere

Before you read
- Make a list of all the different kinds of advertising that you encounter on a daily basis.
- How many of these types of advertisements have you come across already today?
- Which adverts (if any) remain in your mind? Why?

After reading

Working with the text
1. Which diarist …
   a) … points out in an amusing way that adverts can have a strong influence on particular groups such as young people or those with low self-esteem?
   b) … sees the necessity for advertising as a way to make publications cheaper?
   c) … makes light of adverts and shows how they may produce a completely different effect to the one intended?
   d) … takes the adverts seriously and thinks that women are often misused to sell products?
2. Make a list of the print and TV adverts described in the diary entries and say what effect they had on the particular diarist.
3. In your opinion, which of the ads/spots described in the article might not uphold the codes of advertising? Give reasons for your answer.

Language & style
1. Write down the noun form of the following words:
   starved • imply • portray • remind • relax • resign • defend • provocative
2. Compare the register used in the various diary extracts by considering the following points:
   the tone • the vocabulary (e.g. formal/informal/etc.) • the syntax (e.g. long, complicated sentences or short, easy sentences)

Discussion
"Men and women interpret adverts differently." Discuss.
Either write an essay or have a class discussion.

> **Essay writing**
> See *Skills file* on p. 184.
>
> **Having a discussion**
> See *Skills files* on pp. 191 & 192.

Advertising is everywhere

ADVERTISING is everywhere: on the small screen, the big screen, the street, in the news practically everywhere you look. But what do people really think of it?

Oona King, Labour MP
7.30am I feel it's a bit early to watch Angela Rippon doing high-leg kicks in a micro-miniskirt, so I switch off the TV. [...] Before switching off, I see an ad for the new Peugeot 607 and ask myself what a woman's half-starved, semi-naked body has to do with a V6 engine. [...]

Midday Another journey, another billboard and this time it's alcohol – cognac. The ad reads: "Rules? I make them up as I go along." It shows a very beautiful woman, silk dress slit to the crotch, oozing sex and availability. Again, this implies she's yours so long as the price is right. There's no getting away from it: members of my gender are portrayed as whimsical whores, no matter what the product. That is the one rule that never changes. And the one product used to sell all others is the female body. New crime statistics show that, though overall crime is down, violent crime is up. More women being attacked. I'm an old-fashioned type who thinks crime against women is linked to media portrayals of pouting, lusting females who say no but mean yes. [...]

Tamzin Outhwaite, *EastEnders* actor
7am On my way to work, I spot a McDonald's ad which reminds me that I haven't eaten yet. I don't crave McDonald's, but I increase my speed, hoping I can grab a bacon sandwich and a coffee before work.

10am While browsing through *Elle*, I spot an Oasis ad with a healthy-looking girl in red lying on the grass with shiny, scarlet tomatoes all around her. She is smiling with her eyes closed, looking ecstatic. All I can think is how I need to eat more fruit and veg. I don't think: "Must rush to Oasis to buy some new clothes." [...]

11pm Late-night ads always appear more interesting and after a long day, I am relaxing in front of the TV when I see one for *Secret Satin*. It consists of many flashing images of hunky, built-up men, leaving me wondering what the product is. I wait and wait, and eventually it appears. It is a deodorant and an English rose-like girl gives a sexy look. That's it? Is the message that if you wear *Secret Satin* you can be with men like this? [...] I resign myself to the fact that sex sells. [...]

Juliet Soskice, St Luke's ad agency
7.05am Cup of tea. *The Big Breakfast* has some great ad breaks and I'm disappointed when people are snobby about advertising. Without it, there'd be no Channel 4 and your *Weekend Guardian* would cost you a fiver. And advertising is so often a part of the entertainment experience – would *Vogue* be better without all the beautiful photos selling beautiful stuff? [...]

3pm R4's *Today* programme rings to ask if someone can go on to defend the latest IKEA ad, featuring a naked tattooed man, as it's been voted most hated ad of the year by one magazine and best campaign of the year by another. We are all delighted because advertising should be provocative and insightful, treat people intelligently and create debate. Any ad that ridicules or upsets people who don't deserve it is rarely good advertising.

Arabella Weir, author and comedian
4am Woken by screams of 19-month-old son. Feel sure his upset is caused by the ad we spotted yesterday for Holmes Place gym, the place to be for people hoping to lead a leaner, fuller life. He is on the chunky side and may be feeling the subtle pressure of those ads. After all, the woman emerging from the pool does seem to have everything: a good figure, lots of friends, health and a blue swimming costume. Who could ask for anything more?

7.30am Three-year-old daughter insists she must have "grittelly" (read glittery) bra top and nail polish. As am currently not working as a stripper, am puzzled to fathom where such glamorous apparel has been espied. "From the TV." Naturally, where else? [...]

12.45pm [...] Flick through glossy mag and am assaulted by image upon image of thin, gorgeous women, all with posh three-wheeler prams, as far from our food-encrusted buggy as their glistening new Land Rover Discovery is from our beaten up old VW.

From The Guardian, *January 30, 2001.*

Col. 1:
8 **Angela Rippon** former newsreader, and TV personality
14 **billboard** *(AE)* large board used to display posters, usu. at the side of the road
18 **crotch** where one's legs join – **to ooze** *(here fig.)* to clearly suggest
19 **availability** here: willingness to have sex – **to imply** to suggest
22 **whimsical** unpredictable
23 **whore** [hɔː] *(negative)* prostitute
27 **overall** total
31 **to pout** to push one's lips forward to look attractive
37 **to crave s.th.** to really want s.th.
40 **to browse** to leaf through without reading in detail
41 **Oasis** chain of fashion shops
43 **scarlet** bright red
52 **hunky** *(informal)* big, strong and attractive

Col. 2:
4 **to resign o.s.** to accept s.th. which one cannot change
11 **Channel 4** *(GB)* TV station which finances itself by means of sponsorship and advertising
13 **fiver** *(BE informal)* a five-pound note
18 **to go on** here: to be a guest on the programme
24 **insightful** giving a greater understanding of s.th.
34 **lean** having little fat
35 **on the chunky side** having a short strong body
42 **glittery** shiny
45 **to fathom** [ˈfæðəm] to understand s.th. fully – **apparel** *(formal)* clothing
46 **to espy** *(old)* to notice
50 **gorgeous** beautiful – **posh** *(informal)* expensive, elegant

9 Mad for ads

Consumerism

Before you read: One woman in five …
- What/Who would you consider to be a 'shopaholic'? (Do you know anyone who you consider to be a 'shopaholic'?)
- Do you think shopaholism is a serious problem or do you find it amusing?
- Find out about attitudes to shopping amongst your classmates. Find out:
  who enjoys shopping and who doesn't • how much time people spend shopping and what they most frequently shop for • how much on average they spend • how they pay (cash, cash card, credit card, etc.) and/or whether they would prefer to pay by credit card • etc.
  Note any differences in attitudes between boys and girls in your class. Express your findings in a few short sentences.

Working with the text
1. What is retail therapy?
2. a) What words and phrases in the text are used to describe "omniomania"?
   b) Explain the term "omniomania" in your own words.
3. Why are the figures on shopaholism probably inaccurate?
4. What factors may encourage shopaholism?
5. a) What solutions are suggested to deal with the condition?
   b) Which of the solutions do you think might be of use to Elizabeth?
   c) Can you think of any other solutions?

Language
1. Find opposites and synonyms/synonymous phrases for the following verbs:
   Col. 1: to combine (l. 8) • to obtain (l. 28) • to save (l. 51) • to mask (l. 60)
   Col. 2: to combat (l. 19) • to assemble (l. 40) • to protect (l. 45) • to inhibit (l. 46) • to drop (l. 58)
2. Define the following phrases:
   Col. 1: leisure pursuit (ll. 2/3) • low self-esteem (l. 44) • empowerment (l. 66)
   Col. 2: epidemic proportions (l. 4) • anti-depressant (l. 38)

A step further
"Omniomania is reaching epidemic proportions." Discuss causes and solutions.

🎧 One woman in five is a shopaholic

Col. 1:
6 **to overtake s.th.** *here:* to reach a higher level than s.th. else
11 **compulsive** driven by an uncontrollable desire
12 **in debt** [det] owing money to other people

Col. 2:
5 **to reveal** *here:* to show s.th. which had been unknown
9 **pathological** *(informal)* unreasonable

[…] Retail therapy has become one of Britain's most pleasurable leisure pursuits. But the percentage of the population suffering from the serious medical condition of shopping addiction is reaching crisis point, overtaking the number of drug and drink addicts in the UK combined.

Experts believe 10 per cent of the population, and possibly 20 per cent of women, are manic, compulsive shoppers. Most shopaholics are seriously in debt, and the condition has led to family break-ups, depression, homelessness and even suicide.

Known as omniomania, the condition has been known to psychiatrists since the early 1900s but only now is it reaching epidemic proportions. A European Union report recently revealed that up to half of 14- to 18-year-old girls in Scotland, Italy and Spain exhibited symptoms of shopping addiction, with 8 per cent showing signs of a 'pathological compulsion'.

Jim Goudie, a consumer psychologist at Northumbria University, said the stigma of being a shopaholic, and the fact that so few people take the condition seriously, may be masking an even higher number of sufferers.

"Our figures would correlate to research done in the US showing a similar percentage of the population there suffering from shopping problems. But with some people feeling that being a shopping addict is so downright silly, the true statistics could be much higher."

"One of the reasons behind this sudden rise could be that shopping has never been so attractive. Shopping centres are beautiful these days, absolute wonderlands. Store cards are offered at the till and people can obtain handfuls of credit cards with relative ease."

Five credit-card companies are in the process of taking Elizabeth, 31, a businesswoman from Leeds to court. While speaking to *The Observer* she opened her wardrobe to count 26 handbags and 72 pairs of shoes.

"I can't begin to count my clothes, that would take all day," she said. "I guess my real weakness is jewellery, though. I do have quite a lot although most of it is the cheaper stuff."

Elizabeth has been offered *Prozac* by her GP in an attempt to counter her addiction, which he believes is sparked by low self-esteem. She has just sold her flat and paid off an overdraft of £4,700. But she is still shopping.

"It started when Harvey Nichols opened a shop in Leeds," she said. "Everyone in my office was forever rushing off and coming back with bags of lovely stuff but I was saving for a holiday and I felt really left out. I thought, "Stuff it", and went mad buying clothes for my holiday on my credit card. It was a fantastic rush, a great feeling. Then all of a sudden I was just buying stuff all the time. I don't even remember applying for all the cards, they just seemed to appear."

Goudie believes shopping addiction masks deeper problems. "Mostly there is underlying depression and anxiety. Often it can be a disturbed relationship with one's parents. Cold and unemotional parents often lavish presents on children and so they associated that with pleasure."

"Empowerment is also an increasing trend among young, professional women. I had one woman who bought 150 pairs of shoes, shopping gave her a buzz. They take the purchase home, feel guilty, then go back out and shop to combat the depression."

Consumer debt is one of the most rapidly growing national problems in the UK. The National Association for Citizens' Advice Bureaux reported a 37 percent increase in calls on the subject in just two years. Last year CAB advisers received half a million calls concerning shopping debts. [...]

"Our debt calls used to be from people who couldn't pay the gas bill, now it's a multitude of consumer debts," said an association spokeswoman.

The problem is now being taken seriously. At Stanford University in California 24 women are involved in a trial to see whether the condition can be treated by a specific anti-shopaholic drug, similar to an anti-depressant.

Next month the government will assemble a task force to look at the problem of easy access to credit for those who cannot afford to repay what they are spending. Kim Howells, Minister for Consumer Affairs, said: "The Government's aim is to protect the vulnerable without inhibiting a good, innovative market for the vast majority."

Shopping addiction can reach astonishing levels among the rich – this month Sir Elton John admitted going on a £40 million shopping spree in less than two years. [...]

Adrienne Baker, a psychotherapist and author of *Serious Shopping*, said: "Taking illegal substances in excess is one thing, to shop till you drop arouses only amusement."

Baker became interested in omniomania after the suicide of a young friend. The girl died leaving "a plethora of beautiful, unworn clothes" in her flat.

By Tracy McVeigh, The Observer on Sunday, *November 26, 2000.*

Col. 1:
- 16 **to correlate** to correspond
- 21 **downright** completely
- 27 **store card** credit card for a particular shop; customers can pay back the money they owe in installments (Raten)
- 41 *Prozac* (brandname) medication used to control depression
- 42 **GP** short for general practitioner, i.e. medical doctor – **to counter** to deal with
- 43 **to be sparked by s.th.** to be caused by s.th.
- 45 **overdraft** money owed to the bank when one spends more than there is in one's account
- 52 **to feel left out** to feel excluded – **Stuff it** (BE, informal) I can do what I like
- 54 **rush** a strong excited feeling
- 64 **to lavish s.th. on s.o.** to give s.o. too much of s.th.

Col. 2:
- 17 **buzz** a quick feeling of happiness or excitement
- 36 **trial** *here:* test
- 41 **access** ['ækses] being able to get s.th.
- 45 **the vulnerable** *here:* those who are likely to run up debts
- 51 **shopping spree** when one buys a lot at one time
- 58 **to arouse** [ə'raʊz] to cause
- 64 **plethora** (formal) many things; more than one needs

9 Mad for ads

E-tailing

E-tailing
See also the text "Internet shopping 'could divide British society'" in chapter 1, p. 17.

Before you read
- Could you imagine buying or have you ever bought goods or services on the internet? Say why, why not.
- What kind of people or groups might be most interested in shopping on the internet?
- What advantages/disadvantages does this type of shopping have?

Working with the text
1. Make a table in which you list the advantages and disadvantages of net shopping according to the text.
2. a) Explain what the writer means by a "digital divide" (Col. 3, l. 4) in Britain.
   b) What factors do you think could cause this type of divide?
3. According to the report how might the present distribution system be improved in the future?

Mind maps
See *Skills file* on p. 180.

Language
Make a mind map of all the words and phrases in the text concerned with 'e-commerce'.

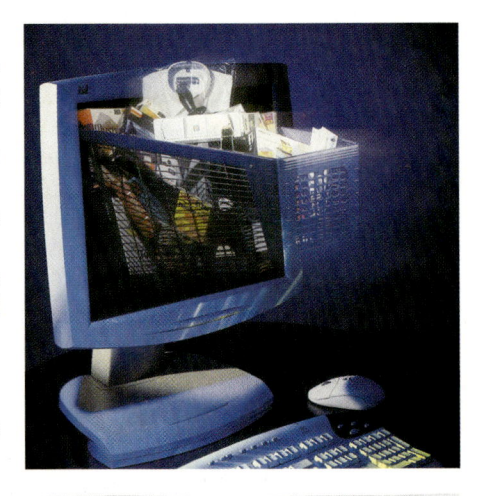

Shopping on the net could jam the roads

Spates of e-road rage are forecast if the popularity of shopping over the internet keeps growing at its current rate.

The prediction is just one conclusion of a detailed report on the impact of e-commerce on transport and logistics by the University of Bradford.

It says residential areas could be overwhelmed by fleets of delivery vans carrying growing volumes of web-ordered goods. Shoppers freed from the weekly supermarket run may then use their cars for other trips, causing an upsurge in traffic and driver frustration.

Peter James, one of the report's authors, said that despite the current shake-out in e-commerce, the trend for internet shopping would have a major impact on everyone's lives over the next decade.

"There could be many benefits, such as easier shopping, lower costs within supply chains and greater access to local shops for the disabled and elderly, and to world markets for small companies. But there could also be disadvantages such as more transport," said Professor James. [...]

The report confirms the positive effects of e-business include its improvement of distribution efficiency, reduction of waste and costs to consumers, and the creation of broader markets for small producers, especially in remote regions.

However, these are offset by the negative effect of a greater use of air freight, extra delivery van traffic and an increased demand for warehousing at strategic locations such as the M1/M62 interchange. Supermarkets could also be closed as shopping patterns change.

Peter Hopkinson, a senior lecturer in business strategy and the environment, said the research showed that the new economy was concentrated in London and the southeast. "There's currently a digital divide between people and regions who can access and develop e-commerce and those who can't," he said.

The report's authors point out that the situation could change rapidly. While growth in home shopping would be based on the existing infrastructure of supermarkets, parcel carriers and collection points in the short term, when it reached 5–10 per cent of total retail sales significant change would occur.

This would include development of pick centres, closure of supermarkets, and the creation of new distribution channels such as purpose-built drop-off and collection networks. [...]

By Sue Law, The Times Higher Educational Supplement, *April 20, 2001.*

Col. 1: *1* **spate** many things happening suddenly – *9* **to overwhelm** to present s.o. with an excessive amount of s.th. – *12* **run** *here:* visit – *14* **upsurge** sudden, big increase – *16* **shake-out** closing companies due to strong competition
Col. 2: *1* **supply chain** network of e.g. companies, involved in product supply – *2* **the disabled** *Behinderte* – *9* **distribution efficiency** low cost delivery of products – *11* **broader** *here:* bigger – *12* **remote** far from towns and cities – *13* **to offset s.th.** to balance s.th. – *16* **warehousing** storing of goods – *17* **M1/M62 interchange** *(GB)* where two motorways meet – *19* **pattern** habit
Col. 3: *12* **parcel** package – *15* **retail sales** selling of products by shops – *18* **pick centre** place where a customer's order is assembled – *20* **drop-off** place where goods are left to be collected later

Mad for ads 9

Project 1: Reaching teenagers

Work in a group of three or four.
You are part of the Nascar advertising team (see pp. 138–139) which wants to put together a magazine ad that will appeal especially to teenagers – both male and female.
First you need to find out more about this section of the population.
- ▶ Put together a survey on "the interests and preferences of teenagers". (You could include a mixture of multiple choice and open questions about topics such as preferred foods and drinks, TV viewing habits, preferred reading material, tastes in music, spare time activities and so on.)
- ▶ Carry out your survey in class. Combine all of your results on one sheet of paper. Work out the trends which apply to the majority of the class.
- ▶ In your advertising teams decide on an outline for the ad using the data you have gathered. Then design your advertisement in detail.
- ▶ Present your ad in class referring to the findings in your survey.

Project 2: Internet Project

Work in a group of three or four.
The Mall of America is a huge shopping centre in Bloomington, Minnesota. Visit its website at www.mallofamerica.com/ and find out the following facts and create a dossier on the Mall:
- ▶ its size and location
- ▶ the type of stores you can find there
- ▶ the services on offer other than the possibility to shop
- ▶ the types of entertainment for families
- ▶ the Mall's impact on the local economy (e.g. as regards employment, its importance as a tourist attraction and so on).

Project 3: Glossary

Work in a group of three or four.
Design and produce a glossary of terms for advertising & consumerism.
- ▶ Collect words from the chapter.
- ▶ View glossaries available on the Internet and choose relevant terms to include from them.
- ▶ Arrange your terms logically (i.e. A–Z and/or thematically)

If possible, process your data on a computer and print it out for your classmates to view.

Project 4: A TV spot

Work in a group of three or four.
You work for a large supermarket chain in Britain which wants to increase online sales. In your team work out a scenario for a TV spot which will bring people's attention to this facility and show its benefits.

10 USA: People, politics, perspectives

What is an American?

Describing the cartoon
1. a) Which aspects of being American are shown in this cartoon? Make a mind map with key words and phrases that come to mind as you look at this cartoon. Include the following subtopics in your mind map:

    entertainment • business • politics • values • architecture • societal problems

    b) Put a minus (-) sign beside aspects you think aren't typically American.
    c) Add any important aspects to your mind map that have been left out of the cartoon.
2. In groups, compare and discuss your mind maps and come up with a list of 10 aspects describing what you think is "typically American".

Mind maps
See *Skills file* on p. 180.

Having a discussion
See *Skills files* on pp. 191 & 192.

Going further
1. Read the following short excerpt from *Letters From an American Farmer*, written in 1782 by Hector St. Jean de Crevecoeur:

    What then is the American, this new man? He is either an European, or the descendant of an European, hence that strange mixture of blood, which you will find in no other country. […] Here individuals of all nations are melted into a new race of men, whose labors and posterity will one day cause great changes in the world. Americans are the western pilgrims, who are carrying along with them that great mass of arts, sciences, vigor, and industry which began long since in the east; they will finish the great circle.

2. Do you think that the description of an American in this excerpt matches what is portrayed in the cartoon? Why or why not?

Check the web
Get more information about Hector St. Jean de Crevecoeur and his works at:
http://xroads.virginia.edu/~HYPER/CREV/home.html

USA: People, politics, perspectives 10

Americans about America …

(1) "For me, [being American] means the freedom to be me. You know, like, if I wanna dance, I can just dance. You know, there's no one tellin' me that I have to be a dancer, that I have to be gymnast or anything like that. It's not dictated, you know. You basically have the opportunity to be whatever you want as long as you can find something or somebody to help you along the way."

Kenye, Sierra Leonian/Indian/Scottish American, teenager, born in the U.S.

(2) "I want to say that I think the best part about being American is getting to learn about the entire world without actually leaving this country. Because, you know, I live here, I get to watch Jamihlah perform African dance, I get to listen to Omar tell me about Malcolm X and all the great African American leaders and about Egypt, and because I have a lot of Hispanic friends, I know a lot of Spanish slang. You're exposed to a lot of different cultures, and it keeps you from being really narrow."

Heather Petersen, Irish/Norwegian American, teenager, born in the U.S.

narrow *here:* narrow-minded

(3) "I have seen negative sides to being an American. I think that as people become Americanized and generations stay here, we lose more in touch of our culture. We lose the backgrounds, we lose the dialect, first of all, because we're Americanizing. Like we change the words. I know my family has. We don't practice the same traditions that we had. I know like, in my house, we've changed a lot of traditions. And I think that that's the sad part. I think that we should keep up with those traditions. That's like the down side of being an American."

Christina, Ecuadorian American, teenager, born in U.S.

(4) "I consider myself a Mexican-American but you can't say that in front of [Latino] people sometimes … because they think you're a sell-out or something. … I mean, right now, we're well-off. … I don't speak a lot of Spanish, and sometimes I say Spanish words that sound like English-Spanglish words. and they say 'you're not really Mexican,' or something. 'You're too white to be Mexican.' It makes me feel real horrible, you know, because I'm proud of my parents and the country they came from … I want to spend my life here. I love the United States; I don't know why. I consider myself a Mexican-American, but not just American, and that's it."

Jaime, Mexican American, teenager, born in the U.S.

sell-out s.o. who has done s.th. against his or her principles
well-off doing well

(5) "There are a lot of positive aspects to this country. The right to vote, respect for human rights and more opportunities, especially for children."

Gilbert Sigua, 41, born in the Philippines

(6) "It's my dream. The American dream, to me, is if you really try hard you can do well. You have more chances. I do feel free."

Tseng Tan-Kiang, 36, born in the People's Republic of China

(7) "It was a child's dream to come to America. America is freedom – of speech, movement, religion, and you can vote. I was born in South Africa, but because I was a non-white, I had none of that freedom."

Nazam Bashid Adam, 54, born in South Africa

Working with the text
1. Summarize each person's statements about being American/living in America and record them in a table with a ***positive aspects*** and a ***negative aspects*** column.
2. a) The top four statements are made by U.S.-born teens, whereas the bottom three statements are from adults who were born elsewhere. What differences are there in the types of comments made by the two groups? Give examples.
   b) What reasons can you think of for these differences?

Style
1. Find typical forms of colloquial English in the statements.
2. Rewrite the sentences you find using formal English.

(1–4) Reprinted by permission of American Documentary, Inc./P.O.V. from the website www.pbs.org/pov/ Copyright © 1999 by American Documentary, Inc./ P.O.V.
(5–7) From "Naturalization Ceremony Fills with Appreciation for Freedom" by Bob Arndorfer, The Gainesville Sun, July 28, 1999.

10 USA: People, politics, perspectives

Becoming American

- Write down the associations that come to mind when you hear the words 'American West' and 'frontier'.

"American Progress" by John Gast, 1872

Working with the picture
1. Look at the picture, and add new aspects to your list from above.
2. a) Why do you think the picture is called "American Progress"?
   b) What does this picture say about how Americans viewed themselves at the time?
3. a) Many immigrants who came to America helped to settle the new frontier. Why do you think they were eager for this chance?
   b) Historians say that the process of settling the frontier helped immigrants to acculturate, or become part of the American culture. Why do you think this might have been the case?
   c) Compare this picture with the one on p. 153. Note down any similarities and differences you notice between the two, and talk about possible reasons for these.

Out of many, one

Before you read
- Which of the following terms best describes American multicultural society, and why?
  melting pot • salad bowl • orchestra • mosaic • pizza
- What words would you use to describe your own society? Give reasons.

Working with the text
1. In your own words, explain the message of Israel Zangwill's play *The Melting Pot*.
2. a) Describe the differences between the immigrants who came to the U.S. at the beginning of the nineteenth century and those who come to the U.S. today.
   b) In view of current demographic trends, what are experts certain will happen as a result of this immigrant influx?
   c) What are likely results of these trends?
3. Explain why many historians argue that in the past those who lived in the U.S. had a more unified idea of what it means to be American.

Language & style
1. Which method, word family (1), similar words with German or French origins (2), or context (3) (see *Skills file: Surviving without a dictionary* on p. 194), will you use to figure out the meanings of these words?
   Col. 1: to pour (l. 10) • central (l. 14) • tremendous (l. 16) • to transform (l. 19) • incoming (l. 25)
   Col. 2: far-reaching (l. 1) • overwhelmingly (l. 7) • shift (l. 10) • rapid (l. 10) • descent (l. 13) • to evolve (l. 27)
2. Rewrite the sentences in which these words occur, but replace them with suitable synonyms/synonymous phrases.
3. How would you describe the style of this text? Give examples from the text to support your answer.

A step further
1. "Today ... there is more emphasis on preserving one's ethnic identity, of finding ways to highlight and defend one's cultural roots." (Col. 3, ll. 24–28). Do you think that this is a positive or a negative trend in the U.S.? Discuss.
2. a) Look at the websites on this page and describe the positions of these organizations about immigration in the U.S.
   b) Which website do you find most convincing? Give reasons for your answer.

> **Check the web**
> Get more information about the FAIR organization at:
> **http://www.fairus.org/**
> the Immigration Forum Orgnization at:
> **http://www.immigrationforum.org/**

USA: People, politics, perspectives

"Welcome to the Land of Freedom" 1887. Drawing by a passenger aboard the "Germanic".

Out of many, one

AT THE BEGINNING of this century, as steamers filled with European immigrants poured into American ports, a Jew from England named Israel Zangwill wrote a play whose story line has long been forgotten, but whose central theme has not. His production was entitled "The Melting Pot" and its message still holds a tremendous power on the national imagination – the promise that all immigrants can be transformed into Americans, a new alloy forged in a crucible of democracy, freedom and civic responsibility.

In 1908, when the play opened in Washington, the United States was in the middle of absorbing the largest incoming group of immigrants in its history – Irish and Germans, followed by Italians and East Europeans, Catholics and Jews – some 18 million new citizens between 1890 and 1920.

Today, the United States is experiencing its second wave of immigration, a movement of people that has far-reaching implications for a society that by tradition pays homage to its immigrant roots at the same time it confronts complex and deeply ingrained ethnic and racial divisions.

The immigrants of today come not from Europe but overwhelmingly from the still developing world of Asia and Latin America. They are driving a demographic shift so rapid that within the lifetimes of today's teenagers, no one ethnic group – including whites of European descent – will make up a majority of the nation's population.

This shift, according to social historians, demographers and others studying the trends, will severely test the premise of the legendary melting pot, the idea, so central to national identity, that this country can transform people of every color and background into "one America".

Just as possible, they say, is that the nation will continue to split into many separate, disconnected communities with no shared sense of commonality or purpose. Or perhaps it will evolve into something in between, a pluralistic society that will hold on to some core ideas about citizenship and capitalism, but with little meaningful interaction among groups.

The demographic changes raise other questions about political and economic power. Will that power, now held disproportionately by whites, be shared in the new America? What will happen now that Hispanics have overtaken blacks as the nation's single largest minority?

[…] Fear of strangers, of course, is nothing new in American history. The last great immigration wave produced a bitter backlash, epitomized by the Chinese Exclusion Act of 1882 and the return, in the 1920s, of the Ku Klux Klan, which not only targeted blacks, but Catholics, Jews and immigrants as well.

But despite this strife, many historians argue that there was a greater consensus in the past on what it meant to be an American, a yearning for a common language and culture, and a desire – encouraged, if not forced by members of the dominant white Protestant culture – to assimilate. Today, they say, there is more emphasis on preserving one's ethnic identity, of finding ways to highlight and defend one's cultural roots.

Adapted from "One Nation Indivisible: Is it History?" By William Booth, The Washington Post, Feb. 22, 1998. © 1998, The Washington Post. Reprinted with permission.

Col. 1: 9 **steamer** a steam ship (one driven by a steam engine) – 12 **story line** plot – 16 **message** ['mesɪdʒ] the point that is to be made – 20 **alloy** ['ælɔɪ] the result of mixing metals together – **to forge** [fɔːdʒ] schmieden – **crucible** ['kruːsɪbl] (lit.) here: Schmelztiegel – 21 **civic** ['sɪvɪk] citizens'

Col. 2: 2 **homage** ['hɒmɪdʒ] respect – 3 **roots** Wurzeln – 5 **ingrained** [--'] difficult to change – 9 **to drive** here: to cause – 17 **severely** [sɪ'vɪəli] greatly – 18 **premise** ['premɪs] idea – 24 **to split** to come apart – 26 **commonality** the state of having s.th. in common – 29 **core** key – 31 **interaction** communicating and working together

Col. 3: 4 **disproportionately** to a comparatively large degree – 12 **backlash** strong reaction against s.th. – **to epitomize** [ɪ'pɪtəmaɪz] to be a typical example of s.th. – 17 **despite** in spite of – **strife** conflict – 20 **yearning** strong desire for s.th.

153

10 USA: People, politics, perspectives

Before you read: Governor Locke's remarks – …
- Would you ever change your nationality? If yes, why, and under which circumstances? If no, why not?

Working with the text
1. How does Governor Locke define the American dream?
2. How is Governor Locke an example of the American dream?
3. Governor Locke states that he hopes these new citizens will give the U.S. their "active citizenship" (l. 29). What do you think he means by this?
4. Does Governor Locke expect these new citizens to completely forget their past ways and traditions in favor of new American ones? Why or why not?
5. What other qualities does he hope these new citizens will give to the country, and (when a reason is given) why?

Language
1. Give the noun form for the following verbs in the text:
   - to nourish (l. 3)
   - to create (l. 4)
   - to contribute (l. 21)
   - to benefit (l. 22)
   - to inspire (l. 33)
   - to improve (l. 33)
2. Give the verb form for each of the following nouns in the text:
   - liberty (l. 5)
   - pursuit (l. 5)
   - preparation (l. 8)
   - immigrant (l. 13)
   - belief (l. 18)
3. Give the opposites for these words:
   - dream (l. 4)
   - belief (l. 18)
   - powerful (l. 9)
   - faith (l. 18)
   - seriously (l. 11)
   - vital (l. 38)
4. a) Form collocations by matching the following verbs and nouns from the text:

to evoke	a new art form
to raise	the cause
to shape	a memory
to build	her hand
to spark	a dream
to advance	a country

   b) Find other nouns to complete these collocations and write your own sentences.

> **Opposites & collocations**
> See *Glossary* on pp. 208–210.

Oath of Allegiance
"I hereby declare, on oath, that I absolutely and entirely renounce and abjure all allegiance and fidelity to any foreign prince, potentate, state, or sovereignty of whom or which I have heretofore been a subject or citizen; that I will support and defend the Constitution and the laws of the United States of America against all enemies, foreign and domestic; that I will bear true faith and allegiance to the same; that I will bear arms on behalf of the United States when required by the law; that I will perform noncombatant service in the Armed Forces of the United States when required by the law; that I will perform work of national importance under civilian direction when required by the law; and that I take this obligation freely without any mental reservation or purpose of evasion; so help me God."

Immigration and Naturalization Service (INS) www.ins.gov

A step further
Remember to use the "Skills files" and "Glossary" to do these tasks.
1. *"This country has made its mark on us, and we have made our mark on this country."* (ll. 23–24) Would you say the same about Germany? Discuss.
2. Read the "Oath of Allegiance" which all of those applying for American citizenship must swear before becoming American citizens.
   a) Look up words that you don't know in a dictionary and then summarize the oath in your own words.
   b) How would you describe the register of this quote, and why do you think that this type of register was chosen?

USA: People, politics, perspectives 10

Governor Locke's remarks – Naturalization Ceremony, July 4, 2000

My fellow Americans: Congratulations on becoming citizens of the United States of America.

I welcome you to a life that is nourished and enlarged by the grandeur of the American dream – the dream of a nation in which all people are created equal, and all are endowed by their Creator with the right to life, liberty, and the pursuit of happiness.

For me, those words evoke the memory of my mother, studying the Declaration of Independence as part of her preparation for the citizenship exam. In my five-year-old eyes, the day she became a citizen, she became a bigger, more powerful person. And I know she felt that way, too. I remember how hard she studied, how thrilled she was to raise her right hand and be sworn in, and how seriously she took her new role as a citizen.

My grandfather was also an immigrant to this country. In his youth, he worked as a domestic servant in Olympia in exchange for lessons in English. Today, I live in the Governor's mansion – just a mile away from the house where my grandfather swept floors, cooked, and washed dishes.

So it has taken my family more than 100 years to travel one mile. But what a journey it has been – a journey of hope, hard work, faith and the belief in the American Dream.

My parents held fast to their faith in America's essential goodness, and did all they could to contribute to it. We are like hundreds of millions of immigrant families, who have both benefited from the American dream and helped shape it.

This country has made its mark on us, and we have made our mark on this country. And that is how American progress is made. This country was built with the blood, sweat and tears of Native Americans and immigrants. And successive waves of immigration have served to renew and enrich the American dream, and contribute to the cultural, spiritual and intellectual wealth of our country. I hope you will make your mark, too.

America needs you. America needs your active citizenship, and your fresh perspective on our most intractable problems. And America needs your cultural contribution, too.

This country is the place where anyone from anywhere can be an individual and can invent, inspire and improve. It may be some of you who'll rub cultures to spark a new art form or world vision. Most importantly, America needs your values, and the wisdom forged from your experiences.

You have powerful traditions of strong families, and fortitude in the face of terrible hardship. Those qualities are vital to keeping our nation focused on service to others, respect for our elders and sacrifice for our children.

Your newly-minted citizenship will help to renew America, and to sustain our pride in being the land of the free, and the home of the brave.

So, on behalf of all the people of Washington State, I congratulate you on your new role as citizens of the United States of America. I implore you to use the power that is now vested in you to advance the cause of hope and opportunity. And I invite you to write the next chapter of America's history of progress toward the goals of freedom and equality for all.

Thank you very much.

---

3 **nourished** [ˈnʌrɪʃt] *here:* encouraged to develop – **grandeur** greatness
5 **to endow** [ɪnˈdaʊ] *(formal)* to give – **pursuit** [pəˈsjuːt] attempt to achieve a goal
7 **to evoke** to bring forth – **Declaration of Independence** U.S.-Unabhängigkeitserklärung
10 **thrilled** very excited
11 **to swear s.o. in** jdn. vereidigen

14 **domestic servant** s.o. who is hired to do tasks in the house
15 **mansion** [ˈmænʃn] very large, luxurious house

20 **to hold fast** to not give up
21 **to contribute** [kənˈtrɪbjuːt] to add to
22 **to benefit** to be helped by s.th.
23 **to make a mark on s.o./s.th.** *(fig.)* to have a certain effect (usually positive) on s.o. / s.th.
26 **to renew** [-ˈ-] to increase the strength of s.th. by repetition – **to enrich** [-ˈ-] to improve s.th.

30 **intractable** [-ˈ---] *(formal)* difficult

33 **to rub** to come into contact and move against each other, creating friction – **to spark** *here:* to inspire
35 **to forge** [fɔːdʒ] schmieden
36 **fortitude** *(formal)* strength
37 **hardship** difficult situation
40 **sacrifice** that which one gives up for the benefit of s.o. or s.th. else
41 **newly-minted** *here:* just received
43 **sustain** keep up
45 **on behalf of** [bɪˈhɑːf] in the interest of or as a representative of
49 **to implore** to urgently ask s.o. to do s.th. – **to vest s.th. in s.o.** *(formal)* to give s.o. s.th.

Speech held by Gov. Gary Locke, Governor of the state of Washington, at the Naturalization Ceremony on July 4, 2000.

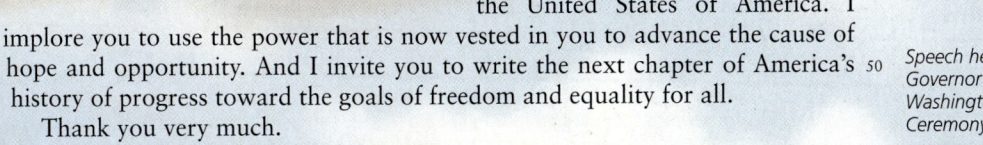

10 USA: People, politics, perspectives

Before you read: Born on the Fourth of July
- Judging by the title, what do you expect the text to be about?

Working with the text
1. Summarize each paragraph in one sentence.
2. a) Why is Ron Kovic bothered by the men helping him out of the car and into the wheelchair?
   b) How do these men treat him?
3. a) Why does the commander refer to Korea and World War II in his speech?
   b) What does the commander mean when he says: "We have to win … because of them!" (ll. 74–77)?

> **Writing a summary**
> See *Skills file* on p. 185.

Language
1. Explain the following examples of figurative speech in your own words:
   to be behind someone (l. 71) • to have one's eyes on someone (l. 82)
2. Replace the underlined words with synonyms/synonymous phrases:
   a) "… where the people from his town had <u>gathered</u> … ." (ll. 26–28)
   b) "When they came to where the speakers' platform had been <u>erected</u>,…" (ll. 33–36)
   c) "… so that their <u>brave</u> sacrifices would not have to be <u>in vain</u>." (ll. 53–59)

Style
1. Where is the literary technique flashback used, and what purpose does this have?
2. How is the commander characterized in this text? Give examples from the text to support your ideas.
3. How would you describe the atmosphere of this text? Give reasons for your answer.

> **Flashback & atmosphere**
> See *Glossary* on pp. 208–210.

A step further
1. During the entire parade and speeches, Kovic and Dugan were never asked to speak about their experiences and feelings. Why do you think that this is the case? Discuss.
2. a) The picture on p. 157 shows a later scene from the film version of this book. The setting is the Republican Convention of 1972. What do you think is going on here?
   b) What do you think the veterans are yelling? What are the Convention delegates thinking?
3. Compare how Ron Kovic is portrayed in the movie scene picture with the text portrayal.

Marine member of a special part of the American Navy
waist [weɪst] *Taille*
to recover to get over an illness or injury
grand marshal person in charge of e.g. a parade
Memorial Day U.S. holiday on May 30 honoring those who have been killed in combat

Born on July 4, 1946, Ron Kovic grew up as an all-American boy with a dream to serve his country. Kovic became a Marine, and experienced the horrors of Vietnam. His combat time ended when he was severely wounded – paralysed from the waist down. Kovic then spent months recovering in hospitals, and was finally able to return home to a life that would never be the same. In this excerpt, he and his friend Eddie Dugan have been asked by people in their hometown to be the grand marshals in the Memorial Day parade. Ron Kovic became famous for his anti-war activism, his fight for veteran rights, and for this book, his memoir of the experiences that made him into a soldier, a veteran and an activist.

Born on the Fourth of July: Annotations

> **Listening comprehension**
> Listen to the song *For America* by Jackson Browne.

3 **cub scout** *junger Pfadfinder* – 8 **to keep in step** (fig.) to walk or run as fast as s.o. else – **Yankee Doodle** title of a Revolutionary War song, here: patriotic – 13 **crepe paper** [kreɪp] long, thin colored paper strips used for decoration – 17 **vet** here: short for veteran – 25 **drum majorette** [ˌmeɪdʒrˈet] a girl or woman in colorful uniform who marches in front and leads the band – 33 **platform** a raised surface upon which speeches or performances take place – 35 **crutches** *Krücken* – 37 **trunk** (AE) the place where you store things (e.g. luggage) in a car – 44 **Legion** short for *American Legion*, U.S. veterans association – 46 **to stagger** [ˈstæɡə] to walk very unsteadily – 55 **dignitary** important person with high rank – 57 **to support** [-ˈ-] to help – 58 **sacrifice** that which s.o. gives up for the good of s.o. or s.th. else – 61 **to measure one's steps** (fig.) to take steps in an exact way – 62 **to jut** to move very suddenly

Born on the Fourth of July

The street was a sea of red, white, and blue. He remembered how he and all the rest of the kids on the block had put on their cub scout uniforms and marched every Memorial Day down these same streets. He remembered the hundreds of people lining the sidewalks, everyone standing and cheering and waving their small flags, his mother standing with the other mothers on the block shouting for him to keep in step. "There's my Yankee Doodle boy!" he'd hear her shouting, and he'd feel embarrassed, pulling his cap over his eyes like he always did.

There were scouts decorating the Cadillac now with red, white, and blue crepe paper and long paper banners that read *welcome home Ron Kovic and Eddie Dugan* and *support our boys in Vietnam*. There was a small sign, too, that read: OUR WOUNDED VIETNAM VETS … EDDIE DUGAN AND RON KOVIC.

When the scouts were finished, the commander came running over to the car with a can of beer in his hand. "Let's go!" he shouted, jumping back in with the heavy guy.

They drove slowly through the crowd until they were all the way up in the front of the parade. He could hear the horns and drums behind him and he looked out and watched the pretty drum majorettes and clowns dancing in the street. He looked out onto the sidewalks where the people from his town had gathered just like when he was a kid.

But it was different. He couldn't tell at first exactly what it was, but something was not the same, they weren't waving and they just seemed to be standing staring at Eddie Dugan and himself like they weren't even there. […]

When they came to where the speakers' platform had been erected, he watched Eddie push himself out of the back seat, then up on his crutches while the heavy guy helped him with the door. The commander was opening the trunk, bringing the wheelchair to the side of the car. He was lifted out by the heavy guy and he saw the people around him watching, and it bothered him because he didn't want them to see how badly he had been hurt and how helpless he was, having to be carried out of the car into the chair like a baby. […]

He pushed himself to the back of the platform where two strong members of the Legion were waiting to lift him up in the chair. "How do you lift this goddamn thing?" shouted one of the men, suddenly staggering, almost dropping him. He tried to tell them how to lift it properly, the way they had shown him in the hospital, but they wanted to do it their own way and almost dropped him a second time.

They finally carried him up the steps of the stage where he was wheeled up front next to Eddie, who sat with his crutches by his side. They sat together watching the big crowd and listening to one speaker after the other, including the mayor and all the town's dignitaries; each one spoke very beautiful words about *sacrifice and patriotism and God*, crying out to the crowd to support the boys in the war so that their brave sacrifices would not have to be in vain.

And then it was the tall commander's turn to speak. He walked up to the microphone slowly, measuring his steps carefully, then jutted his head up and looked directly at the crowd. "*I believe in America!*" shouted the commander, shaking his fist in the air. "*And I believe in Americanism!*" The crowd was cheering now. "*And most of all … most of all, I believe in victory for America!*" He was very emotional. Then he shouted that the whole country had to come together and support the boys in the war. He told how he and the boys' fathers before them had fought in Korea and World War II, and how the whole country had been behind them back then and how they had won a great victory for freedom. Almost crying now, he shouted to the crowd that they couldn't give up in Vietnam. "*We have to win …*" he said, his voice still shaking; then pausing, he pointed his finger at him and Eddie Dugan, "*… because of them!*"

Suddenly it was very quiet and he could feel them looking right at him, sitting there in his wheelchair with Eddie all alone. It seemed everyone – the cub scouts, the boy scouts, the mothers, the fathers, the whole town – had their eyes on them and now he bent his head and stared into his lap. […]

From Born on the Fourth of July *by Ron Kovic, New York: McGraw-Hill Book Company, © 1976, pp. 89 – 93. Reprinted with permission of the McGraw-Hill Companies.*

10 USA: People, politics, perspectives

> **Giving a talk or presentation**
> See *Skills file* on p. 189.

Before you read: Annual meeting of the Bretton Woods Committee
- Create a mind map for the term 'world poverty', and compare yours with those of your classmates'.
- Imagine that you have to give a talk on world poverty. Make an outline for your talk, and ask a partner to look over your outline and give you tips and suggestions.

Working with the text
1. a) According to Colin Powell, what are some important functions of the IMF, the World Bank and the WTO?
   b) Why is it important that America plays a leading role in these organizations?
2. Paraphrase Powell's definition of the term *globalization*.
3. a) What makes it potentially possible to solve the problem of world poverty today?
   b) Summarize the steps that need to be taken/the things that must not be done in order to solve this problem.

Language & translation
1. a) Find as many compound nouns and adjectives as you can in this text.
   b) Translate the sentences in which these words occur.
2. a) Find examples in the text of sentences which use connectives from at least four of the categories in the "Skills file" on page 185.
   b) Rewrite the sentences using different connectives from the same category.

> **Connectives**
> See *Skills file* on p. 185.

> **Analysing style**
> See *Skills file* on p. 181.

Giving a speech
Give a short speech in which you state if you agree or disagree with Colin Powell's definition of globalization, and why. Be sure to use connectives, and try to use rhetorical devices like Powell used in his speech, such as repetition and alliteration.

> **Check the web**
> Get more information about the Bretton Woods Committee at:
> http://www.brettonwoods.org

In July 1944, representatives of the U.S., Britain, France, the Soviet Union and 40 other Allied countries met to discuss how economic and financial prosperity could be established and maintained in the world after the end of World War II. This historic meeting, which took place in Bretton Woods, New Hampshire, came to be known as the Bretton Woods Conference. At that time, a number of important decisions were made and institutions were founded that still exist today, including the founding of the International Bank for Reconstruction and Development (the World Bank) and the International Monetary Fund (IMF). The Bretton Woods Committee meets every year to discuss the changing challenges of the world economic and financial situation. The text below is part of a speech given by Secretary of State Colin Powell at the meeting on April 27, 2001.

🎧 Annual meeting of the Bretton Woods Committee

It is no coincidence that in the early 1940s, as President Roosevelt prepared an isolationist America for war against fascist tyranny, he included freedom from want in his famous four freedoms. It is no coincidence that even while FDR and his administration mobilized our nation for world war, they also began to design the
5 economic architecture of a lasting post-war peace. And it is certainly no coincidence that in 1944, at the Mount Washington Hotel in New Hampshire, the "Live free or die" state, FDR reminded the Bretton Woods delegates that the arrangements they would be making to ensure an orderly, harmonious world would "affect ordinary men and women everywhere and form the basis upon which they will be able to
10 exchange with one another their natural riches of the earth and the products of their own industry and ingenuity."

---

1 **coincidence** s.th. that happens by chance
2 **want** *here:* poverty
8 **to ensure** [-'-] *(formal)* to make certain that s.th. will happen
11 **industry** *here:* hard work – **ingenuity** [ˌɪndʒɪˈnjuːətɪ] skill

And so the IMF and the World Bank and now the WTO are not just about exchange rates, financing infrastructure projects, eliminating trade barriers and structural reform. No. Fundamentally, these instruments are about securing the blessings of liberty and prosperity for more and more ordinary human beings on this planet who wonder if society is there for them.

And I will take every opportunity I have to get the message across to American and foreign audiences alike that in our increasingly globalized world, America's prosperity and well-being are linked ever more closely to expanding growth and stability worldwide. That is why strong United States leadership in the IMF, the World Bank and the WTO is so crucial to America's future and the world's future. [...]

Of course, 57 years ago at Bretton Woods, no one was talking about globalization. The word hadn't even been coined at that time. But that is what they were discussing in reality, globalization in its basic sense, an interconnected world in which national identity and sovereignty are preserved, but in which all countries work together to meet challenges and harvest opportunities, from which no country working alone can derive full advantage.

And that is why I believe the architects of the Bretton Woods system envisioned a world that more resembles the dynamic one we are living in now at the start of the 21st century than it does the static Cold War world that dominated the first four decades of its existence. Globalization, free trade, open markets, the Technology Revolution, economic and political reforms – the potential they hold for humankind is incredible, and the Bretton Woods institutions and the WTO can help the world's people realize it. [...]

And here I want to talk about an enormous challenge that is before us all in this new century, and that is eradicating world poverty. It is a goal that technological advancement and economic growth can put within our grasp at last. Certain fundamental understandings are necessary if in this century we are to liberate more and more of the world's people from the prison of poverty. We must acknowledge first that engagement with the global economy, opening up to trade and investment, is the engine of poverty-easing growth. The last thing nations should do in response to the desperate needs of the ill-housed, ill-fed, uneducated and unhealthy is to adopt policies that have the effect of slowing growth. [...]

Second, we must recognize the investment and education, training and health that stimulates growth, attracts capital, and opens opportunities for the poor.

Third, peace and stability, fair and accountable governance, democracy, respect for human rights and the rule of law – these are the strongest foundations for growth and for the alleviation of poverty. Companies and governments alike must realize that openness, transparency and good government are the building blocks of a healthy investment climate. Political and economic reform must go hand in hand if either is to succeed.

And finally, we must acknowledge that official assistance and private investment alike can play catalytic roles in poverty reduction, provided that they flow to societies that embrace openness to trade, social investment, and good governance. The hard truth is that assistance and investment are ineffective in societies that are closed, corrupt or callous. [...]

I have every confidence that the Bretton Woods and related multilateral economic institutions are finding and will keep finding new and creative ways to contribute to international well-being, that they will not confuse stability with stasis, that they will foster growth generating change, change that frees human potential; in short, that they will not forget those ordinary men and women all over the world who President Roosevelt spoke about when he welcomed the delegates to Bretton Woods on that July day back in 1944.

The U.S. Department of State, www.state.gov

---

12 **WTO** World Trade Organization
13 **barrier** ['bærɪə] s.th. that stands in the way of s.th. else
14 **to secure** [-'-] to get s.th. with a lot of effort
15 **blessing** s.th. good that one is thankful for – **prosperity** [-'---] a financially good situation

21 **crucial** ['kruːʃl] very important

24 **to coin** to invent s.th.

26 **to preserve** to make sure that s.th remains the same
27 **to harvest** *(lit.)* to enjoy the good results of s.th.
28 **to derive** [dɪ'raɪv] *(formal)* to get
29 **to envision** [-'--] to imagine

34 **incredible** s.th. so great that it's almost unbelievable

37 **to eradicate** *(formal)* to get rid of
38 **within one's grasp** *(fig.)* within reach
40 **to acknowledge** [ək'nɒlɪdʒ] to recognize that s.th. is true
42 **engine** ['endʒɪn] *(fig.)* generating force
43 **ill-housed** without good housing conditions

47 **accountable governance** [əˌkaʊntəbl 'ɡʌvnəns] the state of being responsibly governed
49 **alleviation** [əˌliːviˈeɪʃn] *(formal)* reduction

54 **to flow** when s.th. moves continuously
55 **to embrace** [-'-] *(formal) here:* to support enthusiastically
57 **callous** uncaring

60 **stasis** ['steɪsɪs] *(formal)* state in which s.th. does not change or develop
61 **to foster** to encourage

10 USA: People, politics, perspectives

Before you read: The Weak at War With the Strong
- Has your view of the world changed since September 11, 2001? If yes, in which ways? If no, why not?

Working with the text
1. Why will *"nothing ever be quite the same again"* (Col. 1, ll. 4–5)?
2. a) The author refers to the U.S. attitude of "invulnerability". Give examples to explain what he means by this.
   b) What has been the effect of this attitude of "invulnerability"?
3. According to the author, why didn't people see the bombing of the World Trade Center in 1993 as a warning that something worse could happen later?
4. How are those who commit acts of war and those who commit terrorist acts different?
5. a) Why, according to the author, do terrorists hate the U.S.?
   b) What does he recommend the U.S. do to deal with these terrorists?

Language
1. a) The author describes Americans after the terrorist attack to be *"Like a person riding in an armor-plated car who is felled by a virus …"* (Col. 1, ll. 44–46). Do you think that this simile is effective? Why or why not?
   b) Think of either a simile or a metaphor to show what you think of Americans after September 11.
2. Rewrite the following sentences as suggested:
   a) Col. 1, ll. 32–33: *"We welcomed allies, but also acted alone."* (start with *"Not only"*)
   b) Col. 2, ll. 28–31: *"If they ruled a state they would have something to lose …"* (insert *"in 2001"*)
   c) Col. 3, ll. 23–25: *"… we cannot deal effectively with terrorists unless we understand them."* (replace *"unless"* with *"if"*)

A step further
This article was published a few days after the World Trade Center attacks. Do you think that the points made here are relevant for the current world situation? Discuss.

Working with the cartoon
1. What is this cartoon saying about the U.S. national defense against terrorism?
2. Does this cartoon support the points made in the article? Give reasons.
3. Do you agree with the message of this cartoon? Why/Why not?

Annotations: The Weak at War with the Strong

Col. 1: 2 **invulnerability** [ɪnˌvʌlnrəˈbɪləti] being impossible to harm – 5 **irrevocably** [ɪˈrevəkəbli] *(formal)* irreversibly – 6 **breached** *(formal)* broken through – 12 **to violate** [ˈvaɪəleɪt] to do great damage to – 17 **expanse** [-ˈ-] large area of land – 18 **to subject** [-ˈ-] to cause s.o. to experience s.th. bad – 20 **devastation** [ˌ--ˈ-] destruction – 21 **retaliation** [-ˌ--ˈ--] fighting back – 23 **unscathed** [ʌnˈskeɪðd] unharmed – 25 **impregnability** [ɪmˌpregnəˈbɪləti] the state of being impossible to attack – 29 **intervene** [ˌ--ˈ-] to become involved in s.th. to try to influence it – 30 **objective** goal – 31 **to deem** to consider – 37 **aerial shield** *Raketenabwehrsystem* – 38 **to deflect** to keep s.th. from reaching its target – 41 **abiding** [əˈbaɪdɪŋ] lasting a long time – 45 **armor-plated** covered in a protective metal coating – 46 **to fell** *here:* to become infected

Col. 2: 9 **plotter** s.o. who plans and carries out a crime – 10 **to try s.o.** to determine in court if s.o. has committed a crime – **to convict** to say that s.o. is guilty of a crime – 11 **scrupulous** [ˈskruːpjələs] morally right – 13 **mere** [mɪə] unimportant – **aberration** [ˌæbəˈreɪʃn] happening that isn't typical – 17 **dry run** *(fig.)* practice – 19 **assault** [əˈsɔːlt] attack – 31 **to evict** to throw out – 34 **vulnerable** weak – 35 **ordinary** normal – 36 **Tamil Tigers** guerrilla fighters who attack the Sri Lankan armed forces and other political targets – 42 **trapped** caught

Col. 3: 1 **resentment** bitterness – 7 **to champion** to support and promote – 9 **secularism** separation of church and state – 10 **norm** usual state – 11 **to orchestrate** [ˈɔːkɪstreɪt] to organize an action to achieve a certain result – 16 **undisputed** [ˌʌndɪˈspjuːtɪd] not to be questioned – 19 **threatening** *bedrohlich* – 21 **to shrink from s.th.** to avoid s.th. – 23 **to harbor** *(BE harbour)* to protect – 27 **spillover** *(fig.)* resulting effect – 33 **combatant** [ˈkɒmbətnt] s.o. who fights in a war – 42 **claim** [kleɪm] a statement presented as a truth or fact

The Weak at War With the Strong

This is the end: the end of an era, the era of our invulnerability. We will recover physically and even psychologically, but nothing will ever be quite the same again. A barrier has been irrevocably breached: a barrier against the world outside. Until this week our enemies never seriously penetrated our continental shores. But in the attacks on the World Trade Center and the Pentagon, the proud symbols of our global power and influence were violated.

Our invulnerability lasted for more than 200 years. During that time we grew rich and powerful, protected by vast oceans and our great territorial expanse. We fought our wars abroad, subjecting our enemies – Germany, Japan, North Korea and North Vietnam – to devastation. But we were safely beyond the reach of retaliation. Our wars brought us pain, but our home front was virtually unscathed.

Because we have enjoyed our impregnability for such a long time, we came to take it for granted. Concerns about vulnerability never seriously entered our calculations of where, and when, and how we would intervene abroad to bring about objectives we deemed to be desirable.

We welcomed allies, but also acted alone. Even as modern technology shrunk the protection that geography once offered us, we sought invulnerability in more advanced technology. Today our leaders tell us that an aerial shield will deflect all enemy attacks aimed at our shores.

It is a comforting thought, reinforced by our abiding faith in technology and our history of fighting wars on the soil of others. But all that has now been revealed as a fantasy. Like a person riding in an armor-plated car who is felled by a virus, we have been attacked from within – by hostile terrorists commanding our own commercial airliners carrying Americans on their daily journeys across our vast land.

We had a preview of this catastrophe a few years ago. But the 1993 bombing of the World Trade Center, with its relatively minor damage, made little impact on us. We captured the plotters, tried and convicted them within the scrupulous rules of our justice system, and then tried to treat the entire episode as if it were a mere aberration, a quick-passing summer storm, that meant nothing.

But for others, this bombing was merely a dry run for something far bigger – as indeed this most recent assault may be for something we cannot yet imagine. We call those who commited these acts "terrorists" because they operate outside the traditional rules of warfare. They operate this way because they are, virtually by definition, weak by traditional measurements of power and do not command the resources of a state to pursue their aims.

If they ruled a state they would have something to lose: their state would be militarily punished and they would be evicted from power. That is what we call war. Terrorists cannot defeat a state in war. They can only weaken it from within by attacking its most vulnerable point: ordinary people. All terrorist movements – the I.R.A., the Tamil Tigers, the Muslim militants inspired by Osama bin Laden – use this tactic.

Even though we cannot yet be sure who directed and carried out the attacks against us, we do know that there are those in the world who hate us. Trapped between the traditional world in which they were born and the confusing world of modernity in which they inescapably live, they seek a single cause for their confusion, their resentments, their frustrated ambitions and their problems of cultural identity. It is perhaps not surprising that they would focus on the world's most powerful state as the object of their resentment.

They hate us because we champion a "new world order" of capitalism, individualism, secularism and democracy that should be the norm everywhere. We orchestrate a global economic system that dictates what others shall produce, what they shall be paid, and whether or not they will find work. We proudly declare that we are the world's undisputed Number One. Then we are surprised that others might hold us responsible for all that they find threatening in the modern world.

This does not mean that we should shrink from retaliating against those who attack us and the leaders of any state that harbors them. But at the same time we cannot deal effectively with terrorists unless we understand them. It would be a mistake to assume that terrorism is a spillover from the continuing troubles in the Middle East. Even if the Palestinian-Israeli quarrel were settled tomorrow, the war of the traditionalists against the modernizers – the war in which we find ourselves combatants – would go on. What happened this week is part of a global phenomenon not limited to any single geographical area. Today it might be focused in Central Asia, tomorrow in Latin America or Asia.

It is a war in which the weak have turned the guns of the strong against them. This is a war that is showing – despite the proud claims of the globalizers – that in the end there may be no such thing as a universal civilization, of which we all too easily assumed we were the rightful leaders.

By Ronald Steel, The New York Times, September 14, 2001. Copyright © 2001 by the New York Times Co. Reprinted by permission.

10 USA: People, politics, perspectives

FACT FILE

U.S. history and foreign policy

A sense of mission
In the 17th century, the Puritans who settled in the New World were inspired by a mission to set an example for all others, to establish a model community, or a 'city upon a hill' for everyone else to see and copy. Over the course of American history, Americans have defined their role in the world in terms of this 'mission'. Over time, this sense of mission has gone back and forth between two extremes: a) setting an example for the rest of the world from a distance by concentrating on challenges and improvements in the U.S. itself; b) active involvement to promote democracy and the American way in the world outside the U.S. The phases when the focus was more on setting an example and less on U.S. world involvement are called isolationist phases. The periods of active involvement are called internationalist (or interventionist) phases.

From isolationism to internationalism
At the beginning of the republic, the USA was so weakened from the War of Independence against the British (1775–1783) that George Washington advised his successors to follow the policy of 'no entangling alliances' (1796). However, with another American victory against Britain in the War of 1812, President Monroe declared the whole of the Western hemisphere as the U.S. special sphere of interest, and with his Monroe Doctrine (1823) warned the European powers against interference. For most of the 19th century, Americans concentrated primarily on settling the great stretches of land that had become part of the country and on developing their industries and resources.
   Once the continent was almost settled, the U.S. gradually turned towards the outside world, and pursued a more active internationalist policy. The U.S. won a massive piece of territory including California as a result of the Mexican War (1846–1848). Negotiations between America and Japan resulted in Japan opening its harbours for foreign trade in 1853–1854. During 1861–1865, America concentrated on its affairs at home because of a bloody Civil War. The 1880s, however, ushered in the period of imperialism, when the U.S. sought more territory and influence abroad. With its victory in the Spanish American War (1898) the U.S. extended its power to Puerto Rico, Guam, and the Philippines.

Making the world safe for democracy
In the first half of the 20th century the U.S. was torn twice between isolationism and internationalism. Twice the Americans had to decide whether they should intervene in a war between the European powers. And twice, after long deliberation, they decided to become involved "to make the world safe for democracy" (Wilson, 1917). After World War I there was a sharp reaction against such entanglement when the idealistic notions of the U.S. for a peace settlement could not be realized. The U.S. never signed the Treaty of Versailles and did not join the League of Nations. The resulting disillusionment combined with the Great Depression which started in 1929 resulted in a period of isolationism that would last well through the 1930s.
   The majority of Americans wanted to stay out of World War II, but this changed fundamentally after the bombing of Pearl Harbor by Japan on December 7, 1941. After this, the U.S. became directly involved in the fighting in both the European and Asian theatres. By the end of the war and thereafter, the U.S. had established factual dominance in the spheres of business, trade, technology and popular culture, and was in the postion to set the agenda for the greater part of the world. The nation's self-image was put in a nutshell by media czar Henry Luce when he proclaimed the 20th century the "American Century".

The Cold War
After 1945, the Americans waged a campaign against communism, which they considered to be the major threat for the world. Economically they tried to include as many countries as possible in the sphere of the free market; politically they promoted democracy; militarily they guaranteed security to countries within their sphere of influence. Ideologically, the containment of communism was considered a fight of good against evil. During the Cold War, the threat of nuclear war became very real. In the Cuban Missile Crisis (1962), when American spy planes found Soviet missiles in Cuba, a miracle of diplomacy prevented what might have been world destruction. Many Americans believed that the nuclear stand-off prevented direct confrontation with the Soviet Union.

1960s: the over-extension of power
In the Cold War era, world politics were dominated by the two superpowers, the U.S. and the Soviet Union. In this bipolar world, political action did not always have the result of creating a better world. The USA became involved in other (sometimes covert) campaigns to defend the free world that, in hindsight, were ill-advised, and finally over-extended its power in the Vietnam War (c. 1964–1973).

USA: People, politics, perspectives

1970s: detente

The end of this war brought U.S. withdrawal, humiliation and greater reluctance to get involved actively in other foreign engagements. America's faith in itself was shaken, and its isolationist tendencies increased as it focused more on its economic problems and the repercussions of the Watergate (1973–74) scandal on the political system. This was also an age of attempted de-escalation of tensions between the superpowers, an age of detente. Internationally the U.S. was considered rather weak, – a situation which may have contributed to the events in Iran 1979–1981, when over fifty Americans were held hostage in the American Embassy. The military operation to rescue these hostages failed miserably, causing the U.S. even more American humiliation before the world.

1980s: a new confidence

The 1980s, however, were more confident years. Many believed that the economy was becoming strong (although the national debt skyrocketed), and there was renewed international activism. For example, arms were supplied to help Afghanistan fight a Soviet invasion, and, illegally, to Iran and Nicaragua (Iran Contra Scandal of 1986) under the Reagan government. There were military interventions against communism in Grenada (1983) and against international terrorism in Libya (1986). In 1987 Ronald Reagan and Michail Gorbachev signed the INF Treaty, which eliminated all intermediate-range missiles from Europe.

1990s – today: the lonely superpower

With the fall of the Berlin Wall in 1989 and the breaking apart of the Soviet Union, the U.S. became the sole remaining global power, and the Cold War was over. Nevertheless, the U.S. and its global partners still face many dangers. The U.S. tries to stem the threat of hostile third-world countries with nuclear and/or chemical weapon arsenals. After the terrorist attacks on the World Trade Center on Sept. 11, 2001, the U.S. launched a continuing war with its allies to fight the terrorist threat in today's world.

For some, the U.S.' actions have earned it a reputation as global bully, for example during the Gulf War (1991) when it took military action to end Saddam Hussein's invasion of Kuwait. Still, many countries expect and even demand that the U.S. gives them aid in trouble spots around the world, such as the Balkan conflict (1993–1998). Indeed, Americans in general still see it as their mission to promote peace and democracy in the world, yet some are also concerned that the U.S. expends too much of its power abroad and too little at home. The U.S. continues to work to define the boundaries of its new role between the two extremes: that of the key global ally and of the sole superpower who keeps the option open, if necessary, to act alone in its own interests.

Adapted from the Fact File by Dr. Rolf Theis in The New Top Line, *pp. 102–103 (Klett Number 510450).*

---

4 **model** ideal – 20 **to advise** to give s.o. advice – **successor** [sək'sesə] s.o. who takes over a position from s.o. else – 21 **entangling alliances** [ɪnˈtæŋglɪŋ əˈlaɪənsɪz] relations with countries which would require (e.g. military) involvement – 26 **interference** getting involved in s.th. against the wishes of those affected – 32 **massive** ['--] very large – 34 **negotiation** formal discussion to reach agreements – 35 **harbour** a protected area of water where ships remain stationary – 38 **to usher in** to introduce – 46 **intervene** [ˌ--ˈ-] to become involved in s.th. to try to change or influence it – 48 **deliberation** [-ˌ--ˈ--] thinking about s.th. carefully – 51 **notion** idea – 52 **settlement** agreement – 61 **theatre** area of the world in which there is a war – 65 **to put s.th. in a nutshell** (fig.) to express s.th. in a short and clear way – 69 **to wage** to start and continue s.th. (e.g. a war) – 75 **influence** power – **containment** [-ˈ--] keeping s.th. from spreading – 81 **stand-off** *here:* where two powers are an equal threat to each other, meaning a conflict between the two couldn't (theoretically) be won – 89 **hindsight** looking back on s.th. after it has happened and understanding it only then – **ill-advised** not having received good advice – **overextend** to go beyond a reasonable limit – 92 **withdrawl** pulling back, usually after having lost a conflict – **humiliation** [hjuːˌmɪliˈeɪʃn] great embarrassment – 93 **reluctance** [rɪˈlʌktəns] not wanting to do s.th. – 96 **repercussion** [ˌriːpəˈkʌʃn] effect – 102 **hostage** *Geisel* – 109 **to skyrocket** to go up very high quickly – **renewed** that which is started again and/or made stronger – 123 **to stem** (formal) to stop – **hostile** antagonistic – 137 **to expend** (formal) to use

---

Project: Researching historical information

▶ Work in groups of three or four.
▶ Choose one of the time periods presented in the fact file, and do research to find out more information about the facts presented. Use the internet (e.g. the History Channel website at http://www.historychannel.com) for your research. Also be sure to check your local library for relevant books, as well as magazine and newspaper material.
▶ Organize and hold a presentation about one or more of the facts presented.

11 The voice of British politics

Bernie Grant, MP, at the State Opening of Parliament

The House of Commons in session

What do the photos above tell you about British society and politics?

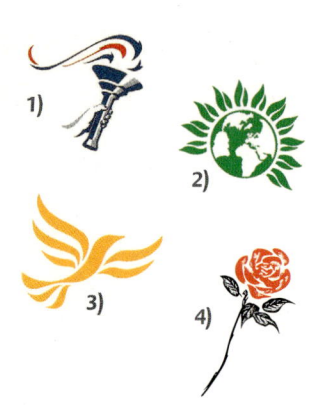

1)
2)
3)
4)

Quiz
Do this quiz in pairs. Compare your answers and then discuss the further questions.
1. Which party has which emblem? Match the emblems on the left to the party:
   a) Labour   c) Social democrats
   b) Conservative   d) Green party

   Discuss: Which parties in your country correspond to these parties? What are their emblems?
2. Which party is currently in power in Britain? Which forms the Opposition?
3. The arrangement of seats in the House of Commons is:
   a) horseshoe   b) two sets of seats facing each other   c) a circle

   Discuss: Which seating arrangement do you think is best for political debate?
4. Most of the 53 nations belonging to the Commonwealth are former British colonies. Which of the following nations:
   a) was suspended from the Commonwealth in 1961 because of its apartheid regime, but rejoined in 1994?
   b) is a former German colony?
   c) is a former Portuguese colony and the first non-English speaking member of the Commonwealth?
   d) is a former British colony, but not a Commonwealth member?

   Grenada • United States • Malta • Canada • Hong Kong • Australia • South Africa • New Zealand • Kenya • Jamaica • Cyprus • Sierra Leone • Tanzania • Nigeria • India • Uganda • Mozambique

   Discuss: What relationship does Germany have with its former colonies?
5. Decide which (if any) of the following statements are true:
   a) Britain has a written constitution.
   b) The British have to carry identity cards.
   c) The official currency of Britain is the Euro.

   Discuss: Why do you think the British have or don't have these things?
6. In the late 1990s, Scotland, Wales and Northern Ireland were given limited powers by the Westminster Parliament to govern themselves. What is this process of delegating power called?

   Discuss: How centralised is government in your country?

Ben Bradshaw, Labour MP for Exeter. Find out more about Ben at his website:
www.benbradshaw.co.uk/

" Quotes from an exclusive interview with Ben Bradshaw, a young Labour MP, have been included throughout this chapter. "

The voice of British politics 11

National identity – an Island race?

Before you read
1. Which of the following do you think is the best test of national identity? Explain why.
   the national football team you support • your racial background • where you were born • where your parents were born • where you (will) pay tax • the language you speak at home • your religion • your nationality according to your passport • anything else
2. What other identities or loyalties may conflict with people's national identity? Discuss the problems that sometimes arise from such conflicts.

'I call myself …'

Ashley Marks, 36, solicitor: 'I call myself Jewish because my religious identity defines me. I was born in Hull and my parents were born in Britain, but I am Jewish first.'

Sabrina Wong, 25, mother: 'I am British. I was born in Hong Kong and my parents are Chinese but I married here and have lived here for eight years.'

Noora Ahmed, 18, student: 'I call myself British because the terms British and British-Somalian mean the same thing to me. I have lived here for four years and my father moved here in the 60s.'

Vanessa Ainscough, 22, music graduate: 'I'm British – if you were born here, you're British, if you weren't, you're not. My dad was born in Jamaica, so what?'

David Golley, 42, student: 'I'm African-British because my mother is Scottish and my father is from Sierra Leone – given the choice on a form between British or "other" I tick "other".'

Patrick McGuinness, 76, retired: 'I'm Irish. I'm from County Down, my accent is strong and Irish and there's nothing about me that's British.'

Hussain Mohammed, 31, van driver: 'I call myself British because I was born in England, grew up in Scotland and I like Scottish things: I drink Irn Bru and I support Celtic.'

Paulina Dandgey, 16, school pupil: 'I call myself Scottish because I was born in Glasgow and this is the country that I'm most proud of – Britishness is fine but it's a bit too English.'

Hussain Shamnez, 24, shop assistant: 'I would say I was Pakistani because I am from there and though I have residence here I still have a Pakistani passport and things there are much more familiar to me.'

From The Guardian, *October 11, 2000.*

Ben Bradshaw:

"The British people feel slightly differently from continental Europeans about European integration because we are an island nation and we haven't been invaded or occupied since the Norman Conquest of 1066, but at the same time I think that people recognize that for the last 55 years we have enjoyed unprecedented peace and security because European countries have learned to cooperate with each other rather than fighting each other. And people recognize that that is a good thing."

Translate this quote into German.

Col 1:
7 **solicitor** *Rechstanwalt*
21 **graduate** person who has completed a course of study at a university

Col 2:
13 **Irn Bru** type of beer
14 **to support** to be a fan of –
Celtic Scottish football team
22 **to have residence** to have the right to live (in Britain)

Working with the text
1. Who is clearly not British/has divided loyalties/is happy to call themselves British?
2. Identify some of the contradictory attitudes expressed in the text. For example, compare the views of Hussain Mohammed and Paulina Dandgey, or Noora Ahmed and David Golley.
3. Where is Patrick McGuinness from? (Find out exactly where this is.) Given the political situation there, would you agree that there's nothing about him that's British? Suggest why he expresses this view.

A step further
1. Find out the criteria for citizenship in Britain on the home office website. Compare them with the criteria for citizenship where you live and discuss the differences.
2. A panel of experts was asked by the BBC Radio 4 'Today Programme' to agree on ten questions that aspiring British citizens could be asked. Try the Today citizenship test yourself at this link: http://www.bbc.co.uk/radio4/today/reports/politics/citizenship.shtml
Write a citizenship test for your own country and try it out on your classmates.

Check the web
Get information about British citizenship at:
http://www.homeoffice.gov.uk

11 The voice of British politics

The future of Britishness

The following text is part of a speech by the former Foreign Secretary, Robin Cook to the Social Market Foundation in London.

While reading
Identify the different areas covered in the speech (e.g. History & tradition; Britain and the USA) and make notes under each heading.

Robin Cook

Check the web
Get more information about Robin Cook at:
http://robincook.org.uk/cook/robin.htm

"This evening, I want to set out the reasons for being optimistic about the future of Britain and Britishness. Indeed, I want to go further and argue that in each of the areas where the pessimists identify a threat, we should instead see developments that will strengthen and renew British identity.

The first element in the debate about the future of Britishness is the changing ethnic composition of the British people themselves. The British are not a race, but a gathering of countless different races and communities, the vast majority of which were not indigenous to these islands.

In the pre-industrial era, when transport and communications were often easier by sea than by land, Britain was unusually open to external influence; first through foreign invasion, then, after Britain achieved naval supremacy, through commerce and imperial expansion. It is not their purity that makes the British unique, but the sheer pluralism of their ancestry. [...]

The idea that Britain was a 'pure' Anglo-Saxon society before the arrival of communities from the Caribbean, Asia and Africa is fantasy. But if this view of British identity is false to our past, it is false to our future too. The global era has produced population movements of a breadth and richness without parallel in history.

Today's London is a perfect hub of the globe. It is home to over 30 ethnic communities of at least 10,000 residents each. In this city tonight, over 300 languages will be spoken by families over their evening meal at home.

This pluralism is not a burden we must reluctantly accept. It is an immense asset that contributes to the cultural and economic vitality of our nation. [...]

Our cultural diversity is one of the reasons why Britain continues to be the preferred location for multinational companies setting up in Europe. The national airline of a major European country has recently relocated its booking operation to London precisely because of the linguistic variety of the staff whom it can recruit here.

And it isn't just our economy that has been enriched by the arrival of new communities. Our lifestyles and cultural horizons have also been broadened in the process. This point is perhaps more readily understood by young Britons, who are more open to new influences and more likely to have been educated in a multi-ethnic environment. But it reaches into every aspect of our national life.

Chicken Tikka Massala is now a true British national dish, not only because it is the most popular, but because it is a perfect illustration of the way Britain absorbs and adapts external influences. Chicken Tikka is an Indian dish. The Massala sauce was added to satisfy the desire of British people to have their meat served in gravy. [...]

To deny that Britain is European is to deny both our geography and our history. Our culture, our security, and our prosperity, are inseparable from the continent of Europe.

Underlying the anti-European case is the belief that there is an alternative future available to Britain. It used to be argued that the European Union is not Europe and that Britain could exist perfectly comfortably as one of a number of European countries maintaining a loose association with Brussels. But with the majority of

---

3 **threat** danger
7 **vast** extremely large
8 **indigenous** [ɪnˈdɪʒɪnəs] native
11 **naval** relating to the navy (Marine) – **supremacy** [sʊˈpreməsɪ] dominance
12 **imperial** relating to the empire – **purity** pure quality – **unique** [juːˈniːk] the only one of its kind
13 **sheer** pure, simple – **ancestry** [ˈænsəstrɪ] family or racial group which you come from
17 **breadth** range, variety
19 **hub** lively centre
22 **burden** problem, heavy load – **reluctantly** unwillingly – **immense** very large – **asset** [ˈæset] positive characteristic, advantage
30 **to broaden** to make wider, to extend

37 **gravy** sauce made of meat juices
39 **prosperity** continuing wealth
41 **underlying** important but not immediately obvious to – **case** argument
44 **loose** [luːs] (informal) not close

non-EU states now clamouring for full membership, the changing geopolitics of Europe have consigned that argument to the past.

Some anti-Europeans now argue that Britain's destiny lies outside Europe, as part of 'the English-speaking world' and a member of NAFTA.

Yet Britain trades three times more with the rest of the EU than we do with NAFTA. The reason why over four thousand US companies have located here is because they want to export to Europe. If they only wanted to sell to NAFTA, they would have stayed at home.

Europe is where our domestic quality of life is most directly at stake, whether the issue is environmental standards, the fight against organised crime, policy on asylum or stability on the continent.

But it is not simply a question of economic and political realism that ties Britain to Europe, compelling as those arguments are. Britain is also a European country in the more profound sense of sharing European assumptions about how society should be organised. The last international survey of social attitudes put Britain squarely within the European mainstream on our approach to social justice and public services, such as health.

There are strong ties of kinship between Britain and North America. These are an immense asset to us in the modern world. The US and the UK are each other's closest allies. But our value as an ally to our friends in Washington is in direct proportion to our influence with our partners in Europe. [...]

None of our European partners, with their own proud national traditions, seem afflicted by this self-doubt and insecurity. The idea that the French, the Germans or the Spanish are attempting to erase their national identities by constructing a 'country called Europe' is the mother of all Euromyths. On the contrary, our partners see their membership of a successful European Union as underwriting, not undermining, their assertion of national identity. [...]

The last of the three perceived threats to Britishness is the new flexibility in our modern constitution.

The devolution of power to Scotland, Wales and Northern Ireland will stand the test of time as one of this Government's most radical and significant achievements. The creation of a Scottish Parliament and Welsh Assembly allows both nations to choose the policies that are right for them through their own democratic structures. In Northern Ireland, devolution was needed for a different reason – to enable the communities of a divided society to share power and to work together to build a common future. In all three cases, I am convinced that our reforms were essential.

Let us put to bed the scare stories about devolution leading to the 'Death of Britain'. Devolution has been a success for Scotland and for Wales, but it has also been a success for Britain. The votes for devolution in the referendums were not votes for separation. They were votes to remain in the United Kingdom with a new constitutional settlement. By recognising the United Kingdom's diversity, devolution has guaranteed its future. It is striking that today opinion polls in Scotland show that support for separation from the rest of Britain is lower than at the time of the referendum four years ago.

Centuries of living together and working together have created enduring bonds between each of the constituent nations that make up Britain. Our future together in a single state is all the more secure if we each respect the distinctive identity that makes some of us Scottish and others Welsh or English. That mutual respect strengthens our common identity as British. [...] In Scotland, the legal and educational systems are important expressions of Scottishness. At a British level, there is a strong attachment to institutions such as the National Health Service, the BBC and the armed forces. In Europe, we work with fourteen other nations to build the Single Market and to use our joint strength in trade negotiations. Action at one level does not invalidate our commitment to work at the other levels. On the contrary, they reinforce each other. [...]

---

45 **to clamour** ['klæmə] **for** to demand, to cry out for
46 **to consign to** to put firmly into
47 **destiny** future
48 **NAFTA** North American Free Trade Agreement

53 **to be at stake** to be at risk
54 **asylum** [ə'saɪləm] *Asyl*

57 **compelling** convincing
58 **profound** deep, meaningful – **assumption** idea, belief
60 **squarely** directly – **mainstream** core

62 **kinship** relationship, tie

67 **to be afflicted by** to suffer from
68 **to erase** to get rid of, to destroy
70 **to underwrite** to support
71 **to undermine** to weaken – **assertion** declaration, expression
72 **perceived** imagined, considered to exist

85 **constitutional** *verfassungsmäßig* – **settlement** agreement
86 **striking** remarkable, very noticeable and important

89 **enduring** long lasting – **bond** tie, link

97 **to invalidate** to make worthless
98 **to reinforce** to strengthen, to support

11 The voice of British politics

*100 **to be confined to** to be limited to*
*101 **aftermath** period of time following an important event*

In our thousand years of history, the homogeneity of British identity that some people assume to be the norm was confined to a relatively brief period. It lasted from the Victorian era of imperial expansion to the aftermath of the Second World War and depended on the unifying force of those two extraordinary experiences. The diversity of modern Britain expressed through devolution and multiculturalism is more consistent with the historical experience of our islands.

Tolerance is important, but it is not enough. We should celebrate the enormous contribution of the many communities in Britain to strengthening our economy, to supporting our public services, and to enriching our culture and cuisine. And we should recognise that its diversity is part of the reason why Britain is a great place to live.

From The Guardian, *April 19, 2001.*

True or false?
Identify the false statements and correct them.
1. Most non EU-states in Europe are keen to become full members of the EU.
2. Multinational companies prefer to locate in Britain mainly because the British speak so many languages.
3. Thousands of American companies have moved to Britain in order to get access to European markets.
4. The British Empire and the Second World War had a unifying effect on national identity, which continues to this day.
5. Robin Cook thinks Britain will benefit from common European policies, for example, on crime and asylum.
6. According to a recent international survey on social attitudes, the British have a lot in common with other Europeans.

Working with the text
1. According to Robin Cook, what are the three areas in which the "pessimists" see a threat to British identity?
2. Summarise his reasons for believing these supposed threats will actually strengthen rather than weaken British identity.
3. What do the examples of Chicken Tikka Massala and London as a global hub demonstrate?

Writing a summary
See *Skills file* on p. 185.

Language
1. a) Complete the questions below using the adjectives in the box and adding the correct prepositions. *Example:* Are you … the future of British identity?
   Are you *optimistic about* the future of British identity?
   i) Is Britain's 'special relationship' with America … a pro-European foreign policy?
   ii) How … trade with Europe is the British economy?
   iii) Are the benefits of immigration … cultural contributions?
   iv) If the Anglo-Saxons aren't … the British Isles, where did they come from?
   v) You say the British … confusion about their national identity. What is the reason for this?
   vi) Why was Britain so … to foreign invasions in the past?
   vii) You mention you are … the importance of tolerance, but add that it isn't enough. What do you mean by this?
   viii) Some British people are … closer political integration with Europe because they say that it will lead to a super-state run by the French and the Germans. Where do you stand on this?
   ix) Is British national identity … surviving devolution, in your view?
   b) Suggest how Robin Cook might answer the questions.

capable
dependent
afflicted
indigenous
~~optimistic~~
confined
vulnerable
aware
consistent
opposed

The voice of British politics 11

2. Copy and complete the table with the missing corresponding verbs, nouns and adjectives.

Verb	Noun	Adjective
...	...	strong
to widen	...	...
...	breadth	...
...	...	rich
to separate	...	...
...	distinction	...
...	...	diverse

The legacy of Empire

Before you read

● All of the countries below used to be part of the British Empire. What do you know about them and what problems do you associate with them? Consider possible ethnic, religious, cultural, economic, linguistic and geographical/territorial problems.
    Pakistan and India • Israel and Palestine • Afghanistan • Iraq • Northern Ireland • Gibraltar • Sri Lanka • Zimbabwe

Check the web
Get more information about the British Empire at:
http://www.british empire.co.uk/

Jack Straw, Foreign Minister (2002) sparked controversy by saying: "A lot of the problems we are having to deal with now are a consequence of our colonial past." In the following statements other top commentators say what difference they think the imperial past made to the role that Britain plays in the world today.

"Because of the British Empire and the incredible sprawl that it achieved, Britain has interests and responsibilities on a global scale. Where Jack Straw is wrong is to assume that so many global problems were caused by the Empire. The problems were always there – but the Empire allowed two centuries of respite from the bloodshed that had been there before and which was likely to come again."
    Andrew Roberts, historian

Find the expressions in this statement which mean: area which has grown rapidly and irregularly • period of rest from s.th. unpleasant • violence

"There is a direct link between failed states and contemporary Islamic terrorism. States like Afghanistan and Pakistan have had huge difficulties in fulfilling the aspirations of their citizens and developing genuine legitimacy because they were hamstrung by borders that made no ethnic, cultural, linguistic or even geographic sense imposed by imperial powers. Discontent at illegitimate regimes led to protest, protest has been crushed and its root causes have not been dealt with. Result: violent terroristic activism. Iraq is inherently unstable. So is the Sudan."
    Jason Burke, Chief Reporter, The Observer

Find the expressions in this statement which mean: present day • hope, aim • official acceptance • to restrict, to make difficult • unhappiness • to squash, to defeat • basic cause • by nature

"Britain's withdrawal from the Empire often left a great deal of unfinished business. In the case of partition (e.g. Ireland, the British Raj, and the Palestinian mandate), the creation of new states was based primarily on religious affiliation making it harder for post-colonial states to build multi-cultural societies. In other parts of the world, borders were left unresolved (e.g. Belize-Guatemala; Guyana-Venezuela), giving rise to dangerous tensions. In Africa, the 'Westminster model' proved difficult to sustain and even more difficult to replace once it had been discredited. Britain's colonial past is not glorious and the first step is to recognize this, but it does provide an opportunity to contribute to a resolution of these problems."
    Victor Bulmer-Thomas, Director, Royal Institute of International Affairs

Find the expressions in this statement which mean: separation • in the first place • attachment, close connection • undecided • serious problems and conflict • to continue to use • to reject, to lose trust in s.th.

From *Observer Worldview*, Sunder Katwala, November 17, 2002.

11 The voice of British politics

Working with the text: The legacy of Empire

Which of the following reasons were given in the statements to support the view that the British Empire was responsible for current global problems?

a) The failure of the British to realise how serious certain local problems were.
b) The imposition of artificial borders that the local people did not accept.
c) Political decisions favouring one group over another.
d) Economic exploitation.
e) The citizens did not accept the new regimes that replaced the British rulers.
f) The efforts by the British to win the support of influential local groups.
g) The building of roads, railways and schools.
h) The failure of the British to solve territorial disputes.
i) The parliamentary system of government that the British 'exported' to the colonies.
j) Racial prejudice shown by the British, and lack of understanding of the local culture.
k) Attempts by British missionaries to convert the local people to Christianity.
l) The introduction of the concept of nationalism, which was new in many parts of the world.
m) The spread of the English language.

Language

Expressing cause and effect: Look at the expressions in the boxes below and find examples in the statements. Look at how each example is used in context and rephrase each sentence with an expression from the other box. *Example:*

Example: <u>Cause:</u> *Many global problems today are the legacy of Britain's colonial past. (l. 3)*
         <u>Effect:</u> *Britain's colonial past has created many global problems today.*

Expressing cause	Expressing effect
to be a consequence of	to lead to
because of	to result in
because	to have as a consequence
to be caused by	to have as an outcome
to be down to	to create/produce
resulting from	to give rise to
to be due to	Consequently, …
to be a legacy of	As a result, …
	Therefore, …

A step further

Work in pairs or small groups. Read the "Fact file" opposite. Choose one of the key events in the history of Britain's links with Europe and the Commonwealth. Research the causes and effects of this event and report your findings to the class.

Ben Bradshaw on the Commonwealth:

"The Commonwealth is something that came out of the Empire, and it's more of a club of nations who meet to discuss issues. It doesn't have a great deal of power or influence in the world. It's a way of Britain staying in touch with former colonial countries, although interestingly, countries are queuing up to join the Commonwealth: Mozambique recently, although a former Portuguese colony, has joined. Cameroon, another former German colony has joined, so some countries do see some desirability in joining. But in terms of influence and importance in the global scheme of things, I don't think one should overestimate the importance of the Commonwealth. And most people in Britain now think that our main fora for influence and activity is the European Union, NATO, the United Nations and other international institutions."

What relations do Germany, Holland and France have with their former colonies? Compare them with Britain's network of links with the Commonwealth.

The voice of British politics

FACT FILE

The Commonwealth

The Commonwealth, formerly the British Commonwealth of Nations, is an association of 54 independent nations, plus several British dependencies such as Bermuda, the Falkland Islands and Gibraltar. Most members used to be part of the British Empire. Any nation wishing to join must be independent, and its application must be acceptable to existing members. The symbolic head of the Commonwealth is the British monarch.

Members of the Commonwealth have special links with the United Kingdom and with each other. All members are equal and agree to work together towards world peace, the encouragement of trade, the defence of democracy and improvements in human rights, health and education. During World War II, Commonwealth forces played an important role in the war effort. Critics say that the Commonwealth is pointless, or little more than an exclusive club. However, Commonwealth nations united to oppose apartheid in South Africa, and they encourage joint cultural activities and sports events, particularly the Commonwealth Games, which are held every four years.

Key events: The Commonwealth & Europe

1931 The British Commonwealth of Nations is founded.

1947 India, known as the "Jewel in the Crown" of the Empire, becomes independent. Other colonies follow. This period of de-colonisation is generally peaceful, and most of the newly independent states decide to join the Commonwealth.

1961 South Africa is suspended from the Commonwealth because of its apartheid regime.
Britain applies to join the Common Market (European Communitiy). France vetoes the application, arguing that Britain's links with the USA and the Commonwealth are still too strong.

1972 Britain joins the Common Market.

1982 Argentina invades the Falklands/Malvinas Islands and Britain recaptures them in the "Falklands War".

1991 Britain signs the Single European Act at Maastricht, the Treaty on the European Union.

1994 South Africa rejoins the Commonwealth after the abolition of apartheid and the election of President Nelson Mandela.
The Channel tunnel linking Britain and France is opened.

1995 Nigeria is suspended from the Commonwealth because its regime is considered to be undemocratic (reinstated in 2000).
Cameroon and Mozambique (the latter an ex-Portuguese colony) join the Commonwealth.

1997 Hong Kong is handed back to China.

2002 The British government considers handing Gibraltar back to Spain.
Zimbabwe is suspended from the Commonwealth because it is considered that people in Zimbabwe do not have adequate democratic rights, e.g. the right to vote in free democratic elections.

Check the web

Get more information about the Commonwealth at:
http://www.thecommonwealth.org/

11 The voice of British politics

The Monarchy

🎧 **Ben Bradshaw on the monarchy:**

"I think this [the monarchy as head of state] has got much to do with history and tradition. I think if you were creating a constitution from scratch now in the 21st century, you wouldn't put a hereditary Monarch at the top of it. But I think in many of those countries including many in Europe that have constitutional monarchies, they work pretty well. You have a non-political head of state who is above politics, who is a unifying figure in that country. And I think as long as the pomp and the circumstance is not too much that those countries that have constitutional monarchies like Britain, Denmark, the Netherlands are pretty contented with them, and in the absence of a better or more attractive alternative, are happy to stick with them. I think it's important that the monarchies constantly modernise themselves and reform. And in Britain's case, of course, our monarchy and the institutions of the monarchy are a huge tourism attraction which many people argue would not be the case if we had an elected president who was a former politician or something like that."

What are the pros & cons of having an elected or non-elected head of state in your opinion?

Politics and the Prince

In September 2002 a number of letters which Prince Charles, the Prince of Wales, had sent to members of the government were leaked to the press. The leaks began with a letter to Tony Blair, the Labour Prime Minister, in which the Prince accused the Government of treating farmers worse than ethnic and other minorities. Many Labour MPs felt that Prince Charles was wrong to get so involved in politics, while the Prince publicly defended his right to voice his concerns.

St James's Palace: "It's part of the Royal Family's role to highlight excellence, express commiseration and draw attention to issues on behalf of us all. The Prince of Wales takes an active interest in all aspects of British life and believes that, as well as celebrating success, part of his role must be to highlight problems and represent views in danger of not being heard. But this role can only be fulfilled properly if complete confidentiality is maintained."

Ian Davidson, Labour MP: "If he wants to be involved in politics, then he should consider standing for election. Let's not kid ourselves that Prince Charles is a representative of ordinary people. This is someone who was born with a mouthful of silver spoons, a mega-wealthy farmer looking for things to do, so he fires off letters."

Ben Pimlott, Warden, Goldsmiths College: "It says something about the state of the current media that with war looming and the economy teetering, hours of airtime and acres of newsprint should be devoted to the epistolary habits of a powerless prince. Few more harmless activities could be devised for an heir to the throne than writing dyspeptic letters that civil servants probably answer anyway. No constitutional issue is involved. It is odd that this should be seen as a Left/Right issue, that with views ranging from far left to disgruntled Colonel to endearingly cranky, the prince is impossible to place anywhere on the spectrum. Frivolous past Princes of Wales often got ticked off for spending too much time at the racetrack. It seems harsh that the present idealistic one should get into trouble for being too serious."

---

2 **to express commiseration** to express sorrow and sympathy when s.th. sad has happened, e.g. when s.o. has died – **on behalf of** as representative of
6 **confidentiality** secrecy
8 **to kid o.s.** to believe s.th. that isn't true
12 **warden** official
13 **to loom** to be close and bring problems – **to teeter** to be unstable, to be on the point of collapsing
14 **epistolary** in the form of a series of letters
16 **dyspeptic** pessimistic
18 **disgruntled** angry, unhappy – **colonel** [ˈkɜːnəl] officer in the army – **endearing** likeable
19 **cranky** strange – **frivolous** silly
20 **to tick s.o. off** to speak angrily to s.o.
21 **harsh** very severe and unkind

Tony Wright, MP: "This is an extremely foolish and dangerous thing to do. If you are a member of the Royal family I am afraid you sign up to not getting involved in contentious issues. The Prince is of course, entitled to private conversations with MPs in government as he will be required to do as King and, indeed, as members of the Royal family have done through the ages. As King, however, he will be in no position to be seen to be taking sides. That is a line he must not cross. It's all part of the contract I'm afraid."

Stephen Haseler, chair, Republican movement: "Prince Charles should not be involved in politics. If you or I could have the influence Prince Charles has we would rather like it. He is using his position to apply pressure on Ministers on political, if not always directly party political, issues. But fox hunting, traditional architecture and GM foods are all highly contentious political issues and Prince Charles is acting as a lobbyist for what I would call traditional England. The central Monarchist argument is that the Monarchy is above controversy – that is the only reason for us to continue with it. This is becoming impossible to sustain. Tony Blair should have the courage of his convictions and ask this political prince to stop using his influence for partisan causes. If he continues to be political, Blair ought to start proceedings to change the system."

David Green, Director, Civitas: "The moral justification for allowing Prince Charles, as heir to the throne, to have direct access to ministers is that he represents the common good. In a democracy, Parliament must have the last word, but political parties often represent special interests and frequently make laws to suit vested interests at the expense of the wider population. A ban on fox hunting, for instance, would be class legislation, and the public interest demands a 'live and let live' attitude. So long as he voices what he honestly believes to be the common good, Prince Charles should send the Government as many letters as he wants."

Countryside Alliance spokesman: "This is a matter between Prince Charles and 10 Downing Street. It is none of our business and should be none of the media's business either."

Michael Jacobs, General Secretary of the Fabian Society: "It's often said that the monarchy has entirely ceremonial functions within the unwritten British constitution. But this is not strictly true. The monarchy assents to Acts of Parliament, appoints Prime Ministers and dissolves Parliament. Under convention these powers are not exercised politically. But they could be: a monarch could refuse, for example, to assent to an Act if he or she found it politically or morally repugnant. This has in fact happened within living memory – ten years ago the Belgian King abdicated for a day in order not to sign into law abortion legislation passed by the Belgian Parliament. An expedient was created through which the King's brother took the throne for a day to sign the act. It isn't impossible to imagine a British monarch having similar moral objections to legislation on, say, human cloning or even on reform of the constitution itself.

The problem with an unwritten constitution is that the political power may not be used – but it is still there. This is why the Fabian Society's Commission on the Future of the Monarchy is examining the case for codifying the sovereign's powers in law and removing the areas of discretion which could be used politically. It is sometimes said that reform of the monarchy is the slippery slope to republicanism. But it might equally be argued that removing the potential for political involvement would help protect the monarchy – not least from the kind of accusations of political interference that have been made this week."

From *The Guardian*, September 29, 2002.

---

25 **contentious** controversial

33 **GM** gene manipulated

36 **to be above s.th.** to not be involved in s.th. – **controversy** discussion, argument, dispute
37 **to have the courage of one's convictions** to be prepared to take a risk and take action based on what you believe
39 **proceedings** formal or legal action

43 **vested interest** strong personal reason

54 **under convention** in practice

56 **repugnant** horrible, disgusting

58 **to abdicate** to resign from the position of monarch (*abdanken*) – **abortion** *Abtreibung*

66 **discretion** rule which is not fixed
67 **on a slippery slope** becoming worse in a way which is difficult to stop

70 **interference** intervention, involvement

11 The voice of British politics

> **Check the web**
> One of Charles' letters was printed in *The Guardian*. You can find it at this website:
> http://www.guardian.co.uk/uk_news/story/0,3604,799954,00.html

Working with the text: Politics and the Prince
1. a) Summarize the view expressed in each statement in your own words.
   b) Say whether you agree or disagree giving reasons.
2. a) Make a table showing the arguments in favour of (justifying) and the arguments against Prince Charles' letters. Wherever possible include the reason given for the view expressed.
   b) Which arguments do you find the most and least convincing? Why?
3. Make a mind map with as much information as possible from the statements on the role and duties of the Monarchy. (Add further information if possible.)
4. Which other issue, apart from the role of the Monarchy, was highlighted by the leaks? Do you consider this issue to be more or less important? Give reasons.

Language
1. Explain the following terms in your own words:
   to draw attention to (l. 2) • to take an active interest in (l. 3) • to be involved in (l. 7) • to be devoted to (l. 14)
2. Explain the difference between being "entitled" to do something (l. 25) and being "required" to do something (l. 26). What do you think a head of state should be entitled to do and what should they be required to do?

Your view
Has Charles overstepped the mark or are his letters to Ministers a valuable example of public duty? Discuss.

> 🎧 **Listening comprehension**
> *Listen to Ben Bradshaw talking about Britain's role in Europe.*

Britain in Europe

About the euro: An open letter to the PM's Press Secretary

Dear Alastair Campbell,

There are some things I ought to know which I don't, and if I don't know, it's a fair bet that quite a proportion of the population doesn't either. I am, to be honest, very confused and muddled about Europe. For decades it's seemed to be just about trade and frankly, if the headlines were about trade, let alone treaties, I'd read something else less boring. […]

But now it seems a great deal more than that. Our country seems to be joining itself politically, economically and militarily to a kind of foggy, amorphous mass
10 called Europe. When the fog clears, what will we see? A federal Europe, working much as does the USA, with a two-party system, one egging on and another holding back; or a Soviet Union, with little use for electors at all, but a central government that knows best?

Either way, or even if there is a third middle way, what we seem to be losing, and
15 without discussion, is democracy itself and the two party system we are accustomed to. Is this or is this not the case? I'm writing to you because someone has to let us know what is going on, and you as Press Secretary seem to be the man. So bear with me.

I am not suggesting that to abandon the democratic system is necessarily a bad
20 thing: the mob have always been in favour of crucifixion, castration, capital punishment and so forth, and have heavily relied upon our politicians to represent its best side, not its worst – but it's a pretty momentous thing to do and I think we should be told.

---

5 **muddled** unsure
6 **let alone** still less
7 **treaty** official written agreement usu. between two or more countries
9 **amorphous** shapeless
11 **to egg s.o. on** to encourage s.o. to do s.th.
17 **to bear with s.o.** to have patience and take the time to listen to what s.o. is saying
20 **crucifixion** killing by nailing s.o. to a cross (like Jesus) –
capital punishment penalty of death

The voice of British politics

I am neither Europhile nor Europhobe, but one of those irritating 'don't knows.' Now that I actually want to know, I meet only proselytisers for or against, with enormous budgets going towards the pros. You are meant to be impartial on this kind of issue, I believe, so tell us.

Okay, so the Euro makes trading easier, and when it's been going a while prices will be standardised across Europe, so we'll all pay the same for our cigarettes and grappa. That's fine by me, just a bit dull.

But what about democracy? The great thing about that system of government, the one we're used to, is that you can throw the bastards out. But when we are properly 'in' Europe, how can we do this?

We will be run by civil servants not elected politicians. Europe will decide what is a crime and what is not. And how are Europe's judges appointed? Do you know? I certainly don't. Do they prefer Napoleonic law or our innocent-until-proved-guilty sort of stuff?

And what representation do we the British people get within their counsels? We have no clout, no status, we are 60 million people about to meld with another 200 million or so, one of 27 envisaged nations, and more to come. Is this how we want our children's future to be? Perhaps you could persuade me, Mr. Campbell, that all this is okay, that my worries are groundless? That democracy stands supreme?

I understand that in the new Europe we will still be able to raise our own taxes. But what is the point of doing this if European decree tells us where we must spend it? The Westminster assembly will be to the European assembly as Scotland is to Westminster's, all but swallowed up. I daresay we will have minor initiatives, like road bumps, for a time, but for how long? The great reforming zeal of the joyless bureaucrats will enter into all areas of our national life, as if our own little Cromwells weren't bad enough. They will act in our interests, naturally, but please remember that Stalin, welding together the great Socialist Soviets of the union, always believed himself to be acting in the best interests of that union, KGB and all.

As voters we are accustomed to make a decision between (in effect) two parties with different views: the majority party 'in power' to put the pro points, with an 'opposition' to put the case against, and sometimes to be able to persuade the other side. By and large the system has worked well. But all this is to change. We are in effect to be 'ruled' from Brussels. Unelected civil servants, motivated and moderated by personal feelings rather than accepted political allegiance – or are at any rate unknown to us – are, on current form, to issue a stream of dirigiste rulings, which we must obey. Is this any different from the Soviet style of doing things? Every one in the Soviet Union voted, but for individuals, not parties. Their problem being what I fear ours will be, that they couldn't throw the bastards out.

Are we to have a President? What sort of President? Who will elect him? He won't be like the US president, because we won't be in the old familiar left/right party system. Will he be like the French president, a figurehead? Will he be like our Prime Minister? No, because ours is voted in from the party in power, and 'the party in power' in Europe doesn't make sense. People need leaders, and the more flamboyant the better, and where are you to find them?

So tell me, Mr Campbell, how is it meant to work? It may well be that I have got things wrong. I read in a pro-Europe booklet that in ten years time it is envisaged that the Euro will be as powerful as the dollar, and an equal world-policing force to the USA. Is this the ambition, a second great power to face up to US imperialism, and if so what consequence is this going to have for world peace?

Please let me know, Mr. Campbell, and give it your best shot, because I'm beginning to get worried, and if I am, a whole lot of others will be feeling the same.

Fay Weldon

http://www.yougov.com/, 2002

---

25 **proselytiser** people who try hard to make you change your opinion or beliefs about s.th. (usu. religious)
34 **civil servant** person who works for the government or state (Beamte)
39 **to have no clout** to have no say or strength, power
47 **road bump** raised part in a road to make cars drive more slowly – **zeal** great enthusiasm
57 **allegiance** [əˈliːdʒəns] support for
58 **dirigiste** bureaucratic, undemocratic

Fay Weldon
Fay Weldon was born in England in 1931 but grew up in New Zealand. She studied economics and psychology at the University of St Andrews in Scotland.
She worked on the problem page of the Daily Mirror and then as a copywriter for the Foreign Office. She then embarked on an extremely successful career as an advertising copywriter.
Her first novel, The Fat Woman's Joke, was published in 1967, but by then she had already written some fifty plays for radio, stage, or television. She has published over 20 novels, collections of short stories, television movies, newspaper and magazine articles.
In October 2002 Fay was named the first writer-in-residence at The Savoy Hotel in London.

11 The voice of British politics

Working with the text: About the euro …

1. Complete the following sentences:
   a) Fay Weldon clearly doesn't like civil servants who are …
   b) She obviously thinks politicians should be …
   c) She probably prefers judges who are …
   d) She certainly thinks leaders should be …
   e) She firmly believes the British people should be. …
   f) She sincerely hopes Alastair Cambell will be …
2. a) Explain briefly why and on behalf of whom Fay Weldon wrote the letter.
   b) What does this tell you about Britain's relationship with Europe at a political level? And at a personal level?
3. What two contrasting visions of Europe does she outline?
4. To what extent is she a supporter of democracy?

Language

1. a) Find the opposites of the words underlined in the sentences below.
   b) Rewrite the sentences without changing their meaning using the words you have found.
      i) *I am very <u>confused and muddled</u> about Europe.* (ll. 4–5)
      ii) *You are meant to be <u>impartial</u> on this kind of issue.* (ll. 26–27)
      iii) *Perhaps you could persuade me […] that my worries are <u>groundless</u>.* (ll. 41–42)
      iv) *He won't be <u>like</u> the U.S. president.* (ll. 62–63)
      v) *People need leaders, and the more <u>flamboyant</u> the better.* (ll. 66–67)
2. Explain the following words from the text:
   a fair bet (l. 3) • frankly (l. 6) • to be accustomed to (ll. 15/16) • Europhile (l. 24) • Europhobe (l. 24) • to be run by (l. 34) • to appoint (l. 35) • to act in s.o.'s interests (l. 49) • to give s.th. your best shot (l. 73)

Style

1. Describe the tone and language of the letter. Choose from the words in the box, giving examples from the letter to support your answer. (Look up any words you don't understand.)
2. Do you think Fay Weldon's tone is appropriate, in view of who she is and who she is writing to? Give reasons.

A step further

1. Pick out ten key questions that Fay Weldon puts to Alastair Campbell. Draft a reply in the style which a press secretary would use in a letter to a member of public.
2. Refer back to the text on pp. 166–168 ("The future of Britishness"): How do you think Robin Cook would reply to Fay Weldon?

Describing tone & language
informal • formal • neutral • biased • chatty • pompous • demanding • polite/rude • bossy • wordy • deferential • challenging • persuasive • tentative • worried • flowery • hesitant • direct • lively • aggressive • business-like

Politics & the media

🎧 **Ben Bradshaw on politics & the media:**

„ It's very important, I think, in a democracy that you have a vigorous, free and independent media. Very important in terms of uncovering corruption and wrong-doing and scutinizing government policies. It helps governments make the right decisons, but I think sometimes our media in Britain is also very trivial and tends to concentrate on gossip, tittle-tattle and personalities rather than on the meat of politics and the decisions that are being made that actually affect peoples' lives. They tend to cover politics as a soap opera rather than as a serious business, which impacts on peoples' lives and I regret that.

The voice of British politics

On the other hand the Sun actually helped the Labour Party to get elected in 1997, so in a way the politicians use the media too.

I think politicians have realized that it's important to use all forms of communication that there are, but the influence of the newspapers should not be overestimated because – as a former journalist, I think that ordinary people are quite intelligent enough to make a judgement when it comes to voting based on their own views and their own experiences rather than allowing themselves to be told how to vote by the newspapers. For many, many years *The Sun* always supported the Conservative Party, but still a majority of Sun readers still voted Labour, so you cannot simply *extrapolate a newspaper's editorial view and assume that all its readers vote in that direction.

Modern parties like New Labour have been accused of becoming Americanized in the way they exploit the media. What I mean by this is that they rely heavily on spin, speaking sound bytes, concentrate on image rather than content, and also letting policy be dictated by opinion polls and focus groups. Do you think this is a fair criticism?

I don't think it's a criticism. It's just a statement of fact that in the modern media age where we have 24-hour electronic media, politicians need to change the way that they operate. We do not any longer fight elections or try to get our message across by standing on a soap box in the middle of a marketplace or in a drafty village hall, because most people would not bother to turn out to listen to us. But most people do watch television, listen to the radio, read newspapers, so those are the media through which politicians try to communicate. And in terms of using opinion polls and focus groups, it's also quite important in an age when it's quite easy for *vociferous pressure groups and others to make their voices heard, it's quite easy for politicians to think that they are speaking on behalf of the majority. And one of the useful things about focus groups and opinion polls is that they give you a much more accurate or scientific impression of where public opinion is, which of course is a very important fact for politicians when they are deciding whether or not to implement a policy.

> 1. How and why have politicians changed the way they operate? Do you see this as a positive or negative development?
> 2. Describe how politics and politicians are represented in the media in Germany.
> 3. To what extent do you think the media influences the voters in Germany?

* **to extrapolate** to examine facts and make statements about the future
* **vociferous** loud

Stage-managing the Surf Summit

Before you read

- What is most important in order for a politician to be successful? Put the following points in your own order of importance and add other ideas of your own. Discuss your order with others in your class.
  appearance • what is said (content/policies) • frequent appearances on TV/radio, etc. • public meetings (e.g. summits) with other international politicians • sex appeal

> **Having a discussion**
> See *Skills files* on pp. 191 & 192.

Stage-managing the Surf Summit

When it came to matters of the media, Jonathan Bendall was a wholehearted disciple of the Art of Anticipation. Which is otherwise known as keeping the bastards waiting.

Bendall knew that the sight of food can throw dogs into a feeding frenzy, a raw, primitive call of the wild that has no limits and allows no mercy, yet in anticipation of that food, a dog will slaver and come quickly to heel. So it was Bendall's custom to keep the media in constant anticipation, telling them what they were going to get, and when. In the meantime he would watch them sit up and drool. (He also relied heavily on the principle of idleness, which states that dogs will eat almost anything as long as they don't have to go looking for it.)

Out of this grew the idea for what came to be known as the Surf Summit.

2 **anticipation** expectation

4 **frenzy** excited, uncontrolled and sometimes violent behaviour
5 **mercy** pity (*Gnade*)
6 **to slaver** ['slævə] / **to drool** to dribble, to let saliva fall from the mouth – **to come to heel** to come and stand next to its owner

11 The voice of British politics

*12 **inspired** clever and new*

*14 **portentous** important in affecting future events*

*19 **to shove** [ʃʌv] to push roughly*

*22 **gaze** look (Blick) –*
***lest** to prevent (s.th. from happening)*

*26 **to be plagued with** [pleɪɡd] to be full of s.th. bad –*
***impoverished** poor – **over-indulged** spoilt, having been given too much*
*28 **to suffice** to be enough*
*30 **gilding** thin layer of gold paint*
*32 **to hone** to shape, to create*

*37 **armoured** protected against weapons*

*43 **the Honours List** list of people who are given a knighthood by the Monarch each year*
*44 **to touch s.o. for s.th.** to ask s.o. for s.th. (usu. money)*
*52 **scraggy** very thin and bony*
*53 **to make a dash** to make a fast journey*
*60 **lad** modern young man*

Check the web
Get more information about Michael Dobbs, including an interview with him about *Whispers of Betrayal* at:
http://www.fireandwater.com/author/detail.asp?aid=3954

It seemed inspired. Bendall would travel or 'surf' around Europe, meeting separately with seven other heads of government in a single day – a day that would, in the portentous words of the press briefing, 'shake up the politics of indifference
15 and kick-start the European economies out of recession.' Well, up to a point. That sort of schedule allowed for no more than forty minutes for each meeting, barely enough time for handshakes and photo-calls. But if modern statesmanship was all about imagery, then those images would be superb. A politician on the move, shoving aside apathy through sheer force of character, his thinning hair tussling in
20 the wind as he ran down stairs, stepped off trains and waved to the carefully prepared camera positions. Look up, young man, look up! And let the world follow your gaze, lest they see the nature of what it is you're standing in …

So the Surf Summit was born, although one early problem emerged. The French President was recuperating from an illness at this holiday home near Porto-Vecchio
25 in Corsica. It seemed so much better for his health than Paris, where the streets were plagued with violent protests by impoverished farmers and over-indulged students. In the circumstances, illness seemed a far better option. The most he agreed to was a video link-up, but at least it was pictures. It would suffice.

Preparations were made, then remade, and at last the day had arrived. As a
30 confident new sun crept across the rooftops of Whitehall and set fire to the gilding on top of the Victoria Tower, Bendall's private secretary checked the schedule one final time. It had been honed by experts and polished by repeated examination until it shone.

At eight a.m., with breakfast television and radio drawing their biggest audiences,
35 Bendall would greet the Irish Prime Minister on the steps of Downing Street. The press communiqué had been agreed well in advance; they only had to sign.

At a quarter to nine Bendall would make the three-minute ride in armoured convoy to Leicester Square where, after a walkabout of precisely ninety seconds, he and the assembled press corps would occupy one of the picture halls of the Moviemax
40 cinema, at which point Monsieur le President would appear many times life size on the screen behind him. Stunning. (It was mere coincidence, of course, that the Moviemax was owned by a close friend of Bendall, who was also a considerable contributor to party funds and soon to be included very publicly on the Honours List. Much less publicly, he would then be touched for a contribution to match the size of
45 the enormous publicity he was pulling from the summit. But that was for the future.)

For today, Bendall would hurry out of the cinema, coat tails flying, to be greeted by a crowd of well-wishers. It was certain that the crowd would consist of well-wishers since every single one of them had been hand-picked and shipped in by party headquarters. Nothing was to be left to chance.

50 He knew where the camera would be positioned. He knew which part of the future to gaze at, forty-five degrees, no higher, otherwise his neck would begin to look scraggy, then, with a theatrical sweep of his arm, he would leave them all behind as he made the six-minute dash to the international terminal at Waterloo, where he would be met by the Swedish Prime Minister, Kristen Svensson. A railway
55 station in south London would seem an unlikely location for an Anglo-Swedish summit but there was no time for Bendall to get to Stockholm. Anyway, the Swede was delighted to cooperate. She and Bendall had always hit it off, their public relationship full of clinches and clutches to the point that some suggested it could only be built on a private and more intimate relationship. Disgraceful suggestion, of
60 course, but it gave him instant sex appeal, made him a real lad, while she'd made it onto the front cover of Private Eye almost as often as Prince Edward.

So, after much synchronized smiling it would be a quick wave through the window of the Eurostar on its way to Brussels. And still only ten-fifteen!

By Michael Dobbs from Whispers of Betrayal, London: HarperCollins, 2000, pp. 165–167.

The voice of British politics 11

Working with the text
1. You are Bendall's personal assistant. Write a checklist of the things you need to do before and after the Surf Summit and make a schedule for the day.
2. Who do you think Bendall is? Describe the image of himself that he wants to convey, and compare this with your own impression of him.
3. What is the Surf Summit? Explain both its official and its real purpose.
4. The passage refers explicitly and implicitly to deals that are struck. What are these deals, and what do the people/groups involved get out of them?
5. Collect examples of irony and hypocrisy in the text and explain their purpose.

Language
1. Explain or give synonyms/synonymous phrases for the following expressions from the text:
    disciple (l. 1) • indifference (l. 14) • barely (l. 16) • to recuperate (l. 24) • well in advance (l. 36) • to leave s.th. to chance (l. 49) • to hit it off (l. 57)
2. What do you understand by the word "statesmanship" (l. 17)? Describe the leader of your own country and discuss the extent to which he or she is 'statesmanlike'.

Your opinion
Discuss the following points in a group or in class and then choose one of them to write a comment on. You should write about 350 words.
1. Politicians today are less interested in the public good than in their public image. Discuss.
2. The success or failure of a politican today depends entirely on the media.

Creative writing
Choose one of the following writing tasks:
a) You are Bendall's Press Secretary. Write the press communiqué to send to the media.
b) You are Bendall's Image Consultant: Write a briefing in which you outline your concept for Bendall's public image.

> **Writing a press release**
> See *Skills file* on p. 205.

Project: Political profile

Work with a partner or in small group.
Choose one of the following and prepare a political profile.
- one of your local MPs
- a British MP (e.g. Ben Bradshaw)
- the perfect politician

Your profile should include the following details:
▶ family background & status
▶ age and education
▶ professional experience outside of politics
▶ political career
▶ main political interests
▶ presence in the media
▶ …

Prepare a multi-media presentation of your MP for your class.

> **Check the web**
> Get more information about German politicans at:
> *http://www.bundestag.de/mdb15/index.html*
> Find out about British MPs at:
> *http://www.parliament.uk/directories/directories.cfm*
> Read about Ben Bradshaw at:
> *http://www.benbradshaw.co.uk/*

Skills file Mind maps

Mind maps are useful for collecting and organizing a large amount of information about a certain topic. You can make a mind map for yourself or as a group. The basic structure of a mind map is always the same.

How to make a mind map
Use a pencil so that you can easily delete things or change their position, if necessary.
1. Write your main topic in the middle of a page and draw a circle around the word or phrase. (Fig. 1)
2. Think of important things directly related to the main topic. Write each idea (subtopic) in a circle around the outside of your first circle. Draw lines connecting the subtopics to the main topic. (Fig. 2)
3. Now add more circles with related ideas around the subtopics. (Fig. 3)

Instead of drawing circles you can use lines with 'branches' for subtopics. (Fig. 4)

Ways of using mind maps
- To brainstorm ideas on a given topic:
  Write the topic heading in the centre circle and add all new and related aspects.

- To organize information from a text (or other source):
  Start with the most important point in the text, add the main subtopics, then add relevant detailed information or quotations from the text.

- To develop word fields:
  Start with the generic term and add all related words.

- To organize arguments:
  Start with the topic of discussion. Add a branch or circle: 'for' and another one 'against'. Continue by adding further branches/circles with arguments 'for' and 'against'.

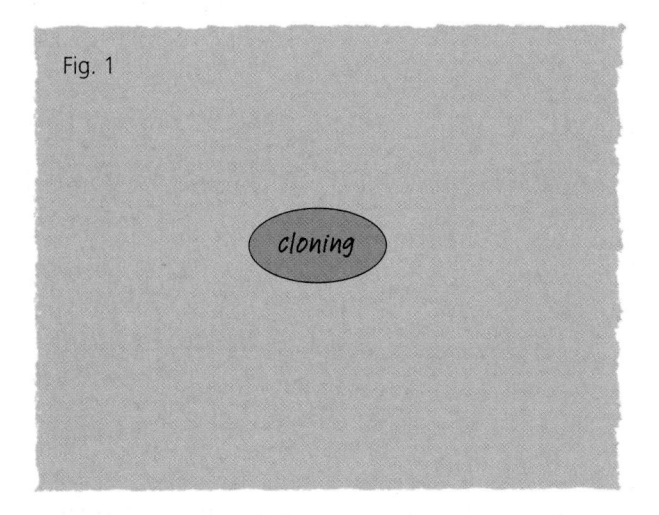

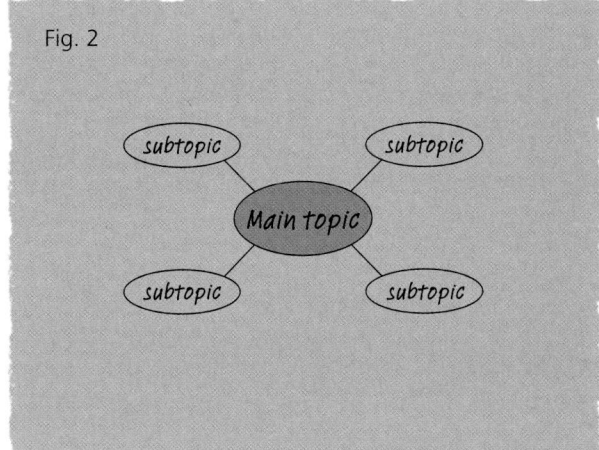

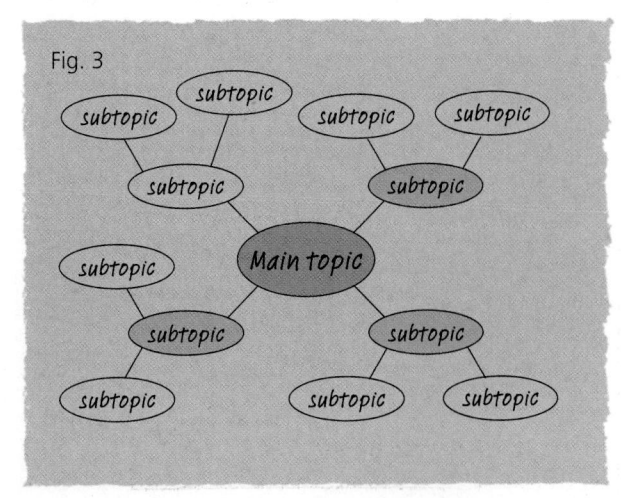

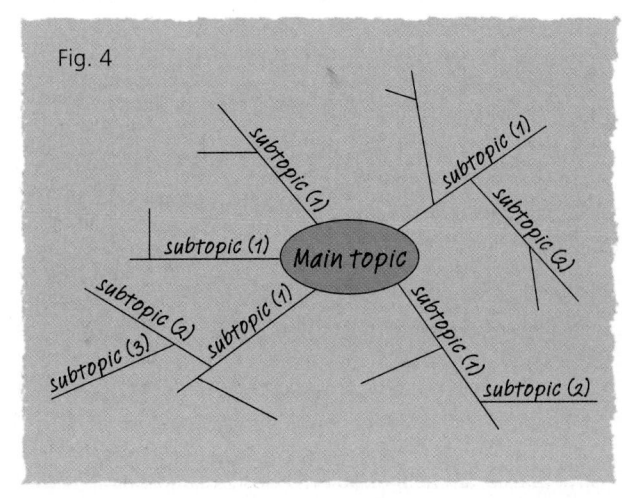

Fig. 1

cloning

Fig. 2

Fig. 3

Fig. 4

Analysing style Skills file

The way a writer uses words, phrases, structure and rhetorical devices defines his or her style. Below are some points to keep in mind when you analyse the style used in a text. For each of your points, be specific (e.g. provide quotes that illustrate your ideas). You can find the highlighted words below in the glossary on pp. 208–210:

Text form
What is the **text form**? Is it a poem, short story, a play, a novel, factual article, letter, essay or a speech?

Text type
What is the **text type**? Identify the author's intention for writing the text: is it primarily argumentative, instructive, narrative, descriptive or expository? Although more than one type may be present in a text, one type is usually dominant.

Text structure
Describe the physical arrangement of the text:
The physical structure of **novels** is usually determined by the sequence of the chapters, whereas **dramas** (plays) are composed of acts and scenes. Most **poems** are made up of **stanzas**. Generally an **essay, comment** or article is composed of a series of paragraphs (sometimes divided by subheadings).
Describe the presentation and development of the **theme**, events, issues and ideas, etc. in the text:
Most texts are built on a carefully planned progression of ideas, details and/or events that should help the reader to understand the point(s) the writer wants to make.
In most novels, **short stories** and dramas this progression of ideas is determined by the **plot**.
The main point of an essay, factual article or a speech is usually presented in the first (or sometimes the last) paragraph, and the following paragraphs contain additional ideas that support and develop this point with various techniques (see the „Skills file: Writing an essay" on p. 184). Poetry contains carefully selected descriptions and **figurative language** which vividly portray ideas, tell stories and/or create emotions.
Decide whether you think the text structure has been successful. Does it help to present important ideas and issues clearly and effectively? Why or why not? What changes would you suggest for the structure?

Register
Register, a writer's language choice in a situation, indicates the type of audience he or she wants to reach, and the relationship that he or she intends to establish with that audience. For example, **formal language** and complex sentence structure keep this relationship more academic and distant, whereas **informal language** and simpler sentence structures often help establish a closer relationship.

There are three aspects to consider when analysing register.
- Vocabulary:
  How would you describe the writer's choice of vocabulary? Is it formal or informal? Do you think the vocabulary is descriptive and concrete or abstract and theoretical? Are a lot of terms used that are specific to a certain scientific field or profession? Does the choice of vocabulary help to create a certain **atmosphere** in the text? Do you think that the choice of vocabulary is appropriate?
- Sentence structure:
  Are most of the sentences simple and short, as is the case for most dialogues, or mainly complex? What other grammatical elements do you notice (e.g. participles, gerunds, infinitives)? Why do you think the writer uses these structures and grammatical elements?
- Tone:
  Describe the **tone**, or the author's attitude toward the subject, the characters and the readers that has been conveyed in the text. How does this tone affect your understanding of the text and your own attitude toward it?

Rhetorical devices
Rhetorical devices (often referred to as "literary devices" or "stylistic devices") involve the use of language in a non-literal sense or in an unusual way. Use of these devices serves a variety of purposes including the organization, emphasis, explanation and varied expression of ideas within a text. The following are examples of rhetorical devices: **alliteration, assonance, hyperbole, irony, simile, metaphor, personification, rhetorical questions, understatement**. The following rhetorical devices are commonly used in talks, but they are also frequently found in written texts:
the repetition of key words and/or ideas for emphasis • quotations and proverbs to support a statement • rhetorical questions to structure the text and to keep the listeners' attention • the usage of personal pronouns (we/our/you) to make the audience feel personally involved.
What function do these rhetorical devices have on the text? What effect do they have on you?

> **Check the web**
> Get more information about rhetorical devices at:
> *http://www.virtualsalt.com/rhetoric.htm*

Skills file   Translating

Guidelines

1. Before you start translating
- Always read the whole text before you start translating.
- Make a note of the main points in your own words in German before you start your detailed translation.

2. First version
- Write your first version in pencil so that you can change and correct things easily.
- Don't translate word for word, but do keep as close to the original as possible.
- Refer to the **Tips and tricks** and to the table of **common problems** on p. 183.
- Don't leave any gaps! In your first version write words or phrases which you can't translate in English. Underline them so that you can find them easily.

3. Second version
- Read through your first version and try to translate any remaining English words from the context. If you can't, look them up in a dictionary.
- Check your translation word for word against the English text and make sure you haven't left anything out. Make corrections as necessary.

4. Final version
- Reread your text and decide if it sounds German. If it doesn't, you haven't translated properly. Think about what you are trying to say and decide how you would say it in German. Make corrections.
- Reread your translation and repeat these steps until you are certain your text is in good German. If you have time, leave the text for a while (e.g. overnight) before checking it for the last time.

Tips and tricks

1. Don't improve texts when you translate. For example, if one verb is used repeatedly in the text use one verb in your translation, even if you think another would sound better.

2. When translating long sentences, define the main clause and translate this first, then translate the other clauses in their order of importance.

3. Try to keep to the same number of sentences in the text and in your translation. (Don't split sentences up or join them in your translation, unless it is really necessary.)

4. Be prepared for your German text to be longer than the English original: English sentences are often shorter than German ones. One of the reasons for this is that, for example, there is often a relative clause in German where in English a participle construction (with -ing form or past participle) is used.

5. You will only be able to translate well, if you read in your own language. Look for texts on similar topics to those you cover in your English lessons in German newspapers, magazines, etc. This will help you translate specific topic-related vocabulary and names of people, groups, etc.

6. Some words and phrases occur in almost all texts and are frequently difficult to translate. Collect these words and phrases in a special file. Some 'false friends' are listed below to start you off.

Common 'false friends'

actual – eigentlich (≠aktuell)
after all – doch, zum guten Schluss (≠nach allem)
brave – mutig (≠brav)
briefcase – Aktentasche (≠Brieftasche)
critic – Kritiker (≠Kritik)
gift – Geschenk (≠Gift)
gymnasium – Turnhalle (≠Gymnasium)
however – jedoch (≠wie auch immer)
to overhear – zufällig mitbekommen (≠überhören)
physician – Arzt (≠Physiker)
rent – Miete (≠Rente)
rubber hose – Gartenschlauch (≠Gummihose)
sensible – vernünftig (≠sensibel)

File continued on next page.

Translating Skills file

Common problems

Problem / Solution	English	German
Present perfect sentences with 'since/for' are usually present tense in German.	I **have had** my car **for** 2 years now.	Ich **habe** mein Auto jetzt **seit** zwei Jahren.
Constructions using past participles and -ing forms can often be translated with a relative clause.	I thanked them for the lovely weekend **spent with them**.	Ich dankte ihnen für das schöne Wochenende, **das ich mit ihnen verbracht hatte.**
	A group of American students **visiting our town** were at college today.	Eine Gruppe amerikanischer Studentinnen, **die unsere Stadt besuchen,** waren heute in der Schule.
The translation of 'it' is not always 'es'. It depends what 'it' refers to.	I couldn't get a seat on the train: **it** was totally crowded.	Ich konnte im Zug keinen Platz kriegen: **er** war total überfüllt.
'you' and 'they' can often be translated with the German *'man'*.	In Britain **you often see** double decker buses.	In Großbritannien **sieht man oft** Doppeldeckerbusse.
'do' or 'did' in positive sentences are used to emphasize the verb. In German you usually need an adverb.	I **did do** my homework!	Ich habe **sehr wohl** meine Hausaufgaben gemacht!
'there is/are' and 'there was/were' are usually translated with *'es gibt'* or *'es gab'*.	**There's** so much to do and see in Atlanta!	**Es gibt** so viel zu tun und zu sehen in Atlanta!
	There was nothing to eat.	**Es gab** nichts zu essen.
An adjective + noun combination in English can often be translated by one noun in German.	**congressional elections** (adjective + noun)	**Kongresswahlen** (compound noun)
'with + -ing form' is best translated with a separate clause beginning with a conjunction (*weil, da, wo, wenn, wobei,* etc.).	Roads are becoming busier and busier **with** more and more people **driving** cars.	Die Straßen werden immer voller, **weil** immer mehr Leute Auto **fahren**.
	With winter **approaching**, they decided to leave.	**Jetzt, wo** der Winter **sich näherte**, beschlossen sie zu gehen.
Passive sentences can often be translated in the active form using *'man'*.	The stolen money **was found** in a phone box.	**Man hat** das gestohlene Geld in einer Telefonzelle **gefunden**.
Translate proper names etc. only when there is a real German equivalent.	**Henry VIII** **Cologne** **Prince Charles**	**Heinrich der VIII.** **Köln** **Prinz Charles**
Don't convert miles to kilometres, pounds to kilogrammes, etc.	She runs **5 miles** every day.	Sie läuft jeden Tag **5 Meilen**.

183

Skills file   Essay writing

An essay is a clearly structured piece of writing in which important points on a topic are presented. Essays are generally written in the present tense.
In an expository essay you explain an idea or set of related facts.
In an argumentative essay you express your opinion and give arguments for and/or against a given topic.

Stage 1: Preparation

- Define the topic clearly.
- Brainstorm ideas and write down what you know about the topic in a mind map, diagram or table.
- If necessary, collect facts, arguments, statistics and other information from other sources, e.g. your library or the internet.
- Formulate your opinion on the topic.

Stage 2: Arranging your material

- Decide on the most important facts, arguments or pieces of information that you want to include in your essay (maximum 5 items).
- For each main argument try to think of two supporting arguments.
- Put your facts or arguments in a logical order.
  For example, you could:
  - start with general ideas and then go on to talk about details.
  - put things into chronological order.
  - start by giving all the arguments in favour and then give all the counter-arguments.
  - follow each argument in favour with a counter-argument.

Stage 3: Writing your essay

The introductory paragraph
- The introductory paragraph should introduce your topic and catch the reader's interest. You could:
  - give a relevant quotation.
  - make a provocative statement.
  - describe a relevant (humorous) personal experience.

- In your introductory paragraph you should also:
  - say clearly what your essay is going to be about in one or two sentences.
  - ask a question or questions which you will answer in your essay.
  - give a brief outline of the problem/topic at present and in the past.

The main paragraphs
- Start a new paragraph for each new idea.
- Begin each paragraph with a main idea or argument and then follow it up with your supporting or counter-arguments (see also Stage 2).
- Write simple sentences.
- Arrange your sentences in a logical order.
- Join your sentences using suitable connectives (see p. 185).
- Use adverbs to emphasize and tone down points.
- Use examples where possible.

The conclusion
- Do not introduce new ideas in your conclusion!
- Make a brief concluding statement summarizing what you have said in your essay.
- Include a quotation or anecdote if you can.

Stage 4: Checking your essay

- Check that all your sentences are complete and that they make sense.
- 'Proofread' your essay: check for grammar, spelling and punctuation mistakes. (Tip: Leave your essay overnight before 'proofreading' it.)
- Write or print out the final version of your essay.

Connectives

Connectives are words and phrases which you use to show a connection between sentences and paragraphs. Using connectives helps readers to follow your ideas more easily because they give your text a clear structure.
Make use of the following connectives in your texts. Keep your own list of personal favourites and add new words and phrases to it when you learn them.

To express a certain order:
to begin with • initially • first of all • first(ly)…, (second(ly)…, third(ly)…, etc.) • next • then • later • finally

To add ideas:
also • as well • in addition • additionally • too • moreover • furthermore

To give examples:
for example • for instance • by way of illustration

To generalize:
as a rule • generally • in general • by and large • on the whole

To express certainty:
clearly • evidently • obviously • undoubtedly

To give a reason:
consequently • that is why • therefore • this is the reason why • as a result

To give an opinion:
in my opinion • to my mind • the way I see it • in my view

To compare or give an opposing opinion:
in the same way • similarly • likewise • equally • on the one hand … on the other hand • in contrast • on the contrary

To conclude:
finally • in conclusion • to conclude • in summary • to sum up

---

Writing a summary

A summary is a short piece of writing in which you restate the main points of a text in your own words.
- A summary is almost always written in the present tense.
- Use your own words and do not copy any phrases or sentences from the text.
- Do not use statistics, numbers, figures, details or quotations from the text.
- Do not give your personal opinion.
- Your final version should be no longer than between one fifth and one third of the length of the original.

A summary of a non-fictional text
In a summary of a non-fictional text, for example, a newspaper article, a report, a factual text, etc. restate the main points or arguments presented in the text.
1. Read through the original text at least twice.
2. In your own words make a note of the main arguments or points in the text. You could:
   - Make a list of key words.
   - Write one sentence to go with each paragraph.
3. Rewrite some or all of your sentences to say what the writer's intention was. You can use the following phrases:
   - The author/writer …
     – points out that …
     – emphasizes …
     – suggests that …
     – describes (how) …
     – concludes by saying that …
4. Link your sentences with connectives (see above).

A summary of a fictional text
In a summary of a fictional text, for example, a short story or extract from a novel, describe briefly what happens in the story or extract and who the main characters are.
1. Briefly describe the characters and the setting.
2. Briefly describe what happens and how the events are connected. Use these phrases:
   - The scene/story/extract …
     – … takes place in …
     – … is set in …
     – … takes place in the present/past/future.
   - The main character is …
   - There are two/three/etc. main characters.
3. Link your sentences with connectives (see above).

Skills file   Making phone calls

Basic guidelines

- Prepare yourself thoroughly.
  - Make notes in English or write out a rough draft of the main things you want to say or find out to give you more confidence and fluency. This is especially important when making formal or business calls.
  - If possible find out the name and number of a direct contact person in advance.
  - Think of things the contact person is likely to ask or say and work out responses.

- Speak clearly and slowly. State your requests clearly and to the point.

- Don't expect to understand every single word that is said.

- Don't worry about making mistakes.

- Be polite! Remember to say '**please**' whenever you ask for information and '**thank you**' whenever you have been given help. Remember: *please* = bitte • *you're welcome/not at all* = bitte schön; gern geschehen

- State telephone numbers as single digits. When the same number occurs twice consecutively you can say 'double' (e.g. 33: **double 3**). 0 = **Oh** (BE & AE) or **zero** (AE)
  Example: 07145 14406: *Oh/zero – seven – one – four – five – one – double four – oh/zero – six*

- When making a social call, give your first name only.
  When making a formal/business call give your first name and surname.
  Address people you know well (friends, people you know socially, people of your own age) by their first names.
  In a formal/business situation address people using '**Mr**', '**Mrs**' or '**Ms**' [mz] + surname.

- Be prepared to spell words, especially people's names and names of places. Useful phrases:
  Would you like me to spell …/that for you? It's spelt … • *I'll just spell that for you. It's …*

- Ask the caller to spell names, etc. for you to avoid confusion. Useful phrases:
  Could you spell …/that for me, please? • *Would you mind spelling …/that for me, please?*

- Repeat information (times, names, addresses, prices, etc.) to be sure that you have understood everything correctly.
  Useful phrases:
  • *Let me just check that I've understood all the information you've given me/asked for correctly. …*
  • *I'll just repeat that back to you to make sure I've got everything down correctly. …*
  • *Let me just check that I've spelt your name correctly. …*
  • *Let me just check that I've written the dates/times/etc. down correctly. …*

- If you don't understand something:
  - Ask the person to repeat what they have just said: *Could you repeat that, please?*
  - Ask the person to explain something in a different way: *I'm sorry, I'm afraid I don't understand what you mean. Could you explain that again, please?*
  - Ask the person to speak more slowly: *Could you speak a little more slowly, please?*

- If you can't hear the the caller properly, ask the caller to speak more loudly:
  I'm sorry, (it's a very bad line,) I didn't quite catch that! Could you speak up a bit, please?

- If you think you've got the wrong number, check and apologize. Don't just hang up. Useful phrases:
  Is that (+ number you want) ? • *I'm sorry, I think I've dialled the wrong number, I'm trying to call (+ number you want).* • *I'm sorry to have bothered you.*

- If the caller has got the wrong number, explain politely. Don't just hang up.
  I'm sorry, but I think you've got the wrong number. This is (+ your number/name/company name). • *I'm sorry, there's no-one here with that name. This is (+ your number/name/company name).*

- Don't interrupt! If you do interrupt, be as polite as possible. There are examples of phrases you can use to interrupt someone or deal with being interrupted in the "Skills file: Useful phrases for discussions" on p. 192.

*Book room for 3 nights from 27th July.
How much?
Evening meals?*

File continued on next page.

Making phone calls **Skills file**

Social calls

Remember to follow the basic guidelines on p. 186.
(See also ideas and useful phrases in the "Skills file: Small talk" on p.188.)

Greeting
Hello! • Hello, this is …[1] • Hello …[2]! It's me, …[1].

Starting a conversation
How are you? • How are you doing? • It's great to hear from you! • I just thought I'd call and find out how you are. • I just wanted to ring and let you know that I'll be in the States in July/etc.

Asking to speak to someone else & passing a call on
Could I speak to …[2], please? • Is …[2] in, please? • Do you know when …[2] will be back, please?
Just a second, I'll go and find him/her. • Hold on a minute, I'll see if he/she's in.

Giving & taking messages
Could you give …[2] a message, please?
I'm afraid he/she can't come to the phone right now. Can I take a message? • I'm sorry, but he/she's not in at the moment. Would you like me to take a message?

Ringing back
Would it be OK to ring back later? • What time can I ring back back till? • I'll ring back in about half an hour, if that's OK. • Could you give …[2] my number, please, and ask him/her to ring me back? • Would you ask …[2] to ring me back, please? You can try ringing again in about 20 minutes if you want to. • He/she should be back at about 10 pm. • Shall I ask him/her to call you back?

Ending a call & saying goodbye
Thanks for ringing! • It was great to talk to you/to hear from you! • Speak to you again soon, I hope. • Bye! • Take care. • All the best.

Formal calls

Remember to follow the basic guidelines on p. 186.

Greeting
Hello/Good morning./Good afternoon. … *. (This is) …[1] speaking. • Can I help you? • What can I do for you?

Asking to speak to someone
Can I speak to …[2], please? • Can you put me through to …[2], please? • I'd like to speak to someone in your … department.

Holding the line & putting calls through
Please hold (the line). • One moment, please. • I'll connect you with …[2]./with the … department. • I'll put you through (to …[2]/to the … department).

When someone isn't available …
I'm sorry, …[2] isn't here/available at the moment/today/etc.

Getting the right extension, etc.
Can you give me …[2] 's extension number, please? • I'd like to receive more information about … . • I'm calling about … .
• I can give you his/her extension number/ voice mail number/fax number / e-mail address. It's …[3].

Giving & taking messages
Would you like to leave a message? • Can I take a message? • Would you like me to pass on a message? • Could you pass on a message, please?

Ringing back
Shall I ask him/her to call you back? • Could you call back later/in half an hour/etc., please? • Could you ask him/her to call me back, please? My number is …[3] • Can I call back later? • I'll call back later/in half an hour/etc. , if that's OK. • When would be the best time to call back?

Ending a call
Thanks for your call!/Thanks for calling! • Thank you very much for your help! • Sorry I can't be of any more help. • Have a nice day! • Goodbye!

---

[1] Your name.
[2] Name of person you want to speak to.
[3] State telephone number.

[1] Your name.
[2] Name of person you want to speak to.
[3] State telephone/extension number.
* Name of company.

Skills file Small talk

Small talk is light (casual) conversation. It is a way of showing interest in others, communicating in a friendly way and avoiding conflict at all times! At a social event, like a party, you might spend the whole time in casual conversation. At a business meeting, on the phone, at an interview, etc. you can start (and end) with a few minutes of small talk.

Topics for small talk

- The weather (especially popular in Britain!)
- A journey (to or from the place where you are)
- Where you live./Where your conversation partner lives
- Your family and/or your conversation partner's family (if you know them)
- A recent/well-known TV programme or film
- Tips about what to see and do in a certain town or city (i.e. cultural events, attractions, restaurants, local specialities, etc.)
- Sport (e.g. a current international sports event)
- A vacation
- Where you/your conversation partner went to school or university
- What you/your conversation partner do for a living
- Hobbies and interests
- An experience/event that you and your conversation partner are both currently involved in or have been involved in
- A non-controversial item in the news

Useful phrases

Starting a conversation
Hi!/Hallo!
What are you up to?
Do you mind if I join you?
Nice to see you (again)!
How are you?
How are you doing?
How are things?

Filling time
Well, …
Actually, …
Let's see, …
Let me think, …

Finding a topic
Did you see … on TV last night/at the weekend/etc.?
Have you seen the new [James Bond] film yet?
Did you read about [that terrible train crash] in the newspaper this morning?
Terrible/Beautiful weather, isn't it?
How was your journey?
How did you get here?
What made you decide to come here?
Have you ever been here before?
Who do you think is going to win [the football match] this evening?

Responding & showing surprise
Really?
I don't believe it!
That's incredible!
Well, I've never heard of anything like that before!
That's the funniest/most interesting/strangest thing I've heard in ages!
I've never thought of it like that before.
I couldn't agree more!
That's funny! Exactly the same thing happened to me the other day/two weeks ago/etc.

Using question tags
You know …, don't you?
He's …, isn't he?
It hasn't …, has it?

Finishing a conversation
It was nice talking to you!
Goodness/Oh no, is that the time?
Excuse me,/What a shame, I've got to go now.
Hope to see you again soon.
Hope you get home safely.
Take care.
Give my regards to … .
Don't forget to say hello to … for me!

Giving a talk or presentation — Skills file

Preparation

1. Gather material on your topic.
   - Brainstorm to find ideas on the topic and make a mind map.
   - Find information from relevant sources (library, school books, the internet, newspapers, etc.)
2. Choose which main points you want to talk about.
3. Make a set of prompt cards in English, which you can look at during your talk to remind you of what you want to say. (See below.)
   - Use one card for each of your points. Give each card a suitable title.
   - Write down the key words, phrases, and vocabulary which you will need.
   - Note down any examples or quotations.
   - Note down any visual aids (OHPs, photographs, posters, flip charts, etc.) which you want to use.
   - Use colour markers to help you identify things on your cards easily when you are speaking.
4. Arrange your prompt cards in a logical order. You could present points:
   - in terms of importance, from the most to the least important (or vice versa).
   - chronologically.
   - in favour and then all those against.
   - in favour and against one after the other.
5. Make a prompt card for your introduction. To catch the listeners' attention you could start with:
   - an interesting question or fact
   - a quote or joke
   - a picture or cartoon on an OHP transparency.
   Note the key words, phrases etc. that you will need on your prompt card.
6. Make a prompt card for your conclusion.
   - Note the point(s) you want to emphasize.
   - Write down key words and phrases.
   - Make a note of a final quotation or example to use.

Giving the talk or presentation

Practise your talk or presentation out loud preferably in front of a mirror or ask a friend/relative to listen to you!

1. Speak slowly and clearly!
2. Use short, clear sentences.
3. Vary your voice so that you don't sound boring. For example, emphasize particularly important points by speaking a little more loudly.
4. Look at your audience as often as possible. Don't look at your prompt cards all the time.
5. Try not to make distracting movements such as waving your hands, etc.
6. Smile! (But don't laugh nervously!)
7. Start by introducing yourself (if necessary) and your topic. Finish by thanking your audience for listening and asking if anyone has any questions.

Useful phrases

Good morning/afternoon, my name is ... • Today I'm going to talk about ... • The subject of my talk today is ... • Can everyone hear me alright? • Can everyone see the board/screen/etc.? • Please tell me if you can't hear me properly/can't see the board/screen/etc. • I'd like to begin by (+ verb in -ing form) • Let me start by saying a few words about ... • Let me give you an example. • If you look at the chart/graph/cartoon, you'll see that ... • As you can see on the chart/graph/cartoon/etc. ... • I'd like to finish/conclude by (+ verb in -ing form) • Let me finish by (+ verb in -ing form) • Finally ... • Thank you very much for your attention. • Thank you very much for listening. • I hope you've all enjoyed my talk. • If you have any questions, please feel free to ask. • I'd be happy to answer any questions.

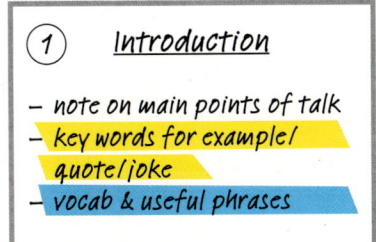

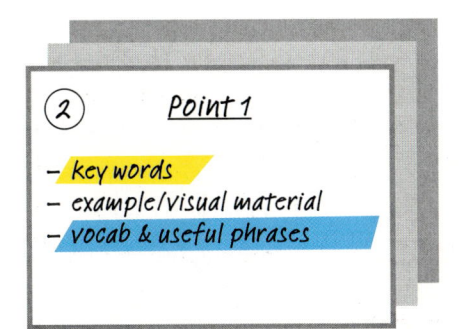

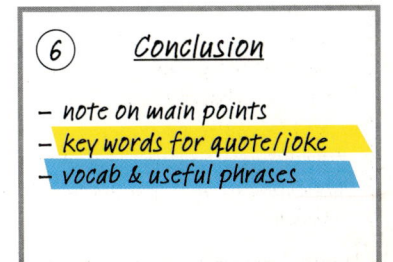

---

① Introduction
- note on main points of talk
- key words for example/quote/joke
- vocab & useful phrases

② Point 1
- key words
- example/visual material
- vocab & useful phrases

⑥ Conclusion
- note on main points
- key words for quote/joke
- vocab & useful phrases

Skills files — Illustrations & photographs/Cartoons

Illustrations & photographs

Types of pictures
photo • (graph) • print • transparency • slide • painting • drawing • sketch • picture • illustration • image • collage • electronic image • snapshot • skyline • panorama • close-up • action photo • still (from a film)

Saying what a picture is of
- This is a photo/an illustration of … .
- This photo was taken in … .
- The illustration shows …
- In this illustration/photo you can see (that) …

Saying where things are in a picture
on the right-hand/left-hand side of the picture • in the centre • in the foreground • in the background • at the top • at the bottom • in the upper right-hand corner • in the lower left-hand corner

Adjectives of style & colour
colour • black & white • bright/dull • hand-painted/hand-drawn/drawn by hand • clear/in focus • blurred/not in focus/out of focus • lifelike • to scale/not to scale • posed/staged

Describing the impression a picture makes
- The person in the picture looks … (+ adjective, e.g happy)
- The photo/illustration supports the point made in the text that …
- The photo/illustration gives you the impression that …
- The impression I get from this photo is that …
- The illustration makes me feel … (+ adjective: e.g. worried).
- The colours the artist has chosen make me feel … (+ adjective: happy/sad/worried/etc.)
- In my opinion the illustration would be better, if … (+ simple past: e.g.if it was more life-like)

Cartoons

Cartoons are funny but critical. When looking at a cartoon the most important thing is to try to work out what point the cartoonist is making. Generally the point is made by a combination of the text and the illustration, so it is important to analyze and understand both.

Illustrations generally show caricatures of well-known people or particular stereotypes. To understand a cartoon, you need to recognize and define the person or group of people illustrated.

Text can be in one or all of the forms below. All text is relevant!
- A caption (a statement in quotation marks under the illustration). You need to work out who is speaking.
- A speech bubble, or speech bubbles.
- Other text, for example, on a sign or poster illustrated in the cartoon.

Phrases for talking about cartoons

Describing the cartoon
The cartoon consists of an illustration of … . • The illustration shows … • There is a caption under the cartoon, which is spoken by … . • There is a caption under the cartoon, which says "…". • In the (first) speech bubble it says "…". • The text in the speech bubble is spoken by … • The figure is a stereotype of … • The figure is a caricature of … • The drawing is detailed/clear/sketchy/abstract.

Talking about the point
The cartoonist is making fun of … • The cartoonist is satirizing … • The cartoonist is making the point that … • The cartoon is funny because of the misunderstanding between … . • The cartoon is funny because of the discrepancy between … .

Giving your opinion
I think/I don't think the cartoon is (very) funny because … • I get the joke./I don't get the joke. • I get the point./I don't get the point. • I think/I don't think the cartoon is easy to understand because … • I agree/I don't agree with the point the cartoonist is making because …

Tips for an interview

Before the interview:
- Find out as much as you can about the business or institution where you will have your interview.
- Try and think of questions that you might be asked, and practice answering them in front of a mirror. Also, choose some discussion phrases (see "Skills file" on p. 192) that you think will be useful and practice using them as well.
- Have a friend ask you these questions (plus some surprise ones) and give you a critique of how you have answered them.
- Think of a few "intelligent" questions to ask the interviewer about the business or institution. These questions should show that you already know something about the business or institution.
- Dress nicely and arrive between 10 and 15 minutes early so that you can collect your thoughts before the interview begins.

During the interview:
- Smile and maintain eye-contact with your interviewer (although it isn't a good idea to stare at him or her)!
- The interviewer knows that you are nervous, so he or she might try to lighten the atmosphere with small talk (see "Skills file" on p. 188). Be prepared to chat with him or her for a short time on this level.
- Speak clearly and not too quickly! It is alright to pause for a moment and think about what you want to say.
- If necessary, ask your interviewer to repeat or explain a question. This also gives you more time to think!
- Do not answer questions with merely a *yes*, *no*, or *I don't know*! This is your chance to give information about yourself that should convince your interviewer that you are the right person for the job! However, make your answers clear and concise.
- If possible, ask your question(s) to show your interest in the business or institution.
- Thank your interviewer at the end.

After the interview:
- After a short time, send a short follow-up e-mail or letter thanking your interviewer and expressing your interest in the position again. If you haven't been told when the decision will be be made, ask politely when you can expect a reply.
- If you don't get the job this time, don't worry! Try and think of what you can do better next time, and work on these aspects. Like with any other skill, the more you go through interviewing, the better you will get!

Having a discussion

- Use the phrases on p.192.
- Always be polite!
- Look at the people you are talking to but don't stare at them.
- Don't interrupt unless you feel it is really necessary.
- Listen carefully to what other people are saying.
- Keep to the point.
- Don't talk too much.

Leading a discussion

A discussion leader:
– introduces the discussion and the participants.
  - *(As you know,) our discussion today is about …*
  - *On my right/left I have … (name of person or group), who is/are in favour of/against …*
– makes sure the discussion is held in an orderly way and that participants are always polite to each other.
– chooses whose turn it is to speak.
  - *Who would like to open the discussion?*
  - *… , would you like to open the discussion?*
  - *The next person to speak is … , followed by … and then … .*
– makes sure everyone has an equal chance to speak, including people who are shy.
  - *Is there anything you would like to say, …?*
– makes sure no one person monopolizes the discussion.
  - *I'm sorry to interrupt you, but I'm afraid you'll have to stop there.*
  - *Sorry, but I must give the others a chance to put forward their arguments now.*
– makes sure that only one person is speaking at a time.
  - *Please wait your turn, you'll have a chance to speak in a minute!*
  - *If you'd just let … finish, please.*
– notes down the most important points and summarizes the discussion at the end.
  - *Time is running out, so I'd like to sum up what we've been discussing.*
  - *We heard from … that …*
– always remains neutral (i.e. doesn't give his/her own opinion).
– thanks everybody for taking part at the end.
  - *Thank you for taking part in the discussion!*

Skills file   Useful phrases for discussions

To make a suggestion:
- Let's consider ...
- I suggest/propose that you/we ...
- I suggest/propose + (verb in -ing form)
- What do you think about ...?
- If I were you, I would ...

To respond to a suggestion:
- That's a good idea!/Fine!
- OK/Yes, why not?
- OK, if you want, I don't really mind.
- I think it would be a better idea to talk about/consider ...
- Couldn't we look at this/do this another way? What about ...?
- I'm not sure (if that's such a good idea). How about ...?

To ask for an opinion:
- What do you think/feel about ...?
- What is your view/opinion on/about ... ?
- What would you say?

To give an opinion:
- As far as I'm concerned ...
- I think/feel/believe/am of the opinion that ...
- To my mind ...
- In my opinion .../In my view ...

To agree:
- You are (quite/absolutely) right.
- That's a very good point!
- Absolutely!/Exactly!
- I agree (with you/Susi/etc.).
- You have a point.
- You might/could be right.
- I think you're right to a certain extent/up to a point.

To disagree:
- I disagree (entirely/with some of the things you said/etc.)
- I'm sorry, but I completely disagree.
- Stop exaggerating!
- I think you're oversimplifying things.
- That's an interesting point, but ...
- That's not the point.
- You've missed the point (entirely).

To interrupt someone:
- Sorry to interrupt, but (could you please explain/repeat the point you just made).
- Excuse me for interrupting, but (I don't understand what you just said).
- Sorry for interrupting but (can I please say something/make a point?)

To deal with being interrupted:
- Can I just finish what I was saying, please?
- Just a second. I haven't quite finished.
- Would you let me/allow me to make my point, please.
- You could at least let me finish my sentence!

To change the subject:
- There is something else that I'd like to say ...
- Have you ever thought of/considered ...
- On the other hand ...
- Try looking at things another way/from a different angle.
- I'd like to bring up another point/point out something else.

To return to the original subject:
- Lets get back to what we were saying/discussing.
- Let's get back to the point.
- As I was saying before, ...
- Getting back to what we/you/... said earlier ...

To ask for further explanation:
- Did I get that right?
- Do you really mean that ...?
- Did I understand correctly that you think ...?
- Could you explain what you just said/the point you just made/etc. again, please?
- Could you give me/us a concrete example, please?

To say that a point has been misunderstood:
- I'm sorry, but ...
  ... that's not what I meant to say (at all)!
  ... I think you've got the wrong end of the stick!
  ... you've got me (completely) wrong.
  ... you've (completely) misunderstood me.
  ... that's not what I was trying to say!
  ... I didn't make myself clear. I'll try and explain again.

Collecting words   Skills file

Where to write new words
- On cards with the word in English on the front and the definition in English (and the German translation) on the back.
- In a vocabulary book: use a small ringbinder so that you can add pages and move pages around as necessary.
- On the computer.

Don't just write German translations to go with new English words. Always write an explanation or give a synonym or opposite in English!

Ways of collecting & organizing words

Be flexible: choose the method for collecting and organizing words which best suits your needs at a particular time.

- Alphabetically (A–Z): This is good as a reference system and you have plenty of space for definitions. You can find words easily, but you have to know what the word is in the first place. It is a good method to use in addition to the other methods listed below.

- By writing synonyms and opposites: Group together words with similar meanings, e.g. **pretty, nice, lovely**, or with their opposites, e.g. **pretty ≠ ugly**.

- In word families: When you note a new word, include the other words which can be formed from it, e.g. the verb, adjective, adverb, etc. Also make a note of the word with its prefix or suffix (see opposite). This is a good way of quickly increasing your word power!

- In collocations: Make a note of words which are often written together (verb + preposition, verb + noun, etc.) Always try to learn words with their collocations, e.g. **to make allowances, to break the news**.

- In semantic fields: Group words according to topics. Include nouns, adjectives, verbs, idioms, phrases, etc., e.g. **School: to attend, to be absent from, to play hooky; classroom, hall, staff room, gymnasium;** etc.

- In mind maps by topic (see p.180): Start with the topic heading and add all the words which come to mind in a logical way. This is a good way of collecting words on a particular theme, however you generally don't have much space in a mind map for definitions.

Prefixes

A prefix is added to the beginning of a word to change its meaning.

To give a word a **negative** or **opposite** (≠) meaning add:

Prefix	Example
in-	active ≠ **in**active
im-	possible ≠ **im**possible
il-	literate ≠ **il**literate
ir-	relevant ≠ **ir**relevant
un-	happy ≠ **un**happy
dis-	to like ≠ to **dis**like
de-	to stabilise ≠ to **de**stabilise

To show an **increase** (+) or **decrease** (-):

Prefix	Example
over- (+)	to heat – **over**heat
out- (+)	to grow – to **out**grow
super- (++)	natural – **super**natural
under- (–)	to pay – to **under**pay
sub- (–)	standard – **sub**standard

Others:

Prefix	Meaning	Example
inter-	between/among	**inter**national
pre-	before	**pre**-school
post-	after	**post**-war
trans-	across	**trans**atlantic
counter-	against	**counter**revolution
pro-	for	**pro**-abortion
anti-	against	**anti**-smoking
re-	again/back	**re**read
mis-	wrong/bad	to **mis**understand

Suffixes

A suffix is added to the end of a word to give it a different meaning, usually to make a verb or adjective into a noun:

Suffix	Example
-ence	to differ – differ**ence**
-ment	to improve – improve**ment**
-ion/-ation/-ision	to nationalize – nationaliz**ation**
-er/-or	to teach – teach**er**/to act – act**or**
-ing	to begin – beginn**ing**
-ness	happy – happi**ness**
-(i)ty	difficult – difficul**ty**
-th	true – tru**th**

193

Surviving without a dictionary

It is very important that you read a text once through without looking up any words. Try to understand the gist, i.e. the basic meaning of a text. You don't need to understand all the details and words at first to understand the general meaning of each sentence! Here are some other techniques that will help you to 'survive' without a dictionary when you come across words you don't know:

1. Try to identify the word family. Part of the word may well be related to another English word which you already know. Look out for prefixes, suffixes and compounds, e.g. *disapproval* = *approve* + prefix & suffix.

2. Many English words are of French or German origin, so think about whether there is a similar word in your own language or other foreign languages you know, e.g. discipline – *Disziplin*.

3. See whether the words and sentences before and after the word (the context) can help you to understand it! Can you guess the meaning by the context? Or can you understand the sentence without needing to understand that particular word?

4. Does the sound of the word help? Say the word out loud, e.g. "Ping!".

Using an English-English dictionary

A good English-English (monolingual) dictionary gives you much more information than just the meaning of a word. It will provide you with:
- the different forms of a word.
- the class of the word (noun, verb, adverb, etc.).
- the pronunciation (phonetics).
- the different meanings.
- grammatical information, e.g. if the word takes an object; whether a noun is countable; etc.
- examples showing how the word is used in context.
- the prepositions, etc. commonly used with the word.
- idioms, etc. in which the word is commonly used.

Tips for using an English-English dictionary
- Before looking up a word identify whether it is a verb, noun, adjective, adverb, etc.
- When you have found the entry for the word make sure you look at the meaning for the correct class of word.
- Read any examples and/or additional information which the dictionary gives you about the word.
- Take your time to read the entry carefully. Don't just look at the first entry or entries. Make sure you find the entry which matches the use of the word in the given context.

In the dictionary entry on p. 195 the following additional information is given in the extra column.

◆◆◆◇◇ = importance of a word. The more black squares, the more important the word is.
ADV = adverb
PHRASE = common phrase using the word
PRAGMATICS = a word is used in a particular way to show more than meaning. There is a definition of when and how to use the word or phrase, the feeling created and an example.
ADV after v = the word is an adverb used with a particular verb. The adverb always comes after the verb in the sentence.
N-COUNT = word is a countable noun and must be used in the singular with a determiner (the/a/my/etc.).
INFORMAL = word or phrase is usually used in informal conversations, personal letters, etc.
ADJ: ADJ n = word is an adjective and must be used in front of the noun or noun phrase.

N-SING: prep the N = a singular noun which always has 'the' in front of it and has a preposition before it.
SPOKEN, BRITISH = used mainly in speech and mainly in Britain (not in America)
N-UNCOUNT = uncountable noun. Uncountable nouns do not have a plural form and always take verbs in the singular.
AMERICAN = used mainly in America (not in Britain)
VERB = word is a verb.
V *onto* n = word is a verb which takes the preposition *onto* followed by a noun.
V-ERG = verb which can be used with or without an object.
V n = verb followed by a noun.
COMB = combining form. Word is joined to another usually with a hyphen (-).
be V-ed = word is used in the passive.

Using an English-English dictionary — Skills file

Dictionary page

This dictionary entry was taken from *PONS Cobuild English Learner's Dictionary*, Klett number: 517922

---

back 1 adverb uses

back /bæk/. In addition to the uses shown below, **back** is also used in phrasal verbs such as 'date back' and 'fall back on'. ◆◆◆◆◆

1 If you move **back**, you move in the opposite direction to the one in which you are facing. *The photographers drew back... She stepped back from the door... She pushes back her chair and stands.* **2** If someone moves **back and forth**, they repeatedly move in one direction and then in the opposite direction. *He paced back and forth. ...tossing a baseball back and forth.* ADV / PHRASE

3 If someone or something goes **back** somewhere, they return to the place where they were before. *I went back to bed... Smith changed his mind and moved back home... I'll be back as soon as I can.* **4** If someone or something is **back** in a particular state, they were in that state before and are now in it again. *Denise hopes to be back at work by the time her daughter is one.* **5** If you give or put something **back**, you return it to the person who had it or to the place where it was before you took it. If you get or take something **back**, you then have it again after not having it for a while. *She handed the knife back... Put it back in the freezer... You'll get your money back.* **6** You can say that you go or come **back** to a particular point in a conversation to show that you are mentioning it again. *Going back to the school, how many staff are there?* **7** You use **back** in expressions like **back in London** or **back at the house** when you are giving an account, to show that you are going to start talking about what happened or was happening in the place you mention. *Meanwhile, back in New York, Sid was back to his old tricks.* **8** If something is or comes **back**, it is fashionable again after it has been unfashionable for some time. *Consensus politics could easily come back.* ADV / ADV / ADV / ADV PRAGMATICS / ADV PRAGMATICS / ADV

9 If you put a clock or watch **back**, you change the time shown on it so that it shows an earlier time. ADV: ADV after v

10 If you talk about something that happened **back** in the past or several years **back**, you are emphasizing that it happened quite a long time ago. *The story starts back in 1950, when I was five. ...that terrorist attack a few years back.* **11** If you think **back** to something that happened in the past, you remember it or try to remember it. *I thought back to the time in 1975 when my son was desperately ill.* • to **cast your mind back**: see **mind**. ADV PRAGMATICS / ADV

12 If you write or call **back**, you write to or telephone someone after they have written to or telephoned you. If you look **back** at someone, you look at them after they have started looking at you. *If the phone rings say you'll call back... Lee looked at Theodora. She stared back.* ADV

13 If someone or something is kept or situated **back** from a place, they are at a distance away from it. *Keep back from the edge of the platform.* **14** If something is held or tied **back**, it is held or tied so that it does not hang loosely over something. *Her hair was tied back.* ADV / ADV: ADV after v

15 If you lie or sit **back**, you move your body backwards into a relaxed sloping or flat position. *She leaned back in her chair and smiled.* **16** If you look or shout **back** at someone or something, you turn to look or shout at them when they are behind you. *Nick looked back over his shoulder... He called back to her.* ADV: ADV after v / ADV

back 2 opposite of front; noun and adjective uses

back /bæk/ **backs. 1** A person's or animal's **back** is the part of their body between their head and their legs that is on the opposite side to their chest. See picture headed **human body**. *She turned her back to the audience. ...the victims were shot in the back.* ◆◆◆◆◆ N-COUNT

2 If you say that something was done **behind** someone**'s back**, you disapprove of it because it was done without them knowing about it, in an unfair or dishonest way. *You eat her food, enjoy her hospitality and then criticize her behind her back.* **3** If you tell someone to **get off** your **back**, you are telling them angrily to stop criticizing you or putting pressure on you. **4** If you say that you will be glad **to see the back of** someone, you mean that you want them to leave. **5** If you **turn** your **back on** someone or something, you ignore them, leave them, or reject them. *Stacey Lattisaw has turned her back on her singing career.* **6** If someone or something **puts** your **back up** or **gets** your **back up**, they annoy you. PHRASE PRAGMATICS / PHRASE INFORMAL / PHRASE INFORMAL PHRASE / PHRASE INFORMAL

7 If you **break the back of** a task or problem, you do the most difficult part of what is necessary to complete the task or solve the problem. *We've broken the back of inflation in this country.* PHRASE

8 The **back** of something is the side or part of it that is towards the rear or farthest from the front. *...a room at the back of the shop. ...the back of her neck... Her room was on the third floor, at the back.* **9 Back** is used to refer to the side or part of something that is towards the rear or farthest from the front. *...the back door. ...the back seat of their car. ...the back garden.* **10** You can use **back** in expressions such as **round the back** and **out the back** to refer generally to the area behind a house or other building. *He had chickens and things round the back.* **11** You use **back** in expressions such as **in the back** and **out back** to refer to the area behind a house or other building. You also use **in back** to refer to the rear part of something, especially a car or building. *He would be out back on the patio cleaning his shoes... I sat in back.* **12** If you are wearing something **back to front**, you are wearing it incorrectly, with the back of it at the front of your body. If you do or write something **back to front**, you do or write it the wrong way around. *He wears his baseball cap back to front... The picture was printed back to front.* N-COUNT / ADJ: ADJ n / N-SING prep the N SPOKEN, BRITISH / N-UNCOUNT prep N AMERICAN / PHRASE

13 The **back** of a chair or settee is the part that you lean against when you sit on it. **14** The **back** of a piece of paper or an envelope is the side which is less important. *...the back of a postcard.* **15** The **back** of a book is the part nearest the end. *...the index at the back of the book.* **16** In team games such as football and hockey, a **back** is a player who is concerned mainly with preventing the other team from scoring goals. N-COUNT / N-COUNT: the N / N-COUNT: the N / N-COUNT

17 • **off the back of a lorry**: see **lorry**. • to **have your back to the wall**: see **wall**.

back 3 verb uses

back /bæk/ **backs, backing, backed. 1** If a building **backs** onto something, the back of it faces in the direction of that thing or touches the edge of that thing. *...a ground floor flat which backs on to a busy street.* **2** When you **back** a car or other vehicle somewhere or when it **backs** somewhere, it moves backwards. *He backed his car out of the drive... The train backed out of Adelaide Yard.* **3** If you **back** a person or a course of action, you support them, for example by voting for them. *...a new witness to back his claim that he is a victim of mistaken identity.* ◆ **-backed** *...government-backed loans to Egypt.* **4** If you **back** someone in a competition, you predict that they will win, and usually you bet money that they will win. *It is upsetting to discover that you have backed a loser.* **5** If a singer **is backed** by a band or by other singers, they provide the musical accompaniment for the singer. **6** See also **backing**. ◆◆◆◆◆ VERB V onto n / V-ERG V n / VERB V n / COMB VERB V n / VERB: be V-ed

195

Skills file Letter writing

Personal letters

A personal letter is a letter you write to someone you know well on a personal basis, e.g. a friend or relative. There are no special rules which you have to follow when you write to people you know well. The model letter below shows you what an informal letter generally looks like in English. You can use informal language in a personal letter, as if you were speaking to the person.

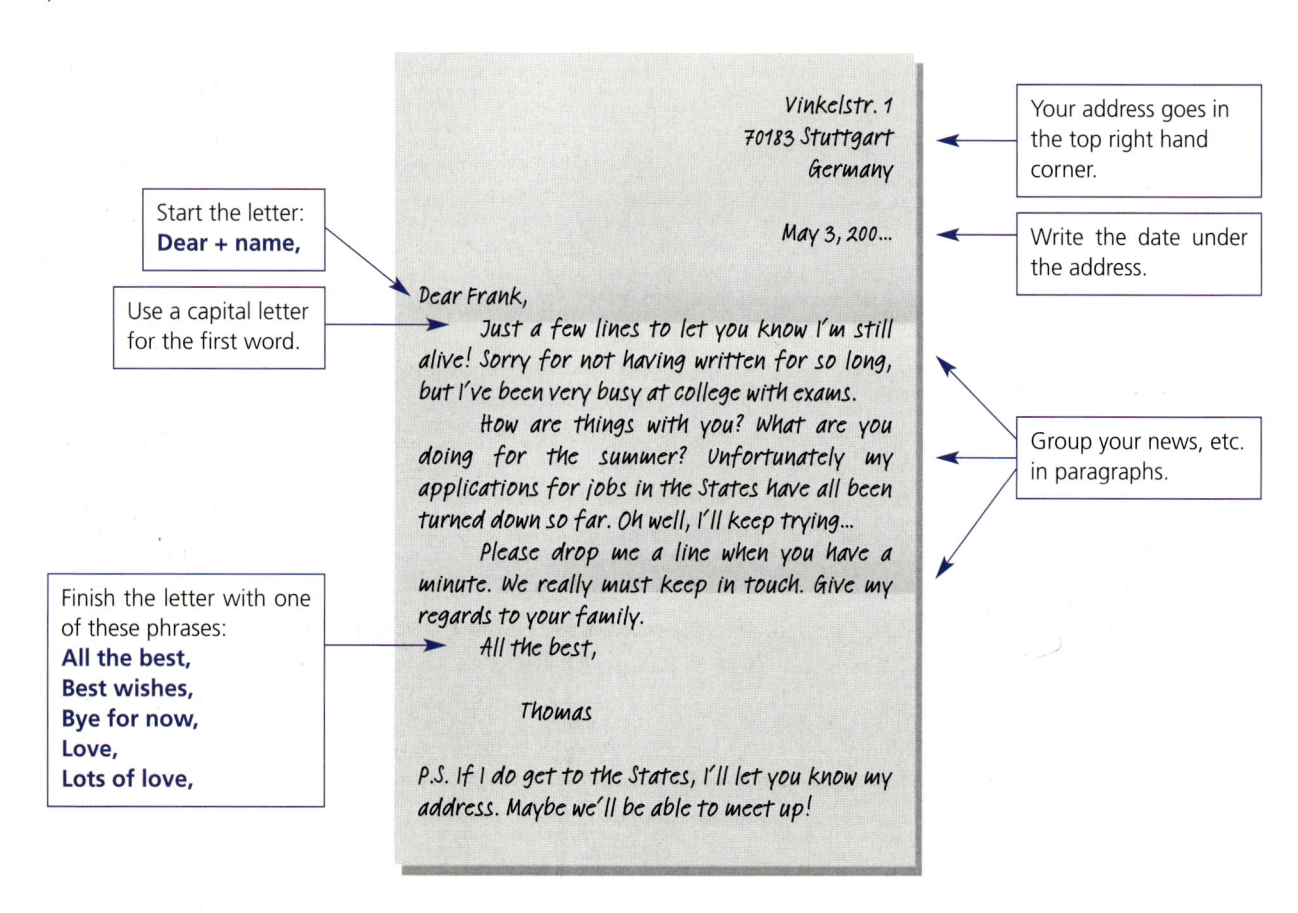

Your address goes in the top right hand corner.

Write the date under the address.

Start the letter: Dear + name,

Use a capital letter for the first word.

Group your news, etc. in paragraphs.

Finish the letter with one of these phrases:
All the best,
Best wishes,
Bye for now,
Love,
Lots of love,

Vinkelstr. 1
70183 Stuttgart
Germany

May 3, 200...

Dear Frank,
  Just a few lines to let you know I'm still alive! Sorry for not having written for so long, but I've been very busy at college with exams.
  How are things with you? What are you doing for the summer? Unfortunately my applications for jobs in the States have all been turned down so far. Oh well, I'll keep trying...
  Please drop me a line when you have a minute. We really must keep in touch. Give my regards to your family.
  All the best,

  Thomas

P.S. If I do get to the States, I'll let you know my address. Maybe we'll be able to meet up!

Salutations & complimentary closes

The salutation you choose in a formal letter (see p. 197) depends on whether you know a person's name, sex, etc. The complimentary close depends on the salutation you have used. Follow the guidelines below.

! Americans usually close formal letters with: **Sincerely yours** or **Yours truly**

Salutation	When used	Complimentary close
Dear Sir or Madam	to a company and when you don't know person's name or sex	Yours faithfully
Dear Madam	to a woman, when you don't know her name	Yours faithfully
Dear Sir	to a man, when you don't know his name	Yours faithfully
Dear Mr Brown	to a man, whose name you know	Yours sincerely
Dear Ms Brown	to a woman, whose name you know	Yours sincerely
Dear Jenny	to a person you know well	Best wishes / Yours

Salutation the way a person is addressed at the beginning of a letter   **Complimentary close** the phrase used before signing off

Letter writing Skills file

A letter of application

Letters of application are personal **formal letters**. (**Commercial correspondence** refers to formal letters written in a business context, i.e. from one company to another, see *skills file* 'A business letter'.
There are different ways of layouting these types of letters. The model letter below is in 'block form', which is probably the best to use because it is accepted everywhere.

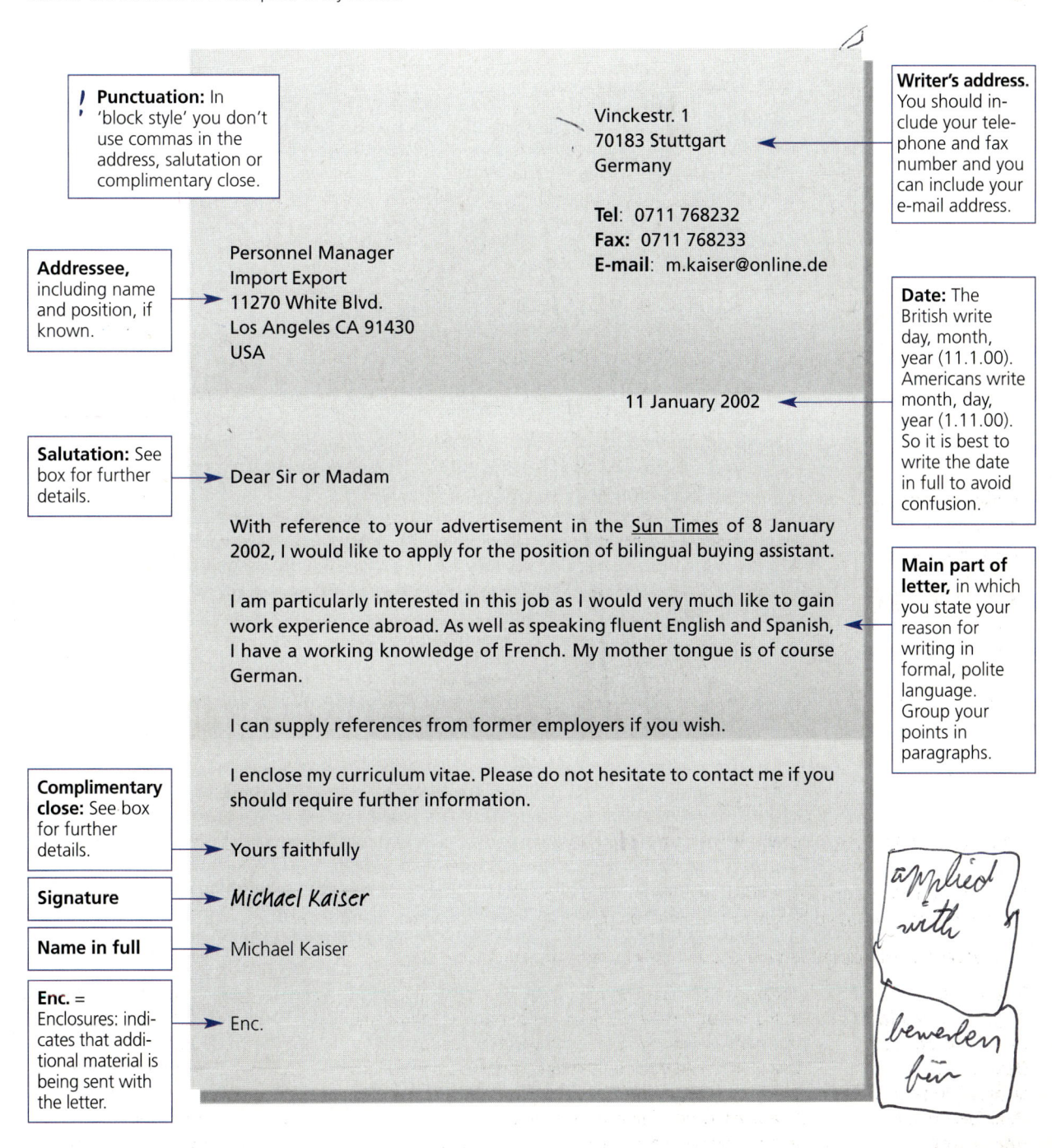

Punctuation: In 'block style' you don't use commas in the address, salutation or complimentary close.

Addressee, including name and position, if known.

Personal Manager
Import Export
11270 White Blvd.
Los Angeles CA 91430
USA

Vinckestr. 1
70183 Stuttgart
Germany

Tel: 0711 768232
Fax: 0711 768233
E-mail: m.kaiser@online.de

Writer's address. You should include your telephone and fax number and you can include your e-mail address.

11 January 2002

Date: The British write day, month, year (11.1.00). Americans write month, day, year (1.11.00). So it is best to write the date in full to avoid confusion.

Salutation: See box for further details.

Dear Sir or Madam

With reference to your advertisement in the <u>Sun Times</u> of 8 January 2002, I would like to apply for the position of bilingual buying assistant.

I am particularly interested in this job as I would very much like to gain work experience abroad. As well as speaking fluent English and Spanish, I have a working knowledge of French. My mother tongue is of course German.

I can supply references from former employers if you wish.

I enclose my curriculum vitae. Please do not hesitate to contact me if you should require further information.

Main part of letter, in which you state your reason for writing in formal, polite language. Group your points in paragraphs.

Complimentary close: See box for further details.

Yours faithfully

Michael Kaiser

Signature

Name in full

Michael Kaiser

Enc. = Enclosures: indicates that additional material is being sent with the letter.

Enc.

197

Skills file Letter writing

A business letter

There are no rules for the layout of business letters and most companies have their own 'house style'. However, there are some common features.
- This sales letter from GiLa's Diner, laid out in block style, is a typical example of a modern business letter.
- Short forms are used (we're, you're) for a personal touch. Use long forms in more formal writing.
- Remember the **KISS** rule: **K**eep **I**t **S**hort and **S**imple.
- Remember the **5 Cs** rule: **C**ourteous, **C**oncise, **C**omplete, **C**oherent, **C**orrect.

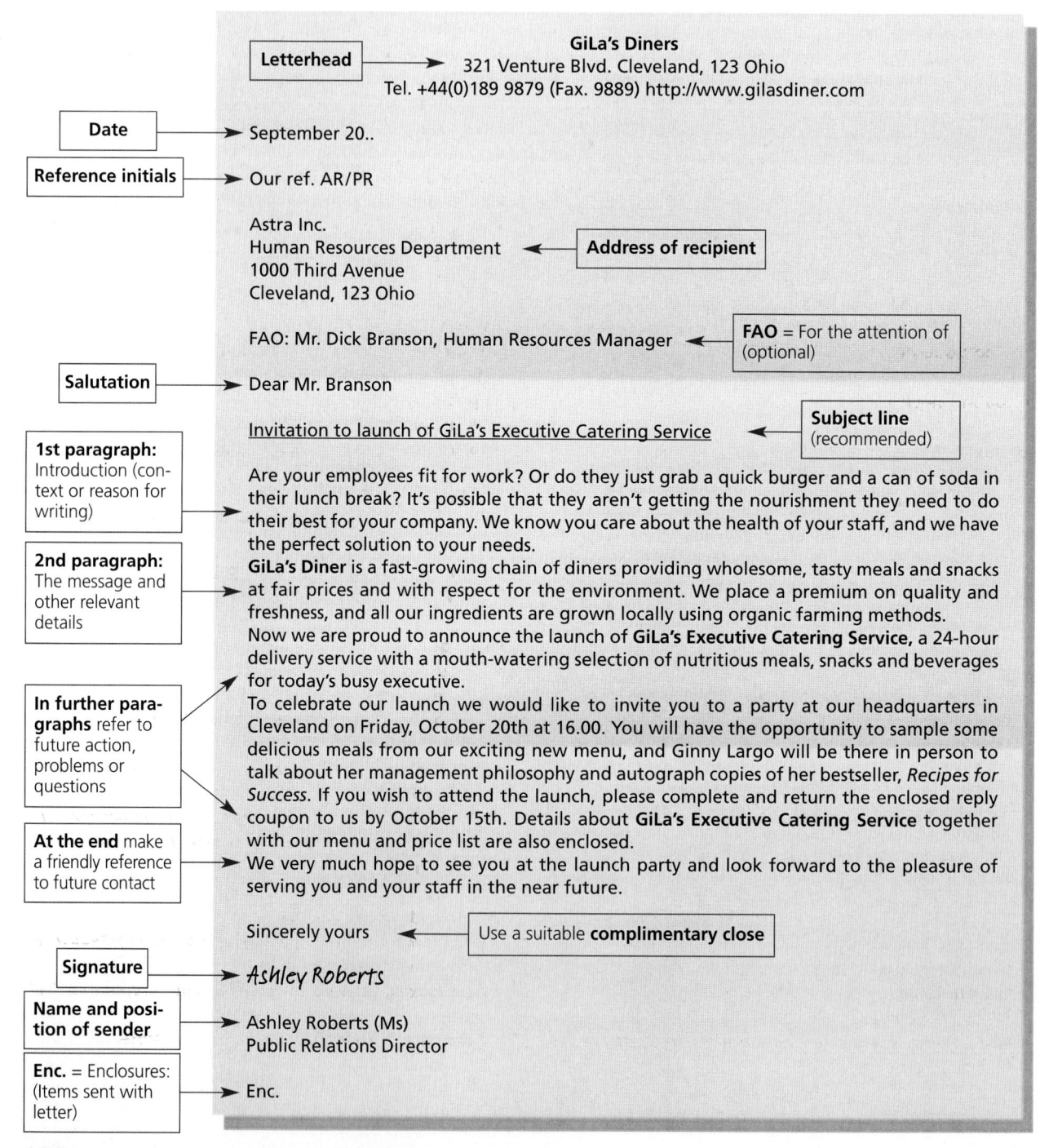

Letterhead →
GiLa's Diners
321 Venture Blvd. Cleveland, 123 Ohio
Tel. +44(0)189 9879 (Fax. 9889) http://www.gilasdiner.com

Date → September 20..

Reference initials → Our ref. AR/PR

Astra Inc.
Human Resources Department ← **Address of recipient**
1000 Third Avenue
Cleveland, 123 Ohio

FAO: Mr. Dick Branson, Human Resources Manager ← **FAO** = For the attention of (optional)

Salutation → Dear Mr. Branson

Invitation to launch of GiLa's Executive Catering Service ← **Subject line** (recommended)

1st paragraph: Introduction (context or reason for writing)
Are your employees fit for work? Or do they just grab a quick burger and a can of soda in their lunch break? It's possible that they aren't getting the nourishment they need to do their best for your company. We know you care about the health of your staff, and we have the perfect solution to your needs.

2nd paragraph: The message and other relevant details
GiLa's Diner is a fast-growing chain of diners providing wholesome, tasty meals and snacks at fair prices and with respect for the environment. We place a premium on quality and freshness, and all our ingredients are grown locally using organic farming methods.
Now we are proud to announce the launch of **GiLa's Executive Catering Service**, a 24-hour delivery service with a mouth-watering selection of nutritious meals, snacks and beverages for today's busy executive.

In further paragraphs refer to future action, problems or questions
To celebrate our launch we would like to invite you to a party at our headquarters in Cleveland on Friday, October 20th at 16.00. You will have the opportunity to sample some delicious meals from our exciting new menu, and Ginny Largo will be there in person to talk about her management philosophy and autograph copies of her bestseller, *Recipes for Success*. If you wish to attend the launch, please complete and return the enclosed reply coupon to us by October 15th. Details about **GiLa's Executive Catering Service** together with our menu and price list are also enclosed.

At the end make a friendly reference to future contact
We very much hope to see you at the launch party and look forward to the pleasure of serving you and your staff in the near future.

Sincerely yours ← Use a suitable **complimentary close**

Signature → *Ashley Roberts*

Name and position of sender →
Ashley Roberts (Ms)
Public Relations Director

Enc. = Enclosures: (Items sent with letter) → Enc.

Useful phrases for business letters

Explaining the purpose of the letter:
- We are writing/I am writing ...
  - ... in connection with ...
  - ... with reference/regard to ...
  - ... to advise you of ...
  - ... to confirm ...
  - ... to let you know ...
  - ... to tell you that ...
  - ... to ask/enquire ...
  - ... to ask/enquire whether ...

Stating a reference:
- Thank you for your letter of 26th July.
- Many thanks for your letter dated 26th July.
- We/I refer to your order for 2000 ABC Widgets.
- I have received your enquiry regarding our new widgets.
- Further to our telephone conversation today, ...
- With reference to your fax of June 5th, ...
- With regard to your enquiry of June 5th about ...

Giving good news:
- I am delighted to tell you that ...
- You will be pleased to hear that ...

Giving bad news:
- We regret to inform you that ...
- I am afraid that ...
- We are sorry to have to tell you that ...

Making a request:
- Please ... (direct)
- Please could you ... (less direct)
- Could you possibly ...?
- We would be grateful if you could/would ...
- We would be much obliged if you could ...
- I would appreciate it if you could ...

Offering help:
- If you wish, we would be happy to ...
- Would you like us to ...?

Giving information:
- We wish to inform you that ...
- We are pleased to inform/advise you that ...

Enclosing documents:
- I am enclosing ...
- Please find enclosed ...
- Please find attached ... (e-mail attachment / papers fixed to letter with paper clip/etc.)

Thanking:
- Thank you for sending me ...
- Many thanks for ...
- I am grateful to you for ...
- I am much obliged to you for sending me ... (formal)

Apologising:
- I am sorry about the delay in replying.
- We were (very/extremely/most) sorry to hear about the problem.
- We regret that this problem has happened.
- We apologise for any inconvenience caused.

Setting deadlines / Insisting / Threatening:
- Please ensure that the goods reach us by (+ deadline).
- We must insist on payment by (+ deadline) at the latest.
- If the goods do not reach us by (+ deadline), we will ... (+ threat).

Assuring:
- Please rest assured that we will do our utmost to help you.
- We assure you that we will do our best to put the matter right.
- We promise to look into the matter immediately.
- You can count on us to ensure smooth delivery in future.

Making concessions:
- We agree to reduce the price by (percentage/sum of money).
- We are happy to grant you a discount of 3 % on the goods.
- We will let you have the goods at a reduced price of ... .

Closing remarks:
- If you have any questions, please do not hesitate to call me/us on (+ tel. no.).
- Should you have any questions, feel free to contact me/us.
- If you require further information, please do get in touch/ask.
- Should you require further details, please contact us again.
- If we can help in any way we would be happy to be of assistance.

Referring to future contact:
- I look forward to hearing from you soon/meeting you next week/seeing you on the 29th.
- I am looking forward to receiving your proposal/order/replay.
- I hope to receive your comments in due course.

Skills file   Writing a CV

CV is short for 'Curriculum Vitae'. There are no rules about how to write a CV in English. Use the following 'Dos and Don'ts' and the model CV below as a guide.

Dos and Don'ts

dos
- Do include skills and interests which are relevant to the job, if possible.
- Do give the English equivalents of German terms, where possible.
- Don't write more than one page.
- Don't necessarily include a photo, unless asked to.
- Don't use handwriting for your CV.
- Don't sign your name at the end.

Curriculum Vitae

Name:	Michael Kaiser
Address:	Dinkelstr. 1, 70183 Stuttgart, Germany
Telephone:	++ 49 / 711/234567
E-mail:	m.kaiser@on-line.de
Date of birth:	22.3.1982
Nationality:	German
Schools:	1992–1998: Pfeiffer Comprehensive School (*Realschule*)
	1998–2000: College of Languages, Stuttgart
Qualifications:	School leaving certificate (*Realschule*) (1998)
	Diploma in English & Spanish for bilingual secretaries (2000)
Work experience:	July 1999– September 1999: cashier at McDougall's, Stuttgart
	July 2000– September 2000: office assistant in the export department of Busch, Stuttgart
Further skills:	Fluent in English and Spanish, working knowledge of French
	Good computer skills (Word, Excel)
	Driving license
Hobbies:	Tennis, member of local theatre group responsible for posters and advertising

References:
Mr Peter Meier,   Ms Hannelore Schwarz,
Export manager   Personnel Manager
Busch,   McDougall's,
Jahnstraße 11   Königstraße 128
70023 Stuttgart   70031 Stuttgart

capable
(able (syn.))

Projects & group work Skills file

Finding information

Create an 'information centre' in which you keep a record of where to find information.

Find and keep a record of:
- the name, address, e-mail address, telephone and fax number of:
  - your local library.
  - the nearest university or college library.
  - your twin-town association (if your area has one).
  - the nearest newsagent or bookshop which stocks English newspapers and magazines. (Tip: Try your nearest main station.)
- the website addresses of:
  - search engines in America and the UK.
  - schools and colleges in America and the UK.
  - youth organizations in America and the UK.
  - political parties in America and the UK.
  - newspapers, magazines in America and the UK.
  - government agencies in America and the UK.
- the names of any members of your class who have contacts (penfriends, relatives, friends, etc.) in the English speaking world, and who might be willing to help you.
- the names of any members of your class or people in your neighbourhood who have an English-speaking parent/parents and who might be willing to help you.

Collect brochures from travel agencies and tourist information bureaus.

Collect material while you are on holiday (leaflets, magazines, postcards, advertisements, menus, timetables, etc.).

Add information and addresses to your files whenever you find new material.

Doing a project

How you go about doing a project will depend on the assignment. These tips are very general.

1. Read the information you are given about the assignment carefully.
2. In your groups, brainstorm to find ideas about:
   - what you all already know about the topic.
   - which aspects you want to concentrate on.
   - where you can find information.
   (See "Skills file" on p. 180.)
3. If necessary, decide which points are more important (concentrate on these) and which are less important (and can possibly be left out).
4. Decide which tasks each member of the group are going to do. Make sure the workload is divided equally amongst you.
5. If not specified in the assignment, decide how you want to present your material. You can produce:
   - a talk using visual aids. (See "Skills file" on p. 189.)
   - a video.
   - a cassette or CD.
   - a leaflet.
   - a brochure.
   - a file of written information.
   - a poster or wall chart.
   - a written report. (See "Skills file" on p. 206.)
6. Remember to keep a record of your sources, i.e. where you found material, where quotes or extracts from original material are taken from, etc.

Projects in *Challenge 21* • Band 2

- User's Guide (p. 23)
- Decision making: Choosing the right applicant (p. 40)
- Research & present: The changing world of work (p. 41)
- Discussion & Survey: Drug testing (p. 41)
- International e-tailing (p. 55)
- Research and report – local action (p. 75)
- Instruction manual (p. 89)
- Fishbowl discussion: Project Blue Book (p. 105)
- Immigrants in Germany (p. 117)
- Lifestyle magazine launch (p. 133)
- Reaching teenagers (p. 149)
- Internet project (p. 149)
- Glossary (p. 149)
- A TV spot (p. 149)
- Researching historical information (p. 163)
- Political profile (p. 179)

Useful websites (general information)

Search engines
www.google.com
www.altavista.digital.com
www.excite.com
www.lycos.com
www.yahoo.com
GB
www.searchuk.com *(Search engine for GB only)*
www.bta.org.uk *(British Tourist Association)*
www.britcoun.org *(British Council)*
USA
http://usinfo.state.gov/usa/infousa/ *(U.S. Dept. of State)*
www.whitehouse.gov *(U.S. Government)*
www.nytimes.com *(New York Times)*
Find more websites in the *Check the web* boxes in each chapter.

Skills file Questionnaires & surveys

Before doing a survey

It is important to have a clear idea of what kind of information you hope to get from your survey.

1. Write one or two sentences describing your topic and explaining why you are doing the survey. (Later you can include these sentences at the start of your questionnaire so that the people you ask (interviewees/participants) have a clear idea of what the survey is about.)
2. Briefly state what you expect the results of your survey to be – or give alternatives.
   I think the survey will show/prove that …
   The survey might prove that … . On the other hand, it might show that …
3. Decide how many people you want to interview and which social groups they should belong to. For example, is the age of participants important? Should they be male or female? Should they have a certain job or hobby?

The questionnaire

The success of a survey depends largely on how good your questions are. If possible, ask an independent person to answer your questions before you carry out the survey to make sure your questions are clear.

1. Decide what type of questions you want to ask.
   - Your choice of question type will depend on the type of information that you hope to get and on the amount of time that you want to spend on the survey.
   - The most common types of questions are described in the box opposite.
   - Your questions need not all be of the same type, but it is best not to include too many different types.
2. Always keep the aim of your survey in mind when you are formulating questions.
3. Word your questions clearly and concisely. Use formal language.
4. Don't ask too many questions (between 10 and 15 is usually enough).
5. Put your questions in a logical order.
   - questions relating to particular aspects together.
   - Start off with simpler, more general questions and then go on to more detailed questions.
   - Your last question can be an open-ended question giving interviewees the opportunity to give further information on the topic.

Types of questions

- **Multiple choice questions**
  The interviewee chooses from one (or more) of a given set of answers.
  Which of the following is not a US state?
  a) Hawaii ❏
  b) Texas ❏
  c) Bangladesh ❏
  d) North Dakota ❏

- **Yes / No questions**
  Questions that can be answered 'Yes' or 'No'.
  Do you exercise more than three times a week?
  ❏ *YES*
  ❏ *NO*

- **Graded questions**
  The interviewee has to choose to what extent they agree/disagree with, do/don't do, like/don't like, etc. the thing in question.
  How often do you eat fruit and vegetables on average per day?
  ❏ *never*
  ❏ *less than three times*
  ❏ *more than three times*

- **Open-ended questions**
  Questions to which the interviewees must give their own answer. These questions usually begin with a question word: **who**, **what**, **when**, **where**, **why** or **how**.
  How, in your opinion, could the recycling system in your area be improved?
  _____
  _____

- **Advantages (+) & disadvantages (–)**
  Multiple choice, yes/no and grades questions:
  + Can be answered quickly and easily. Are easy to evaluate.
  – Answers are not detailed or personal.
  Open-ended questions:
  + Answers are detailed, personal and individual.
  – Questions take much longer to answer. Answers are more difficult to evaluate.

File continued on next page.

Questionnaires & surveys   Skills file

Carrying out the survey

1. Don't try to make people take part in the survey or to answer particular questions if they don't want to. Participation should always be voluntary.

2. Explain to interviewees why you are doing the survey, who you will be presenting the results to and in what form you will be presenting them.

3. It is usually best to conduct anonymous surveys: that is, without keeping a record of the names of the people you interview. However, in order to evaluate the results it can be important to make a note of certain personal details, for example, age and sex. If you do need this information, explain why to the interviewee.

4. Explain exactly what interviewees are expected to do.
   - Be prepared to give more details if necessary.
   - Be prepared to explain what certain questions mean as the interviewee is doing the survey.

5. If you want to make an audio or visual recording of the interview (and especially if you want to use the recording in your presentation), ask participants for their permission.

6. Smile and always be polite!

Useful phrases for talking to interviewees:

- *Excuse me, I'm carrying out a survey on ... for a school project. Would you be prepared to answer a few questions?*
- *It shouldn't take long.*
- *It should only take a few minutes.*
- *Don't hesitate to ask me, if any of the questions are unclear.*
- *Ask, if you're not sure what any of the questions mean, won't you?*
- *Thank you very much for your participation.*
- *Thank you very much for taking part in the survey.*

Analyzing & presenting results

1. Combine all your results on one sheet of paper.

2. Where possible, present your findings in graphic form using graphs, diagrams, pie charts, bar charts, etc. (See "Skills file" on p. 207.)

3. Look for similarities and differences in the responses. Try to come to basic conclusions and explain why you think particular results were found.

4. Compare the results with the results that you predicted. If there are differences, think of reason(s) why you think this might have occurred.

Useful phrases for talking about the results of a survey:

- *The objective/aim/goal of our survey was to ...*
- *In this survey we wanted to find out ...*
- *(Approximately) one-fourth/one-third/20%/only two of the participants said ...*
- *Our findings indicate that ...*
- *A(n) (overwhelming/slight) majority/minority of the participants indicated that ...*
- *The survey results prove/show/suggest that ...*
- *As we expected, the survey showed ...*
- *Surprisingly, ...*
- *The results of the survey were completely different to the results we had expected.*
- *On the basis of these results, we have come to the conclusion that ...*
- *As a result, ...*
- *We are of the opinion that ...*

Skills file Memos/Agendas

Memos

Memos are letters or reports written to people within an organisation (internal communication). E-mails are gradually replacing memos, but have the disadvantage of not automatically providing a record on paper of important information (unless printed out). 'Memo' is short for memorandum. 'Memos' is short for memoranda or memorandums.

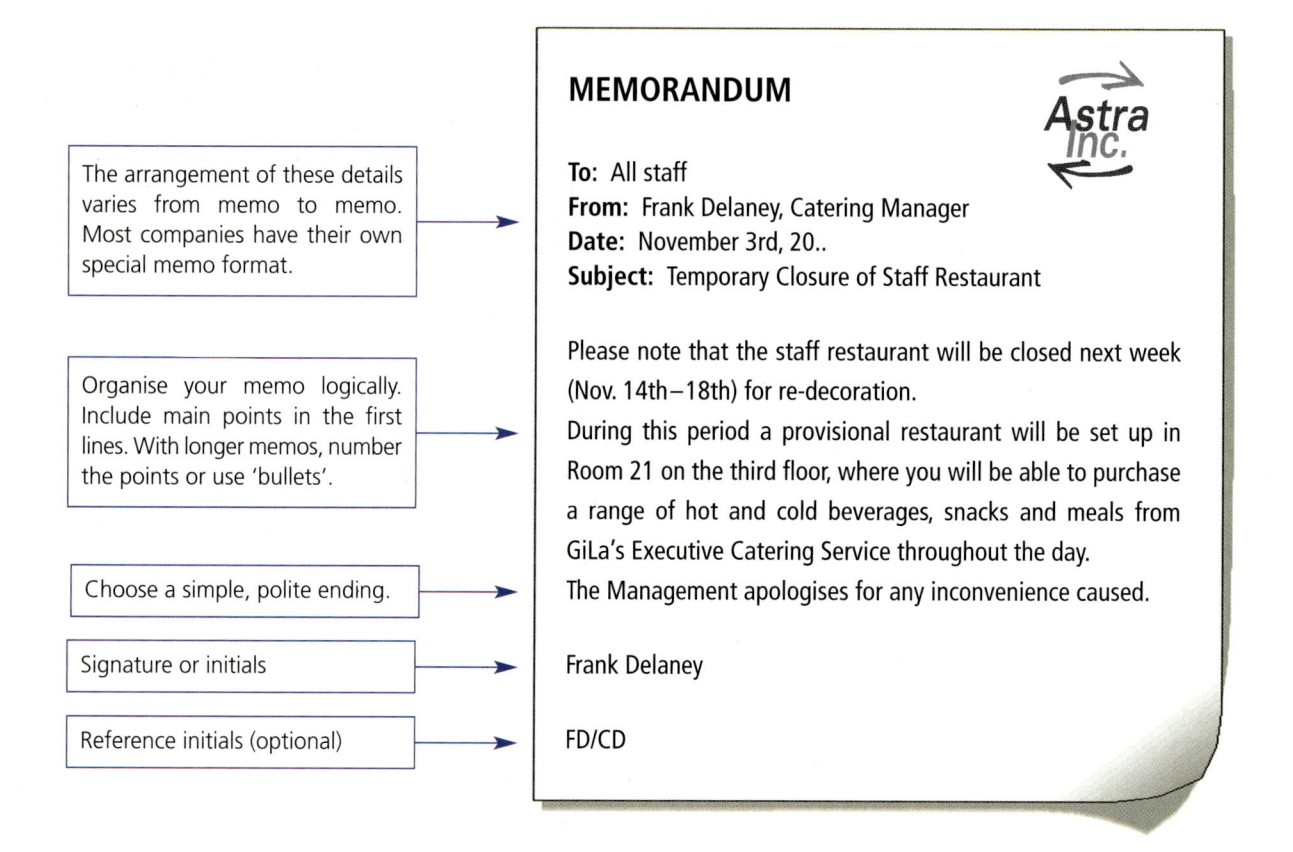

> The arrangement of these details varies from memo to memo. Most companies have their own special memo format.

> Organise your memo logically. Include main points in the first lines. With longer memos, number the points or use 'bullets'.

> Choose a simple, polite ending.

> Signature or initials

> Reference initials (optional)

MEMORANDUM   *Astra Inc.*

To: All staff
From: Frank Delaney, Catering Manager
Date: November 3rd, 20..
Subject: Temporary Closure of Staff Restaurant

Please note that the staff restaurant will be closed next week (Nov. 14th–18th) for re-decoration.
During this period a provisional restaurant will be set up in Room 21 on the third floor, where you will be able to purchase a range of hot and cold beverages, snacks and meals from GiLa's Executive Catering Service throughout the day.
The Management apologises for any inconvenience caused.

Frank Delaney

FD/CD

Agendas

An agenda is a list of points to be discussed in a meeting. People invited to the meeting are usually sent the agenda in advance so that they have time to prepare.
Start with the title, date, time and venue (place) of the meeting, followed by a list of the points to be discussed in order.

The first points are often:
- Apologies for absence
- Matters arising from last meeting

The last points are often:
- A.O.B. (any other business), i.e. any other relevant matters not included in the agenda.
- Date of next meeting

Management Meeting

Date: 28 August 20..
Time: 2pm – 3.30pm
Venue: Conference Room, Block B

AGENDA
1. Matters arising from last meeting
2. Spring collection
3. Price review
4. Customer complaints
5. Problems with supplier
6. A.O.B.

A press release   Skills file

Organisations make use of press releases to promote a product or service or to present a positive public image without the expense of advertising. They are usually sent to a wide range of media groups, including newspapers, radio, TV, trade publications and internet news sources. Editors do not want to give the impression they are providing free advertising, so press releases should be written in a professional news style offering newsworthy information.

Guidelines for press releases

- Use a letterhead (optional).
- Write PRESS RELEASE at the top under the letterhead.
- Write the date and contact details.
- Write FOR IMMEDIATE RELEASE or, if not for immediate release, HOLD UNTIL … (+ date)
- Include an attention-grabbing headline.
- In the first paragraph give key information based on the '5 Ws' (who, what, when, where, why), and also how.
- Keep the press release short (max. 500 words)
- Try to use: quotes where appropriate • statistics to support claims • short description of company including information about products/services.
- Follow news not advertising style. Avoid: too many adjectives • overstatement • exclamation marks (!!!) • self praise
- Enclose or offer photos.
- Always end with "–30–" or ### three lines below the end of the text.

GiLa's Diners
321 Venture Blvd. Cleveland, 123 Ohio
Tel. (0216)1234 (Fax. 1235) http://www.gilasdiner.com

PRESS RELEASE

November 17, 20..
Contact:
Ashley Roberts, Public Relations Director
Phone: (0216)1234-9

FOR IMMEDIATE RELEASE

"LET'S GO ORGANIC!"
GiLa's Diners and Alliance of Organic Farmers announce partnership

GiLa's Diners and the Alliance of Organic Farmers today announced a partnership with the slogan "LET'S GO ORGANIC!" to promote awareness in young Americans of healthy eating and care of the environment. To mark the occasion, Ginny Largo, founder and President of the successful chain of diners, promised a donation of $10,000 to fund educational programs and class trips to certified organic farms. In a keynote speech, Largo said "We are always looking for new opportunities to serve our customers and help the community. Young people and the environment are our most precious resources."

GiLa's Diners provides wholesome, tasty meals and snacks at fair prices and with respect for the environment. Premium is placed on quality and freshness, and all ingredients are grown locally using organic farming methods. September saw the launch of **GiLa's Executive Catering Service**, a 24-hour delivery service with a mouth-watering selection of nutritious meals, snacks and beverages for today's busy executive. This concept is proving especially popular among young professionals.

A survey conducted by the Alliance of Organic Farmers reports a growing demand among American teenagers for food free of chemical additives. Also, 83% of children under 12 would prefer organic food "if it tastes good". **GiLa's Diners** meets their needs. In 2002 it won the award "Best Munchies" in a poll conducted by the "Food 4 Kids" website, http://www.food4kids.com.

Photos available on request.

"–30–"

Skills file Writing a report

Basic guidelines

Length
Reports can vary in length according to the depth of study leading up to them.

Common features
- *Title or title page*
- *Table of contents*
- *Introduction / Summary / Terms of reference / Procedures* stating the purpose and scope of the report.
- *Findings* (= main part of the report) giving the results of investigations. Key facts should be clearly identified by numbering or the use of bullet points.
- *Conclusion(s)* giving an analysis of the facts or findings
- *Recommendations* i.e. action recommended by the writer on the strength of the findings and conclusions
- *Appendices* (graphs, diagrams, statistics, etc. referred to in the report)
- *Bibliography and/or References* (titles of books, magazines, etc. used in finding information for the report or related to the subject of the report)

Form & style
- Reports should be kept simple.
- Language used should be concrete rather than abstract.
- Use shorter words and shorter sentences rather than long and complicated formulations.
- The date can be written at the top or under the signature at the end.

GiLa's Diners

Proposal to Launch Executive Catering Service

Terms of reference
Ginny Largo, President, has asked for a report about the market potential of special catering service to executives.

Procedures
The Marketing Department has conducted extensive research on this subject and analysed the findings.

Findings
1. 87% of executives interviewed eat regularly at GiLa's Diners.
2. GiLa's Diners is generally perceived as an upmarket and socially responsible classic family diner providing quality and convenience.
3. Most respondents were critical of their company's cafeteria. 45% never use it. Common reasons were: 'slow service', 'low quality', 'no vegetarian meals', 'tasteless food', 'downright unhealthy'.
4. Competition is limited to downmarket fast-food takeaways.
5. Executives are prepared to pay a premium for health food, especially the 18–45 age group.

Conclusions
There is a clear gap in the market for an executive catering service. Executives value speed and quality over price and GiLa's Diners already has high brand recognition among an increasingly health-conscious target group. However, it is still seen primarily as a traditional family diner.

Recommendations
I recommend that an executive catering service be introduced, tailored to the target market. The existing brand image of wholesome family dining must be adapted to project a slicker, more professional image.

Dolores Gregory

Marketing Manager

February 17th 20..

Talking about statistics — Skills file

Describing current trends
Use the present progressive to refer to current trends and developments.
Unemployment is rising again. • *The rich are getting richer and the poor are getting poorer.*

Decimals
In English decimals come after the 'point' (not 'comma').
2.5   *two point five*
3.06   *three point oh six*
0.53   *(nought) point five three* or *(zero) point five three*

Zeros in a billion
1,000,000,000   (modern AE/BE:) *a billion*;
                      (formerly in BE: *a thousand million*)
1,000,000,000,000   (modern AE/BE:) *a thousand billion*;
                      (formerly in BE:) *a billion*

Money
£5.20   *five pounds twenty (pence)*
€98.99   *ninety-eight euros ninety-nine (cents)*
$23,454m   *twenty-three thousand, four hundred and fifty-four million dollars*

Describing an increase
to rise/a rise • *to increase by/an increase of/an increase in* • *growth*

Describing a decrease
to decrease/a decrease • *to drop/a drop of/a drop in* • *to decline/a decline*

Adjectives & adverbs
sharp(ly) • *slow(ly)* • *steady/steadily* • *continuing/continual(ly)* • *gradual(ly)* • *significant(ly)* • *insignificant(ly)* • *negligible/negligibly* • *large* • *high* • *small* • *dramatic(ally)*

Examples: *Sales figures have risen sharply over the last two years.* • *There has been a steady decline in the sales of mobile phones.* • *Growth is expected to be negligible.*

Expressing numbers & figures
the figures for the last year/the last month/etc. • *the latest figures* • *the total number of ...* • *a (significant/insignificant/etc.) number of ...* • *a (high/etc.) percentage of ...* • *a majority/minority of ...*

Qualifiers
a total of • *over* • *under* • *nearly* • *more /less/fewer than* • *the same number as* • *the same amount of* • *fifty per cent/ (a) half of* • *twenty-five per cent/a quarter* • *twice as many* • *three times as many* • *roughly* • *approximately* • *around/ about* • *exactly* • *precisely*

Types of graphs
graph[1] • chart • pie chart[2] • bar chart[3] • diagram

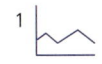

Types of surveys
survey • opinion poll • questionnaire

Describing graphs & tables, etc.
• *The figures in the table show that ...*
• *As you can see from the graph, ...*
• *The dotted line on the graph represents ...*
• *The pie chart compares ...*
• *The figures prove that ...*
• *The statistics suggest that ...*
• *This table gives information about ...*
• *The diagram makes it clear that ...*

207

Glossary abbreviation – flashback

This glossary explains literary terms and terms which you need to understand when working with texts and completing tasks in English.

abbreviation short form of a word or phrase made by leaving out some of the letters or only using the first few letters of a word, e.g. 'Rd' is the abbreviation for 'Road'.

acronym short form of a phrase in which a new 'word' is made by using the first letters of the words in the phrase. For example, AIDS is an acronym for Acquired Immune Deficiency Syndrome.

alliteration repetition of sounds, especially consonants, either at the beginning of each word in a group or on certain syllables within each of the words, e.g. 'seven singing sisters'.

allusion reference to well-known person or event. These persons or events may come from a historical, religious or literary context.

antagonist the character who is opposed to or in conflict with the main character in a novel, play or story (protagonist).

antonym see glossary entry for *'opposite'*.

assonance repetition of the same or similar vowel sounds within stressed syllables of neighbouring words, e.g. 'on the dole with nowhere to go'.

atmosphere the dominant feeling or mood in a text often created by the author's use of setting and description.

character person in a piece of fiction whose personality develops through action, description, language and way of speaking. Flat characters lack depth and represent constant, non-changing types rather than full personalities. Round characters are like real people who can change and develop.

characterization how a character is presented. When a character is presented directly, the narrator or another figure tells the reader what the character is like. When a character is presented indirectly, the reader has to find out what the character is like by analysing his or her actions, thoughts, words, etc.

cliché description of a group of things or people in a way that has been done so often before that it is no longer interesting. See also glossary entry for *'stereotype'*.

climax the most intense point in a novel, short story or drama. This point in the plot often coincides with the crisis or turning point, when the protagonist experiences a dramatic change that will better or worsen his situation.

collocation words which often appear combined as a unit (e.g. to take a photo, a good laugh)

colloquial language synonym for *'informal language'*. A 'colloquialism' is a colloquial word or phrase.

comment short essay giving your opinion on a topic (usually about 200 words).

connotation additional meaning of a word beyond its dictionary definition(s).

curriculum vitae (CV) short formal written account of personal details, education, work experience, etc. usually sent with a letter when applying for a job. (See "Skills file" on p. 200.)

denotation actual meaning of a word as defined in a dictionary.

drama piece of fiction, also known as a play, usually written for performance on stage, in films or on TV. It is characterized by dialogue and stage directions. It may be written as poetry or prose.

essay piece of writing usually between 300–600 words.

euphemism device used to make something unpleasant sound nicer by expressing it in a more pleasant, less direct way, e.g. 'to pass away' is a euphemism of 'to die'.

exposition structural element at the beginning of a longer text, in which the main characters are introduced, the setting is described, and first indications of the atmosphere and tone are made.

falling action the part of a fictional text which occurs after the crisis has been reached, when the conflict is resolved and there is a clear reduction of suspense.

fictional not real, invented by an author.

figurative language words (figures of speech) used in an imaginative, abstract context rather than with their literal definitions. Metaphors, similes, and personification are examples of figurative language, e.g. "girls are like cats". The term *imagery* is a synonym for *figurative language*.

flashback interruption of the chronological order of a text in order to go back in time and show what happened earlier.

foreshadowing anticipating events that will occur later in the story.

formal language used to address people you don't know very closely. Formal style shows detachment and respect. Typical of it are the use of precise and often difficult vocabulary, full forms and frequently long, complex sentences.

genre type of text, e.g. poetry, drama and fiction, non-fiction.

hyperbole statement which is exaggerated for effect, e.g. 'The way he put his car keys on the desk indicated that he had a fleet of Cadillacs parked outside'.

imagery see glossary entry for *'figurative language'*.

informal language relaxed, personal and subjective communication. Typical of it are the use of fairly simple language, short forms, uncomplicated sentence patterns and fillers.

irony in its strictest sense, a statement expressing the opposite of what is really meant, whereby the reader is expected to realize the true meaning, e.g. saying: "What a lovely day!", when the weather is terrible.

literal meaning of a word as defined in a dictionary.

literary devices synonym for 'rhetorical devices'. (See "Skills file" on p. 181.)

metaphor way of describing something by saying it is something else, e.g. journalists are vultures.

narrator the narrator is the person who tells a story in a novel or short story. The narrator is not identical with the author. If the story is written as if someone was telling it themselves, using the 'I' form, the narrator is a first-person narrator. The first-person narrator can only tell you what he/she does, thinks, and feels, so he/she always has a limited point of view. A third-person narrator is not a character in the story, but stands outside it. The story is told in the third person (he/she/they). The point of view of a third-person narrator can be limited or omniscient (unlimited).

non-fictional true to life; the writer refers only to real people and places and to events that do or did take place.

note making writing down in short form information you are given from a written source.

note taking writing down in short form information you are given from a spoken source.

novel long and complex fictional story, written in prose, which typically includes characters, setting(s) and a plot.

opposite (also known as **antonym**) word or term which has roughly the opposite meaning of another word, e.g. soft ≠ hard.

parody fictional text which imitates the form or language of a well-known piece of writing.

personification technique of presenting animals, plants, objects, the forces of nature or abstract ideas as if they were human beings and possessed human qualities, e.g. "Atlanta was young for her years."

plot the author's careful selection and arrangement of related events. A plot, found in most novels, short stories or dramas, typically consists of a conflict, which develops during the rising action and reaches a climax, which is then followed by falling action and finally a resolution of the conflict.

poem writing divided into single lines that express ideas, experiences and feelings through the use of descriptive and figurative language. Traditional poetry uses four poetic devices: metre (the regular pattern of stressed and unstressed syllables); stanza (the usually regular number of lines which form a unit); rhythm (the sound pattern which is created primarily by the metre); rhyme (the repetition of the same or similar sounds, often found at the ends of words). Modern poetry often does not have a regular rhythm or rhyme scheme (the pattern created by rhymed words).

point of view perspective or position from which the *narrator* presents the story to the reader. (See also glossary entry for *'narrator'*.)

project a major assignment which usually involves some kind of research.

prose writing which is used for articles, essays, and novels, short stories and most dramas. This type of 'everyday language' is composed of lines of various lengths which flow together and are divided into paragraphs.

protagonist the main character in a novel, play or story.

pun play on words, e.g. 'The sole has no feet and therefore no soul, poor soul.'

quotation a quotation is a sentence or phrase taken word for word from another source. If you quote someone or quote from a text you use the exact words spoken or written, usually to support an argument.

report factual text written objectively describing a particular event or point.

rhetorical devices synonym for 'literary devices'. (See "Skills file" on p. 181.)

rhetorical question question to which an answer is not expected but is used for emphasis or organizational purposes.

rising action structural element of a fictional text, marked by an increase in suspense and an intensifying of the conflict.

sarcasm bitter or aggressive remark used to express disapproval or mockery.

satire a humorous fictional text intended to criticize certain conditions, events or people by making them appear ridiculous. It differs from comedy in that it tries to correct and improve rather than to be only funny.

science fiction literary genre in which fantastic adventures take place on Earth, on other planets or in other worlds, mostly in the future. Fictional technological developments and inventions play a major part in this genre.

setting the place and time in which the action in a piece of writing occurs.

short story short fictional narrative which typically has a tight plot, and is limited in theme, setting, number of events and characters.

simile a simile describes someone or something as being like something else, e.g. she runs like a hare.

speaker the voice speaking in a poem, which is not necessarily identical to the voice of the author.

stage direction author's notes in a drama on how it is to be performed.

stanza group of lines in a poem (see entry for *'poem'*).

stereotype a fixed set of general characteristics that people believe are typical of a particular group of people or things. (See also glossary entry for *'cliché'*.)

suspense feeling of tension and expectation about what is about to happen in a book, play or film, etc.

symbol an object which stands not only for itself but for some abstract idea as well, e.g. the dove is often used as a symbol of peace.

synonym a word or term that means the same or nearly the same as another, e.g. clever/intelligent.

technical term word or phrase used in a special field of knowledge, e.g. word processor.

text form kind of text, e.g. comment, novel, report, manual.

text type classification of texts based on the writer's intentions, e.g. argumentative (also called persuasive: tries to convince the reader of a certain point of view), instructive (neutral texts telling the reader what to do or how to do something), narrative (tells the story of a fictional or non-fictional event in chronological order), descriptive (describes people, places, objects) or expository (explains and analyses complex topics or issues).

theme the central idea or 'message' in a text. A theme is an abstract idea that is not usually stated directly but may be demonstrated through the use of symbols or recurring events and/or images.

tone writer's attitude towards the subject, character(s) and especially towards the reader, as reflected in the text. The tone can be e.g. serious or playful, humorous or solemn, arrogant or modest.

turning point structural element of a fictional text, marking a change in the conflict or suspense.

understatement statement that is deliberately weak, putting less emphasis or importance on s.th. than it deserves, often used in the form of irony.

utopia fictional text dealing with an ideal society, place or world.

word family a base word plus the other words which can be formed from it e.g. the noun, verb, adjective, or adverb forms, combinations with prefixes and suffixes, etc.

word field a group of words relating to the same topic or category. A word field can include nouns, adjectives, verbs, phrases, etc.

Most of the words explained in the annotations in this book are listed here in alphabetical order with their German meanings. The German meaning is given for the use of the English word in the given context.

A

to abandon [əˈbændən] (p. 97) aufgeben
to abdicate (p. 173) abdanken
aberration [ˌæbəˈreɪʃn] (p. 160) Verirrung, Irrtum
abiding [əˈbaɪdɪŋ] (p. 160) bleibend
abortion (p. 173) Abtreibung
to abound (p. 111) sehr zahlreich sein
to be above s.th. (p. 173) über etw. stehen
to keep abreast (p. 45) auf der Höhe der Zeit bleiben
abrupt [əˈbrʌpt] (p. 58) abrupt, plötzlich
absently (p. 103) (geistes)abwesend
abuse [əˈbjuːs] (p. 64) Missbrauch
abyss [əˈbɪs] (p. 98) *hier:* Weite
to accelerate [əkˈseləreɪt] (p. 58) beschleunigen
access [ˈækses] (p. 147) Zugang – **to access s.th.** *BE:* [ˈ--], *AE:* [-ˈ-] (p. 11) *hier:* zugreifen auf etw.
accountable governance [əˌkaʊntəbl ˈɡʌvnəns] (p. 159) verantwortungsvolles Regieren
accountancy firm (p. 45) Buchhaltungsfirma
accountant (p. 46) Buchhalter(in)
acid *(slang)* (p. 102) LSD
to acknowledge [əkˈnɒlɪdʒ] (p. 159) anerkennen, zugeben
to acquire [əˈkwaɪə] (p. 24) erwerben (p. 42) annehmen, sich aneignen
actuator [ˈæktʃueɪtə] (p. 80) Schalter
to address [-ˈ-] (p. 93) *hier:* etw. angehen, sich einer Sache annehmen
adequacy [ˈædɪkwəsɪ] (p. 32) *hier:* Fähigkeit
adjustment pains [əˈdʒʌstmənt] (p. 128) Anpassungsschwierigkeiten
to admit s.o. (p. 88) jdn. hereinbitten
in advance (p. 83) im Voraus, vorab
adverse [ˈædvɜːs] (p. 38) nachteilig
advert *(informal)* (p. 45) Anzeige
advice [-ˈ-] (p. 131) Rat
to advise (p. 163) raten
aerial shield (p. 160) Raketenabwehrsystem
affiliate (p. 93) Partnerunternehmen
to affirm (p. 102) bestätigen
to be afflicted by (p. 167) leiden an
affluent [ˈ---] (p. 115) reich, wohlhabend
to afford s.th. [-ˈ-] (p. 87) sich (etw.) leisten
to afford (p. 93) *hier:* geben; bieten
aftermath (p. 98) schreckliche Folgen; (p. 168) die Zeit nach einem wichtigen Ereignis (*hier:* der zweite Weltkrieg)
to come of age (p. 106) mündig/ erwachsen werden

agony (p. 98) Qual, Verzweiflung
to have an air of (p. 46) den Anschein haben
airlock (pp. 95, 96) Luftschleuse
albeit [ɔːlˈbiːɪt] (p. 141) obgleich, auch wenn
to alert (p. 107) warnen
alien (p. 107) Ausländer/in
allegedly (p. 139) angeblich
allegiance [əˈliːʒəns] (p. 175) Treue
alleviation [əˌliːviˈeɪʃn] *(formal)* (p. 159) Linderung
entangling alliances [ɪnˈtæŋɡlɪŋ əˈlaɪənsɪz] (p. 163) verpflichtende Bündnisse zwischen Staaten
alloy [ˈælɔɪ] (p. 153) Legierung
to alter (p. 82) ändern
alternating [ˈɔːltəneɪtɪŋ] (p. 58) wechselnd, abwechselnd
amazed [-ˈ-] (p. 128) erstaunt
ambitious [æmˈbɪʃəs] (p. 93) ehrgeizig
amorphous (p. 174) unstrukturiert, formlos
to amount to (p. 123) hinauslaufen auf
ampersand (p. 13) das Zeichen & für ‚und'
to amplify (p. 59) verstärken
ancestry [ˈænsəstrɪ] (p. 166) Abstammung, Herkunft
at right angles (p. 13) in rechtem Winkel zueinander
Anglo [ˈæŋɡləʊ] *(informal)* (p. 117) *hier:* Englisch – **Anglos** *(informal)* (p. 111) Kurzform für englischsprechende und -stämmige Amerikaner
anguish [ˈæŋɡwɪʃ] (pp. 88, 98) Qual, Schmerz
annoying (p. 128) ärgerlich
anorexia [ˌænˈrɪksɪə] (p. 117) Magersucht
anticipation (p. 177) Erwartung
anxiety [æŋˈzaɪətɪ] (p. 123) Sorge
to be anyone's guess (p. 143) weiß der Himmel
apparel *(formal)* (p. 145) Gewand
appeal (p. 21) Reiz
application fee (p. 115) Anmeldegebühr
application (p. 101) Verwendung
to apply (p. 93) verwenden
apprehensively (p. 123) besorgt
appropriate (p. 143) angemessen
to appropriate [əˈprəʊprɪeɪt] (p. 141) sich zu Eigen machen
to be apt to be (p. 131) wahrscheinlich etw. sein
arc (p. 97) Bogen
ardent (p. 139) begeistert
staging area (p. 107) Aufmarschplatz; *hier:* Ausgangspunkt
argot [ˈɑːɡəʊ] (p. 11) Argot, Slang

arid [ˈærɪd] (p. 59) trocken
Armageddon (p. 98) globale Katastrophe
to be armed with (p. 107) *hier:* ausgerüstet sein mit
armor-plated (p. 160) gepanzert
armoured (p. 178) gepanzert
to arouse [əˈraʊz] (p. 147) hervorrufen, erregen
solar array (p. 95) Solaranlage
to aspire to [əˈspaɪə] (p. 69) nach etw. streben
assault [əˈsɔːlt] (p. 160) Angriff
assertion (p. 167) Behauptung
asset [ˈæset] (p. 166) *(fig)* Vorteil
assiduously (p. 139) gewissenhaft
associate professor (p. 111) C3-Professor
to assume [əˈsjuːm] (p. 109) annehmen – **to assume a position** [əˈsjuːm] (p. 82) eine Position einnehmen
assumed to be (p. 26) vermutlich
assumption (p. 167) Überzeugung, Annahme
asylum [əˈsaɪləm] (p. 167) Asyl
to snap to attention (p. 103) zackig Haltung annehmen
audacious [ɔːˈdeɪʃəs] (p. 45) kühn
target audience (p. 111) Zielgruppe
augmented (p. 77) erweitert
availability (p. 145) *hier:* sexuelle Verfügbarkeit
awash (p. 97) überflutet

B

bachelor (p. 123) Junggeselle
backlash (p. 153) Gegenreaktion
badge (p. 19) Abzeichen
ballistic missile (p. 95) Raketengeschoss
to ban (p. 143) etw. verbannen, verbieten
old banger *(BE, informal)* (p. 129) Klapperkiste
bank statement (p. 131) Kontoauszug
bank (p. 83) *hier:* Reihe
barmy [ˈbɑːmɪ] *(BE, informal)* (p. 129) bekloppt
barrier [ˈbærɪə] (p. 159) Schranke
bashfully (p. 88) schüchtern
batch [bætʃ] (p. 87) Stapel – **a batch of** (p. 87) *hier:* einige
battered (p. 143) geschlagen
to keep s.th. or s.o. at bay *(fig.)* (p. 46) jdn. in Schach halten
to be intimate (p. 13) vertraut sein
to be one's cup of tea *(informal)* (p. 32) jemandes Fall sein
beacon [ˈbiːkn] (p. 101) Leuchtfeuer
bead (p. 121) Perle

A – Z   bear with – compact

to bear with s.o. (p. 174) sich gedulden, ertragen
bearing (p. 38) Auswirkung
bed sore (p. 82) wundgelegene Stelle
bedsit *(BE)* (p. 82) Einzimmerwohnung
beermat (p. 132) Bierdeckel
to beg for (p. 117) bitten um, betteln um
on behalf of [bɪˈhɑːf] (pp. 155, 172) im Namen von
behemoth [bɪˈhiːmɒθ] (p. 95) Gigant
benefit (p. 117) Vorteil
to benefit (p. 155) profitieren
benison *(formal)* (p. 98) Segen; Wohltat
to berate [bɪˈreɪt] *(formal)* (p. 131) schelten
to besiege [bɪˈsiːdʒ] (p. 104) belagern, bedrängen
to bet on s.th. *(fig.)* (p. 79) auf etwas setzen
to be better off (p. 69) besser dran sein
to bid (p. 109) bieten; ein Angebot machen
billboard *(AE)* (p. 145) Reklametafel
biodiversity (p. 59) Artenvielfalt
bionics (p. 93) *hier:* Verbindung von Natur und Technik
to blame s.o./s.th. (p. 115) jdm./etw. die Schuld geben
blessing (p. 159) Segen
to be blindsided *(AE)* (p. 131) unliebsam überrascht werden
to shed blood (p. 74) Blut vergießen
to bloom (p. 117) (auf)blühen
to blot out (p. 102) verdecken
blue-chip (p. 45) finanziell potent
blue-collar worker (p. 111) Arbeiter(in)
board member (p. 43) Vorstandsmitglied
boarded-up (p. 15) mit Brettern vernagelt
to bolt up (p. 102) hochfahren
bond (p. 167) Band
border-patrol agent (p. 107) Grenzpatrouille, -streife
to borrow (p. 46) *hier:* Kredit aufnehmen
he is not bothered (p. 87) es stört ihn nicht
the bounds of s.th. (p. 95) die Grenzen von, Beschränkung
boundary [ˈbaʊndrɪ] (pp. 13, 59, 111) Grenze
to hit the brakes *(informal)* (p. 107) auf die Bremsen treten
bravura [-ˈ--] (p. 33) Bravour
etiquette breach (p. 13) Verstoß gegen die Etikette
breached *(formal)* (p. 160) durchbrochen
breadth (p. 93) (Band-) Breite; (p. 166) Größe, Ausmaß
to break new ground *(fig.)* (p. 93) Neuland betreten
brewer (p. 73) Brauer(ei)
to bridge a gap *(fig.)* (p. 131) eine Kluft überbrücken
to brief s.o. (p. 103) informieren

to be on the brink of s.th. *(fig.)* (p. 87) kurz vor etw. stehen
briskly (p. 32) flott
broad (p. 148) weit, breit
to broaden (p. 166) erweitern
broking firm (p. 46) Maklerfirma
brow (p. 109) Stirn
to browse (p. 145) durchblättern, überfliegen
bulletin board (p. 21) *hier:* Schwarzes Brett
bunk (p. 102) Etagenbett
buoyant [ˈbɔɪənt] (p. 121) *schwimmfähig*
burden (p. 166) Last
burgeoning [ˈbɜːdʒənɪŋ] *(lit.)* (p. 48) wachsend, blühend
to burst (p. 13) *hier:* heraussprudeln
business as usual (p. 59) wie gewohnt
to buy s.th. *(informal)* (p. 64) *hier:* jdm. etw. abnehmen/abkaufen, glauben
buzz (p. 147) *hier:* Kick
by-product (p. 89) Nebenprodukt, Begleiterscheinung

C

cadre [ˈkɑːdə] (p. 93) Kader, Führungsgruppe, Expertengruppe
cairn [keən] (p. 97) Steinhügel
a tough call *(fig.)* (p. 87) schwierige Situation – **to be on call** (p. 37) Bereitschaftsdienst haben
callous (p. 159) gefühllos, abgestumpft
to campaign for [kæmˈpeɪn] (p. 43) sich einsetzen für
capital punishment (p. 174) Todesstrafe
to capitalise on s.th. (p. 42) Kapital schlagen aus
fleet cars (p. 67) Firmenwagen
carbon dioxide [ˈkɑːbn daɪˈɒksaɪd] (p. 58) Kohlendioxyd
store card (p. 147) Kundenkarte
case (p. 166) *hier:* Argument
to make a case for *(fig.)* (p. 67) sich positionieren als
cast off (p. 102) weggeworfen
cast-iron judgement (p. 38) unumstößliches Urteil
Caucasian [kɔːˈkeɪʒn] (p. 111) Weiße(r) (inzwischen wenig gebräuchlicher Begriff)
to err on the side of caution (p. 63) im Zweifelsfall lieber zu vorsichtig sein
to cease [siːs] (p. 98) aufhören
Celtic (p. 165) schottische Fußballmannschaft
Census Bureau (p. 125) Institution vergleichbar mit dem Statistischen Bundesamt
to challenge (p. 54) in Frage stellen
to champion (p. 160) eintreten für, sich engagieren für
Chartered Surveyor *(BE)* (p. 17) staatlich geprüfter Sachverständiger
to chatter (p. 15) schwatzen, plappern

cheat (p. 46) Betrüger
the funky chicken (p. 131) Ententanz
chief executive (p. 43) Generaldirektor(in) – **Joint Chiefs of Staff** (p. 103) Stabschefs
chilly (p. 121) kühl, emotionslos
chit chat (p. 123) Geplauder
chore (p. 21) lästige Pflicht, unangenehme Arbeit
chuckle (p. 13) Kichern – **chuckles** (p. 67) Gekicher
chunk (p. 139) Batzen; Brocken
on the chunky side (p. 145) untersetzt, gedrungen
to cite [saɪt] (p. 67) nennen
city council (p. 115) Stadtrat
civic [ˈsɪvɪk] (p. 153) bürgerlich
civil engineer (p. 95) Bauingenieur(in)
civil servant (p. 175) Beamter
claim [kleɪm] (p. 160) Behauptung
to clamour for [ˈklæmə] (p.167) lautstark fordern, schreien nach
clear-cut (p. 71) klar, eindeutig
to clench one's fists (p. 97) die Fäuste ballen
clock speed (p. 79) Taktfrequenz
complimentary close (p. 11) Gruß-, Schlussformel
clout [klaʊt] (pp. 48, 111, 115) Schlagkraft, Macht – **to have no clout** (p. 175) kein (politisches) Gewicht haben
cluster (p. 78) Bündel – **to cluster** (p. 97) sich drängen, sich scharen
to clutter (p. 13) (unordentlich) voll stopfen
coalface (p. 121) Streb
to cobble together (p. 79) zusammenschustern
co-chair (p. 43) eine/r von zwei Vorsitzenden
cogeneration facility [fəˈsɪlətɪ] (p. 67) Kombinationskraftwerk
to coin (p. 159) prägen
coincidence (p. 158) Zufall
collateral (p. 46) Sicherheit (zur Erlangung eines Kredits)
kerbside collection (p. 71) Abholsystem
colonel [ˈkɜːnəl] (p. 172) Oberst
to comb [kəʊm] (p. 97) *hier:* streifen
to combat [ˈ--] (p. 43) bekämpfen
combatant [ˈkɒmbətnt] (p. 160) Kämpfer
combustion engine (p. 65) Verbrennungsmotor
to come flaming down *(fig.)* (p. 98) erglühend herabstürzen – **to come of age** (p. 106) mündig/erwachsen werden – **to come to heel** (p. 177) bei Fuß gehen
to express commiseration (p. 172) Anteilnahme aussprechen
commitment (p. 121) Engagement
commonality (p. 153) Gemeinsamkeit
to compact [-ˈ-] (p. 63) zusammenpressen

compassion (p. 143) Mitgefühl
compelling (p. 167) zwingend – **compellingly** (p. 21) *hier:* unwiderstehlich
to compile [-'-] (pp. 11, 109) zusammenstellen
complacent [kəmˈpleɪsnt] (p. 121) selbstzufrieden
to file a complaint (p. 143) eine Beschwerde einreichen
complementary (p. 78) entgegengesetzt und gleichzeitig ergänzend
complimentary close (p. 11) Gruß-, Schlussformel
to comprise [-'-] (p. 63) bestehen aus, umfassen – **comprising** (formal) (p. 79) bestehen aus, umfassen
compulsive (p. 146) zwanghaft
to concede [kənˈsiːd] (p. 48) zugeben
concurrent (p. 93) gleichzeitig
to condemn [kənˈdem] (p. 32) *hier:* sich disqualifizieren; (p. 87) jdn./etw. verurteilen
to condense (p. 11) komprimieren
condiment ['---] (p. 116) Gewürze, Soße
to confess (p. 109) gestehen, zugeben
confidentiality (p. 172) Vertraulichkeit
to be confined to (p. 168) beschränkt sein auf
conflict ['--] (p. 80) Widerspruch; Konflikt
to confound [-'-] (p. 111) *hier:* über-/unterdurchschnittlich
Congressional Black Caucus (p. 115) Kongressausschuss afroamerikanischer Abgeordneter
congressional district (p. 115) Kongresswahlbezirk
consciously (p. 13) bewusst
consequence ['---] (p. 38) Folge; Konsequenz
to take s.th. into consideration (p. 54) etw. bedenken, etw. berücksichtigen
to consign to the past (p. 167) in Vergessenheit geraten
consoling [-'--] (p. 121) tröstlich, beruhigend
constant companion ['--] (p. 123) Lebensgefährte/-gefährtin
constituency [kənˈstɪtjuənsi] (p. 117) Wahlkreis, Wählerschaft
constituent [kənˈstɪtjuənt] (p. 115) Wähler
constitutional (p. 167) verfassungsmäßig
to constrain (p. 65) einschränken, behindern
constraint [-'-] (p. 95) Beschränkung, Zwang
containment [-'--] (p. 163) Eindämmung
contentious (p. 173) kontrovers, umstritten
to contract [-'-] (p. 11) *hier:* verkürzen
to contribute [kənˈtrɪbjuːt] (pp. 58, 111, 155) beitragen

pension contributions (p. 127) Rentenbeiträge
controversy (p. 173) Kontroverse, Auseinandersetzung
under convention (p. 173) in der Praxis
to convey (pp. 13, 21, 143) etw. überbringen, übermitteln
to convict (p. 160) für schuldig erklären
to have the courage of o.'s convictions (p. 173) Zivilcourage haben
to convince s.o. (p. 32) jdn. überzeugen
to cope with s.th. (p. 25) zurechtkommen mit
copywriter (p. 45) Werbetexter
core (fig) (p. 153) Kern – **core demographic** (p. 139) *hier:* Zielgruppe – **to be at the core of s.th.** (p. 127) von zentraler Bedeutung sein
cornucopia [ˌkɔːnjʊˈkəʊpɪə] (p. 141) Fülle, Füllhorn
Corp. (p. 109) Abkürzung für "corporation" = Unternehmen
to correlate to s.th. (p. 147) ew. entsprechen
cost-conscious (p. 141) kostenbewusst
to count on (p. 67) auf jdn./etw. zählen
to counter (p. 147) *hier:* umgehen mit; behandeln
countless (p. 46) unzählig
county commission (p. 115) Kreisrat
to have the courage of o.'s convictions (p. 173) Zivilcourage haben
to let s.th. take its course (p. 87) einer Sache ihren Lauf lassen
to court (old use) (p. 115) umwerben
courtesy of (p. 143) *hier:* dank etw.
coveted [ˈkʌvɪtɪd] (p. 117) begehrt
coy (p. 33) geziert, kokett
to crack s.th. (informal) (p. 115) aufbrechen
crackpot (informal) (p. 88) Spinner
to craft (p. 139) anfertigen, geschickt herstellen
crag (p. 97) Fels
cramped (p. 96) eng
cranky (p. 172) verschroben
to crash out (informal) (p. 37) einschlafen, einpennen
to crave s.th. (p. 145) verrückt nach etw. sein
creditor (p. 46) Gläubiger
movie credits (p. 11) Abspann
creed (p. 74) Kredo, Überzeugung
to creep (p. 96) *hier:* sich ranken; (p. 102) kriechen
crepe paper [kreɪp] (p. 156) Krepppapier
crepitation [ˌkrepɪˈteɪʃn] (p. 98) Prasseln
crescent [ˈkresnt] (p. 98) Sichel
petty crime (p. 127) Kleinkriminalität
to have a criminal record (p. 127) vorbestraft sein
to be at a crossroads (p. 123) am Scheideweg stehen
cross-tempered (p. 36) schlecht gelaunt

crotch (p. 145) Schritt (*Körper*), Unterleib
crucial [ˈkruːʃl] (p. 159) äußerst wichtig
crucial (p. 121) äußerst wichtig
crucible [ˈkruːsɪbl] (lit.) (p. 153) *hier:* Schmelztiegel
crucifixion (p. 174) Kreuzigung
to crumple (p. 95) zusammenbrechen
to crunch (p. 129) knacken
crutches (p. 156) Krücken
cub (p. 19) Wölfling (junger Pfadfinder) – **cub scout** (p. 156) junger Pfadfinder
to be one's cup of tea (informal) (p. 32) jemandes Fall sein
current (p. 82) (elektrischer) Strom
curve (p. 115) *hier:* Trend

D

daresay (p. 36) sich denken können
to make a dash (p. 178) losstürzen
to date (p. 45) bis heute
daycare (p. 43) Kinderbetreuung
day-labor yard (p. 109) Sammelplatz für Tagelöhner
to dazzle (p. 25) blenden (fig.)
to be in debt [det] (p. 146) verschuldet sein
decanter [-'--] (p. 89) Karaffe
Declaration of Independence (p. 155) Unabhängigkeitserklärung
decline (p. 141) Rückgang
to decline (p. 89) ablehnen
dedicated (p. 141) engagiert
to deem (p. 160) erachten, halten für
to defer (p. 116) verschieben
to deflect (p. 160) etw. abwehren
degree (p. 111) (Schul-, Universitäts-)Abschluss
deliberately (p. 32) absichtlich
deliberation [-ˌ--ˈ--] (p. 163) Überlegung
delivery van (p. 15) Lieferwagen
demise [dɪˈmaɪz] (formal) (p. 46) Ende
demographic (p. 111) demographisch, die Bevölkerung(sentwicklung) betreffend; (p. 117) Altersgruppe
to deny s.th. [-'-] (pp. 48, 87) etw. abstreiten
to depict (p. 139) darstellen
to derive [dɪˈraɪv] (formal) (p. 159) beziehen – **to derive from** (p. 107) kommen/sich ableiten von
desertification [dɪˌzɜːtɪfɪˈkeɪʃn] (p. 59) Vordringen der Wüste
desire (p. 24) Wunsch – **desired** [dɪˈzaɪəd] (p. 121) erwünscht, ersehnt
despair (p. 99) Verzweiflung
despite (p. 153) trotz
first destination (p. 26) *hier:* erste Tätigkeit nach dem Hochschulabschluss
destiny (p. 167) Schicksal
to detain [-'-] (formal) (p. 107) in Haft nehmen, festsetzen
to detect (p. 83) entdecken
detergent (p. 67) Reinigungsmittel
devastation [ˌ--ˈ--] (p. 160) Verwüstung

A – Z device – exhilarating

device [dɪˈvaɪs] (pp. 76, 80) Gerät, Vorrichtung – **self-monitoring device** [dɪˈvaɪs] (p. 127) Gerät zur Selbstkontrolle
to devour [dɪˈvaʊə] (p. 48) verschlingen
digestion (p. 128) Verdauung
dignitary (p. 156) Würdenträger
in digs (BE, informal) (p. 129) zur Untermiete
to dilute (p. 121) auflösen; hier: schwächen
to dim (p. 98) langsam ausgehen
dimness (p. 88) Dämmerlicht
dinky [ˈdɪŋkɪ] (p. 79) niedlich, schnuckelig
dirigiste (p. 175) dirigistisch
to hit the dirt (informal) (p. 107) sich auf den Boden schmeißen
the disabled (p. 148) Behinderte
discarded (p. 102) ausrangiert, weggeworfen
to discern [dɪˈsɜːn] (p. 98) erkennen
to discharge [-ˈ-] (p. 73) entladen; ablassen
discount store (p. 15) Discountladen
discretion (p. 173) Ermessen
disgruntled (p. 172) verstimmt
in dismissal (p. 89) als Signal zum Aufbruch
to dispense [-ˈ-] (formal) (p. 130) erteilen
to disperse [-ˈ-] (p. 97) sich auflösen – **dispersed** [-ˈ-] (p. 115) verstreut
disposal [dɪˈspəʊzl] (p. 71) Beseitigung, Entsorgung; (p. 131) Müllschlucker – **at one's disposal** (p. 25) verfügbar
to dispose of s.th. [-ˈ-] (p. 63) beseitigen
disproportionately (p. 153) unverhältnismäßig viel bzw. stark
to disrupt [-ˈ-] (p. 48) stören, unterbrechen
distinctive (p. 50) charakteristisch, unverwechselbar
in distress (p. 101) in Not
distribution efficiency (p. 148) Effizienz bei der Auslieferung
congressional district (p. 115) Kongresswahlbezirk
to disturb (p. 87) beunruhigen
to diversify [-ˈ---] (p. 42) Tätigkeits- und Produktpalette erweitern
diversity (p. 50) hier: Vielfalt (an Nationalitäten)
to divert one's thoughts [daɪˈvɜːt] (p. 88) sich ablenken
docking maneuver (p. 95) Ankopplungsmanöver
doggedly (p. 25) beharrlich
domestic servant (p. 155) Hausangestellte/r
to donate (p. 48) spenden
donor (p. 87) Spender
to be doomed (p. 45) zum Scheitern verurteilt sein
downright (p. 147) ausgesprochen

to draft (p. 113) entwerfen
to draw (p. 67) hier: auslösen – **to draw the line** (fig.) (p. 87) eine Grenze ziehen, aufhören –
drawn from (p. 38) basierend auf
to dread (p. 128) grauen
to dream up (p. 71) sich etw. ausdenken
drive (p. 24) Bedürfnis, Trieb – **to drive** (p. 153) hier: (an)treiben
drop-off (p. 148) Abholstelle
drought [draʊt] (p. 59) Dürre(periode)
drum majorette [ˌmeɪdʒrˈet] (p. 156) Tambourmajorin
dry run (p. 160) Testlauf
to dub (p. 109) nennen
duct (p. 95) Luftschacht
to dump (p. 45) hier: zu Dumpingpreisen verkaufen; (p. 71) abladen
spurt of dust (p. 97) Staubwolke
dwelling (formal) (p. 80) Wohnung
dyslexic [dɪˈsleksɪk] (p. 42) legasthenisch
dyspeptic (p. 172) übelgelaunt, stinkig

E

wage earner (p. 111) Verdiener
ebony [ˈebnɪ] (p. 109) schwarz (wie Ebenholz)
echelon [ˈeʃəlɒn] (p. 143) Niveau, Rang
edgy (p. 139) nervös
higher education (p. 26) höhere Bildung
distribution efficiency (p. 148) Effizienz bei der Auslieferung
to egg s.o. on (p. 174) jmd. antreiben
elaborately [ɪˈlæbrətlɪ] (p. 13) kompliziert, auf komplexe Weise
elderly [ˈeldəlɪ] (n.) (p. 82) ältere Leute, Senioren
Electoral College (p. 117) Wahlmännergremium
electorate (p. 115) Wählerschaft, Wahlberechtigte
elusive [ɪˈluːsɪv] (p. 67) hier: schwer erreichbar
to embrace [-ˈ-] (formal) (p. 159) hier: annehmen
to emerge (p. 97) auftauchen – **emergence** [-ˈ--] (pp. 73, 79) Aufkommen; Entstehen
eminent [ˈ---] (p. 87) angesehen, bedeutend
to emit [ɪˈmɪt] (p. 13) ausstoßen; (p. 58) ausstrahlen, aussenden
emotive (p. 143) emotional
to emphasize [ˈemfəsaɪz] (p. 95) betonen
empire-builder (p. 42) hier: jmd., der sich ein Wirtschaftsimperium aufbaut
empowerment (p. 115) Macht, Machtgewinn
to enable (p. 93) ermöglichen
endearing (p. 172) liebenswert
to endow [ɪnˈdaʊ] (formal) (p. 155) ausstatten mit

enduring (p. 167) dauerhaft
enforcement [-ˈ--] (p. 73) Durchführung, Durchsetzung
to engage in (formal) (p. 21) sich an etw. beteiligen
engine [ˈendʒɪn] (p. 159) Motor, Antrieb – **combustion engine** (p. 65) Verbrennungsmotor – **to gun an engine** (p. 139) den Motor aufheulen lassen
to engulf [-ˈ-] (p. 21) vollkommen einnehmen; (p. 102) verschlingen
to enhance [ɪnˈhɑːns] (p. 93) verbessern
to enlist s.o. (p. 76) jdn. anwerben
to be enmeshed in (p. 121) verstrickt sein in
enormous [ɪˈnɔːməs] (pp. 25, 102) riesig
to enrich [-ˈ-] (p. 155) bereichern
to ensure [-ˈ-] (formal) (pp. 93, 158) sicherstellen
entangled [ɪnˈtæŋgld] (p. 48) verwickelt, verheddert – **entangled photons** (p. 78) ein Paar Photonen, deren physikalische Eigenschaften miteinander gekoppelt sind – **entangling alliances** [ɪnˈtæŋglɪŋ əˈlaɪənsɪz] (p. 163) verpflichtende Bündnisse zwischen Staaten
enterprising (pp. 27, 42) unternehmungslustig
entrepreneur [ˌɒntrəprəˈnɜː] (p. 42) Unternehmer
to envisage s.th. [ɪnˈvɪzɪdʒ] (p. 83) sich etw. vorstellen; etw. vorhaben
to envision [-ˈ--] (p. 159) sich vorstellen – **to envision** (p. 95) sich vorstellen; planen
epistolary (p. 172) Brief-
to epitomize [ɪˈpɪtəmaɪz] (pp. 94, 153) verkörpern, darstellen
equipped [ɪˈkwɪpt] (p. 125) vorbereitet, gerüstet
to eradicate (formal) (p. 159) ausrotten
to erase (p. 167) ausradieren
to err on the side of caution (p. 63) im Zweifelsfall lieber zu vorsichtig sein
to espy (old) (p. 145) erspähen, erblicken
essential (p. 24) (unbedingt) erforderlich
etiquette breach [ˈetɪket] (p. 13) Verstoß gegen die Etikette
event marketing (p. 141) Verkaufsveranstaltung
eventually (p. 32) schließlich
to evict (p. 160) herausschmeißen, entfernen
to evoke (p. 155) wachrufen
exchange (p. 11) hier: Wortwechsel, Austausch
to exchange a glance (fig.) (p. 103) sich ansehen, Blicke austauschen
chief executive (p. 43) Generaldirektor(in)
exhilarating [ɪgˈzɪləreɪtɪŋ] (p. 97) (freudig) erregend

expanse – graduate A – Z

expanse [-'-] (p. 160) Weite (des Landes)
to expect s.o. (p. 32) jdn. erwarten
to expend (formal) (p. 163) verwenden
expenditure (p. 141) Ausgaben
expletive ['---] (p. 143) Fluch, Schimpfwort
to be exposed to (p. 143) etw. ausgesetzt sein
exposition (p. 11) hier: lange Ausführungen
prolonged exposure [-,- -'--] (p. 93) unter der langfristigen Einwirkung von
to express commiseration (p. 172) Anteilnahme aussprechen
exquisitely [ɪkˈskwɪzɪtlɪ] (p. 143) kunstvoll
extended (p. 93) länger – **extended family** (p. 117) Großfamilie
extension (p. 87) Erweiterung, Ausdehnung
extent [-'-] (p. 27) Maß, Ausmaß
to what extent (p. 46) inwieweit
to extrapolate [ɪkˈstræpəleɪt] (p. 15) hochrechnen, extrapolieren; (p. 177) hier: von einer Sache auf eine andere schließen
to tear one's eyes away [teə] (fig.) (p. 143) wegschauen

F

fabulous ['fæbjələs] (p. 130) sagenhaft
face it (informal) (p. 117) Machen wir uns nichts vor
to fade [feɪd] (pp. 67, 89, 130) (ent)schwinden – **to fade away** (p. 96) schwächer werden
to fail (p. 67) scheitern, versagen
faintly (p. 98) schwach
to have faith in s.o. (p. 64) jdm. vertrauen
to fall out (p. 48) hier: sich (zer)streiten
fallout (p. 104) radioaktiver Niederschlag
extended family (p. 117) Großfamilie
famine ['fæmɪn] (p. 59) Hungersnot
to fathom ['fæðəm] (p. 145) verstehen
fatigue [fəˈtiːg] (p. 95) hier: Materialermüdung
fear-mongering (p. 22) Furcht verbreitend
feasible ['fiːzəbl] (p. 87) möglich, machbar
oxygen feed (p. 98) Sauerstoffbehälter
to feel left out (p. 147) sich ausgeschlossen fühlen
to fell (p. 160) hier: niederstrecken
to fend for oneself (p. 64) für sich (selbst) sorgen
fertility [fəˈtɪlətɪ] (p. 87) Fruchtbarkeit
feverishly (p. 87) fieberhaft
fierce [fɪəs] (p. 48) erbittert, heftig; (p. 97) hier: glühend; (p. 99) grausam
to fight a rearguard action (p. 48) zu spät etwas zu verhindern suchen
to file a complaint (p. 143) eine Beschwerde einreichen

fine print (p. 109) hier: Kleingedrucktes
to be fined (p. 36) zu einer Geldstrafe verurteilt werden
accountancy firm (p. 45) Buchhaltungsfirma – **broking firm** (p. 46) Maklerfirma
to fish s.th. from s.th. (p. 131) aus etwas herausangeln
to clench one's fists (p. 97) Fäuste ballen
fiver (BE informal) (p. 145) Fünf-Pfund Note
flamboyant (p. 42) extravagant
to come flaming down (fig.) (p. 98) erglühend herabstürzen
fleet cars (p. 67) Firmenwagen
flexi-work (p. 127) Gleitzeit, gleitende Arbeitszeit
to float shares (p. 43) Aktien auf den Markt bringen
to flog (informal) (p. 143) etw. verscheuern
to flood (p. 125) überfluten
to roll on the floor (fig.) (p. 11) sich auf dem Boden wälzen vor Lachen
to floss (p. 131) sich die Zähne mit Zahnseide reinigen
to flow (p. 159) fließen
fluctuating ['flʌktʃueɪtɪŋ] (p. 102) schwankend
fodder (p. 143) Futter
to follow (p. 67) hier: etw verfolgen, nachgehen
to fool around (informal) (p. 64) sinnlos herumspielen
foot restraint (p. 95) Fußhalterung
forecast (p. 46) Prognose
to have foresight (p. 46) Weitblick haben
to forge [fɔːdʒ] (pp. 153, 155) schmieden, schaffen
fortitude (formal) (p. 155) (innere) Kraft
to foster (pp. 95, 159) fördern; (p. 115) hier: verstärken
founder (p. 43) Gründer(in)
franchise ['fræntʃaɪz] (pp. 43, 50) in Lizenz vergebenes Unternehmen
fraud (p. 46) Schwindler
to freeze one's tail off (slang) (p. 64) sich einen abfrieren
frenzy (p. 177) Raserei
to frequent (p. 25) (oft) besuchen
fridge [frɪdʒ] (p. 129) Kurzform für refrigerator: Kühlschrank
fringe (p. 113) Rand
frivolous (p. 172) leichtsinnig, unbekümmert
front-line support (p. 37) Telefonservice; Kundenbetreuung
froth [frɒθ] (p. 109) Schaum
fuel cladding (p. 63) Schutzverkleidung
to fulfill (p. 93) ausführen; verwirklichen
fulfillment (p. 67) Erfüllung
trust fund (p. 131) Treuhandfonds

funeral pyre [paɪə] (p. 98) Scheiterhaufen
the funky chicken (p. 131) Ententanz
funny (p. 95) hier: merkwürdig

G

gap (p. 111) Kluft, Unterschied
garage sale (p. 109) Garagenverkauf
gas-guzzling ['gʌzlɪŋ] (p. 64) spritfressend
to gather (p. 58) sich ansammeln, zusammenkommen; hier: sich verdichten
gaze (p. 178) Blick – **to gaze** [geɪz] (p. 97) jdn./etw. anstarren
gear (p. 77) Zahnrad
generously (p. 116) großzügigerweise
genetic screening (p. 87) Genuntersuchung
geostationary orbit [,dʒiːəˈsteɪʃnrɪ] (p. 101) geostationäre Umlaufbahn
gerbil ['dʒɜːbl] (p. 19) Wüstenspringmaus
germanium [dʒəˈmeɪnɪəm] (p. 79) Germanium
to get s.o. out of a jam (fig.) (p. 109) jdm aus der Patsche helfen – **to get s.th. over to s.o.** (p. 64) (eine Idee) verständlich machen, etw. rüberbringen
gilding (p. 178) Vergoldung
gimmik ['gɪmɪk] (p. 45) Spielerei
to give in (p. 123) nachgeben – **to give s.th. the green light** (p. 143) grünes Licht für etw. geben
to exchange a glance (fig.) (p. 103) sich ansehen, Blicke austauschen
to glance (p. 74) blicken
glare [gleə] (p. 98) greller Schein
to gleam (p. 98) schimmern
glimmer (p. 71) Schimmer; hier: Anzeichen
glitter (p. 98) Glitzern – **glittery** (p. 145) glitzernd
GM (gene manipulated) (p. 173) genmanipuliert
at a go (p. 132) auf einmal – **to go on** (p. 145) hier: (als Gast in einer Fernsehsendung) auftreten – **to go on one thing** (p. 79) hier: für einen bestimmten Zweck verwenden
to gobble ['gɒbl] (p. 132) verschlingen
godfather (p. 73) Pate, hier: Vorreiter
goofily (p. 13) auf alberne Weise
gorgeous (p. 145) hinreißend
gouache [guˈɑːʃ] (p. 32) Gouache
accountable governance [əˌkaʊntəbl ˈgʌvnəns] (p. 159) verantwortungsvolles Regieren
GP (p. 147) Kurzform f. general practitioner: praktischer Arzt, praktische Ärztin
to grab s.o. (informal) (p. 64) jdn. packen
graduate (p. 165) Hochschulabsolvent – **to graduate** ['grædjueɪt] (p. 111) einen (Schul-)Abschluss machen

215

grainy (p. 103) unscharf, körnig
grand marshal (p. 156) Oberkommandierender einer Parade
grandeur (p. 155) Größe
to take s.th. for granted (pp. 121, 128) etw. für selbstverständlich nehmen
to grasp (fig.) (p. 130) verstehen, begreifen – **within one's grasp** (fig.) (p. 159) in greifbarer Nähe
grassroots movement (p. 48) Volksbewegung
gravy (p. 166) Soße
grazed [greɪzd] (p. 19) aufgeschürft
greed (p. 42) Gier, Habgier
to grill s.o. (fig.) (p. 32) jdn. in die Zange nehmen
to break new ground (fig.) (p. 93) Neuland betreten
grubby (p. 15) schmuddelig
to be anyone's guess (p. 143) weiß der Himmel
guide [gaɪd] (p. 107) Führer(in)
gulf (p. 67) Kluft
to gun an engine (p. 139) den Motor aufheulen lassen
guy (informal) (p. 12) Typ, Kerl

H

habitat (p. 59) Lebensraum (von Pflanzen und Tieren)
hall (p. 128) hier: Wohnheim
hallowed ['hæləʊd] (p. 11) hier: altehrwürdig, traditionell
handout (p. 64) Zuwendung, Almosen
handy (p. 113) praktisch
to harbor (BE harbour) (p. 46) in sich tragen; (p. 160) Unterschlupf gewähren – **harbour** (p. 163) Hafen
hardship (p. 155) Not, Elend
harmonisation (p. 127) Harmonisierung
harrowing (p. 143) entsetzlich, grauenvoll
harsh (p. 172) hart
to harvest (lit.) (p. 159) (Früchte) ernten
to hassle with s.o. ['hæsl] (p. 125) mit jdm. streiten
to wreak havoc [riːk] (p. 17) etw. total durcheinander bringen
hazy ['heɪzɪ] (p. 98) hier: verschwommen
to head for a fall (fig.) (p. 46) in sein Verderben rennen
headland (p. 97) Landspitze
to have a heavy heart (fig.) (p. 109) bedrückt sein
heated (p. 54) hier: hitzig, erregt
by heaven (p. 64) Bei Gott!
heavy (p. 103) hier: groß
one heck of (slang) (p. 95) ein irrsinniger ...
to come to heel (p. 177) bei Fuß gehen
heritage (p. 98) Erbe
high street (BE) (p. 17) Haupteinkaufsstraße – **high-profile** ['prəʊfaɪl] (p. 42) Aufsehen erregend – **high-wire act** (p. 94) Drahtseilakt

hindsight (p. 163) Rückblick
to hit (informal) (p. 141) erreichen – **to hit the brakes** (informal) (p. 107) auf die Bremsen treten – **to hit the dirt** (informal) (p. 107) sich auf den Boden schmeißen
to hoard (p. 132) horten
ho-hum (p. 94) na ja; langweilig
to hold fast (p. 155) festhalten an – **to hold out** (p. 109) nicht nachgeben – **to hold s.o. hostage** (p. 163) jdn. als Geisel festhalten
homage ['hɒmɪdʒ] (p. 153) Huldigung
to hone (p. 178) (fig.) zurechtfeilen
honest-to-goodness (p. 50) ehrlich, echt
the Honours List (p. 178) Liste der Titel- und Rangverleihungen
to be hooked by s.th. (informal) (p. 21) von etw. total begeistert sein
to hold s.o. hostage (p. 163) jdn. als Geisel festhalten
hostile ['hɒstaɪl] (pp. 99, 163) feindselig
wee hour (p. 128) frühe Morgenstunde
householder (p. 34) Haushaltsvorstand
to hover ['hɒvə] (p. 102) herumstehen, herumhängen
hub (pp. 67, 166) (fig.) Zentrum, Mittelpunkt
to huddle up (AE) (p. 13) die Köpfe zusammenstecken
hue (p. 98) Farbe
humiliation [hjuːˌmɪli'eɪʃn] (p. 163) Demütigung
hunched (p. 33) gekrümmt
hunky (informal) (p. 145) sexy, knackig
hurdle (p. 67) Hürde
to hype (p. 21) Rummel um etw. machen
hyper-activity [ˌhaɪpræk'tɪvətɪ] (p. 127) Hyperaktivität
hyphenated (p. 113) hier: in zwei Kulturen verwurzelt (mexikanisch - amerikanisch)
hypocrisy [hɪ'pɒkrəsɪ] (p. 54) Scheinheiligkeit

I

idle ['aɪdl] (p. 131) faul, träge, müßig
ill-advised (p. 163) schlecht beraten – **ill-housed** (p. 159) in schlechten Verhältnissen wohnend
imaged (p. 97) abgebildet
immense (p. 166) riesig, enorm
imminent (p. 46) (nahe) bevorstehend
immutable (formal) (p. 139) unveränderlich
impact ['--] (p. 101) Aufprall; (pp. 59, 109) Auswirkung
to impair (p. 103) beeinträchtigen
imperial (p. 166) das britische Weltreich betreffend
implausible [ɪm'plɔːzəbl] (p. 15) unwahrscheinlich
to implore (p. 155) anflehen, inständig bitten

to imply (pp. 25, 145) andeuten, implizieren
imposing (p. 32) beeindruckend
impoverished (p. 178) verarmt
impregnability [ɪmˌpregnə'bɪlətɪ] (p. 160) Uneinnehmbarkeit, Unverletzbarkeit
impressive (p. 73) beeindruckend
in vitro fertilization (p. 87) künstliche Befruchtung
inalienable [ɪ'neɪlɪənəbl] (formal) (p. 131) unbestreitbar
incentive [ɪn'sentɪv] (p. 50) Anreiz
incident ['ɪnsɪdnt] (p. 101) Vorfall
to incinerate [ɪn'sɪnreɪt] (p. 63) verbrennen – **incineration** [ɪnˌsɪnr'eɪʃn] (p. 71) Verbrennung
income (p. 111) Einkommen
to incorporate [ɪn'kɔːpreɪt] (p. 82) enthalten
incredible (p. 159) unglaublich
incredulously (p. 32) ungläubig, skeptisch
indecisive (p. 54) unschlüssig, unentschlossen
indelible [-'--] (p. 111) dauerhaft, unauslöschlich
indigenous [ɪn'dɪʒɪnəs] (p. 166) einheimisch
indigo (p. 13) indigoblau
induced [ɪn'djuːst] (p. 58) verursacht
industry (p. 158) hier: Fleiß
inevitable (p. 46) unvermeidlich
inexorably [-'----] (p. 32) unerbittlich
influence (p. 163) Einfluss – **to influence** (p. 54) beeinflussen – **influential** (p. 24) einflussreich
influx ['ɪnflʌks] (p. 8) Zustrom
ingenuity [ˌɪndʒɪ'njuːətɪ] (pp. 25, 158) Einfallsreichtum
ingrained [--'] (p. 153) verwurzelt
inherently (pp. 21, 76) von Natur aus
initial [ɪ'nɪʃl] (p. 54) anfänglich – **initially** [ɪ'nɪʃlɪ] (p. 82) anfangs, ursprünglich
innuendo [ˌɪnjʊ'endəʊ] (p. 143) zweideutige Anspielung
insanity (p. 104) Wahnsinn
inside (p. 32) hier: eingeweiht
insight (p. 99) Erkenntnis – **insightful** (p. 145) einsichtsvoll
inspired (p. 178) genial
instant (p. 24) unmittelbar, sofortig
to be instilled with a feeling (p. 43) etw. eingeflößt bekommen
insult ['--] (p. 131) Beleidigung
insurance agent [ɪn'ʃʊərns ˌeɪdʒnt] (AE) (p. 88) Versicherungsvertreter
integral ['---] (p. 54) wesentlich
to interact (p. 12) hier: direkt/sofort reagieren – (p. 80) hier: Informationen austauschen
interaction (p. 153) Interaktion
interchange (GB) (p. 148) (Autobahn)Kreuz
vested interest (p. 173) persönliches Interesse

interface – mockery A – Z

interface (p. 79) Schnittstelle
interference (pp. 163, 173) Einmischung – **to run interference** (fig.) (p. 104) hier: sich gegen einen Einwand wehren
to interlock (p. 88) ineinander stecken; verschränken
International Monetary Fund (IMF) (p. 48) Internationaler Währungsfonds
to intervene [ˌ--'-] (pp. 160, 163) einschreiten
to be intimate ['ɪntɪmət] (p. 13) vertraut sein
intimidating (p. 25) bedrohlich
intolerable [-'----] (p. 123) unerträglich
intractable [-'---] (formal) (p. 155) hartnäckig
to invalidate (p. 167) entkräften
invaluable (p. 42) von unschätzbarem Wert
investigative [ɪn'vestɪgətɪv] (p. 27) forschend, wissbegierig
invulnerability [ɪnˌvʌlnrə'bɪlətɪ] (pp. 46, 160) Unverwundbarkeit
irreverent (p. 143) respektlos
irreversible [ˌ--'---] (p. 59) bleibend, unumkehrbar
irrevocably [ɪ'revəkəblɪ] (formal) (p. 160) unwiderruflich

J

to get s.o. out of a jam (fig.) (p. 109) jdm. aus der Patsche helfen
jealousy ['dʒeləsɪ] (p. 131) Eifersucht
jinx (p. 94) Unglück, Fluch
joint (p. 139) hier: (billiges) Restaurant, Bude – **Joint Chiefs of Staff** (p. 103) Stabschefs
cast-iron judgement (p. 39) unumstößliches Urteil – **to withhold judgement** (p. 54) nicht vorschnell urteilen, sich mit seinem Urteil zurückhalten
to juggle (p. 25) miteinander vereinbaren
jumble ['dʒʌmbl] (p. 109) Durcheinander – **jumbled** (p. 97) (kunterbunt) gemischt
junk (p. 109) Trödel, Gerümpel
just so many (p. 67) nur
to justify (pp. 48, 88) rechtfertigen
to jut (p. 156) (plötzlich) heben, hervorstrecken

K

to keep in step (fig.) (p. 156) Schritt halten – **to keep on the road** (fig.) (p. 45) mit etw. weitermachen – **to keep pace** (p. 115) Schritt halten – **to keep s.th. short and sweet** (p. 11) (fig.) etw. kurz und knapp halten
kerbside collection (p. 71) Abholsystem
to key in s.th. (p. 83) etw. eingeben, eintippen
to kid o.s. (p. 172) sich etw. vormachen
kingpin (informal) (p. 141) wichtige Person

kinship (p. 167) Verwandtschaft, Beziehung
to have a knack for s.th. [næk] (fig.) (p. 42) ein Händchen für etw. haben
to knock out (p. 95) hier: zerstören

L

lack (p. 25) Mangel
lad (p. 178) junger Mann
to lag behind (p. 115) zurückbleiben hinter (fig.)
landfill (p. 71) Deponiegelände
lathered (p. 109) schäumend
laundry ['lɔːndrɪ] (p. 129) schmutzige Wäsche
to lavish s.th. on s.o. (p. 147) jdn. mit etw. überhäufen
lawn (p. 67) Rasen
to leaf through (p. 88) (ein Buch) durchblättern
lean (p. 145) schlank
paternity leave (p. 25)/**maternity leave** (p. 39) Elternurlaub
legacy ['legəsɪ] (p. 116) Vermächtnis
Legion (p. 156) American Legion, Organisation amerikanischer Veteranen
leisure ['leʒə] (p. 69) Freizeit
lest (p. 178) damit nicht
let alone (p. 174) geschweige denn
level (p. 36) hier: Tunnel
to take the liberty of doing s.th. (p. 89) sich die Freiheit nehmen, etwas zu tun
to be licked (slang) (p. 48) erledigt sein
to give s.th. the green light (p. 143) grünes Licht für etw. geben
to be less likely (p. 38) weniger wahrscheinlich sein
the likes of (p. 42) wie zum Beispiel
to draw the line (fig.) (p. 87) eine Grenze ziehen, aufhören – **in line with** (p. 48) entsprechend
lingo (pp. 11, 143) Jargon
to live in the shadows (p. 109) im Verborgenen leben
loaded (p. 89) geladen
loafers (p. 13) Halbschuhe, Slipper
loan (p. 46) Kredit
to mark a location (p. 107) einen Ort markieren
long-drawn (p. 99) lang anhaltend – **long-duration** [djʊə'reɪʃn] (p. 93) von langer Dauer
longing (p. 96) Verlangen
to loom (p. 172) drohen
loose [luːs] (p. 166) lose, locker
the whole lot (p. 15) alles
lunar surface (p. 102) Mondoberfläche
lurch (p. 143) Ruck, Hereinbrechen

M

madman (p. 89) Verrückte(r)
mainstream (pp. 73, 116) vorherrschend; (p. 79) allgemein gebräuchlich; Standard-; (p. 167) Mitte, Kern

to maintain (pp. 34, 48) (aufrecht)erhalten – **maintenance-level spending** (p. 141) Ausgaben, auf einem bestimmten Niveau halten
to make a mark on s.o./s.th. (fig.) (p. 155) seine Spuren hinterlassen
with all the makings of (p. 107) mit allen Voraussetzungen für
managerial [ˌmænə'dʒɪərɪəl] (p. 116) Manager-
to manipulate [mə'nɪpjəleɪt] (p. 83) hier: handhaben, bedienen
mansion ['mænʃn] (p. 155) Villa, Herrenhaus
maple-trimmed (p. 139) mit Ahornholz gefertigt
marginal (p. 141) unwesentlich
Marine (p. 156) Mitglied einer bestimmten Abteilung der US-Marine
marital status (p. 34) Familienstand
to make a mark on s.o./s.th. (fig.) (p. 155) seine Spuren hinterlassen
to mark a location (p. 107) einen Ort markieren
to market to s.o. (p. 111) Produkte verkaufen an eine bestimmte Zielgruppe
marketeer [ˌ--'-] (p. 45) jmd., der im Marketingbereich arbeitet
marquee personality (p. 139) Star
to marvel ['--] (p. 97) staunen
to mask (p. 113) verbergen
massive ['--] (p. 163) riesig
maternity leave (p. 38) Elternzeit, Mutterschaftsurlaub
mayoral race ['meərl] (p. 111) Wahlkampf um das Bürgermeisteramt
meandering [mi'ændrɪŋ] (p. 130) hier: äußerst unterschiedlich
to measure one's steps (fig.) (p. 156) gemessenen Schrittes gehen
Memorial Day (p. 156) U.S. Feiertag zu Ehren der im Krieg Gefallenen
mentally arrested (p. 88) geistig zurückgeblieben
mercy (p. 177) Gnade
mere [mɪə] (p. 160) bloß
merit (p. 73) Leistung, Verdienst
mesquite [mes'kiːt] (p. 107) Buschlandschaft
to mess around with (informal) (p. 87) herumpfuschen an, herumspielen
message ['mesɪdʒ] (p. 153) Botschaft
methamphetamine (p. 22) Methamphetamin
methane ['miːθeɪn] (p. 58) Methan
Middle America (p. 139) amerikanische Mittelschicht
mid-level (p. 111) mittlere(r)
to be of the same mind (fig.) (p. 36) gleicher Meinung sein
mint (p. 48) Pfefferminz
ballistic missile (p. 95) Raketengeschoss
moaning [məʊn] (p. 98) Stöhnen
mockery (p. 139) Hohn, Spott

model (p. 163) vorbildlich, ideal
to monitor ['mɒnɪtə] (p. 82) überwachen
to have moral fiber (p. 64) inneren Halt/Rückgrat haben
mouldy ['məʊldɪ] (p. 129) schimmelig
to be moved (p. 22) bewegt sein –
  mover (p. 109) Möbelpacker
movie credits (p. 11) Abspann
muck (p. 129) Dreck
to muddle along (p. 121) weiterwursteln, sich durchwursteln – **muddled** (p. 174) unsicher, konfus, durcheinander
to mumble (p. 32) murmeln
murky (p. 143) düster
to murmur (p. 32) murmeln

N

NAFTA (North American Free Trade Agreement) (p. 167) nordamerikanische Freihandelszone
nail-biting (p. 94) spannungsgeladen
narrow (p. 151) hier: engstirnig
nasty (p. 95) böse, unangenehm
natal ['neɪtl] (p. 95) Geburts-
native-born ['neɪtɪv] (p. 111) im Land (als Amerikaner) geboren
naval (p. 166) Marine-, See-
to negotiate [nɪ'gəʊʃɪeɪt] (p. 121) hier: (eine schwierige Situation) bewältigen – **negotiation** (p. 163) Verhandlung
neuter (p. 123) geschlechtslos
newly-minted (p. 155) hier: nagelneu
nicety ['naɪsətɪ] (p. 13) hier: Nettigkeit
nickel (AE) (p. 94) Fünf-Cent Stück
night-vision goggles ['gɒglz] (p. 107) Nachtsichtgerät
nimble (p. 11) flink
nitrous oxide ['naɪtrəs 'ɒksaɪd] (p. 58) Distickstoffmonoxid
to be noble (p. 131) hier: ehrlich sein
nondescript ['---] (p. 88) unauffällig, unscheinbar
to note (p. 67) bemerken; anmerken, feststellen
notification (p. 46) Benachrichtigung, Mitteilung
notion (p. 163) Idee, Vorstellung
notwithstanding (p. 116) zum Trotz
nourished ['nʌrɪʃt] (p. 155) hier: genährt
novel (p. 93) neu(-artig)
nudging (p. 95) stupsend
to numb (p. 143) betäuben
to put s.th. in a nutshell (idiom) (p. 163) um es kurz und bündig zu sagen

O

obedient [əʊbiːdɪənt] (p. 82) gehorsam
objective (p. 160) Ziel
obvious (pp. 46, 54) offensichtlich
occupant ['ɒkjəpənt] (p. 80) Bewohner
occupation (p. 24) Beruf, Beschäftigung
to occur to one (p. 12) in den Sinn kommen
20-odd (p. 15) etwa 20 – **at odds with** (p. 48) im Konflikt mit

off planet (p. 93) fern der Erde
to be better off (p. 69) besser dran sein
on offer (BE) (p. 25) im Angebot
to offset s.th. (p. 148) ausgleichen; aufwiegen
offshoot (p. 73) Ableger
offspring (p. 125) Nachwuchs
old banger (BE, informal) (p. 129) Klapperkiste
onsite … utilization (p. 93) hier: Material im Weltraum verwenden
to ooze (here fig.) (p. 145) strotzen vor
to oppose (p. 48) sich widersetzen – **as opposed to** (p. 111) im Gegensatz zu
oppressive [-'--] (p. 121) erdrückend; hier: trostlos
orbit (p. 101) Umlaufbahn – **geostationary orbit** (p. 101) geostationäre Umlaufbahn – **polar orbit** (p. 101) Umlaufbahn über die Pole – **orbiting** (p. 93) sich auf einer Umlaufbahn befinden
to orchestrate ['ɔːkɪstreɪt] (p. 160) ans Werk setzen, organisieren
ordinance ['---] (p. 73) Verordnung
ordinary (pp. 42, 160) gewöhnlich, normal
ore (p. 71) Erz
ostensibly [ɒs'tentsɪblɪ] (formal) (p. 73) angeblich
out of pawn (p. 36) ausgelöst (Pfand)
to be out (informal) (p. 37) pennen
outcast teen (p. 21) jugendlicher Außenseiter
outcome (p. 38) Ergebnis; Resultat
outlay (p. 141) Aufwendungen
outright (p. 71) ohne Umschweife, gleich
overall (p. 145) gesamt
overdraft (p. 147) Kontoüberziehung
overdue (p. 46) überfällig
to overextend (p. 163) sich übernehmen
to overhear (p. 103) zufällig mitbekommen
over-indulged (p. 178) verwöhnt
overlooker (p. 36) Aufseher(in)
oversight (p. 116) Versehen
to overtake s.th. (p. 146) überholen
overtly [-'--] (p. 143) offen, unverhohlen
to overwhelm (p. 148) überwältigen
to owe (p. 143) hier: etw. verdanken
oxygen feed (p. 98) Sauerstoffbehälter

P

to keep pace (p. 115) Schritt halten
to pacify ['pæsɪfaɪ] (p. 107) beruhigen
pack (p. 46) Rudel; Meute
adjustment pains [ə'dʒʌstmənt] (p. 128) Anpassungsschwierigkeiten
paleoclimatology [ˌpælɪəklaɪmə'tɒlədʒɪ] (p. 101) vergleichende Wissenschaft der vorzeitlichen klimatischen Verhältnisse auf der Erde
panel (p. 67) Gremium
paneled (p. 113) holzgetäfelt

virgin paper (p. 71) fabrikneues, nicht durch Recycling hergestelltes Papier
parcel (p. 148) Paket
particularly [pə'tɪkjələlɪ] (p. 111) besonders
to pass a hand across the forehead (p. 89) hier: sich mit der Hand über die Stirn fahren
paternity leave (p. 25) Elternzeit, Vaterschaftsurlaub
pathological (informal) (p. 146) krankhaft
patter (p. 98) Platschen
pattern (p. 82) hier: Regelmäßigkeit; (p. 148) Muster
paucity ['pɔːsətɪ] (formal) (p. 95) Mangel, geringe Zahl oder Menge
pavement (p. 132) Gehsteig
out of pawn (p. 36) ausgelöst (Pfand)
pay package (p. 48) Einkommen plus Sonderleistungen
to pay off (p. 117) sich auszahlen
PDA (p. 127) personal digital assistant, Palm Computer
peak (p. 45) Höhepunkt
pebbled (p. 98) Kieselstein-
to peer (p. 48) (hervor)schielen
pension ['penʃn] (p. 132) Rente – **pension contributions** (p. 127) Rentenbeiträge
people on high (p. 121) Leute von Rang und Namen
to perceive (p. 167) wahrnehmen
perennial (p. 98) ewig
to persist (p. 139) an einer Gewohnheit festhalten
to peruse [pə'ruːz] (formal) (p. 32) sorgfältig durchsehen, prüfen
Petri dish (p. 87) Petrischale
petty crime (p. 127) Kleinkriminalität
to philander [fɪ'lændə] (p. 131) tändeln
photon (p. 78) Photon
pick centre (p. 148) Versandzentrum, Auslieferungslager
to pick up people (p. 25) hier: aufgabeln
pickle (p. 132) saure Gurke
pilgrimage (p. 99) Wallfahrt, Pilgerfahrt
pimp (p. 143) Zuhälter
to pin down (fig.) (p. 111) jdn. aufhalten, jdn. festnageln/festlegen
pitch (informal) (p. 111) Verkaufstaktik, Masche
plagued [pleɪgd] (p. 141) geplagt – **to be plagued with** (p. 178) hier: verstopft sein mit
plain (p. 97) Ebene
platform (p. 156) Podium, Bühne
to give on a silver platter (fig.) (p. 64) auf einem Silbertablett servieren
to play out (p. 93) weitermachen, fortfahren mit
to plead [pliːd] (p. 95) bitten
to pledge s.th. (p. 36) etwas verpfänden – **to pledge** (p. 74) versprechen

plethora *(formal)* (p. 147) Fülle
plotter (p. 160) Verschwörer
to plummet (p. 46) stark fallen, abstürzen
to plunge s.o. into s.th. (p. 143) jdn. in etw. hineinversetzen
polar orbit (p. 101) Umlaufbahn über die Pole
policy maker (p. 121) Leute, die politische Entscheidungen treffen
at the polls (p. 115) bei Wahlen
to pool (p. 111) zusammenlegen
portentous (p. 178) gewichtig
portfolio (p. 127) *hier:* Auswahl
to portray (p. 139) darstellen
posh *(informal)* (p. 145) vornehm
postpartum (p. 22) nach der Entbindung (auftretend)
to postpone (p. 116) hinausschieben; (p. 45) verschieben; hinausschieben
potent ['--] (p. 58) stark; hochwirksam
to pout (p. 145) einen Schmollmund machen
to power (p. 67) antreiben
to praise (p. 54) loben
to precede (p. 13) vorangehen
precious ['preʃəs] (pp. 11, 54) wertvoll – **precious few** ['preʃəs] (p. 131) recht wenige
precipitous [prɪ'sɪpɪtəs] (p. 97) steil
predicament [prɪ'dɪkəmənt] (p. 101) Dilemma, Zwangslage
to predict (p. 111) vorhersagen
to prefer (p. 111) bevorzugen
premise ['premɪs] (p. 153) Idee
to preserve (p. 159) wahren, erhalten
to have bad press *(fig.)* (p. 87) einen schlechten Ruf bekommen
pressure (p. 82) Druck
proceedings (p. 173) Verfahren
proficiency [prə'fɪʃnsi] (p. 111) Können, Kenntnisse
profound (pp. 22, 167) tief
to project [-'-] (p. 77) projizieren
social action projects (p. 48) Sozialhilfeprogramme
prolonged exposure (p. 93) unter der langfristigen Einwirkung von
to promote (p. 38) fördern
to be prompted (p. 82) veranlasst werden; ermuntert werden
to pronounce (p. 32) verkünden
propensity *(formal)* (p. 139) Hang, Neigung
quantum property (p. 78) Quanteneigenschaft
proposed (p. 67) geplant, beabsichtigt – **proposition** [,--'--] (p. 125) *hier:* Angelegenheit
to propound (p. 143) propagieren
prosaic [prəʊ'zeɪɪk] *(formal)* (p. 95) langweilig, prosaisch
proselytiser (p. 175) Bekehrer, Missionar
prospect ['--] (p. 87) Aussicht

prospective (p. 45) potenziell
prosperity [-'---] (pp. 159, 166) Wohlstand
to prove to be (p. 141) sich erweisen als
to pry (p. 11) neugierig sein; herumschnüffeln
public amenity [ə'mi:nəti] (p. 69) öffentliche Einrichtung – **to go public** (p. 43) in eine Aktiengesellschaft umgewandelt werden
pulp [pʌlp] (p. 48) Fruchtfleisch – **to pulp** (p. 71) einstampfen
pundit (p. 21) Experte
purchasing power ['pɜ:tʃəsɪŋ] (p. 111) Kaufkraft
to purge (p. 96) reinigen
purity (p. 166) Reinheit
pursuit [pə'sju:t] (p. 146) *hier:* Beschäftigung; (p. 155) Streben
to put [pʌt] (p. 102) Golf: einlochen – **put aside** (p. 139) lassen wir beiseite – **to put s.th. in a nutshell** *(idiom)* (p. 163) um es kurz und bündig zu sagen – **to put up with** (p. 131) etw. hinnehmen, sich etwas gefallen lassen
funeral pyre ['paɪə] (p. 98) Scheiterhaufen

Q

quantum property (p. 78) Quanteneigenschaft
to quarrel ['--] (p. 121) streiten
quest (p. 93) Mission, Suche
quid [kwɪd] *(informal)* (p. 128) britisches Pfund
to quiz [kwɪz] (p. 128) ausfragen

R

mayoral race ['meərl] (p. 111) Wahlkampf um das Bürgermeisteramt
radiance ['reɪdɪəns] (p. 97) Leuchten
radiation shielding (p. 63) Strahlenschutz
to rage (p. 99) *hier:* wüten
railings (p. 132) Geländer
to rally (p. 48) jdn. für etwas mobilisieren
rampart (p. 97) Wall
range [reɪndʒ] (pp. 25, 43) Palette – **to range** (pp. 37, 93) gehen (von...bis)
ratings (p. 22) Quoten
ratio (p. 48) *hier:* Einkommensunterschied
to rattle around *(informal)* (p. 11) herumgeistern
ravine [rə'vi:n] (p. 97) Schlucht
to reach a stage (p. 25) an einem Punkt ankommen
to reap [ri:p] (p. 95) ernten, als Gegenleistung bekommen
to fight a rearguard action (p. 48) zu spät etwas zu verhindern suchen
reasonable (p. 129) *hier:* preiswert
reassurance (p. 71) Beruhigung
receiver [rɪ'si:və] (p. 45) Konkursverwalter

recent ['ri:snt] (p. 111) kürzlich
reckless (p. 97) leichtsinnig; (p. 131) rücksichtslos
to recoil from [-'-] (p. 109) zurückschrecken
to have a criminal record (p. 127) vorbestraft sein
track record (p. 45) Erfolgsbilanz
to recover (p. 156) sich erholen, genesen
to recuperate (p. 178) sich erholen, genesen
redistricting (p. 115) Neuordnung von Wahlbezirken aufgrund sich verändernder Bevölkerungszahlen
redneck *(negative, informal)* (p. 139) Prolet
reduction (p. 141) Abnahme, Rückgang
to make s.o. redundant [-'--] *(BE)* (p. 45) jdn. entlassen
to refuse [rɪ'fju:z] (p. 125) sich weigern
regardless of (p. 34) ungeachtet
to reinforce (p. 167) stärken, stützen
rejection letter (p. 25) schriftliche Absage
to release [-'-] (p. 67) freisetzen
reliable (pp. 32, 67, 130) zuverlässig
reluctance [rɪ'lʌktns] (p. 163) Abneigung, Widerwillen – **reluctantly** (p. 166) widerwillig
to rely on [rɪ'laɪ] (p. 42) sich auf etw. verlassen
remains (p. 102) Überreste
remote tool (p. 63) ferngesteuertes Gerät; Roboter – **remote** (p. 148) entfernt; abgelegen – **remotely** (p. 83) aus der Entfernung
to renew [-'-] (p. 155) erneuern – **renewable** (p. 65) erneuerbar – **renewed** (p. 163) erneut, wiederholt
renowned [rɪ'naʊnd] (p. 87) berühmt
repercussion [,ri:pə'kʌʃn] (p. 163) Auswirkung
repetitive [-'---] (p. 37) monoton
to replace (p. 67) ersetzen
replicable ['replɪkəbl] (p. 93) reproduzierbar – **to replicate** ['replɪkeɪt] (p. 87) kopieren, nachbilden
to reproach s.o. (p. 69) jdm. Vorwürfe machen
repugnant (p. 173) abstoßend
reputation (p. 117) Ruf
reputedly [rə'pju:tɪdli] (p. 123) vermeintlich, angeblich
requisite ['rekwɪzɪt] (p. 95) notwendig
rescue tracking (p. 101) Lokalisierung zum Zweck der Rettung
resentment (p. 160) Ärger, Groll
to reside [rɪ'zaɪd] *(formal)* (p. 82) *hier:* sich aufhalten – **to have residence** (p. 165) eine Aufenthaltsberechtigung haben
residue ['resɪdju:] (pp. 63, 67) Rest, Rückstand

to resign [rɪˈzaɪn] (p. 43) zurücktreten – to resign oneself to s.th. (p. 145) sich mit etw. abfinden
response (p. 37) Antwort
restrained (p. 37) beschränkt, begrenzt
foot restraint (p. 95) Fußhalterung
retail sales (p. 148) Einzelhandelsumsatz – retailer (p. 45) Einzelhändler – retailing (p. 126) Einzelhandel
to retaliate (p. 160) Vergeltung üben – retaliation [-ˌ--ˈ--] (p. 160) Vergeltung
to retrieve (p. 101) bergen
to reveal (p. 146) enthüllen
revenue stream [ˈrevnjuː] (p. 67) Einnahmequelle
reverie (p. 139) Träumerei
to reward (p. 27) belohnen
ridicule (p. 21) Spott – ridiculous [rɪˈdɪkjələs] (p. 129) lächerlich
rift (p. 48) Riss
at right angles (p. 13) in rechtem Winkel zueinander – on the right track (fig.) (p. 67) auf dem richtigen Weg sein
rigorous [ˈrɪgrəs] (p. 73) streng, genau
rim (p. 97) Rand
rival [ˈraɪvl] (p. 48) Rivale
road bump (p. 175) Bodenschwelle – to keep on the road (fig.) (p. 45) mit etw. weitermachen
roar (p. 96) Dröhnen
to rock (p. 13) schaukeln
to roll on the floor (fig.) (p. 11) sich auf dem Boden wälzen vor Lachen
roots (p. 153) Wurzeln – to set roots (fig.) (p. 22) Wurzeln schlagen – to trace one's roots (p. 115) seine Herkunft angeben mit
to rotate (p. 45) drehen
rotten (p. 64) verzogen
to round up (p. 107) hochnehmen
to rub (p. 155) reiben; hier: (mit anderen Kulturen) in Berührung kommen
run (p. 148) hier: Besuch – dry run (p. 160) Testlauf – to run interference (fig.) (p. 104) hier: sich gegen einen Einwand wehren
rush (p. 147) Rausch (fig.)
ruthless (p. 46) rücksichtslos, schonungslos

S

sabbatical (p. 32) Freistellung, Sabbatjahr – on sabbatical (p. 94) freigestellt
sacrifice (pp. 155, 156) Opfer
to sail close to the wind (p. 32) etwas Riskantes oder Gefährliches machen
salary (p. 45) Gehalt
garage sale (p. 109) Garagenverkauf
saliva [səˈlaɪvə] (p. 94) Speichel
saltmarsh (p. 59) Salzsumpf
sample (p. 132) Kostprobe
sane [seɪn] (p. 87) normal; zurechnungsfähig
satisfied (p. 24) erfüllt; zufrieden

say (p. 115) hier: zum Beispiel
to scan (p. 102) absuchen
scarce [skeəs] (p. 69) knapp – scarcely [ˈskeəslɪ] (p. 97) kaum
scarlet (p. 145) scharlachrot
to be scarred by s.th. [skɑːd] (p. 141) gezeichnet sein von etw.
scary [ˈskeərɪ] (p. 87) unheimlich, Furcht erregend
school board (p. 115) Schulbehörde
scorched (p. 129) angebrannt
score (p. 15) hier: jede Menge
to scour (p. 99) scheuern; hier: wegschwemmen
scraggy (p. 178) dürr
to screech (p. 139) hier: mit quietschenden Reifen fahren
to scrub (informal) (p. 95) hier: (aus dem Programm) streichen
scrupulous [ˈskruːpjələs] (p. 160) gewissenhaft
seal (p. 95) Siegel – to seal [siːl] (p. 63) versiegeln; abdichten
secularism (p. 160) Trennung von Kirche und Staat
secure [-ˈ-] (p. 63) sicher, solide – to secure [-ˈ-] (p. 159) erwerben
to seduce (p. 33) verführen
to seek out (p. 125) suchen, ausfindig machen – to seek to do s.th. (p. 111) streben nach, versuchen etw. zu tun
seldom (p. 129) selten
self-esteem (p. 147) Selbstachtung
self-monitoring device [dɪˈvaɪs] (p. 127) Gerät zur Selbstkontrolle
to sell out (slang) (p. 48) hier: Prinzipien aufgeben – sell-out (p. 151) Verräter
to send a shiver down one's spine (fig.) (p. 87) es einem eiskalt den Rücken hinunterlaufen lassen
senescence [sɪˈnesns] (p. 117) Altern
sensitivity (p. 143) Empfindsamkeit
sentence (p. 32) hier: Urteil
sequential (p. 102) regelmäßig, fortlaufend
servant (old use) (p. 11) Diener
service job (p. 111) schlecht bezahlte Dienstleistung
to set one's sights higher (fig.) (p. 116) sich höhere Ziele stecken – to set roots (fig.) (p. 22) Wurzeln schlagen
to settle for (p. 109) sich zufrieden geben mit – settlement (pp. 163, 167) Übereinkunft, Regelung
severely [sɪˈvɪəlɪ] (p. 153) außerordentlich
to live in the shadows (p. 109) im Verborgenen leben
shake-out (p. 148) Schrumpfungsprozess, Pleitewelle
shallow (p. 97) flach
to be shaped by s.th. (p. 54) geformt werden
shareholder (p. 48) Aktionär(in)

to float shares (p. 43) Aktien auf den Markt bringen – tranche of shares (p. 46) Aktienpaket
to shed blood (p. 74) Blut vergießen
sheer (pp. 46, 166) rein
sheik (p. 64) Scheich
to work shifts (p. 37) Schicht arbeiten
shiver (p. 87) Schauer, Schauder – to send a shiver down one's spine (fig.) (p. 87) es einem eiskalt den Rücken hinunterlaufen lassen
shopping spree (p. 147) Einkaufstour
to be shorn of his locks (fig.) (p. 48) hier: seine Vorbildfunktion verlieren
to keep s.th. short and sweet (p. 11) (fig.) etw. kurz und knapp halten
shortcoming (p. 76) Mangel, Fehler
to shove [ʃʌv] (p. 178) stoßen
shovel (p. 64) Schaufel
to shrink from s.th. (p. 160) vor etw. zurückschrecken
shrub (p. 59) Busch, Strauch
to shuttle (p. 42) hin- und hertransportieren
shyster (p. 46) Gauner
sibling (p. 38) Geschwister – siblings [ˈ--] (p. 131) Geschwister
on the chunky side (p. 145) untersetzt, gedrungen
to side with s.o. (p. 73) sich auf jds. Seite schlagen
sideshow (p. 87) hier: Nebensache
to sift through (p. 102) sichten, durchgehen
to sigh [saɪ] (p. 109) seufzen
to set one's sights higher (fig.) (p. 116) sich höhere Ziele stecken
simultaneously [ˌsɪmlˈteɪnɪəslɪ] (p. 45) gleichzeitig
sincerity [sɪnˈserətɪ] (p. 88) Aufrichtigkeit
to skin (p. 48) häuten – to skin s.o./s.th. alive (fig.) (p. 48) hier: auseinander nehmen
to skyrocket (p. 163) in die Höhe schießen
slab (p. 79) Scheibe
slag (BE rude) (p. 143) Schlampe
to slaver [ˈslævə] (p. 177) geifern
slender (p. 96) schlank
slightly (p. 38) leicht
slope (pp. 64, 97) Hang – on a slippery slope (p. 173) schiefe Bahn, gefährlicher Weg; hier: auf direktem Weg
to slump (p. 103) sich fallen lassen (z. B. auf einen Stuhl)
to smack (p. 11) eine runterhauen
smokestack (p. 97) Schornstein
smooth (p. 113) hier: flüssig
smugly (p. 71) selbstgefällig
snafu [snæfˈuː] (AE:slang) (p. 94) Schlamassel
it's a snap (fig.) (p. 11) das ist ein Kinderspiel
to snap to attention (p. 103) zackig Haltung annehmen

snuff (p. 139) Schnupftabak
sobriety [səʊˈbraɪɪtɪ] (p. 132) Nüchternheit, Ernst
social action projects (p. 48) Sozialhilfeprogramme
solar array (p. 95) Solaranlage
sole (pp. 95, 98) einzig
solicitor (p. 165) Rechtsanwalt
some (p. 111) *hier:* ungefähr
soothing (p. 21) beruhigend
bed sore (p. 82) wundgelegene Stelle
at source (p. 69) an der Quelle
to spark (p. 155) *hier:* (er)wecken, hervorrufen – **to be sparked by s.th.** (p. 147) verursacht werden durch
spate [speɪt] (p. 73) Flut, große Menge, Reihe – **spate** (p. 148) Flut; Schwall
clock speed (p. 79) Taktfrequenz
spent (p. 63) verbraucht
spillover (p. 160) Resultat
spine (p. 85) Wirbelsäule – **to send a shiver down one´s spine** *(fig.)* (p. 87) es einem eiskalt den Rücken hinunterlaufen lassen
to spit (p. 132) spucken
splendour [ˈsplendə] (p. 97) Glanz, Pracht
to split (p. 73) spalten – **to split** (p. 153) (auf)spalten – **to split up** *(informal)* (p. 127) sich trennen
spouse (pp. 34, 131) Gatte, Gattin
to sprinkle (p. 143) (aus)streuen, verspritzen
water spout (p. 101) Wasserhose
spurt of dust (p. 97) Staubwolke
to squash [skwɒʃ] (p. 95) zerdrücken
squarely (p. 167) direkt, genau
squat [skwɒt] (p. 97) niedrig
to squint (p. 32) schielen
to reach a stage (p. 25) an einem Punkt ankommen
to stagger [ˈstægə] (p. 156) schwanken, wanken
staging area (p. 107) Aufmarschplatz; *hier:* Ausgangspunkt
stainless steel (p. 63) Edelstahl
to be at stake (p. 167) auf dem Spiel stehen
stance [stæns] (p. 73) Haltung, Einstellung
standing (p. 15) *hier:* augenblicklich; (p. 46) Ansehen, Ruf, Status
stand-off (p. 163) *hier:* Patt(situation)
stark (p. 73) krass
to starve (p. 129) hungern
stasis [ˈsteɪsɪs] *(formal)* (p. 159) Stillstand
state legislature (p. 115) Parlament eines Bundesstaates
marital status (p. 34) Familienstand
steadfastly (p. 97) unerschütterlich
steamer (p. 153) Dampfer
stainless steel (p. 63) Edelstahl
to stem *(formal)* (p. 163) aufhalten

to keep in step *(fig.)* (p. 156) Schritt halten – **stepping stone** (p. 95) Sprungbrett *(fig.)*
to measure one´s steps *(fig.)* (p. 156) gemessenen Schrittes gehen
stern (p. 104) ernst
to sting (p. 103) *hier:* treffen, schmerzen
stitched [stɪtʃt] (p. 82) genäht
stock car (p. 139) Tourenwagen
stepping stone (p. 95) Sprungbrett *(fig.)*
store card (p. 147) Kundenkarte
story line (p. 153) Handlung
strain (p. 19) Belastung, Stress
stranded (p. 101) gestrandet; festsitzend
to get the strap *(fig.)* (p. 36) Prügel bekommen
revenue stream (p. 67) Einnahmequellen – **to stream** (p. 46) *hier:* über den Bildschirm laufen
strife (p. 153) Konflikt; Unfriede
striking (p. 167) bemerkenswert
stringent [ˈstrɪndʒənt] (p. 73) streng, hart
stuff *(informal)* (p. 37) *hier:* Arbeit – **stuff it** *(BE, informal)* (p. 147) was soll's
to subject [-´-] (p. 160) unterwerfen
subsidy [ˈsʌbsɪdɪ] (p. 73) Subvention
to subsist on (p. 32) leben (von)
substitute (p. 12) Ersatz
subtle [ˈsʌtl] (p. 54) subtil
successor [səkˈsesə] (p. 163) Nachfolger
succour [ˈsʌkə] *(formal)* (p. 46) Beistand
to be sucked toward s.th. (p. 95) herangesaugt werden zu
to sue (p. 49) verklagen
to suffice (p. 178) genügen
to be suited to s.th. (p. 11) passen – **to not suit s.o.** (p. 132) jdm. nicht (gut) stehen
sullenly (p. 103) mürrisch, missmutig
sunscreen (p. 130) Sonnencreme
to sup *(old use)* (p. 36) trinken
supervision (p. 63) Aufsicht
supply-chain (p. 148) Versorgungskette
to support [-´-] (pp. 37, 131, 156) unterstützen – (p. 165) Anhänger/Fan sein
supremacy [sʊˈpreməsɪ] (p. 166) Vormachtstellung
surface [ˈsɜːfɪs] (p. 101) Oberfläche – **lunar surface** (p. 102) Mondoberfläche
to surmount (p. 97) krönen mit etw.
to surpass [-´-] (pp. 111, 115) übertreffen
to surround (p. 79) umgeben
Chartered Surveyor *(BE)* (p. 17) staatlich geprüfter Sachverständiger
to sustain (pp. 21, 155) aufrechterhalten; (p. 103) erleiden
sustainable (p. 17) aufrechtzuerhalten; (pp. 65, 73) nachhaltig; (p. 71) nachwachsend

to swear (p. 132) fluchen – **to swear s.o. in** (p. 155) jdn. vereidigen
to keep s.th. short and sweet (p. 11) *(fig.)* etw. kurz und knapp halten
to swill *(informal, negative)* (p. 139) (runter)kippen

T

tabloid (p. 104) Boulevardzeitung
to tack [tæk] (p. 121) *hier:* sich hin und her bewegen
to freeze one´s tail off *(slang)* (p. 64) sich einen abfrieren
to let s.th. take its course (p. 87) einer Sache ihren Lauf lassen – **to take s.th. for granted** (pp. 121, 128) etw. für selbstverständlich nehmen – **to take s.th. into consideration** (p. 54) etw. bedenken, etw. berücksichtigen – **you can´t take it with you** *(humorous saying)* (p. 64) du kannst es nicht mit ins Grab nehmen – **to take the liberty of doing s.th.** (p. 89) sich die Freiheit nehmen, etwas zu tun
to talk s.o. in on top of s.o. (p. 107) jdn. zu einer anderen Person (hin)führen
Tamil Tigers (p. 160) Guerillakämpfer in Sri Lanka
tang (p. 96) *hier:* (scharfer) Geruch
tap (p. 143) Wasserhahn
target [´--] (p. 73) Ziel – **target audience** (p. 111) Zielgruppe
to be one´s cup of tea *(informal)* (p. 32) jemandes Fall sein
to tear one's eyes away [teə] *(fig.)* (p. 143) wegschauen – **tear-jerking** [tɪə] (p. 143) mitleidheischend, kitschig
to teeter (p. 172) schwanken
telescience (p. 93) Telescience (Remote-Betrieb von wissenschaftlichen Einrichtungen)
tense (p. 96) *hier:* gespannt
to have tenure [ˈtenjə] (p. 87) auf Lebenszeit angestellt sein
theatre (p. 163) *hier:* Kriegsschauplatz
thin (p. 15) *hier:* spärlich
to think twice about s.th. (p. 54) lange über etw. nachdenken
think-tank (p. 109) Expertenkommission
threat (p. 166) Bedrohung
threatening (pp. 54, 160) bedrohlich
thrill (p. 94) aufregend
thrilled (p. 155) erregt, begeistert
to be at one another´s throats *(fig.)* (p. 73) sich an die Gurgel gehen
to tick s.o. off (p. 172) jmd. schelten, kritisieren
tinge [tɪndʒ] (p. 13) Hauch, Spur
to tip (p. 143) (weg)werfen
token (p. 113) Merkmal
remote tool (p. 63) ferngesteuertes Gerät; Roboter
to topple (p. 116) *hier:* etw. / jdn. stürzen

to get in touch (p. 37) sich in Verbindung setzen – **to touch s.o. for s.th.** (p. 178) jmd. um etw. anpumpen
a tough call [tʌf] *(fig.)* (p. 87) schwierige Situation
to trace back (p. 11) zurückverfolgen – **to trace one's roots** (p. 115) seine Herkunft angeben mit
track record (p. 45) Erfolgsbilanz – **on the right track** *(fig.)* (p. 67) auf dem richtigen Weg sein – **to track** (p. 82) jdm. nachspüren
trailer park (p. 139) Wohnwagenplatz
to be trained on (p. 83) gerichtet sein auf
trait [treɪt] (p. 87) Eigenschaft
tranche of shares [trɑ:nʃ] (p. 46) Aktienpaket
transition (p. 58) Wechsel, Übergang
to translate (p. 115) *hier:* Wirkung haben
transparency (p. 103) Folie
trapped (p. 160) gefangen
treaty (p. 174) Vertrag
tremendous (p. 11) enorm
trial (p. 147) *hier:* Versuch(sreihe)
to trigger (p. 46) auslösen
triple (p. 95) dreimal, dreifach – **to triple** (p. 111) (sich) verdreifachen
trunk *(AE)* (p. 156) Kofferraum
truss (p. 95) Gerüst
trust fund (p. 131) Treuhandfonds
to trust s.o. on s.th. (p. 131) jdm. vertrauen in bezug auf
to try s.o. (p. 160) vor Gericht stellen
tumbleweed (p. 129) vom Wind umhergewehtes Präriegewächs
turd *(vulgar)* (p. 103) Scheißhaufen
to turn out (p. 109) sich entwickeln – **to turn out to be** (p. 115) sich herausstellen als
turnout rates (p. 115) Wahlbeteiligung
to twinkle (p. 97) funkeln
twist (p. 80) *hier:* Neuartigkeit; das Besondere

U

unchecked (p. 17) unkontrolliert
unconditionally (p. 121) bedingungslos
to undergo (p. 59) durchlaufen
underlying (pp. 54, 166) zugrunde liegend
to undermine (p. 167) schwächen
to underwrite (p. 167) unterstützen, stärken
undisputed [ˌʌndɪˈspjuːtɪd] (p. 160) unbestritten
to unfold (p. 101) *hier:* sich entwickeln
unimpeachable *(formal)* (p. 46) untadelig
unique [juːˈniːk] (pp. 12, 50, 166) einzigartig
unsavoury (p. 25) widerwärtig, widerlich
unscathed [ʌnˈskeɪðd] (p. 160) unversehrt

unscintillating [ʌnˈsɪntɪleɪtɪŋ] (p. 97) nicht funkelnd
unsuspecting (p. 48) ahnungslos
upbringing (p. 38) Erziehung
upmarket (p. 73) anspruchsvoll
upsurge (p. 148) Zunahme
to usher in (p. 163) (ein neues Zeitalter) einleiten
utilization [ˌjuːtlaɪˈzeɪʃn] *(formal)* (p. 93) Nutzung – **onsite ... utilization** (p. 93) *hier:* Material im Weltraum verwenden
utterly (p. 121) total, völlig

V

vaguely [ˈveɪɡli] (p. 13) *hier:* leicht
van (pp. 67, 109) Lieferwagen
vapor [ˈveɪpə] (pp. 58, 67, 97) Dampf
vast (p. 166) *hier:* überwältigend
veg [vedʒ] (p. 129) *Kurzform für vegetables:* Gemüse
in this vein (p. 123) in derselben Art
velocity [vɪˈlɒsəti] (p. 95) Geschwindigkeit
venom (p. 99) Gift
venture [ˈventʃə] (pp. 45, 46) riskantes Unternehmen
venue [ˈvenjuː] (p. 143) Ort – **venue** [ˈvenjuː] (p. 11) *hier:* Forum, Treffpunkt
to verify (p. 15) (über)prüfen
vessel *(formal)* (p. 101) Schiff
to vest s.th. in s.o. *(formal)* (p. 155) jdm. etwas verleihen – **vested interest** (p. 173) persönliches Interesse
vet (p. 128) *Kurzform für veterinarian* [ˌvetrɪˈneərɪən] Tierarzt, Tierärztin; (p. 156) *hier:* Veteran *(Kurzform)*
via [vaɪə] (p. 19) über, via
vibrant [ˈvaɪbrənt] (p. 69) lebendig, dynamisch
vigorous [ˈvɪɡrəs] (p. 73) eifrig, heftig
to violate [ˈvaɪəleɪt] (p. 160) verletzen – **to violate s.th.** (p. 78) verstoßen gegen etw
virgin paper (p. 71) fabrikneues, nicht durch Recycling hergestelltes Papier
virtually (pp. 67, 115) praktisch, so gut wie, nahezu
vital (p. 22) lebenswichtig – **vital signs** [ˈvaɪtl] (p. 83) Lebenszeichen
vitrification (p. 63) Verglasung, Einschmelzen in Glas
vitrified (p. 63) etwas zu Glas schmelzen
vociferous (p. 177) lautstark
volcanic eruption (p. 58) Vulkanausbruch
voter registration (p. 115) Eintragung ins Wählerverzeichnis
to vow (p. 48) geloben
vulnerable (p. 160) verwundbar
the vulnerable (p. 147) verletzliche Personen

W

wage earner (p. 111) Verdiener
to wage (p. 163) (Krieg) führen

waist [weɪst] (p. 156) Taille
want (p. 158) *hier:* Not
WAP-enabled (p. 15) WAP-fähig (WAP = Wireless Application Protocol)
warden (p. 172) Rektor
warehousing (p. 148) Lagerung
warping (p. 95) Krümmung
to be wary of s.th. [ˈweəri] (p. 73) vor etw auf der Hut sein, sich vor etw. in Acht nehmen
to waste (p. 99) *hier:* loswerden, verlieren
water spout (p. 101) Wasserhose
watershed (p. 143) Wasserscheide, Trennlinie; *hier:* Zeitpunkt, vor dem für Kinder ungeeignetes Material nicht gezeigt werden darf
to weave on one's feet [wiːv] (p. 109) torkeln
wee hour (p. 128) frühe Morgenstunde
weeping *(fig.)* (p. 74) weinend
well-off (p. 151) gut dran
18-wheeler (p. 94) Lastwagen mit 18 Rädern
whimper (p. 46) Winseln
whimsical (p. 145) launenhaft
white-knuckle maneuver [ˈwaɪtˌnʌkl məˈnuːvə] *(BE manoeuvre)* (p. 94) waghalsiges Manöver
whore [hɔː] *(negative)* (p. 145) Hure
wiggle room *(fig.)* (p. 95) (Fehler)Spielraum
wildlife (p. 59) Tier- und Pflanzenwelt
wiring (p. 80) Stromkabel
wit (p. 11) Geist, Witz
with all the makings of (p. 107) mit allen Voraussetzungen für
withdrawal (p. 163) Rückzug, Abzug
to withhold judgement (p. 54) nicht vorschnell urteilen, sich mit seinem Urteil zurückhalten
woe (p. 65) Kummer
womb [wuːm] (p. 74) Mutterleib
to work shifts (p. 37) Schicht arbeiten
blue-collar worker (p. 111) Arbeiter(in)
worthy (p. 95) lobenswert
wound [wuːnd] (p. 82) Wunde
wounded [ˈwuːndɪd] (p. 156) verwundet
wrap-around (p. 83) rundum, umfassend
to wreak havoc [riːk] (p. 17) etw. total durcheinander bringen
writ large *(lit.)* (p. 143) mit Riesenbuchstaben, überdeutlich
WTO (World Trade Organization) (pp. 43, 159) Welthandelsorganisation

X, Y, Z

to yak [jæk] (p. 11) *(AE slang)* schnattern, quasseln
day-labor yard (p. 109) Sammelplatz für Tagelöhner
yearning (p. 153) Verlangen
zeal (p. 175) Eifer

Solutions

Just for fun (p. 10)
acronyms:

B4N	bye for now
CSL	can't stop laughing
F2F	face to face
FYA	for your amusement
FYI	for your information
ILY	I love you
LMK	let me know
MYOB	mind your own business
OTOH	on the other hand
rehi	hallo again
STYS	speak to you soon
TYVM	thank you very much
WB	welcome back
xoxoxo	kisses (x) & hugs (o)

emoticons:

<:-(	annoyed
:( )	loudmouth, talks all the time, or shouting
(:-D)	big grin (smile)
:-@	screaming
@>--->---	a long-stemmed rose
[:-)	wearing a walkman
}{	face to face
{}	no comment

emoticon beginners use too many emoticons: i.e. more than one per paragraph or three per mail!

capitals mean you are shouting. It's common to use all lower case but very bad chat-style to use all upper case!

Photo captions (p. 18)
left: "Video days: Tom Nutt in Bristol shows his cub badge to his mother in Cambridge over the computer link."
right: "Keeping in touch: Gill Nutt as she appears on her children's screen. 'It has changed my life,' she said."

Slogans (p. 135)
1. British Telecom, telephone company
2. CNN, news broadcaster
3. Weight Watchers Frozen Meals, food producer
4. TicTac mints, sweet manufacturer
5. Jaguar, luxury car manufacturer
6. Nike, sports clothes & equipment
7. McDonalds, fast food
8. Alka Seltzer, pharmaceuticals: medicine for indigestion, pain, colds

Acknowledgements

The editors wish to thank all authors, publishers and literary agencies who have given permission to use copyright material. Sources are given next to the texts. The following list acknowledges copyright holders who are not identical with the publishers quoted and also gives specifications requested by copyright holders.

Every effort has been made to locate owners of copyright material, but in a few cases this has not proved possible and repeated inquiries have remained unanswered. The publishers would be glad to hear from any further copyright owners of material reproduced in this book.

p. 24: From *The Management Guide to Motivating*, by Kate Keenan. London: Horsham: Ravette Books, 1995; p. 25: Approximately 600 words from ABOUT A BOY by Nick Hornby (Victor Gollancz, 1998) Copyright © Nick Hornby, 1998. Reproduced by permission of Penguin Books Ltd.; p. 26: HESA: Higher Education Statistics Agency, http://www.hesa.ac.uk/Press/sfr46/sfr46.htm; p. 36: (top text) Found in *Victorian Women: A Documentary Account of Women's Lives in Nineteenth Century England, France and the United States*, by Erna Olafson Hellerstein, Leslie Parker Hume, and Karen M. Offen, Stanford University Press, 1981; p. 46: Extract from *In a Land of Plenty* by Tim Pears published by Black Swan. Used by permission of Transworld Publishers, a division of The Random House Group Limited; p. 48: © Telegraph Group Limited, 2000; pp. 58-59: NERC: www.nerc.ac.uk; p. 64: From the article "What about Energy in the Future? Let our Kids Find Their own Oil." by Art Buchwald, *Washington Post*, April 28, 1977. Reprinted with permission from the author; p. 73: © *The Economist Newspaper Limited*, London, June 3, 1995; p. 110 (U.S. population figures): U.S. Census Bureau, www.census.census.gov; p. 140: From AdAge.com, www.adage.com; p. 145: From the article "Lie back and think of profits", *The Guardian*, January 30, 2001

Picture Credits

Every effort has been made to locate owners of copyright material, but in a few cases this has not proved possible and repeated inquiries have remained unanswered. The publishers would be glad to hear from any further copyright owners of material reproduced in this book.

Cover photos: 4 MEV, Augsburg, 3 Getty Images (PhotoDisc), München, 2 NASA, Washington, D.C., 1 Corbis (RF), Düsseldorf; p. 8: 1, 2, 4, 5, 6, 7 *The Spectator Limited*, London, 3 SIPRESS *(The New Yorker)*; p. 19: South West News Service, Bristol; p. 30: MEV, Augsburg; p. 34: *The New York Times* (P. Steiner), New York; p. 40: MEV, Augsburg; p. 42 left: Action Press (BIC Pictures), Hamburg; right: Corbis (Chenet), Düsseldorf; p. 44: BANX *(The Week)*; p. 49: Corbis, Düsseldorf; p. 56: Cartoonists & Writers Syndicate/c (KAL), Rolling Hills Estates, CA; p. 59: U.S. Environmental Protection Agency, Washington, DC; p. 63: Magnox Electric, Berkeley, Gloucestershire; p. 67 top: General Motors; p. 67 bottom: Rocky Mountain Institute, Snowmass, CO 81654-9199; p. 69: Car Free Cities Brochure; p. 70: Klett-Archiv, Stuttgart; p. 70: (cartoon) Scott Willis, San José, CA; p. 72: Cartoonists & Writers Syndicate/c (KAL), Rolling Hills Estates, CA; p. 74: MEV, Augsburg; p. 77 left: Dyson GmbH, Köln; right: MEV, Augsburg; p. 78: Cinetext, Frankfurt; p. 90 (astronaut): DPA, Frankfurt; p. 90 (earth): The Tech Museum of Innovation, San Jose, CA; p. 91: DPA, Frankfurt; p. 93: DPA, Frankfurt; p. 96: Corbis (A Mark/Sygma), Düsseldorf; p. 98: The Tech Museum of Innovation, San Jose, CA; p. 100 top right: The Tech Museum of Innovation, San Jose, CA; bottom left: Greenpeace, Hamburg; p. 101: Gulf of Maine Aquarium; p. 103: Cinetext, Frankfurt; p. 106 left: reproduced with permission from Hispanic Business Inc. (www.hispanicbusiness.com); right: Corbis (SABA/Dannemiller), Düsseldorf; p. 107: Andy Singer, St. Paul, MN; p. 108: Sergio J. Hernandez, Acton, CA; p. 110: (fig. 1) Population Reference Bureau, www.prb.org, (fig. 2–3) U.S. Census Bureau, www.census.census.gov; p. 113: Photo of Pat Mora reprinted with permission from the publisher Arte Público Press, University of Houston, TX; p. 114: Reuters, Berlin; p. 117: Photograph by Firooz Zahedi for Latina Magazine; p. 118: *Guardian News Service Limited,* Manchester; p. 122: *The Spectator Limited,* London; 123: *Guardian News Service Limited,* Manchester; p. 124: Population Reference Bureau, www.prb.org; p. 128: *The Spectator Limited,* London; p. 129: *The Spectator Limited,* London; p. 131: Corbis, Düsseldorf; p. 132 top left, top middle, top right, bottom right: MEV, Augsburg; bottom left: Getty Images (PhotoDisc), München; p. 134: Klett-Archiv, Stuttgart; p. 137: Klett-Archiv, Stuttgart; p. 144: B. Smaller *(The New Yorker)*; p. 147: Corbis (RF), Düsseldorf; p. 148: MEV, Augsburg; p. 149 left: Chris Gregerson; right: Mall of America, Bloomington, MN 55425; p. 150: *The Spectator Limited,* London; p. 152: Corbis, Düsseldorf; p. 153: Corbis, Düsseldorf; p. 155 (flag): MEV, Augsburg; p. 157: PWE Verlag P.W. Engelmeier, München; p. 160: Tribune Media Services (Drew Sheneman), Chicago, IL; p. 164 top left: AP, Frankfurt; p. 164 top right: Mirror Syndication International, London; p. 164 bottom left: Ben Bradshaw, London SW1A 0AA